I0100672

THE LITTLE GIRL AT THE BOTTOM OF THE PICTURE

The Little Girl at the Bottom of the Picture

A JOURNEY OF SELFLESS DISCOVERY

Jeremy White

WLP

White Lines Press

Copyright © 2023 by White Lines Press

All rights reserved. No part of this book may be reproduced in any manner whatsoever without written permission from the publisher, except in the case of brief quotations embodied in critical articles and reviews.

Designations used by companies to distinguish their products are often claimed as trademarks. All brand names and product names used in this book and on its cover are trade names, service marks, trademarks, and registered trademarks of their respective owners. The publisher and the book are not associated with any product or vendor mentioned in this book. None of the companies referenced within the book have endorsed the book.

Some names have been changed to protect the privacy of certain individuals.

Contents

Preface

"John Hart is your father" is seared in my wife's brain when AncestryDNA sucker-punches her at work in Baton Rouge in 2018. Raised by a loving adopted family, Edie had altruistically submitted a sample in hopes of healing an unknown woman's nearly fifty-year-old wound. *The Little Girl at the Bottom of the Picture: A Journey of Selfless Discovery* immersively reveals how the resulting bombshell propels the two of us into this beautifully epic, transformational adventure that resolves a trio of daunting mysteries, including one plaguing an enthusiastic horde of gangster-adjacent Ukrainian Americans for two-thirds of a century.

The heart of this powerful story about healing is Edie's utterly selfless agenda. It's also what sets it apart, as far as this tenured cynic can tell, from other books involving searches for biological family. Edie successfully dodges all the traps that could have turned our unicorn of a story into a darker version of the insane yet heartwarming tale that it is. With a smattering of bittersweet moments, *The Little Girl* is heavy on happy reunions, including a mind-blowing, poetic parental reunion of sorts, one involving a local bookstore, no less.

It's also worth noting this story occurs on the eve of 2020. A post-COVID read brings several themes to the fore, including social and racial justice, police brutality, and the value of science. Additionally, insidious homophobia in 1950s Middle America lies at the root of our heartbreaking titular mystery. *The Little Girl* also reminds us of a recent time when air travel was less perilous and we could safely hug strangers. In an age characterized by sickening inhumanity, this work celebrates the best of our humanity. Transcending issues of genealogy, *The Little Girl* appeals to readers seeking empathy in a divided land, and authentic beauty in an increasingly ugly world.

Acknowledgments

I'm forever grateful to my peer reviewers, including (but not limited to) Odelle Hadley, Steven Landry, Melinda Deslatte, Pamela Sandoz, Jared Kendall, Knick Moore, Sunny Weathers, Robert Mann, Rob Payer, Julie Baxter-Payer, Mike and Shannon Cavell, and my mom, Laura Swire. My sincerest apologies to those who endured my first draft.

A huge thank you to Jay Grymes for going above and beyond in providing definitive weather data. Baton Rouge's best-ever weatherman went so far as to write complete daily overviews, detailed weather patterns in PowerPoint, and custom-made an animated gif showing precipitation over eight particular days.

My deepest appreciation goes to LeAnne Weill, Beth Colvin, Rachel Stevens, Case Duckworth, Patrick O'Neal, and Justin Hart for patiently fielding constant, random messages from a debut author battling a daunting case of imposter syndrome during an isolating pandemic. A thank you goes to my book coach, Martha Bullen, who introduced me to the publishing industry's quirks, and led me to my editor, Dave Aretha, and his valuable insight.

Susan Mustafa, thank you for your friendship, support, and encouragement. Not every debut author has a *New York Times* best-selling author at their disposal for invaluable feedback. Thank you for being there.

This book wouldn't have happened without the cooperation of many people, some you'll meet on the following pages, including my wife, Edie, whose immense love, support, and patience allowed this project to materialize. Our reluctant hero is an intensely private person who's come to realize her incredible story begs to be added to the human narrative. I'm eternally grateful to my bride for trusting me with putting her and her family on the printed page for the world to fall in love with.

1

Three Suits—All Aces

It was predawn in the middle of February 2018 at our home in Baton Rouge, Louisiana. My wife, Edie, typically a night owl, had quietly gotten up sometime before me. Upon awakening in our darkened bedroom, I instantly knew where she was.

The previous two mornings, we had received life-altering emails from seemingly incredible people we hadn't previously known. The two of us were like little kids excitedly waking up on Christmas morning, anxious to see what awaited in the inbox.

Edie, wrapped in a white, cat-adorned robe, sat at her desk in our office, awash in the glow from the hand-me-down computer. Three images, attached to a new message sent overnight from two time zones away, slowly loaded on the monitor.

The first showed an adorable little girl and a beautiful woman with a warm gaze. Bundled up in winter gear, both wore wool caps and broad smiles. In the background was lots of water, with what looked like mountains on the horizon against an overcast sky.

In the next photo, the same darling little girl was being held by a handsome man with piercing brown eyes on a rocky beach. A craggy, tree-lined bluff projected a bit into the water behind them.

The still-adorable, grinning girl wore a different outfit in the third pic. Sunlight from the left highlighted her blonde locks and lit the face of an older, white-haired man with her; he also shared a smile. He wore glasses and a couple days of gray stubble.

I silently studied the last photo as my eyes continued to fully awaken. Coffee would have to wait.

After a few seconds, I looked back to see that my winsome wife of over twenty-five years was staring straight ahead at that third picture. I was witnessing the love of my life look upon—for the very first time— her biological father.

It wasn't yet six on a so-far caffeine-free Wednesday. Just like the past two, nearly equally insane mornings, Edie would be at work on time.

It all stemmed from a decision she had made nearly two months before, in the early evening of Christmas 2017, in the living room of my widowed mother-in-law, who goes by a childhood nickname. Ducky and her husband, the late Dr. James Wade O'Neal Jr., did a bang-up job raising their four kids about a half-hour's drive west of the capital city, in their rural, four-bedroom house. Edie reached her fateful decision as we listened to her older brother Patrick speak about recently connecting with a biological cousin who made artisan soap in New Orleans.

The O'Neals adopted Patrick and Edie, each at birth. My wife and her blond brother are not biologically connected. Nevertheless, they share an incredible bond. After giving birth to Wade and Kellie early in their marriage, Ducky struggled with a series of miscarriages for years. She and Doc adopted Patrick in 1964. Six years later, they were blessed with curly-haired Edie, whom Wade still calls "Red."

With over a dozen years separating Edie from her two elder siblings, she bonded with Patrick well before learning that she was adopted. That newly discovered fact as a preteen only proved to strengthen their connection, especially when people would point out the "obvious" family resemblance between the two. The pair of secret-keepers typically just nodded along, often together, in social settings. Ironically enough, the two nonbiological O'Neals are, by far, the most Irish-looking of the bunch.

My in-laws' youngest came into their lives via private placement through Ducky's OB-GYN, Dr. Tony Leggio. They gave their baby girl the same name as Doc O'Neal's older sister, better known as Aunt Neenie. "Edris Ann" is on Edie's birth certificate, dated November 30, 1970. I married the fourth Edris in the family's history.

I first saw the fetching high school valedictorian in Louisiana State University's West Laville Hall, where I served as a resident assistant. I was newly back on campus to resume my mechanical engineering studies after taking a year off to join the Naval Reserve. Edie, a future Marine Corps officer candidate, came tromping through the lobby in combat boots, camouflage cutoffs, and a red USMC T-shirt highlighting her voluminous auburn mane, leaving a fiery trail in her wake. With the most adorably badass sense of purpose I'd ever seen, Edie halted just long enough to staple a flyer to the bulletin board with surprising authority, before resuming her captivating march out the front door with more bills in her freckled hands.

A handful of us guys, who were chatting near the front desk before she entered from the main hall, were left speechless.

"Well," I recall finally saying, "that was interesting."

Some twenty-seven years later—despite a persistent, almost debilitating reticence to speak about her awesome self—Edie would tell an exuberant woman in Indiana about her upbringing in a small South Louisiana town with one flashing traffic light. Maringouin, French for "mosquito," is an agricultural community near the Atchafalaya Basin.

"I was really blessed," she told this Indiana woman in their guffaw-filled initial phone call, months after that Christmas at Ducky's. Kellie, her older sister, who grew up to become a caring nurse and mother of five, took care of Edie like she was "her little baby doll." Big Sis and Wade both maintain Red got away with "bloody murder" in comparison, Edie explained.

"I work at Pennington Biomedical Research Center. It's part of the LSU campus," Edie told the Indianan. "We do a lot of clinical trials, research. My boss does a lot of work with the military." Edie, a zoology grad, ensures that millions of dollars' worth of research, primarily aimed at improving the health and nutrition of our deployed troops, goes smoothly.

My wife was raised by a respected family with a strong work ethic. Wade is president of a bank. Kellie's husband, Mike, is a lawyer, as is Patrick.

Meanwhile, their brother-in-law with a local satire site—the smartass from down the bayou who married Doc and Ducky's youngest—told jokes on the internet. As a junior college football officiating crewmate would remind me whenever he saw me with Edie: I had outkicked my coverage.

"I was never any good at dating," Edie would eventually write a newly discovered relative, explaining how I completely lucked out. "I either obsessed over someone who wasn't available or interested—not that I ever did anything but gawk from afar, because I didn't have a clue—or got unwanted attention." My bride since 1992 went on to say, "I went out with Jeremy because I had no interest, and he was finally going to be the guy I went out with and have nothing come of it."

A year before the fateful Christmas at Ducky's, Edie and I spent the final week of 2016 with Patrick and his engaging wife, Yvette, at their home in Fort Worth, Texas. He informed his little sister that he planned to submit a sample to AncestryDNA in hopes of learning about his biological family.

We went back the following Memorial Day weekend for a U2 concert. My wife did not ask about DNA results because Patrick did not bring up the topic.

Edie is persistently concerned about upsetting others, to the point that she'll put off communicating with them, using the time instead to agonizingly determine the perfect way to reach out. Their feelings come before hers. This can prove somewhat problematic when attempting to make potentially feather-ruffling decisions. Inaction is her default position in these situations.

Nevertheless, this is probably the most ideal trait anyone could have for what would become a yearlong-plus exercise in discretion, patience, and empathy, three suits in which my wife is all aces. My hand, despite getting stronger along the way, is still no match for hers, especially in the patience department. There's no way in hell I would've put up with me for this long.

Seven months after the concert with Patrick and Yvette, they joined us and Ducky in her living room, after everyone else had gone home following a day filled with family, food, and gifts. Patrick used the occasion to tell us about his Ancestry findings. His cool, soap-making cousin Emily in the Crescent City represented his closest match thus far. My mother-in-law's genuine excitement about the news only amplified when Edie soon said she'd also submit a sample.

Ducky, only slightly less spry than when she played high school basketball during the Truman administration, had always been eager to help her adopted children find out where they came from. However, Doc O'Neal, who passed away in 2010, didn't feel the same way.

"It was Dad's decision not to learn anything about my birth parents," Edie would later inform more newly discovered kin, "aside from possibly being told they were LSU students."

When her "Edie Bean" said she was ready to embark on the search, Ducky bolted for the closet that housed the adoption records. The box contained only letters about attorney fees and who handled the adoption. Nevertheless, Ducky would eventually prove willing to shake down whomever she had to—including Dr. Leggio's widow, as well as the OB-GYN who took over his practice—in order to help her baby find her birth mother.

"My mom can be a bulldog," Edie would inform the Indiana woman on the phone. "If she gets on a task," Edie laughed, "she'll harass people until they relent."

My wife instinctively, and politely, vetoed Ducky's help. This would be Edie's journey to embark upon and—more importantly—lead, a fact that she'd have to remind me of a few times.

"Mom is a Pandora's box of an entirely different magnitude," she would tell a dear friend, "with discretion out the window."

Edie is the last person on Earth who would ever bust into someone's life unannounced like the Kool-Aid Man. She was not at all driven by a need to know about her bio family. Rather, her motivation was utterly selfless.

On December 26, 2017, the day after that evening at Ducky's, Edie and I would celebrate twenty-five years of marriage. In that quarter century, we never discussed her biological family. She told me during our engagement that she had no desire to know about them. The closest we ever came to discussing it was when she shared with me a brief composition titled "If You Were My Mom"—a few sweet words she would tell her birth mother should the opportunity ever arise.

Edie was totally happy not knowing about her bio folks, especially since it carried a risk of pain to someone else.

"I was blessed with a loving family and wanted for nothing," she'd eventually write. "I did not want to risk the possibility of opening an old wound that someone may have tried to leave in their past and move beyond. However, as I got older, I began to wonder more often if maybe I was preventing a wound from fully healing by keeping to myself, rather than making myself available to be discovered by someone who might have a lingering question as to whether they had made the right decision."

As Patrick continued sharing his exciting discoveries in Ducky's living room that Christmas evening, Edie began to ponder her age, and that of her birth mother, assuming she was still alive. If it wasn't already too late, Edie was ready to take action to alleviate a stranger's presumed burden.

My wife likes to say she was just putting herself out there, in AncestryDNA's database, in case someone was looking to connect, looking to finally close—after almost fifty years—an undoubtedly heartbreaking chapter in their life. Edie's humility prevents her from conceding that sending off a vial filled with her saliva was an altruistic act.

I've spoken with enough people to know that not all searches of this type have a happy ending. Most folks who've told me about their families' experiences with online DNA database services, like Ancestry and 23andMe, said they involved unpleasant surprises. If and when someone connects with a long-lost biological family, they run a significant chance of either causing, or becoming embroiled in, a bunch of strangers' drama. Think about it: Who puts their child up for adoption because everything in their life is going great?

And once you're out there, you're out there. The internet is forever. Spit in a vial, and you've released a skeleton key to open countless cans of worms, a key you can get back as much as you can unblow a whistle.

She'll never say it, so I will. My intensely private wife willingly put herself at risk for untold emotional pain and mental anguish, all for someone she didn't know, who might not have even been among the living.

That decision poetically led to the greatest, most surreal, transformational experience of our lives. An experience in which my life partner stumbled into solving a gut-wrenching, sixty-five-year-old family mystery.

A family with proud connections to some of the most notorious criminals in this nation's history.

A family in which many of its numerous members rightfully see my bride as a bona fide miracle.

2

Or Closer

Edie received her AncestryDNA kit on the third day of 2018. I had to show my civilized wife how to spit, at least with enough volume to fill the sample tube to the prescribed level. She dropped it in the mail the next day.

Precisely one month after receiving her kit, Ancestry sent Edie an email notification. Her results were available.

She initially ignored the message, for two reasons. The first was low expectations set by the modest pace of Patrick's discoveries. One year into his search, the closest match he found was in the second-cousin range, according to Ancestry's estimation.

The second reason she lacked a sense of urgency to investigate was timing; the Saturday notification arrived amid the madness of Carnival season. Edie and I were responsible for a forty-foot-long Mardi Gras float hauling the second-oldest continuously rolling krewe in Baton Rouge's largest annual parade. Known for risqué, irreverent humor, Spanish Town Mardi Gras is a throwback to Carnival's satirical roots. STMG would roll for the thirty-eighth time in exactly one week, and we still had giant foam penis heads to fashion.

In addition to working on parade stuff, Edie spent that first weekend of February taking care of weekly business back home in Maringouin.

For the past six years, she crossed the Mississippi River, usually on Sundays, to tend to an aging motherly figure in her life.

"The closest experience I had to a set of grandparents," Edie would eventually explain, "are a couple I refer to as my 'other parents.' They owned the house my family rented when they first moved into the town where I grew up."

Earle and Hugh Wagley also owned and ran the Maringouin Western Auto for years. Known affectionately as "Eel and Poppa," they never had kids of their own. The Wagleys befriended their new tenants. In return, the O'Neals shared their youngest with them. Edie became Eel and Poppa's baby, too.

The two families had adjacent fishing camps on Grand Isle. Both sets of parents took turns driving the cutest redhead three and a half hours to Louisiana's only inhabited barrier island, where she swam, fished, and collected other cherished childhood memories.

Poppa passed away in 2012. That's when Wade began helping his baby sister serve as Earle's caretaker. It's all part of their longstanding promise to the beloved woman—considered my wife's second mom—that she'd finish her years in her own home.

"We have sitters stay with her around the clock," Edie would later write, "and I visit each week to manage her affairs and make sure she is as comfortable as possible."

At sunup Monday, February 5, Edie shared something from Ancestry with Patrick and Yvette on our four-person Facebook Messenger thread.

"We haven't done J's kit yet, but my results came in," Edie reported with a screenshot of her "ethnicity estimate." Great Britain was tops with thirty-five percent. Next was a surprising twenty-eight percent Eastern European. Ireland/Scotland/Wales came in at fifteen percent, while Scandinavia got six.

"Very cool," Patrick replied with a nod to her potential Soviet Bloc roots. "You're a commie."

"She do like her vodka," I chimed in with a Russian flag emoji.

"Fascinating!" Yvette replied. "What's next?" our hip Latina sister-in-law asked. "Did you get the app?"

"Didn't know about the app," Edie answered as she installed Ancestry's software on her phone, "but downloading it now." The email notification, she added, "didn't indicate anything better than 700-plus possible fourth cousins, so I probably won't do any digging til after Mardi Gras."

Tuesday morning, with a full week of Carnival season to go, Edie "just happened" to check out the newest app on her iPhone during a break.

I was back in our home office sending her a just-completed float graphic. "Lame ol Dongs" was laid out in the *Game of Thrones* font, complete with a flaccid penis extending from the first L. Edie promptly loved my work with a trio of big red hearts. I began typing a reply when she grabbed my attention.

"Ho.lee.shit," Edie posted in our chat thread. A screenshot from her phone soon followed. "So that just happened," she quickly added.

The image she shared was topped by the white initials "JH" against an olive block. Below that was a man's name, in black and white. A little lower was the line "Predicted Relationship: Parent/Child." At the bottom, another read in a contrasting color, "Confidence: Extremely High."

Also extremely high? Our shared confidence that my wife's never given birth.

"John Hart is your father" is seared in Edie's memory.

"Wow," was the best I could initially muster. "Any idea who/where he's at?"

"Not yet," Edie answered.

"Damn."

I was suddenly laconic.

John Hart had joined AncestryDNA the previous year, Edie soon discovered.

"Perfect timing," I noted, just as she sent the Ancestry screenshot to the O'Neals in Fort Worth.

"This is why I should stay offline at work," Edie led off in the four-person thread.

"Oh. Shit," Patrick quickly replied.

"Yea, verily," his little sister confirmed.

"I can't focus!" Yvette exclaimed. "Patrick is driving."

"Holy crap, Edie," Patrick posted after parking, a few minutes before midday. "You okay? That's a heavy thing to learn."

"Yeah," she assured her concerned brother. "I'm trying to crank out a shit-ton of reports at work today, and I go into a series of meetings in an hour. I'm going to be grateful there aren't any readily visible links on social media, and try to set this revelation aside for a bit."

"Still going to be a challenge," Patrick warned. "Hang in there."

He checked back in a few hours later.

"How you doing?" Patrick asked. "I'm gobsmacked. Can't imagine where you're at."

"Getting ready to leave work," Edie answered. "Had to accomplish something, even if it was for someone who's already started Mardi Gras vacation." My wife was also "considering the distinct possibility that this guy's first clue that I exist might not occur until the next time he checks his account. I have to allow some time for that to happen. I am not freaking out; I hope he doesn't. Maybe he knew," Edie said of her existence. "Maybe he didn't. Maybe it's why he took the test. Maybe it's not."

Patrick suggested that if John Hart believed he had a child out in the world, then perhaps he joined Ancestry to find them. And if he didn't know about Edie's existence, Patrick said, "Boy won't he be surprised." He then advised his baby sister, "Either way, if you haven't heard anything in a while, contact him. It'll send him an email that someone on the site has contacted him. I know that's a bold step. But hey," he added, "when a door opens..."

"I'm just trying to think about how you or Jeremy would feel if you suddenly got an email from your alleged child you've not known for forty-seven years," my wife revealed.

"I know. It's sticky," her brother empathized. "I can say that I would be stunned, shocked, amazed, even afraid, but I would definitely want to know if there was a child of mine out there. Especially as I got older."

"The way I see it," Yvette injected, "he's on Ancestry for a reason as well."

"I agree with Pat and Yvette," I posted just past 6 p.m.

Still flummoxed by that morning's surprise, Edie brought up Ancestry's email notifications. "My settings are to get weekly email notifications of new DNA matches," she said. "I don't think I ever saw the email where it told me I had a parent/child match."

The email notification that Edie saw did in fact say she had 700-plus possible fourth cousins. However, my wife, an award-winning copy editor, had not fully appreciated the subsequent "or closer" qualifier, largely due to the meager expectations informed by Patrick's findings.

I'd also like to point out that, at the very moment she learned the name of the man who fathered her, my love enthusiastically approved of "Lame ol Dongs." I'm still not sure how to interpret that.

So what now? What do you do after that kind of bombshell? Well, in this case, my puzzle-loving Marine dusted herself off, got her bearings, and soon realized that she could use it to her benefit.

Ancestry's common-relative feature allowed her to see which of her other myriad DNA matches were also related to her bio father. When John Hart exploded onto the scene, he effectively separated all the puzzle pieces according to which side they fit in: paternal or maternal. Without that bombshell, they would have been all jumbled together, thus making the task of correctly placing them much harder.

But who was John Hart? Of all the possible men out there with the less-than-unique name, which one was Edie's father? Where did he live? Ancestry offered no additional personal information to go on.

There were, however, a few visible family trees, constructed by others on Ancestry. Two days before the parade, Edie saved three documents—publicly available family trees for John Wilson Hart, Joseph Edward Hart, and Justin Hart—to begin mapping out her paternal family.

That same Thursday, I cut out heads of fourteen men recently implicated for being dicks in the "Me Too" movement. I then attached their faces to the giant pink phalluses that would serve as manipulable oars on our Viking-ship-themed Mardi Gras float, honoring the memory of our krewe's beloved cofounder, a proud Norseman who'd gone on to Valhalla in early December.

Friday saw tons of last-minute preparations ahead of Saturday's bacchanal. We caught our first Bacchus parade in New Orleans on Sunday with our good friends the Cavells. From there it was Lundi Gras (Fat Monday), Fat Tuesday, and Ash Wednesday, which was also doubling that year as Valentine's Day.

In short, Edie had lots of distractions to help keep her mind off her new, still-jarring reality. They also kept her from instinctively jumping into the puzzle without any real sense of how to begin, which is what she did shortly after the Lenten season began.

My determined wife stumbled around on the internet for a few days, only to be further confounded by dead leads. Frustrated, Edie realized that her ad hoc methodology was getting her nowhere.

Sometimes, when faced by the seemingly unsolvable, the best course of action is to do what my bride did: Step away for a while, and come back at it with a fresh set of eyes.

Or, in this case, two.

3

Google Fu

Saturday, February 17, 2018, was a mostly cloudy day with a trace of rain in Baton Rouge. The high was 82 degrees Fahrenheit (one shy of tying a record), with a low of 62. Winds were light and variable. It also would have been Doc O'Neal's eighty-fifth birthday.

My father-in-law was a hardcore Catholic. Annual pilgrimages to the Manresa House of Retreats and everything. As South Louisiana's season of revelry gave way to one of self-reflection, I imagine Doc would agree that we can only be unburdened from our shortcomings by a savior. So his daughter turned to one in her time of need.

Beth Colvin had worked with Edie at *The Advocate*, the state's largest newspaper. Together, they spent many late nights making last-minute changes before presses cranked out the next day's edition.

From the day they first met, the two hit it off. Edie's a bit selective when it comes to choosing friends. Not long after she started working at the paper, she told me Beth was her "hero." Except for maybe Patrick, I've never heard my wife use that word to describe anyone else in her life.

The admiration between the two women is mutual. Beth later tapped Edie to copy edit a national quarterly. "Edie caught this huge mistake," Beth told someone in the publishing organization, regarding a math error that their auditors and CFO had missed. "I'd trust her to proof my last will and testament."

Edie messaged Beth on Facebook just after 10 a.m. Saturday. "No rush," she insisted, "but if you're free to chat."

The married mother of two young girls was going fishing with her family. "What's up?" Beth answered from the passenger seat.

"So I submitted an AncestryDNA sample."

"Oh," Beth responded. "Did you find some relatives?"

"Sort of," Edie answered with the "John Hart is your father" screenshot.

"WHOA," Beth replied.

"Yeah," Edie agreed.

"Well," Beth led, "he knew it was possible, surely? And he got the same message."

"Perhaps. My brother didn't notice he got a message for a couple months," Edie explained. "This came in two weeks ago."

To ensure such messages don't get ignored, Ancestry really should develop an algorithm that knows when to start email subject lines with "HOLY SHIT! HOLD ON TO YOUR BUTT!!!"

Edie said she hoped that her John Hart hadn't died since the last time he logged into his account. "That would be slightly tragic," she observed.

"Quite," Beth concurred. "Does it give you any more info?"

"Not really." After noting how her apparent father's account had no family tree available to glean from, Edie told Beth about a close paternal match named Justin Hart, "a possible first cousin with a tree that might provide more insight, and lots more distant possibilities."

Beth asked about contacting John Hart. "Are you going to message him?"

"Probably," Edie answered. Since Ancestry's settings offered monthly updates, she initially considered waiting another couple weeks to message him. "The mom knows I'm out there; dad might not."

Edie soon reconsidered the timing of her initial message to John Hart's Ancestry account, though, after mentioning that Ducky and the rest of the non-Texas O'Neals knew nothing yet of the nearly two-week-old bombshell. "Think I might try to compose one today, since time may be of the essence," Edie said, "and more important than practicing patience at this point."

"I agree," Beth replied.

"And, it so happens to be my known dad's birthday," Edie said of the man who wouldn't have been cool with any of this, prompting a succinct observation from Beth.

"That's. Crazy."

While the Colvins fished, Edie tested the Ancestry waters on her own a little more, with no luck. Mercifully, we had a distraction that afternoon.

Sharing a birthday with Doc that Saturday was my podcast co-host Sunny Weathers. We were at The Chimes Restaurant before 5 p.m. for his fortieth birthday dinner because our engaging friend with a great name has the sleep patterns of a man twice his age. Thanks to my hilarious pal's even more laughable bedtime, Edie and I were back home by early evening, as were the Colvins.

At 9:09 p.m., Beth asked about Edie's message to John Hart. "Did you send it?"

"Yep," her friend revealed.

"Anything yet?" Beth messaged back.

"Nope."

"Fingers crossed."

"Not like I'm checking constantly," Edie winked.

"I cannot find the appropriate emoji for this reply." The north Louisiana native with famously expressive eyebrows said, "I'm sure you can imagine my face."

Edie concurred with a laugh, before imagining how such an initial conversation might go down. "Omg, so, like, hey, I might be your daughter you never knew existed. PM me?"

"So call me maybe?" Beth lyrically responded, drawing a much-needed guffaw from her friend.

"We must laugh," Edie declared. "God help me if the results hadn't come amidst Mardi Gras prep."

"I want to Google John Hart SO BAD," the crafty holder of a master's degree in library science admitted. "I have little faith in my Google Fu with so little to go on."

With a couple weeks' worth of Googling the name "John Hart" under her belt, Edie informed Beth, "So many out there."

"The Lone Ranger was John Hart," Beth soon discovered. Doubts about her search engine acumen had succumbed to her curiosity. "A John Hart signed the Declaration of Independence."

"Ooh," Edie cooed.

Another impressive late-night collaboration between two lauded former copy desk denizens was afoot. Seconds later, Edie shared her theory about Justin Hart.

"The alleged first cousin is probably actually a half-brother," she said, "and he has lots of stuff in his tree." When Beth asked if Edie had messaged her ostensible sibling as well, my wife replied, "Not yet. I should probably at least give bio-dad first dibs."

About that time, Edie noticed Justin Hart hadn't logged into Ancestry since last October, prompting her to further debate when to reach out to him. "Seriously," she wondered about their apparent father, "how often do men sixty-five-plus check email?"

"Depends on the man, probably," Beth commented.

Justin had over 2,500 people listed in his family tree. "I kinda jack-potted," Edie reported, "at least in terms of someone doing the work, not necessarily the results."

Beth then said she'd searched for images of Justin Hart.

"Ooh," Edie responded.

"Creepy smile pictures by the zillions."

"Eek."

None of the creepy photos, fortunately, matched the profile picture that Edie's Justin had uploaded to his Ancestry account.

"Ooh," is how Edie announced a link to his LinkedIn page, marking the first time in history that site's ever proven useful, much less exciting.

Fewer than fifteen minutes after poo-pooing her digital sleuthing abilities, Beth found Justin's Facebook profile.

"Gahhhhhhh!" Edie reacted.

"He's got family members tagged on Facebook," Beth said of her friend's apparent new sibling.

"Oh god," Edie replied, "I think I love him already."

My wife and I were at our respective computers in our shared office, where I futilely tried to help with the cyberstalking. Everything was happening so fast, I hardly had time to appreciate that the baby of the O'Neal family apparently had a baby brother of her own out there.

"On Ancestry, his mom is Shirley, and she died in Seattle in October 2014," Edie reported to her research partner. "I think he lives near my aunt for whom I'm named," she said of Aunt Neenie.

Meanwhile, at the Colvins' residence, Beth was spending her Saturday evening scanning the potential can of worms, as deeply as possible, to thoroughly inform her dear friend on how best to proceed.

"He went to Evergreen College. SUPER HIPPY DIPPY," Beth emphasized. "Good news: I searched 'John Hart' AND 'Justin Hart' AND Seattle. Got nothing. I would think, if John had passed on, that search would turn up an obit right quick."

Minutes later, Beth posted a link to a page for a University of Washington Law School affiliate instructor named John Hart. His areas of expertise included constitutional law and civil rights, as listed below his headshot. "I've got nothing more concrete there than eye structure and dimples," Beth admitted about her latest find.

"Yeah," Edie noted the resemblance to Justin Hart, "that's the same face."

"If that IS John Hart," Beth declared, "that's my wheelhouse. I can tell you his whole life in under an hour."

For the next twenty minutes, the two women went down a rabbit hole, discovering all sorts of details about this particular John Hart.

His sixty-one-year-old wife, Kimerly, served as director of the Seattle Art Museum. The ages of their two daughters, however, indicated that Edie and Beth were likely on the wrong trail. That didn't stop me, though, from studying the picture of the redheaded, fair-skinned Kimerly, looking for facial similarities with my love.

"I'm getting far afield," Beth apologized.

"This is more than I've accomplished in two weeks," Edie insisted as the clock reached ten. "My brother is going to be so jealous," she added. Patrick's discoveries had come from states much more red than Washington, politically speaking. "He resisted attempts at contact because so many of his matches were from Mississippi and Alabama," Edie explained.

"Here's Justin's mom." Beth shared a link to an obituary for Shirley Hadley, listed on Justin's tree as a parent. "'She often experienced strife and conflict with her family, and experienced many traumatic events as a young woman in particular,'" our internet PI quoted from the obit.

Moments later, Beth found a Facebook profile for Justin's apparent maternal half-brother, Mason Hadley.

"Ol' Mason's a ginger, too," Beth noted. "Well, his beard is."

Edie examined Shirley's information, made publicly available on Ancestry because Justin had marked her on his tree as deceased. "When I click on his mom, it shows she has a son with each of two men, but all four of them are private," Edie said of the two fathers and their sons.

"So far, I can't put Shirley and John together," Beth messaged. "But they must've been. I mean, obviously."

After briefly revisiting the rabbit hole containing John Hart the law school instructor, an increasingly bemused Beth wrote, "This is all a huge mystery and I want to start getting people on the phone." It was nearly 10:30 on a Saturday night.

Two minutes later, she posed a pivotal question. "Where did Ethel Lee Moore die?" Beth asked about Edie's apparent paternal grandmother.

"Perry, Florida," Edie passed along, "June 27, 1992." Four months before that, Ethel Lee Moore's husband, Edie's ostensible grandfather, had died in Hendersonville, Tennessee.

With ninety minutes until Sunday's arrival, Beth found a 2012 obituary for Ethel Lee Moore's daughter, Collee Wilson. "John I. Hart" was listed as one of Collee's five surviving siblings. Another was "Joseph E. Hart, Jr.," even though Justin's tree said Uncle Joseph had passed away in 2010, two years before Aunt Collee.

"Typo in the tree?" Beth postulated.

"Quite possibly," Edie told Beth. "Damn, you're good."

"Not quite there yet. I haven't found John," Beth maintained before pivoting to another one of Collee's surviving siblings. "I found LeMerle, too, at numerous West Coast addresses. Mainly leaving comments in funeral notices, bless her heart," she said. "She has a weird name. She was easy."

Minutes later, Beth found Uncle Joseph's 2010 obituary. Like Justin's tree, it indicated he died two years before Aunt Collee passed, contradicting whoever approved her 2012 obit to run as-is.

"Obit writer for Collee screwed up?" Beth pondered.

"We've known it to happen," her former newspaper colleague said.

Beth also noted John wasn't mentioned in his brother's obituary.

"Might they have been so estranged as to not know?" my tired wife hypothesized about Uncle Joe's obit omit.

"But how could there be another Joseph E. Hart Jr. with sisters named LeMerle Milsom and Collee Wilson?" Beth countered. With less than an hour of Doc's birthday remaining, she reported, "The best I can tell, John still walks among us."

While Beth determined the mortal state of her friend's biological father, Edie investigated other John Harts.

"There's this guy, whom I know nothing about," Edie sent with a link to a Facebook account. No information was publicly available about this John Hart, except for the nattily dressed man's profile pic. Bespeckled and gray-haired, he did sort of resemble Edie's late Uncle Joseph.

"On it." Beth quickly came back with details about the man's family to dismiss the lead. "I can't cross any of those people back to our people."

Beth also admitted she'd exhausted all apparent leads from the children of Edie's paternal grandparents, although she did run across the bowling scores of Rudy, Aunt Katy Ann's husband in Hendersonville, Tennessee. "He's set to bowl on Wednesday with his team."

Damn. She really is good.

"Damn you, Joe Jr.," Beth lamented, "why didn't you list your brother?"

"John's looking like a possible black sheep," his daughter acknowledged.

At 11:31 p.m., Beth shared the Facebook page for Uncle Joseph's widow, a Minnesotan named Muriel.

"Further confusion," Edie soon countered with an obituary for Joan Hart. "This is Joe Jr.'s wife, as listed on Justin's tree."

"Wut," Beth replied. "Joe Jr.'s obit clearly says HIS WIFE MURIEL."

"And the kids' names don't match," Edie gleaned from the obituaries for Uncle Joseph and his first wife, Joan.

"Muriel might be a second wife that doesn't get along with the progeny of the first wife," Beth proposed.

"Whoa," Edie responded. "Both Joe Jr. and Joan had two sons and one daughter. Joan's daughter is Jean; Joe's daughter is Jeanne."

Beth then noticed the two obits listed the same names for the kids' spouses. "There's some nicknames in play, wanna bet?" she said about Edie's potential first cousins, before taking aim at the newspaper that printed the vexing death notices. "This joint in Minnesota needs literate obit writers; I think we can go ahead and establish that. I had an uncle Stanley we called Randy for no apparent reason, and they also called my uncle Larry that. But we had more sense than to put that in the obit."

"O.M.G." Edie realized, "Dueling obits."

Beth soon found a Facebook profile belonging to Edie's cousin Jean/Jeanne in the Gopher State. Edie then discovered Jean/Jeanne had a son named Tony.

"WHY CAN WE FIND EVERYONE BUT JOHN," Beth wrote. "THIS IS MAKING ME NUTS."

At one minute before midnight, Edie self-induced a brief panic attack by making connections that weren't there. "I'm going off on too many tangents now," she admitted.

"Same," Beth concurred. "I'm tired. Gonna go to bed."

"Sounds good," Edie told her friend. "This has been tremendous. Thank you again."

"We've at least found you a stack of people to reach out to," Beth noted. "Alllll the second cousins!"

Within the minute, after agreeing to suspend the search for the night, Beth added, "Real quick: Justin was born in Seattle?"

"Hm," Edie replied, "just closed browsers."

"OPEN 'EM," the savior instructed. "I JUST FOUND STUFF."

4

More of You

Sunday, February 18, 2018, in Baton Rouge began with low clouds that cleared throughout the day and into the evening. The high was 80 degrees, with a low of 60. Winds were light and variable.

At 12:06 a.m., Beth sent Edie the names of ten Harts likely related to Justin Hart. The list included John I. Hart and Cherish Hart.

Edie's browser tabs were coming back to life. "Cherish is in all his Facebook posts," she said of Justin's photos.

Beth discovered the same Cherish Hart served on the board of a nonprofit in the Seattle suburb of Renton, Washington. Given that Cherish shared a home address with Justin, Beth surmised the two were married.

"Justin was a ginger as a kid," Red realized after coming across a Facebook photo of a young li'l bro with a giant grin. His chin rested on his youthful mother at the foot of a sunny, tree-dotted hill.

The caption of Justin's public post read, "Hadley said to me this morning, when I was looking at my mother's funerary paperwork, 'Daddy, I want to talk to my grandma.' I said, 'We can honey, any time you want. Grandma is all around us; just tell her what you want to say.' I don't know what prompted this—DNA, subconscious wavelengths, thought—but Mom, wherever you are, we love you. We miss you. We feel your presence in our lives in many ways. Happy Mother's Day."

Beth soon sent three words. "I found him."

Edie sent back three exclamation points.

"Degree of confidence: middling," was Beth's caveat regarding a Whitepages listing for John Irving Hart in Austin, Texas. Both Perry, Florida, and Renton, Washington, were listed as previous locations for him. "I like to double-verify Whitepages," she said, "but it's usually decently accurate. Still working."

Moments later, Beth found a "semi-sketchy family tree website" indicating that John Irving Hart married Shirley Ann Stubb in Miami in February 1973. It also showed Justin's mom would later take the surname Hadley.

"Yep," Edie confirmed, "Justin's tree says she was married that date in Florida. Justin also has a 2014 picture of sibling Rachel Sears, from Austin."

"Full sibling?" Beth asked. "She'd have to be John's, because Shirley only had two," Beth said of Justin Hart and Mason "Ginger Beard" Hadley.

"Not sure," Edie conceded about Justin's social media post. "He just labeled the pic 'sibling beach time.'"

While Rachel wasn't on Justin's tree, Beth found the Austin resident and her Edie-like locks on Facebook.

"Justin's in one of her pics," Beth informed my wife. "Dat curly hair."

"She was born about the time I was a senior in high school," Edie noted.

An excited Beth then learned Rachel was cousin to Erica Milsom, daughter of Aunt LeMerle Milsom, John Hart's sister who knows lots of dead folks on the West Coast.

"John HAS to be her dad and Justin's and yours!" Beth told Edie. "SHE'S A GINGER—or was when she was younger."

"So all of our hair darkened up as we went along," Edie concluded about John Hart's children. It was 1:03 a.m.

Literally overnight, my wife went from baby girl of the O'Neals to big sister of a growing new family, complete with a seventeen-year age span between Edie and Rachel, surpassing the fourteen years that separate Wade and Red. Aside from the tsunami of emotions that accompany such a realization came an inescapable change in Edie's reality. Up until that moment, for over forty-seven years, actual family resemblances were strictly for other people.

After finding more photos of Rachel, who looked remarkably like a young Edie, Beth treated herself to a much-deserved "celebratory maybe-found-Edie's-lost-family wedge of blueberry/blood orange pound cake." While cutting in the dark, in an attempt to not wake her husband, Beth's knife "chinked off the knife he left there when he apparently went to get himself a decidedly less celebratory wedge of cake."

Believe it or not, the two of us actually managed to get some sleep, even if it was only a few hours. With daylight came an announcement from someone who's fond of chickens.

"Good morning, E and J!" Yvette messaged us around 8:30 a.m. on our four-person thread. "Do you have any interest in seeing *Hamilton?*"

"Hey, good morning!" I replied minutes later. "We actually bought a membership to this upcoming season of Broadway Across America at the Saenger Theatre specifically because that's one of the shows." We had picked the same Sunday night performances as our friends the Cavells so we could drive down to New Orleans together.

"Y'all recover from Mardi Gras?" Patrick asked. "Looks like y'all were having a blast."

"Pretty much, although last night knocked me for a loop." I teased, "Friend's surprise birthday party."

"You're laying down a fierce pace for your age," my brother-in-law said.

Edie joined in just after 9 a.m. "Fierce is the word a coworker used to describe his parade look," she said of my bad-ass Mardi Gras beard.

"You continue to outdo yourselves," Patrick said with a laugh. "Edie and Jeremy Spanish Town pics are always my favorites."

"Y'all gonna be online for a while?" I asked before sharing an animated GIF dramatically declaring "BREAKING NEWS."

Edie posted seconds later, "My eyes are still blurry because my archivist friend got on my AncestryDNA case til 2:00 a.m."

I immediately followed her message with another animated GIF. This one showed a cigarette-smoking Samuel L. Jackson instructing people in *Jurassic Park* to "HOLD ON TO YOUR BUTTS."

"Holding!" Yvette hollered.

"Tell us!" Patrick exclaimed. "We've been reluctant to ask."

Edie broke the news. "Half-bro outside Seattle."

"Holy fucking shit," Patrick reacted.

"Half-sis, bio dad in Austin," she continued.

"Holy. Fucking. Shit," he reemphasized.

"Eyes, fingers still fuzzy," Edie added.

"The half-bro seems way cool," I threw in.

"I don't think I was holding on to my butt enough," Patrick typed. "Is he on Ancestry?"

"Half-bro has another half-bro on mom's side," Edie replied, "all gingers."

"What?!" he shot back.

"Have you made contact?" Yvette asked.

"Are you overwhelmed by this?" Patrick quizzed. "Because I am."

"Um, yeah," Edie answered both queries. "Brief message sent yesterday to bio dad."

Patrick then clarified how he was feeling overwhelmed. "In a good way," he told his baby sister. "Something about there being more of you makes me happy."

My brother-in-law gut-punched me with that just as I was sending, "Her friend Beth is a beast of an archivist."

"Is she for hire?" Patrick inquired.

"Probs," Edie replied. "I freelance for her. And she traced like a half-dozen lineages in less than five hours," she said of a working mom who spent the day fishing with her family. "An uncle is bowling Wednesday night, and she found his scores."

"WTF?" Patrick reacted. "Is she Deep State? Holy shit."

"I can't tell if it's the coffee or this convo that has my blood pressure elevated," Yvette interjected. Our java-loving hermana was buzzing. "Seriously."

"Anything on Mom?" Patrick wondered.

"Nada," I chimed in.

"There are probable links to mom," Edie informed us, "but more distant."

"Wow," Patrick said. "I'm blown away. You okay?"

Edie's reply came in the form of Justin's moving Facebook post, wherein his daughter asked about conversing with her deceased grandmother. "That is half-bro and his mom," Edie commented on the photo. Justin's words "about did me in," she said.

"I bet," Patrick agreed.

Edie also mentioned her brief message to John Hart. "That was twelve hours before my friend found bio dad's address and landline number. He was so off the grid it frustrated her. He's the one who took so long. She traced his siblings' kids in no time."

"Half-sis in Austin," I introduced Rachel's Facebook page.

"Damn," Patrick replied. "Sis is a liberal!"

"So is bro," Edie noted, "and photographer."

Upon studying Justin's Facebook photos, Patrick wondered, "Am I projecting, or are there similarities in the eyes?"

"And nose," I added with a picture showing Edie's little brother and sister together as adults.

"Sis also didn't have hair til she was a year old," said Red, who was also bald for her first trip around the sun.

"And she likes Cyndi Lauper," Patrick reported another similarity with our newest in-law. "By the way, we are both crying over here at the sight of your brother," Patrick shared. "Oh, Edie. The world just got bigger and better."

"It feels weird that I stayed up all night scrolling their pages, but I couldn't help it," she said as the two youngest O'Neal kids continued their exchange in the thread.

"Your Dad's got some game!" Patrick exclaimed.

"He's Johnny Gingerseed," Edie dubbed her dad, evoking laughter from an again gobsmacked Patrick.

"Did you message the sibs," he asked, "or just the father of ginger nation?"

"Just the progenitor so far," Edie answered. "Kinda feel like the floodgate might open when I contact the sibs."

"No kidding," Patrick empathized. "Honestly, I'm speechless, so 'no kidding' is the best I can do."

"I already have the best and coolest brother in the world," Edie told Patrick. "This is so much icing on cake."

"Awwwwww," Patrick blushed. "Still, blood brother looks really cool. Sister too. Lord knows this family could use an injection of some cool. Especially liberal cool. Plus the eyes and the nose have me drawn to them."

"Justin's mom was a hippy photographer," Edie passed along.

"Your brother brews his own beer," observed Patrick, who used to do the same. "And you have a beautiful niece, apparently," he added. "And I'm stalking these people."

"Me too," Edie admitted.

"So Dad," the attorney redirected his line of questioning, "does he live in Austin proper? Do you know how old he is? Married? Job? Fuck, Pandora's Box holds a lot of shit."

"Probably seventies," Edie said of John Hart's age. She then shared her biological father's Whitepages listing. It showed his home address and phone number, which my wife was nervously sitting on, wondering if she'd eventually resort to dialing it.

"Looks like dad might have another woman at that address," Edie revealed. "Hallie Hart."

"Interesting," Patrick replied late Sunday morning, around the time Edie usually left to tend to Earle and her round-the-clock sitters.

"I better make my weekly rounds in Maringouin before reaching out to anyone else," Edie said, "or I'll never get out of the house."

"Yeah," Patrick agreed. "How long are you going to keep this under wraps?"

"Uncertain."

"We may have your lineage mapped by the time you get back," Patrick joked. "Your secret's safe," he promised.

In the midst of all this, my ever-thoughtful wife asked about Yvette's DNA results. They had not yet come in.

About an hour after Edie departed for her hometown, Yvette blurted out, "I keep breaking down into tears of freaked-outness."

"Yeah, that is definitely a thing," Edie confirmed after returning home from the west side of the Mississippi River. Her late departure had left no time to pass by Ducky's while excitedly holding so many WTF cards close to her vest.

Plus, Edie had initial correspondence to send to her newly discovered baby brother. She personalized for Justin the same Ancestry message she had sent John some twenty-four hours earlier.

"Hi there," were Edie's first two words to her father. "I was adopted at birth and am now a married adult. I wasn't sure what to expect after sending in a sample to AncestryDNA, but it's extremely confident that I am your biological daughter. This revelation is likely much more surprising for you than it was for me. Please know that I don't wish to cause any turmoil, but I am receptive if you are interested in any further communication or sharing of information.

"Respectfully," she signed off, "Edris White."

After sending her message to Justin, she grabbed a grade-school photograph of herself. It showed Edie wearing a gap-toothed smile while holding her beloved childhood calico cat, Patches. My wife held up the decades-old picture next to a computer image of her little sister's freckled face for a side-by-side shot.

"The eyes have it," Patrick flatly said of their brown peepers. "Also, Edie, I want a copy of that amazing picture of you and Patches."

Along with the requested photo, my wife also shared a fresh snapshot of young Edie and Patches back in their place, hanging just below a picture of a teenaged Patrick. The cottontop lady killer was laying on the ground with his right hand propping up his thick locks, shimmering in the sun.

"Lose that," my brother-in-law insisted. "Holy shit."

Minutes later, Beth popped up on chat, eighteen hours after her celebratory-cake message. "Have you heard from anyone?"

"Not yet," Edie replied. "Just sent a message to Justin." She added that Patrick was "mad impressed" with her skills.

Beth responded, "I have a whole master's degree in Google."

"At one point he asked if you're for hire," Edie relayed. "Then asked if you're Deep State."

"So deep, I'm unaware of it myself."

"Bwahahahaha," Edie wrote back, "or maybe that should be muahahahaha."

Now that she had reached out to Justin, would the floodgates open as Edie predicted? How long would she sit on John's phone number? After almost twenty-four hours, it wasn't getting any less weird.

Nevertheless, we were in bed around ten to hopefully catch up on sleep we didn't get all weekend.

At 10:38 p.m. Central Standard Time, just as we were dozing off, Justin clicked send.

5

The Ideal Emissary

Monday, February 19, 2018, the Capital City saw midmorning fog give way to partly sunny skies and a clear evening. The high was 84, with a low of 62. Winds were light and from the east, with afternoon gusts.

The two of us were up by 6 a.m., anxious to see if Justin had replied. Edie checked her primary Gmail account, as she often does after awakening, although this episode felt a bit more dramatic than most.

No notifications from Ancestry awaited her. Since she had set her account to alert her via email whenever she received a message, Edie left for work without anything new to process.

Around lunchtime, a busy Fort Worth lawyer messaged his little sister.

"Just want to make sure you aren't too overwhelmed by all this new info," Patrick checked in. "No matter what, I love you so. No matter what, you're not in this little adventure alone. Hell, by the looks of it," he added, "alone is like the last thing we are going to be."

"I love you," a thankful Edie replied, "and am so glad you prompted me to embark on this adventure. The abundant and close matches are definitely the overwhelming part." She wouldn't rush beyond her initial messages to John and Justin Hart, Edie insisted. "I'm trying to remind myself that as exciting as all that stuff on the paternal side is, one of my main reasons for doing this was to put it out there in case someone was looking on the maternal side, which looks like it will entail more research."

"I was feeling a little guilty," said the inspiration for this adventure. "Like maybe we didn't think it through too much. But hey," Patrick countered, "it's super cool to see your sibs and read about them. There is so much you in them and vice versa, it's astounding."

Edie reciprocated with enough Catholic guilt for the lot of us. "I was feeling guilty that I got all those close matches right off the bat, and then that I got so excited about them."

"I'm sooooo excited, too," he said of their findings. "It's like we've slipped into some alternate universe where you and I don't exist solely as standalones. Does that make sense? Like now, our existence didn't just begin at birth. It has a history that shaped us, at least genetically." Patrick added, "The thought of more Edies is wonderful."

My laughing bride told her brother, "Careful what you wish for."

"At least your relatives aren't from Alabama. I'd be lying if I said that fact hasn't cooled my jets on an overall search," he replied. "We're ready for road trips whenever you are," Patrick insisted. "I love both Seattle and Austin."

"Yay!" Edie enthused. "I was thinking that would be kinda awesome," she said before addressing John Hart's apparent absence from his other children's lives. "While I haven't seen much evidence of bio-paternal involvement on either sib's social media, it was really neat to see their pics of each other nonetheless; like there's a chance to make a connection there even if the direct link isn't involved."

"Right," Patrick agreed. "We can't kid ourselves; there was a reason we were placed for adoption. I remind myself when I do this Ancestry stuff that it may break my heart, or even someone else's. The latter I have no interest in. I don't want a confrontation. But if we get to know ourselves better through these family members," he continued, "then we are enriched whether our bio parents want to, or can be, involved."

"That's a great reminder and perspective," Red said.

"Anyway, as long as you're cool, I'm cool," her brother reassured. "And I'm here for you to chat. Love you so."

At 2:13 p.m., Beth messaged my wife. "Well, anything?"

Her message went unseen, just like Justin's overnight reply. That changed after work, though, once Edie finally checked Ancestry itself.

"Can I call you?" Edie messaged Patrick at 6:19 p.m.

The two were on the phone by the bottom of the hour. Sixty seconds into their sixteen-minute call, Edie posted in our four-person thread a screenshot of Justin's message.

"Hello, Edie," he addressed his new big sis. "And wow, I am so excited and interested to hear from you! It clearly seems that I am your half-brother, but even if we are not related (if, for example, there is some kind of mistake in the Ancestry database or something), I am excited to meet you, and help you figure out more about your family and history. I have never heard that there was even a possibility of John having another, older child before," a surprised Justin said.

"I would like to know more about you," he insisted, "and would like to answer questions for you, too." After asking about Edie's birth mother, Justin wrote, "I can follow up with John and confirm details for you, too."

Their father was a graduate student at LSU in 1969, after serving in the Army in Vietnam, Justin explained. He described John's stint in Baton Rouge as "very politically active. He had been a minister before the war, and was very much an advocate of peace.

"I did not really grow up with John (just visited)," Justin continued, "so there may be some holes in my own understanding of his history, as I lived with my mother and stepfather until I was an adult." Explaining how he regularly sees and communicates with John, Justin assured, "I can ask questions for you, no problem." He also told Edie that she likely hadn't heard back from John because "he is not very internet savvy," adding, "I had him do the DNA test for my own research purposes.

"What questions do you have?" he asked. "What would you like to know more about? I am happy to answer anything I can, and follow up with John. I can also imagine this could be a little overwhelming, so don't feel obligated, either. Just know I am happy to hear from you, and to get to know you.

"Thank you for reaching out," her brother wrote. "I am very eager to know more about you.

"All the best," he signed off, "Justin Hart."

In line with the day's theme of not seeing messages from Justin, a busy Patrick and Yvette didn't get to read Edie's latest share that night.

It's hard to believe that Justin could be even cooler and more awesome than we had surmised from his social media presence. I quickly realized Edie's new brother was *the* ideal emissary for her and our burgeoning adventure of discovery. Even if I had the power to do so, I couldn't imagine custom-making one more perfectly suited for my partner.

For the next hour or so, Edie composed a reply. She aimed to strike a balance between unbridled giddiness and cold professionalism. After I lent an approving, second set of eyes, she sent her next few hundred words to Justin just after 8 p.m. Monday.

"Justin, thank you so much for your quick and gracious response!" she wrote. "I am a bit overwhelmed, but excited, too.

"As surprised as you are," Edie noted, "it's possible that I might be a shock to John's system, too. At this point, I don't have any information about my mother or her circumstances, and I realize there's a possibility she may not have informed John that I had been conceived (or that some data entry went awry at Ancestry). I certainly trust your judgment on how and when to broach that subject with John beyond the brief message I already sent him through Ancestry.

"It was pretty startling to get such close matches right off the bat," she shared. "Not wanting to dive in too deep too soon, I've only reached out to you and John at this point. I don't want to rush in and create angst for people who may not know about me. Your response was such a relief!

"It's a little hard to sort out questions right now, so maybe for starters I can answer some instead," Edie prefaced a brief primer on her life. "Like John, I also went to LSU, where I studied zoology and psychology and met the love of my life. We just celebrated our twenty-fifth anniversary. We don't have any children but loved on four fabulous felines for most of those years. We also devote a great deal of our time to political satire and football.

"I don't think I can adequately convey how much I appreciate your message. Biology aside," she continued, "the warmth of your words has me overjoyed, but it's all the more exciting to think we might be siblings!

"I appreciate your openness and look forward to continuing to get to know each other. Please feel free to share as much information with John as you feel appropriate, and to ask me any questions you or he may have.

"By the way, you've made my day! I hope yours is full of joy, too!

"Edie," she simply closed.

After sending the reply, we ate a late supper and tried to distract ourselves with television. Fatigue eventually overtook excitement as the evening wore on, and we made our way to bed.

About an hour later, at the exact moment Monday gave way to Tuesday in Baton Rouge, Justin clicked send again.

6

My New Favorite Word

Tuesday, February 20, 2018, began with early fog yielding to an unseasonably warm, partly sunny day and a clear evening in the Red Stick. The high was a record-tying 87 degrees, with a low of 67. Winds were breezy and from east to east-southeast, with moderate gusts throughout the day.

The creaking floodgates awoke Edie by 4:30 a.m. It was 2:30 a.m. on the West Coast, four and a half hours after Justin had messaged back.

"Edie, you are most welcome!" she read in the predawn hours at her desk. "And first of all, I want to listen to your feeling of being overwhelmed." Justin promised to keep his responses brief, despite wanting to write much more. "Please know that I respect how you feel, and you get to set the parameters here.

"I spoke to John," Justin continued, "and he, too, is completely surprised. He said he never had any idea he had another child before me." While John was happy to talk with his eldest, Justin noted, "His memory isn't always solid due to his age and life history. But if you want to pursue contact with him, I can put you in touch (email might be best), but only if/when you decide you want to do so. He's a sweet man, but easily discombobulated.

"I find the information about your history fascinating," Edie read, "and it sounds like we have some commonalities. I was born about three years after you," Justin wrote, "June 20, 1973. My wife, Cherish, and I have a five-year-old daughter. She is amazing and the light of our lives. As far as I know, she is the only grandchild of John's (given your info). I was also a copy editor (in grad school), and now am a healthcare data analyst. I love political satire, as well, and watch a little football (because Cherish is a big fan)."

"I also want to let you know of your likely half-sister, Rachel, who was born in 1987," Justin offered along with his personal email. "She lives in Austin, Texas.

"Please tell me more about yourself, as you are comfortable in doing so. I am happy to tell you more about me and my life, and to answer other questions you may have." Curious about our cats' names, Justin also asked about Edie's motivation in submitting her DNA, before revealing his. "I did it because I wanted to know more about where I came from. Both John and my mother were ostracized from their families, so I didn't grow up with much contact with them.

With a "most sincerely" smile, he closed, "You made my day, too, by the way."

An hour before sunup, Edie shared Justin's reply with Fort Worth.

"Oh, Edie," Patrick soon replied. "Is he for real? I'm just so happy," he gushed. "Dad sounds like that might need to be a slow build, but Justin sounds like we all got together and designed a family member just for you. And a copy editor. Wow. Gobsmacked is my new favorite word."

"Iknowrite?" my proofreader typed. "I'm trying to compose a response, but I'm just crying over here," Edie shared. "Happy tears."

"Of course," Patrick sympathized. "Me too. And," he added with a laugh, "don't respond, 'Oh, I know about Rachel. We've all been cyber-stalking her, too.'"

"Yeah," Edie concurred, "trying not to say anything he didn't already provide in his messages!"

"Man, how can you narrow the list of questions AND go to work today?" her big brother asked. "So many questions."

Around seven, before heading out the door, Edie wrote her younger brother back. This time, she was a little less guarded.

"Oh, Justin, there are a lot of happy tears in my house right now," she opened. "I did take the DNA test to see if it might help identify my biological parents. In a way, it feels selfish, and I don't want to hurt anyone by reaching out and imposing myself on them. But for a long time, I've considered that there might be at least one or two people out there wondering if they did the right thing, or how things turned out. And time narrows my opportunity to help bring peace to those people by letting them know it's OK.

"And now it's so much more than OK. My life is already blessed with a loving family; I adore my nieces and nephews (and now eight great-nieces and -nephews, too). I dared not hope that I might find a brother who shares common interests, learn of a relatively nearby sister, and have the opportunity to reach out to a sweet man who links us all together.

"I would appreciate the opportunity to email John, and include you in that correspondence," Edie wrote, sharing her email address. "May I ask if you've mentioned our conversation to Rachel?" she queried. "Again, I don't want to impose myself on anyone, but if she would like it, I am happy to also include her when I reach out to John.

"I have lived my whole life in Louisiana, with the exception of one summer during college when I worked at a research station in Wisconsin," Edie led a paragraph about her upbringing.

"More to come!" she wrapped up with a smile. "Have a great day, and I look forward to continuing our conversation!"

That message took her well over an hour to compose. Even when writing much more innocuous things than correspondence to a newly discovered brother, Edie has always employed an exceptionally deliberative style. My wife writes emails like Orson Welles made movies.

As hard as filling a vial with spit was for Edie, hitting send on an email to newly found kin proved much more difficult. I did what I could to provide coaching and reassurances for both tasks.

She headed out the door Tuesday morning with a lot more things to process than the day before. Like Monday, we traded brief, idle chats throughout the day. Topics tended to be far more mundane than what was happening back home.

Later that afternoon, Edie phoned three important people.

"Called Mom, Kellie, and Wade after work to fill them in," she alerted Fort Worth at 7:30 p.m. "Somewhat," she qualified.

During their call, Ducky suddenly remembered that Edie's birth mother was a "very smart LSU student," and that her OB-GYN had all of her information in his files.

Ducky "wondered if we could ask the doc who bought out the practice to dig it up," Edie reported. "Might be a privacy issue," she winked.

"Yeah, I just got off the phone with Mom," Patrick informed us. "She's good. Ready to travel with you like I thought she would. She has me running down Dr. Leggio's wife."

"What did the sibs have to say?" Yvette inquired.

"Wade brought up that bio mom may have put a release in the file," Edie said of her adoption records. "Duck and Kel were both excited. All want to be kept in the loop." She additionally reported, "Kellie had this idea that bio dad was an LSU football player; not sure if she dreamed that."

We knew next to nothing about John. However, we were pretty confident that a minister/Vietnam vet/peace activist was not also a jock.

Patrick chortled, "The truth is faaaaaaaaar more interesting."

Edie then found a third Ancestry message from Justin. "Made myself stay off site at work," she prefaced her baby bro's lunchtime correspondence.

"I am going to send you a very long email with lots of information about my history and John's," Justin forewarned. "It is really meant as a big information transfer for you to have a story. I apologize for it being so long; so long that it exceeds the Ancestry messaging limit. I won't write such lengthy emails all the time," he promised with a grin.

"I will call Rachel and John tonight as I need to talk to them separately," Justin explained. "Rachel is very excited to communicate with
you, too," he said, "but I have to do a little more checking in with them
first. You will get a sense for why from the lengthy email." Edie was
told to also expect a possible email from John.

A smiling Justin closed, "I hope you have a wonderful day, and am
so glad that you have found us."

After again fighting with a misbehaving email account, she found
Justin's promised message. Edie alerted Fort Worth: "2,228 words."

"Dang," Patrick reacted to the length of what had already engrossed
us in Baton Rouge. "That's more like a treatise," he said.

As we read what I dubbed the "Manifestbro," Edie and I enjoyed our
first sips from a bottle of mezcal we'd bought in Cozumel on our twen-
tieth anniversary cruise. We had been saving it for a special occasion.
This seemed pretty damn special.

Around eight, Edie shared Justin's latest message with Fort Worth.

"Though I was never technically adopted, in a way I was," Justin
wrote of his upbringing, "and I feel connected to you already." He
mentioned a longstanding desire to know and connect with family he
had yet to meet.

"Rachel and John do not communicate directly with each other,
presently," Justin revealed. "I will let Rachel explain why, but suffice it
to say that it has been her choice." While Edie was welcome to copy
Justin on emails to either of them, she was warned against including
Rachel in messages to John. "I am their intermediary, and that has been
awkward at times, but it is my hope that someday she and he will be
able to reconcile." Justin's attempts to help Rachel in this regard had
yielded "mixed results," he said. "She is more like him, in some ways,
than I am."

His mom, Shirley, divorced John after only a couple years together,
and left Florida for Northern California with Justin when he was only
nine months old. John soon followed them, settling in San Francisco.
Shirley had full custody, but allowed John to visit his son, up to weeks
at a time. "Some of my earliest memories are of flying a kite in Golden

Gate park," Justin said, "and eating ice cream on the floor of John's apartment (he never had much furniture any time I visited). But my mom remarried when I was about three years old," he wrote, "and we moved to Colorado when I was about four."

Around that same time, circa 1977, John moved back to Florida, where he expanded his ongoing enterprises.

"John started growing and selling marijuana when he was with my mom," Justin informed Edie about their father. "In the years after they split up, he moved from just growing a little bit to actually growing and selling a lot of it. When I would visit him as a kid, it was a bit scary," but not because John is to be feared, Justin reassured. "He is truly one of the most peace-loving, genuine, and kind-hearted people you could meet." Rather, Justin was scared during his visits "because, as you can imagine, the business of selling drugs is not a safe one. Anyway, he went to prison in 1983 and has never gone back to that life.

"And the reasons he got involved in it in the first place are long and myriad, but I see him as a sort of Robin Hood type of character," Justin explained, "always trying to help out the less fortunate and doing so via 'extra-legal' means. He wasn't trying to make a lot of money; he wasn't trying to become some kind of drug kingpin." Instead, John "started doing it because it was 'natural,' during what you might call his hippie phase," his son said, "and then because people he knew needed cash, or lots of pot to get them out of trouble. In fact," Justin declared, "you could say John was the worst drug dealer, because he never really made much money at all. He gave it all away trying to help this person or that person by paying off their drug debts or what have you."

Justin turned ten when John went to prison in 1983. That's when he and six-year-old Mason relocated to San Diego with Shirley and her second husband, Patrick Hadley. Justin lived there until leaving for college in 1991.

"John was released from prison in 1986 in Austin," Justin wrote. "At around the same time, my mother also decided she was done being a parent, and left me and my brother with my stepfather." Effectively motherless, Justin couldn't move in with his father because John was too busy getting back on his feet after years in a Texas prison. "It was certainly a rough time," Justin shared. "I became a surrogate parent figure for my little brother, before I had finished growing up myself. I never moved in with John for more than a summer vacation because," he added, "honestly, I just felt more comfortable with my stepfather and brother. At one point, my stepfather was going to adopt me, but we decided not to do that because there wasn't a clear reason why we would since we had good relationships with John.

"I first went to visit John after he was able to establish the bare minimum of stability for himself after prison in the summer of 1986. He was on parole, then probation for several years, and he lived in a sort of halfway house that first summer. In fact, his room was really just a large closet with no air conditioning, so it was very uncomfortable. He had me stay with a girlfriend," Justin said of Elizabeth, the woman who would become Rachel's mother.

He was thirteen when "John and Elizabeth eventually became involved." The details of this hurtful episode in Justin's life differ greatly between the recollections of John and his son. "They seemed to get along fine," Justin said of the couple. "They weren't in love or anything, just dating. A few months later, though, Elizabeth was pregnant. John was still on probation, could barely scrape together enough money to keep his car running, and didn't even have his own place." While neither were interested in a relationship, "she definitely wanted to have a baby. She may not have been honest with John," Justin proposed. "This is something Rachel and I have talked about. In any case, that whole relationship more or less imploded over the course of the next year."

On his second summer visit to Austin, Justin met his infant sister, two months after Rachel was born in 1987. "John and Elizabeth had enough cordiality to allow that meeting to happen. They never really did again, though," Justin said. "I didn't see Rachel again until she was an adult in 2007."

He continued spending summers in Austin with John until moving to Amherst, Massachusetts, for college. While there, he met and moved in with a young woman, whom he then followed by transferring to

Evergreen College in Olympia, Washington. "She broke up with me just before I got there," Justin said, "but I stayed."

Upon graduation in 1995, he joined Americorps, where he became an English as a Second Language instructor. While in the yearlong program, he met Cherish. After Americorps, Justin enrolled in graduate school in Spokane. He and Cherish were newlyweds in 2001 when they moved to Tokyo for his university teaching gig. "This was part of our dream to see the world," Justin wrote, "and we traveled a decent amount in Asia and Australia during the years we lived there." By 2005, the couple moved to Seattle, where Justin eventually became a data analyst and project manager in the tech industry.

"Our daughter, Hadley, was born in 2012, and is in kindergarten now. My brother Mason lives in Olympia, about an hour south of us," Justin passed along. "John still lives in Austin, though he is regularly up here for health care visits at the Seattle VA hospital." Justin also reported their father "has finally found a partner he could settle down with." John married Hallie in 2008, after decades of unstable relationships.

"He had a few different girlfriends over the years," the emissary explained, "though none of those relationships lasted more than a year or two. John has some physical and emotional issues that certainly have made it a challenge for him to sustain relationships. In addition to his head injuries, he was never close to his family—lots of fighting and strife. He left as soon as he could.

"He was partially deaf from an early age, and maybe that had something to do with the trouble he experienced at home. He has been mostly deaf since 1968," Justin stated. "He lost all of his hearing in his 'good ear' due to a friendly fire accident in Vietnam. That just exacerbated things for him, not to mention the psychological scars of serving in a war."

Justin further mentioned, "I also have an older brother I have never met. His name was Andrew when he was born in either Georgia or Florida," he said of a man who'd be around Edie's age. "My mother tried to find him before she passed away, but she said the orphanage had been destroyed by a fire, and all records were lost. Andrew was not John's child, so like Mason, he isn't related to you, but finding you reminds me that he may still be out there, wondering if he has siblings or family he's never known.

"I hope this isn't too overwhelming," Justin closed. "Stay tuned for another, more succinct communication soon. And please let me know if there is anything in this lengthy story you want to know more about."

Around the time Edie shared Justin's latest with Fort Worth, she apologized to Beth for missing her friend's message yesterday.

"WELL," a still-curious Beth asked, "DID YOU HEAR?!"

"SO. MUCH," Edie answered, alluding to that day's correspondence, including "2,228 words of backstory that I just read."

"WHOA."

"He is even more awesome than his social media profile lets on," Edie proclaimed. "J wants to hug him."

"That's saying something!" Beth remarked.

"He was not only a college copy editor, but got an MFA in creative writing," Edie reported, evoking a trio of exclamation points from Beth.

In his latest message, Justin offered a peek behind his master's degree in fine arts. "Poetry was so vital to my growth and recovery from the abandonment I felt as a child," he wrote.

"All of his siblings are halfs," Edie messaged Beth.

"Mine too!" Beth replied. "Yay, the halfies!"

"He has a relationship with Rachel, but she doesn't have a relationship with John," Edie relayed. "I woke up at 4:30, like I knew there was another message for me to read, then barely made it to work. Now I'm feeling it," my worn-out bride wrote, "as I'm wondering where to begin to respond to this treatise." She added "justin.is.amazing" at 9:35 p.m., just as her elder brother finished reading the Manifestbro.

"Edie," Patrick popped up on the thread, "that's just the most amazing story. Justin seems like a remarkable person. All the more so for that insane childhood. Wow." As for John, he said, "Your daddy is like some kind of pot saint. It's like that Steve Earl song, 'Copperhead Road.'

He learned a thing or two from Charlie, don't you know." Patrick soon added, "Sorry, I know I'm not making sense. Gobsmacked."

Yvette mustered a "MIND BLOWN" sticker.

"Totally understandable," I assured them both.

"How awesome is he?" Yvette marveled.

"Yeah, I'm in awe," Edie said, "dumbfounded at how to adequately respond."

"I trust you can respond in kind," Patrick allayed. "Just tell your story. The O'Neals are so fucking dull," he joked. "You may need to tart it up a bit to keep him awake."

"To keep myself awake at this point," Edie winked.

"I bet," Patrick wrote. "Phew. What a year you've had these past three days."

"Tell your story!" our bold sister-in-law insisted.

"But maybe get some sleep first?" her husband suggested.

"It might not be a choice," a tired Edie conceded. "But I can't leave him hanging."

Following our foursome's volley of goodnights near ten, Edie worked on her response to Justin.

"I am so very grateful to have found you," she composed, "and awestruck by your email. You have absolutely no reason to apologize to me. I am honored that you would share so much of yourself, and hope my paltry attempts to do the same aren't too disappointing.

"While I'm not sure how much I'll be able to accomplish on that front tonight, I wanted to let you know that our previous exchanges motivated me to begin more vigorously exploring the connections Ancestry has exposed on the maternal side, not only for myself, but also to perhaps find a name to share with John.

"More to come later via email," Edie promised. "As exciting as this journey is, I feel I'm fading fast tonight. Thank you so much for your insight, and I will definitely respect the guidance you outlined in your email as we proceed.

"Wishing you peace," she closed, "Edie."

She hit send at 10:45 p.m. A half-hour later, she was still up, asking me for advice on choosing a current photo to serve as her Ancestry profile pic. It proved a tricky task, given my wife's aversion to being photographed.

Some time before midnight, we piled into bed, exhausted, yet almost too anxious to go to sleep, wondering what might be awaiting our discovery come morning.

7

Dude. IT'S A LOT

Wednesday, February 21, 2018, was another unseasonably warm, partly sunny day in Baton Rouge, beginning with overnight fog and ending with a clear evening. The high was a record-tying 86 degrees, with a low of 71. Winds were gusty and mostly from the south.

Once again, Edie woke up before dawn and me. This time, she discovered not one thing delivered overnight from the Evergreen State; instead, *three* things awaited her, all sent late Tuesday night from the West Coast. First was Justin's reply on Ancestry.

"Dear Edie," he reassured with a smile, "you are not disappointing me in any way. Don't worry." Justin said he had spoken with both John and Rachel, and passed along their email addresses to Edie.

"I helped John write an email to you," he alerted. "The reason I helped him write it is because he has a very difficult time typing, organizing his thoughts, and staying on topic. He does a little better when talking," Justin offered, "but his hearing loss and scattered focus do make even that challenging at times. He is still pretty sharp, though." He said that John "just has to struggle through those various issues.

"He also has some memories to share with you about who he thinks most likely would be your biological mother," Justin wrote. "We don't know that this woman really is her, but we are happy to help you in any way we can with figuring that out. I will say," he indicated, "from what little we know so far, it seems like it might be her. John also said he would be willing to do a more precise DNA test at some point if you ever want to get as much certainty as possible that he is your biological father." Justin was also willing to submit to additional testing.

"I look forward to learning more about you and helping you learn more about your family," he reconfirmed. If and when Edie was up to it, Justin was happy to talk on the phone. "I could even arrange to have a three-way call with John and/or Rachel, too. I know that could be even more overwhelming, so don't feel any pressure." He closed his Ancestry message with a wish for restful sleep.

Next in Edie's inbox Wednesday morning was a brief email from Justin. It contained three attached image files.

"I thought I should send you a couple recent photos, too," he shared. "Here are pictures of me and Hadley and Cherish, plus a photo of Hadley with John from last fall," Justin introduced their father's likeness to my berobed wife.

"Looking at your Ancestry user photo," he noted, "I think you look a little bit like John's mother, Ethel," Justin observed. "I know looking at photos can lead to all sorts of questions, but I would think it helpful, too."

John's initial correspondence rounded out the trio that morning. She now had a face to go with her father's first words to her, as promised and aided by Justin.

"Hello, Edie," he greeted his daughter. "I have read your original message to me, and Justin has shared some of your exchanges with me, too. He is also helping me write this email to you (he will explain). I am delighted to hear that you have enjoyed life with a mother and father that loved and shared themselves with you in kind, beautiful, and inspiring ways. Even through the basics you have shared, it is a great expression of the best in human beings. I am happy to correspond with you, and am open to talking on the phone, too.

"The best I can recall, the only probable partner I can remember that would fit the time frame necessary to be your mother was/is a wonderful person. Her name was/is Fran Poray (not sure of the spelling of her last name). I did not know until she was saying goodbye to me that she was actually engaged to another man. As I recall, when she left me, she said, 'John, I love you very much, always will; but I will probably never see you again. I have to pick up my fiancé at the airport. He's landing right now—a photographer. We are going to return to Paris, and get married.'

"Weeks later," John retold, "another woman said, 'I'm Fran's best friend. Her fiancé ditched her. Everyone gave her money instead of gifts. She is embarrassed to come home, to face friends and family. She asked me to find you, ask you if you would have her back.'" John was "too numb to reply to Fran's friend," he remembered.

Fran taught LSU graduate students English as a Second Language while working on a linguistics degree. "She had an open mind and warm heart, a very pleasant person," John recalled. "We only went out twice. I remember her as an accepting, genuine person. But at the time, I was suffering from extreme abuse from law enforcement and politicians in Baton Rouge because of my political views and activism," John said. "I was also struggling with the haunting spirits of Vietnam.

"Here is one incident that happened to me during that time: Two BRPD officers saw me tutoring Isaac Fleming, a teenaged African American, on my front steps. Their profane gestures paralyzed Isaac in fear. That night, they followed me out to my job, running the five and ten o'clock news cameras at WBRZ-TV. A convoy of officers showed up, started shoving and taunting me, and finally abused me in ways you do not need to hear about now. They told me that I had shot an officer, raped, robbed—and none of it was true. It was because I was against the war. It was because I was trying to help the African American people around me.

"This kind of abuse triggered some suicidal thoughts. They merged with thoughts that I might have become a Jekyll-Hyde kind of monster, committing the atrocities I photographed, reported, and tried to stop in

Vietnam. Trying to stop these kinds of things is what got me 'fragged' there. But I didn't let my emotional and psychological crisis keep me from working with others who wanted to create a more peaceful and equal society. I could tell you many stories about this time, but will save those for another day. Basically, these things led to me getting expelled from LSU in the spring of 1970. A few months later, I went to jail for the better part of a year.

"If you can locate your birth mother, and it turns out to be Fran, we'd probably all be happy to share," John wrote from Renton, in town for medical treatment. "I look forward to hearing more from you," he closed.

The floodgates were officially wide-ass open. Edie was less than forty-eight hours removed from first contact with immediate paternal family, and already had the possible name of her birth mother.

Also, nearly as remarkable as John's jaw-dropping email was the apparent fact that Justin failed to reciprocate our cyberstalking. He didn't know what his sister looked like until she uploaded her Ancestry profile pic just before bed.

Edie fired up the Fort Worth chat thread at 6:40 a.m.

"Got an email from John and pics from Justin," she sent before briefing the Texas O'Neals on John and Fran's relationship.

"So you've communicated with your bio father," Patrick responded. "Holy wow. Did your heart want to beat out of your chest when you opened his email?"

"Before I even opened it," Edie replied.

"And then wow again," he commented on the details she passed along. "The hits just keep on coming."

"And I only hit the highlights of his email," she said of her summary. "He worked at WBRZ," Baton Rouge's local ABC affiliate. "He got roughed up by BRPD for being anti-war and tutoring a Black teen."

"Edie," Patrick suddenly inserted a caveat, "we were talking last night, and I hope you know you only need to share what you feel comfortable sharing. We are eating all this up, but please don't think we are being pushy."

My wife responded by sharing John's email in its entirety. "Not exactly the best imagery to start your day with, but...," she prefaced.

"Damn," Patrick replied upon reading. "Just damn." He added, "Mom said that she remembers Dr. Leggio saying your mother was brilliant. I guess that works out."

Edie then sent the image of her father with our darling niece.

"Gobsmacked again," her brother responded. Patrick also chuckled at the father of Ginger Nation's lack of red hair.

"Your beautiful news is like a triple espresso first thing in the morning!" Yvette outpoured. "I'm so in love with this new book of your life! Big love to you, sis."

"Waking up around here has been a lot more exciting," I told them. "Like Christmas morning every day. 'Ooooh! I wonder what's in the inbox this time!'"

"Right?!" Patrick concurred. "It's like a daily serial. Tune in tomorrow." He then asked Edie, "Have you Googled possible mom's name?"

"Yeah, but I don't have Beth's master's degree in it," Edie lamented. "I have no idea how I'm going to accomplish anything at work today."

"I don't either," Patrick offered. "Compartmentalize."

That same morning, Edie passed along John's top suspect to Beth.

"Is Fran still among us?" our researcher asked before 8 a.m. "Or does anyone know?" Beth then gave her dear friend some solid advice. "Also, this is A LOT. Having been kinda through the same thing," she said of recent events, "give yourself processing time."

Meanwhile, I tried to help keep my wife's mind occupied with things unrelated to her jarring, rapidly evolving, new reality, the enormity of which was just starting to settle in. One mundane detail I bothered her with involved a podcast recording that afternoon. Sunny Weathers and I would join our friend Knick Moore in his workshop, which doubled as an audio studio.

Amidst all the insanity that morning, Edie had forgotten her fitness tracker at home, I soon learned. "Barely made it here," she sent me from work. "Almost asked you to come get me before I even got into the office. Dove into a spreadsheet and was doing better until I started trying to type this," she wrote, beginning to lose it again. "Dammit, I knew I should have just stayed focused."

"Need me to do anything?" I asked.

"Not yet," she informed me, "but you're on call."

By midafternoon, she alerted me that she was coming home.

"Yay!" I celebrated.

"Might want to reserve your judgment," she advised.

Eight hours after she told Edie to allow herself time to process today's news, Beth offered another suggestion. "Idea: Let's go get a yearbook."

Edie was game. "When are you free?" she asked.

A smiling Beth soon answered with a link to a downloadable version of the 1969 LSU *Gumbo*. That's where they soon found someone whose parents tragically decided to name them "Shartle."

"Tis unfortunate," Edie rued.

"I found him," Beth reported. Within minutes of broaching the yearbook idea, she shared John's *Gumbo* photo.

"Wow," his daughter replied.

John, more or less, looked like a mid-twenties, mustachioed Justin.

"Looking for Fran," Beth soon updated. "I'm not having luck." After failing to find "Poray," she sifted through "roughly eight million" iterations of "Fran." Names like Fran, Frank, Francis, and Frances proved quite popular.

During their exchange, Edie needlessly apologized for repeating herself, prompting Beth to remind her, "Dude. IT'S A LOT." She reassured her friend, "You're good all the way up until mass murder."

"Did I tell you she was engaged to a photographer?" Edie inquired. Within moments, her friend was soon caught up on John's international Fran dramatics.

"PARIS?" Beth came back. "This whole two-dates-and-I-love-you thing in the '60s floors me. My mom and dad met and married within two weeks. I don't even understand," the self-described momma bear of two girls said. "I want a state police background check before our first date, thankyouverymuch."

Beth searched both Baton Rouge and Paris for Fran. "The Google is turning up jack shit," she said, adding, "These yearbooks take a million years to download." Beth also wondered if Fran never had her yearbook photo taken because it wasn't required. "I never showed up for a damn yearbook in college."

"Fran dumped John," Edie stated, noting an apparent pattern, "presumably before she found out she was pregnant; Justin transferred from college in Massachusetts to Washington to follow a girl who dumped him before he got there." She also pointed out that—like Justin's mom, Shirley—Fran would've "put up a kid for adoption before John and Justin's mom hooked up."

"God bless," Beth exclaimed, having thought of another surname with a similar regional pronunciation. "I didn't even think of Poirier."

"Aha?" Edie hoped.

"Not a Fran," her relentless research partner confirmed a minute later. Frustrated by the Fran-free *Gumbos*, Beth threatened to Google all names that were remotely similar to the one offered by John. "Let me finish the yearbooks for the sixties. Then I want to look at '71 through '74, in case she returned to LSU. Then," Beth added, "let the Googling begin."

Edie responded with more leads. "Ancestry search for similar names in the Baton Rouge area," she sent with a list of five more potential surnames for her potential birth mother.

"God help us," Beth insisted. "Women are SO MUCH HARDER because of maiden names," she said.

"Simultaneously the best argument for and against keeping the one you came with," my wife observed. "If you don't want to get found."

"Also," Beth reported on an incidental finding, "this woman's name is Twinkle. TWINKLE," she stressed. "She was Miss New Orleans."

"But of course she was," Edie commented.

About that time, Patrick had come up with a brilliant suggestion. "I've learned you can download the *Gumbo*, and it's searchable," he messaged from Fort Worth.

"That's what Beth and I have been doing for the past two hours," Edie laughed. "Beth found John's pic," she added with the *Gumbo* screenshot.

"Very cool," a chuckling Patrick answered. "I see you and Justin."

Near 6 p.m., Edie informed Beth, "Jeremy just messaged me to go meet him." My bride had agreed to join us at Knick's after the podcast. "Your family likely misses your company," she told Beth. "Don't get me wrong: I appreciate your help more than you can imagine. I probably need to take a breather and come back fresh to compose a reply to John's email."

"My family is at gymnastics," Beth responded. "I'll give the year-books a perusal and then give it a rest."

Over in Knick's "Murdershop," our podcast trio wrapped up an episode centered around our drunken Spanish Town Parade antics. There was no way in hell I was bringing up any Ancestry-related issues. This would become the last episode we'd record. Our subscribers didn't sign up to learn about the growing insanity in our lives, and frankly, what else would I have talked about?

Edie arrived as we were packing up the recording equipment. This after-show gathering was the first chance for my wife to actually verbalize—with her mouth (not just typing)—everything she had learned in the past few days. If she wasn't in need of such a release, I sure as hell was. Along with Knick's wife, Carole, the five of us finished off the flask of mezcal under their carport as Edie got everyone caught up.

"Surreal," remarked Knick, who was also adopted at birth. He, too, never had a need to find his biological family.

Back home after grabbing dinner, Edie received an update from neighboring Ascension Parish. "Frances Pig," Beth found, "of Phi Mu. Bless her heart." She had expanded her search to include yearbooks from other Louisiana universities, in case Fran earned her PhD elsewhere while teaching ESL to LSU grad students.

"Merci beaucoup," Edie officially suspended the search for the evening, avec appréciation.

Around 7 p.m., Edie began working on her first in-depth message to the man who ostensibly sired her. She sent it six minutes shy of midnight.

Part of the hours-long deliberation included which photograph to share. She settled on a two-month-old photo of us from a memorable silver anniversary dinner in the Silver State. A wall of wine served as backdrop at Hugo's Cellar in Las Vegas. Edie held the freshly cut red rose presented to her upon entering the venerable eatery.

In addition to the photo, her email included a few hundred pains-takingly chosen words.

"Hello, John," she returned his greeting from that morning. "Thank you so much for writing and sharing some of your story with me. This seems to be such an understatement, but I hope I have not startled you too much by reaching out to you and Justin as I have. I got a bit swept up in the excitement of the results Ancestry revealed. The graciousness you and Justin have shown me fills me with joy. I am so grateful for this opportunity to get to know both of you better, and for the picture Justin shared of you and your beautiful granddaughter.

"I also appreciate the information you provided about Fran. An archivist friend is helping me search for clues about her, and I am investigating the links Ancestry provided on the maternal side to see where they may lead. Perhaps our research will converge.

"It heartens me to hear not only your kind words about Fran, but also your conviction to work for justice despite the horrible things you have seen and suffered. Alas, Baton Rouge still has a long way to go in its quest for social justice. The best result of my time at LSU was meeting my husband, Jeremy, who is passionate about speaking truth to power and holding authorities accountable. He also makes me laugh and smile. I've attached a photo of us from our twenty-fifth anniversary celebration in December.

"My story seems a bit mundane, but I have been blessed to be surrounded by a loving family," she introduced her upbringing in the country. "I never felt there was any difference between us other than age; I always felt wanted. I even had a second set of 'parents' in an older couple who had no children but loved us as if we were their own."

In discussing her education, Edie mentioned, "I went to Quantico for Marine Corps Officer Candidate School, but I was only there for eleven days before being sent home after suffering a heat stroke." Her work history included "taking a job back with our hometown veterinarian who was also a state senator. I was his legislative aide, but we worked out of his vet clinic. He is a strong, quiet man who spearheaded improvements in our education system, and kept his promise to serve no more than two terms after defeating a political dynasty."

Edie also wrote about the two of us producing comedy shows. "Within a year, Jeremy went on to launch a satirical publication, with me as its copy editor. He also officiates high school and junior college football, and I've worked high school games with him the past two years.

"I apologize if I've gone on a bit long about nothing spectacular," Edie offered in closing. "I look forward to continuing our communications by email or phone in the near future."

Another indescribably insane day ended with both of us exhausted—physically, mentally, and emotionally. She joined me in grabbing some sleep after sending the message near midnight.

John would stay up much later, alone, composing a much longer, much less coherent reply to his daughter.

8

That's Your Mom

Thursday, February 22, 2018, brought early fog and partly cloudy skies to Baton Rouge. Following a low of 70, temperatures reached 87, tying yet another record high. Winds were breezy and mostly from the southeast.

John's message came in at over 2,500 words. Without Justin's assistance, many of them were difficult to comprehend. Some were downright disturbing.

Two hours after he had sent it, Edie notified Beth.

"Got a message to John about midnight," she informed the archivist at 6:45 a.m. "He stayed up almost five hours to respond." In his reply, John "gave a phonetic spelling of 'Por-shay'" for Fran's last name, "and asked for discretion, as she might not be the one."

I've seen the email. I'm still amazed how Edie was able to glean so many details from it at such an early hour on minimal sleep. Amid all the chaotic prose, she noticed on her first read at the ass crack of dawn that John offered his phone number, along with an invitation to visit the Harts in Renton. I'm not sure how long it would've taken me to spot either tidbit. A week, maybe?

John began with heartfelt pleasantries, effusing through the opening stanzas.

"Good evening, to both of you!" he opened. "Yes, I probably am your father, and I couldn't be happier. You are an inspiration to many, from your comedy website, to the football fields, all the people in your lives well lived. I am proud of you both," he gushed. "You and your husband are veterans, too! Thank you," he offered. "You and your husband both look, feel like very good persons." He also lauded the veterinarian who retired after two terms in the state senate, calling Edie's former employer "an anomaly for Louisiana, America."

John then explained his difficulty typing, "which was a skill, before injuries in the military took a toll." The rest of his sixth paragraph quickly turned into a tale about how, on his first day in Vietnam, he had a pistol shoved in his face by a fellow soldier, a man from whom John was supposed to learn his job. An unarmed pacifist newly arrived at the theater of war, Edie's father was trying to stop his assigned mentor from assaulting a civilian woman at gunpoint by leaning his head into the muzzle.

John also mentioned his "history of head injuries and hearing traumas" prior to his time in Vietnam, only to then meander back and forth between 1968 Southeast Asia and 1964 British Guyana, where he served as a teenage missionary.

Paragraph thirteen started out, "(I see that I have digressed, as I got sleepier, but will leave it in, because even now, it is difficult to be even this clear, and it is important." He was evidently too tired to add a closing parenthesis. The rest of the paragraph led up to John's fragging by three American soldiers. "They chose to throw an explosive device at me from behind while I worked in our Buddhist Graveyard outpost," he wrote, "left me to die."

About one-third into his email, John opened his fifteenth paragraph, "For me, God is Love."

Imagine feeling relieved when your newly discovered bio dad finally changes the topic to religion.

About 1,000 words in came John's phonetic spelling and his request for discretion. That was quickly followed, without any semblance of transition, by a jarring example of institutionalized racism in the Deep South.

"The bailiff," John said of his time before a judge in Louisiana, "he twisted my shirt, lifted me up. 'You can do anything you want in this state,'" he recounted the bailiff's instructions, "'counterfeiting, drugs, prostitution. Just don't F--- with our N-----s.'" I'm confident I need not clarify what words he censored out.

John managed to sprinkle in some solid hippie wisdom around a pair of wild stories from his teenage years in Florida, shortly after he became a minister. One tale involved him using scripture to talk down a man from Appalachia, who was taking his wife and nine kids to Cape Canaveral. That's where, John explained, the man planned to kill his entire family, before turning on himself one of the loaded guns stashed in the trunk of their old Buick. It was all part of his plan to spare them all from the 1,000 years of Armageddon, that—as promised by their snake-handling preacher—would start "if that rocket hits the moon."

The second incident featured John convincing a super-religious octogenarian not to kill himself and his wife of more than fifty years, which the guy had planned to do, but only after the couple had eaten a nice meal. Apparently, the gentleman had convinced himself that his wife's increasingly longer trips to the grocery store were the result of an adulterous affair, and not because she was slowed by old age.

"Once, I was a good listener," John wrote.

Two-thirds through, he offered more thoughts on Fran. "Perhaps, together, we can give her a hug," John proposed, suggesting that "the loneliness, the pains she felt might be shared, wiped away, in a good way."

Two paragraphs of hippie wisdom followed. Then four about John's more recent health issues. That all came ahead of his invitation to stay at Justin and Cherish's home.

In the next—and thankfully last—paragraph, he volunteered his cell number, reiterated his difficulties typing, and suggested a phone call might be better. "I could be more specific, coherent," a self-aware John insisted. He also revisited his inability to reply to Fran's friend, upon the linguist's return from Paris.

"I would have been delighted to see her again, regardless," John maintained. "I was just so numb, I could not process as real what I was hearing."

John wrote of his time in Baton Rouge, "I was getting isolated, did not want to risk a woman being abused by law enforcement. Her friend did not say anything about Fran being pregnant." He closed by informing Edie, "Your efforts not only help you. Your reaching out benefits me, possibly Fran."

Around the same time she messaged Beth, Edie alerted Fort Worth about John's latest message.

"It might rival Justin's email," she prefaced a taste of John's unedited prose. "'Perhaps,'" she quoted her father, "'we are a part of an even deeper, more appropriate family: Those who seek to give of themselves for others, while maintaining a healthy identity, living exemplary, inspiring lives. Thank you.'"

Amid all the disturbing details John included for her, Edie chose to share that lovely sentiment of hippie wisdom. Her choice speaks volumes about the woman I married.

"That made my day!" Yvette proclaimed. She also wondered, "Do you feel like you're in a movie?"

"No," Edie explained, "I could turn that off."

She then admitted, "Yesterday, I got a *bit* overwhelmed, possibly as much from the daunting part of having to talk about myself as all the rest. But I started all this," she countered with a sense of obligation. "And I don't *have* to keep it up, but I do."

"I'd be a wonderful mess," Yvette said, adding, "downright giddy!"

"Yep," Edie confirmed, "that's a pretty spot-on description."

Later that same morning, armed with a new phonetic spelling for their subject, Beth resumed the Fran search.

"So Porche?" she asked. Beth also mentioned possibly searching LSU's student-run newspaper, *The Daily Reveille*, as well as Baton

Rouge area directories for Fran. "I think another good assumption," Beth reasoned, "is that, pregnant and spurned, she wouldn't venture far from family. If that's a dead end," Beth continued, "it may not be her and we need to revisit John's little black book."

A few minutes later, she shared with Edie a new concern. "I'm starting to worry that she didn't always use Fran," Beth said, "since we have Twinkle and Chairman Mao running around." The Google degree holder proposed, "She could've been Mary Frances and used Mary."

"That was my first hunch," Edie revealed, "like I always used my middle name when calling in to a radio show or something."

"Fuck," Beth blurted. "Portier. I didn't search for Portier," she rued.

"OMG," Edie reacted, "but great catch."

As Beth commenced searching for Fran Portier, she and Edie speculated about the intersection between John, Fran, and Fran's fiancé. Beth theorized that perhaps Fran didn't know she was pregnant until she got to France; or maybe she already knew and hoped to dupe her fiancé into believing the baby was his, "assuming she read trashy romance novels and the idea occurred to her."

Edie responded with some math. "Based on a forty-week gestation, I'd estimate my conception to have occurred about 2/22/70," she said on February 22, 2018. "Happy conceptionversary to me," my wife winked, less than five days after finding John on Doc's birthday. "Dear lord, we're bound to make a discovery today if there is any poetic irony in the world."

"Indeed," Beth agreed. "MUST FIND FRAN."

In moments, Edie mentioned a neat yearbook finding. "The German club entry is in German."

Six minutes later, Beth made a much less mundane discovery of her own. "Fran Portier ran track in 1964" at a Baton Rouge high school, she reported.

"What?!" Edie replied.

"Hold please," Beth requested. She soon sent the winsome image of a high school senior named Frances Annette Portier. "And graduated in 1965," Beth noted. "And was in French Club all four years."

"O.M.G." Edie sent back.

"The age is right," Beth added. "She could've easily been a senior or first-year grad student" circa Edie's birth, Beth explained.

"Young and passionate enough to proclaim love after a single/double encounter," Edie supposed.

Within moments, Edie prepared Fort Worth for incoming news with the question, "Happy conceptionversary to me?" Edie forwarded Fran's photo. She also cited the high school senior's yearbook quote, "'I am curious to see what will be the next thing I do.'"

"Dang," Patrick responded, "Beth is a beast."

"This proves nothing," Edie stood fast, "but dang coincidental."

"True," he agreed, still processing the news.

"OOOOOOOOMMMMMMMGGGGGGGG!" Yvette reacted to the resemblance.

With a "damnnn," Edie eventually conceded her incredible likeness to teenaged Fran, but not before citing John's suspect memory. "Given his head trauma," she doubted that Fran was "the one."

Yvette remained unswayed. "EDIE!!!"

"Indeed," her partner concurred.

"I'm no Nate Silver," I prefaced my take, "but I'd put money on her being the one. Wow."

"I may be projecting," Patrick said of Fran's senior photo, "but something about that picture echoes Edie's graduation picture."

"Yep," I concurred.

Edie soon forwarded more Fran pics from Beth, prompting Patrick to draw a conclusion.

"That's your mom," the inspiration for this little adventure flatly told his baby sister.

"Agreed," replied the guy married to Edie for over a quarter of a century. "I recognize that pouty look."

"She may now live in Houston and/or Georgia," my wife came back with a newly found Whitepages record.

"Is there a fainting emoji?" Patrick inquired.

Minutes later, Beth uncovered that Fran attended the University of Southwestern Louisiana, now known as the University of Louisiana at Lafayette, about an hour's drive west of Baton Rouge.

"Picture not available," Beth cited *L'Acadien,* the Ragin' Cajuns' annual, "freshman class of 1966." She soon reported on their subject, "Gone by 1967."

During her yearbook perusals, Beth had compiled a list of male LSU grad students with French-ish names. Her hunch was that the fiancé was a French national who learned English from Fran. That all changed when Beth came across an item for sale on eBay.

"I assumed Paris came to her," she informed Edie. "Non!" Beth corrected. "SHE WENT TO PARIS."

For $15.88, Edie could purchase an eight-by-ten glossy of her presumed mother's senior picture. "1966 Press Photo Fran Portier," read the webpage's title, "Debutante." It also indicated the name of the Sorbonne affiliate where she'd study, "Ecole Pratique de L'Alliance Francaise." Fran had made the Baton Rouge papers after being accepted by the international organization, founded in 1883 by Louis Pasteur, Jules Verne, and others, with the aim of promoting French language and culture around the globe.

"Cher mon dieu," mon cher said.

"That's why we can't find her in Louisiana," Beth explained.

"I kept starting to suggest that," Edie volunteered, "but never did."

Beth soon messaged me with the eBay link.

"Oh wow!" I exclaimed. "That has got to be her mom."

"God bless America," Beth said, "Fran looks like Edie to me."

I thanked our dear friend for her relentless efforts, and quickly shared the eBay page on the Fort Worth thread.

"What in the actual fuck," Patrick marveled at our friend's Google Fu. "Beth is a ninja."

The admittedly "loud," six-foot-tall woman who threw javelin and played high school softball begged to differ. "Beth says she's about as far from a ninja as one can possibly get and still be human," Edie passed along.

"Beth has metaphorical search ninja skills," the lawyer doubled down. "I will not be swayed."

About that time, Beth asked questions of my wife that, as a married couple, Edie and I were not unfamiliar with.

"Is this too much, too fast? Should I stop? Is it getting freaky?"

Rarely an impulsive buyer, my love was snatching up the photo tout de suite.

"I'm OK," Edie answered Beth after a brief lull on their chat thread, "I was just buying the pic on eBay."

"OK." Beth cracked up laughing. "Just tell me and I'll get up out your business."

"Mother of god," Edie soon messaged her friend, "I just found Fran on Facebook."

"OMG," Beth replied. "Look at all the gingers!" She asked, "Are you OK?"

Edie answered with a Facebook photo showing a bikini-topped Fran on a Galveston pier in 1973. Her eye-catching image could easily pass for one of my wife when we met at LSU.

"Holy shit!" is how Beth reacted.

Edie then apologized for not answering Beth's query concerning her state of mind. "Sorry," she said after encountering Fran's most recent Facebook posts, "got distracted by all the right-wing lunacy."

Fort Worth soon learned of the woman's social media presence.

"Fuckers," Patrick said, feigning annoyance on the day's other hot thread, "I have work to do!"

"She's definitely balancing out the Harts," I wrote of Fran's political views.

"Oh shit," he concurred. "You're correct."

I shared Fran's 1973 Galveston photo, but Patrick was already curating publicly available pictures from her Facebook profile. One was Fran's passport photo, signed "Love Fran." Another was taken at her second wedding in 1982.

"Best knockoff yet of my senior pic," Edie wrote, describing the latter image, which depicted a wryly smiling, curly-haired Fran. My five-foot-one wife soon discovered Fran stands at five-three, and likes cats.

"Cool," I replied. "She definitely ain't camera shy like someone I know."

"Last one," her brother posted with a photo of a grade-school-aged Fran in a velvet dress.

"Yeah," Edie surmised, "that about wraps up that mystery right there."

"I haven't said this in earnest in three years," Patrick announced, "but I honestly could use a drink right now. My fucking hands are shaking," he said. "Edie, I'm not quite sure how you're processing this."

"Me either," she responded.

"Hell," I said of Fran's social media, "I can't even process what she's posted in the last four hours." In the time since Beth and Edie had resumed their search for her, Fran had shared on her Facebook wall twenty-eight conspiracy-theory-laden links. Twenty-fucking-eight.

Fran's far-right-wing insanity was taking a toll on Yvette, who miraculously had survived a near-fatal aneurysm years ago. "My brain damage is flaring up!" she alerted us.

"All the cool people are on dad's side," I noted.

Thursday afternoon saw Beth and Edie begin to nail down a plausible narrative to explain how Fran might've given birth and put her child up for adoption in late 1970. Public photos of a globetrotting Fran from around that time filled her profile. Many of the captions proved informative.

In the late '60s, Fran spent summers in Europe. She was often photographed in the company of attractive young men, like Radomir on the Riviera in 1966. Three lads (one shirtless) sat beside Fran on the grass of the Yugoslavian countryside in 1968. A photo from 1967 St. Raphael showed Fran standing on one of the large rocks meeting open, calm water. Behind her was a sailboat, as well as another bikini-clad woman on the rocks, poised to dive in and join a handful of swimmers. "Right before I had to come back to the U.S. and finish LSU," the caption read. "Didn't want to leave!"

However, in 1970—when Edie would've been gestating—Fran's mother joined her daughter for a "tour" of Europe. "They may have stayed away as long as she was pregnant so nobody back home would know?" Edie wondered.

"I don't know," Beth conceded. "There is a significant gap in the pictures," she remarked on the relative dearth of Fran photos from the nine months in question.

The only picture of Fran from that period was taken in front of a windmill in Holland. She and her mother stood some distance from the camera. Edie noted that young Miss Portier wore "loose clothing." The bag slung over Fran's right shoulder only added to suspicion she was hiding something from the viewer.

Meanwhile, the Texas O'Neals began to wonder about the timeline that Beth and Edie had already pieced together.

"What year were you born?" Yvette asked.

After answering, Edie added, "Fran and her mom toured all over Europe that year."

"Uh, yeah they did," Patrick jested, noting that his sister neglected to wrap the word "toured" in quotation marks. After investigating Fran's recent social media posts, he suggested, "Perhaps John is NOT the best person to contact her."

"Y'all haven't seen this morning's email yet," Edie responded. "John asked if he could be the one to contact Fran; given his issues, I'm inclined to ask Justin's guidance on that front. Mind you," she added, "I haven't even begun to trace maternal lineage from Ancestry yet."

"Your father sounds like a sweet man," her brother wrote. "Just like his daughter. You know," Patrick followed up, "without the man part," he qualified.

"She smoked," I commented on a photo of a smoking-hot Fran showing off her shapely gams in short shorts back in the day, "and she still looks fantastic. Edie hasn't smoked," I continued blabbering, "which means she'll look half her age forever."

"Right," the attorney agreed.

My casual lusting after a younger version of my potential new mother-in-law was tempered by her social media presence. If Fran's the one, then Edie had accomplished her quest. Plus, I'd have further confirmation of my wife's ridiculously youthful genetics. However, it would also mean that I'd likely have to meet this woman, and she could very well become an integral part of our lives. I wasn't sure how graciously I could handle discovering that my soul mate was brought into this world by someone who shares Ann Coulter posts with zero snark.

Later that evening, Edie informed Fort Worth about a message she was composing for Justin. It would include her phone number and the day's news of Fran. After sending the message, Edie promised, her efforts would focus on "tracing maternal DNA matches until a response comes" from Justin.

In light of Yvette's concern that lack of sleep might turn Edie into a zombie, I eventually managed to convince my walking-dead wife to get some shuteye, but only after she put a button on the insane Thursday with an update for her younger brother.

"It has certainly been an interesting day," she emailed Justin. "Yesterday, I was a bit overcome with emotions, but my response was delayed mainly because it's a big challenge for me to put myself out there. I am not only appreciative, but in awe of your ability and John's to so openly share your stories. And be forewarned," she said with a smile, "that I also have a tendency to ramble and spurt out every detail as it pops into my head once I uncork the bottle and let myself out."

Following her report on that day's findings, Edie told Justin, "So, it seems like she most likely is John's Fran, but I don't have any scientific evidence linking her to me just yet. Given that and the emotions at play, I'm not yet ready to make the leap of contacting her myself. John asked to be given her contact information, but I thought it best to check in with you first. I don't want to transfer the burden of unraveling this mystery to someone else, nor do I want to introduce any trauma in his life. But as you said," she recalled, "it's important for him to speak for himself and make his own decisions, and I've already introduced this question about what may or may not have happened in his past," she wrote, speaking to her sense of obligation.

"I don't want to impose on your time, but if you would like to call me to discuss this, please feel welcome to do so. Fair warning," she offered with a smile, "I may become an emotional mess and have trouble speaking." She closed, "I look forward to your response either way."

Overnight, her baby brother replied. Twice.

9

Starfleet and My Wife

Friday, February 23, 2018, didn't see much sunshine in Baton Rouge thanks to early fog and persistent clouds that produced close to a tenth of an inch of rain. The high was 76, with a low of 67. Winds were light and mostly from the east.

Edie grabbed some much-deserved extra winks before awakening as day broke. This left her enough time to read, but not reply to, Justin's two emails before heading out the door.

"I would love to talk with you on the phone!" he wrote in the first. "Weekends are probably easiest for me," Justin added with a smile, "but I will make time, any time, too.

"Thank you for your praise, Edie," he continued. "I think that putting myself out there comes naturally for me," the creative-writing-degree-holder noted, "or at least it does now. I always felt so cut off from family, so distant, not really knowing anyone on my mother's side. I feel like I had to overcome some pretty significant challenges as a kid/young adult with a father who was in prison for a very difficult time in my life," Justin recounted, "and a mother who basically quit on us. I am just saying maybe I developed this tendency as part of my coping and recovery from those difficult times in my young life."

Justin also said he'd show John Fran's Facebook pictures, including one taken in her cap and gown. "The graduation picture would have been right around the time he met her," he said. "If he seems pretty sure that is her, I will let you know.

"It seems like we could reach out to her on Facebook," Justin suggested with an assurance for his big sis. "Given how important this is," he recognized, "and the potential confirmation Fran might provide, we would want to honor your wishes precisely, and communicate exactly what you want to be communicated.

"If you are up for it," Justin closed the opening installment of the day's correspondence, "let's talk this weekend," he proposed, still grinning, "about this or whatever you feel like talking about."

His second overnight message came ninety minutes after the first.

"John has confirmed that the Fran you found must be the Fran he knew," Edie learned before work. "He said he was 'very' certain that was her. But even though John is willing to reach out to Fran on your behalf," Justin acknowledged, "I am not sure that it would be the best choice. I am willing to do it; I might be the least likely to cause her alarm or shock. I could even just say I am doing genetic research," he put forth, "and I am trying to confirm if she might be the mother of my half-sister. But I would only make that contact if you asked me to," Justin reassured, "and were certain you wanted me to."

Edie found time during lunch to send him a reply.

"Hi Justin," she wrote of tomorrow, "perhaps we could talk sometime Saturday? My day is wide open, so I can be available at any time that is convenient for you," Edie insisted.

"I'd like to take some time away from tracing family trees," she wrote, referring to her ongoing maternal search on Ancestry, "and dedicate more to thinking this through before our call. If you're a *Star Trek* fan, you might appreciate the analogy that I'm afraid of violating the prime directive." Edie elaborated, "If my birth mom isn't out there looking for/curious about me, and wants to leave the past in the past, I don't want to violate her choice. Seeing you and John on AncestryDNA made it appear more acceptable for me to reach out," she clarified, "as there was evidence you may have been seeking out connections."

Starfleet General Order 1, also known in the *Star Trek* universe as the "non-interference directive," prohibits contact with lesser-developed civilizations to avoid disrupting the natural order of their development. Starfleet and my wife both recognize that not all beings are ready to be greeted by other beings.

"This has all developed so quickly; I feel bad about not yet reaching out to Rachel," Red revealed, "and for being unable to keep up with John's pace! He's writing circles around me," Edie returned Justin's smile, "but I treasure every word from both of you."

In addition to Justin's pair of emails, Edie also awoke to another one from John. The subject line declared "hello, good evening," despite being sent at 3:33 a.m. West Coast time. At 4,721 words, it was twice as long as his previous message. Without Justin's assistance, it proved no easier to follow. I'm not sure how much of it Edie processed before getting ready for work.

Neither is she.

One-fifth of the unreplied message was about Fran. In that non-contiguous twenty percent, John revisited the incident with Fran's BFF. This time, he admitted that he wasn't sure whether or not he was actually too numb to speak at that moment.

The eight Fran-related portions were scattered amongst disjointed ramblings. In them, John touched on varied subjects, including (but not limited to):

- cat thoughts;
- vigorous dancing;
- health issues caused by the VA that might interfere with John's ability to perform with his wife's dance group;
- his day playing with Hadley, and their discussion about cats;
- massage therapy;
- a drunk woman named Audrey who threw herself at John when Justin was fourteen;

- that same woman, three years ago, running up to John during a veterans parade, hugging him, and inviting John and Hallie to visit Audrey and the Jewish war veteran whom John's kindness had inspired her to marry;
- horrors from John's time in Vietnam, including another reference to being fragged;
- an anecdote involving a woman he identifies simply as Jeanie (While there's no context about who this woman is, John does tell Edie about how Jeanie's father met his wife in her native Belgium during World War II while working for the OSS, which, as John explained, was the forerunner of the CIA.);
- repeated abuse John suffered at the hands of various law enforcement agencies, including an encounter with the Louisiana State Police SWAT team;
- how his childhood study of the Bible led him to stump a bunch of ministers when he was just a kid;
- his time in the East Louisiana State Hospital "for the Criminally Insane" in Jackson, Louisiana;
- the five-word, nonsequitur paragraph, "I love the Parkland KIDS!";
- an anecdote about the summer he and a collaborative artist named Karen drove (in a tiny, trashed Honda he bought from an LSU theater grad student) to a liberal Lutheran retreat center outside Nashville, where they joined a group in creating an empathy exercise that involved dancing naked around a bonfire;
- and, of course, John's unique hippie wisdom.

In closing, he mentioned how he and Justin were enjoying getting to know and share with Edie. John again suggested a phone call.

After signing off, he left three short lines. They weren't a postscript, per se, but apparently represented leftover thoughts he typed and neglected to place somewhere before the complimentary close. As a result, the second unassisted email Edie received from her father ended with the line, "No sweat. That time, no one spit in my face, much less urinated on me."

His daughter had wisely set the tangled message aside that morning in the interest of getting ready for work. That's where she was, still on lunch break, when Justin reciprocated her midday reply.

"Saturday would be perfect," he wrote back. After suggesting times, Justin said, "John is with me now, so you could also speak with him, too, if you wish.

"And I love *Star Trek!*" he announced. "I have seen every episode of every series, but have never been to a convention or anything. I just really enjoy science fiction, the concepts of us someday being a civilization that is much better, much fairer, and more just than we are today. So I appreciate the prime directive reference, and I will follow your lead.

"Don't feel bad about not reaching out to Rachel yet," he allayed. "She is very eager to communicate with you, though I will add, she already feels like you two may bond over the search for absent family since she went through that with me about twelve years ago," Justin explained, "though, of course, she always knew I was out there, and John, too." With a grin, Justin relayed Rachel's promise to be patient.

"I am glad you are treasuring John's words," he began to wrap up. "Don't be afraid to tell him to slow down/turn down the volume, though," Justin insisted. "He knows he is effusive. He isn't the best at regulating that outflow, and doesn't mind being asked to scale it back.

"Looking forward to talking to you tomorrow." Justin closed the latest testament to his awesomeness with a wish for a wonderful day.

Edie soon alerted me about their plans.

"Phone call tomorrow," she messaged. "Justin loves *Star Trek*," Edie winked.

"I'd expect nothing less," I said of my seemingly flawless brother-in-law, who happened to also work at a winery on weekends. The wine rack behind us in the Hugo's Cellar picture led Justin to wonder if we were "vinophiles." That led me to wonder if I should feel a bit intimidated.

As my wife reached the end of what had been the wildest, most surreal workweek one could imagine, her dear friend checked in. She told Beth about the scheduled phone call.

"How exciting!" Beth remarked. "How are you doing?"

"Uncertain," a deliberative Edie answered. "I'll try to compose my thoughts in the morning before the call," she said. "They're willing to contact Fran."

"That's nice of them," Beth replied. "Maybe do about thirty-seven hours of yoga before," she advised.

Edie laughed before seeking a second opinion. "AM I crazy to mentally question whether there could've been another who slipped his mind?" she wondered. "Just because I haven't connected her to my maternal matches yet?"

"No," Beth attempted to reassure my wife, "not at all."

"Or is it just my reluctance to contact someone who didn't sign up for a DNA match?" Edie further questioned.

Beth reminded her friend, "All she can tell you is no."

"That's why I'm leaning toward having them make contact," Edie reasoned. "At least John knows her."

Beth concurred. "Also," she observed, "did that man have a thing for redheads or what?"

"And short girls," Edie threw in. "Current wife is shorter than me."

I forgot to mention earlier that John's email also included Hallie's height.

Edie made it home around 6 p.m. to discover Patrick and Yvette had sent a DVD copy of *Flirting with Disaster*. In the film, Ben Stiller sets out across the country with his wife, as played by Patricia Arquette, to find his biological parents.

In thanking North Texas, she told them about the upcoming call with a father and brother she discovered days before. "Together?" a confused Patrick asked, unaware that the elder Austinite was visiting the Renton Harts.

"John is at Justin's," Edie clarified. "If all four—John, Fran, Justin, and Rachel—were in Austin/Houston this weekend," she admitted, "I might've had to make a road trip."

She then reported, "John, Justin, and Rachel tend toward OCD," a trait my wife shares with all three. The tidbit came from Justin in another message about their dad's communication issues, ahead of their first phone call.

"John has been giving massages since he was a kid," Fort Worth also learned from the redhead long known for offering spontaneous shoulder rubs to those seated at the table following meals with the O'Neals. Like John, Fran was licensed as an adult, something Edie learned from the woman's "multitudinous pics."

"That's really fortuitous she has all those pics," Patrick noted, "and they're public."

"Yep," my private wife agreed. "Justin is willing to contact her if that's what I want," Edie revealed, "through Facebook."

"You ready for that?" Patrick wondered.

"Not sure."

"Then hold off until you are," he advised. "You have waited a looooong time," he reminded his sister. "Get it right for you."

"If she had shown up as an AncestryDNA link," Edie asserted, "I would be less hesitant."

"Good point," Patrick granted.

"We're going out for dinner tonight," Edie signed off, "so I won't be trying to track her tree back to any of my matches."

Despite the colossal amount of processing yet to be done, my wife had already started comparing Fran's lineage—as revealed by the copious family details she shared on social media—to Edie's maternal matches on AncestryDNA. She didn't need to know about her birth mother, at least not until John needed to know. My Molly Marine was officially on a mission.

The two of us got away from all that, though. Shared company and comfort food at a nice Italian restaurant somewhat soothed our growing anxiousness over tomorrow's further-life-changing phone call.

10

Kind of Like Dancing

Saturday, February 24, 2018, started with overnight fog before mostly clear skies settled into the Red Stick throughout the day and evening. After a morning low of 68 degrees, temperatures reached 84, Baton Rouge's fourth record-tying high in five days. Winds were breezy with moderate daytime gusts from the southeast.

For the first time since the previous weekend, Edie slept past sunup. Just like the last two mornings, she awoke to discover a new, four-digit-word-count email from John.

At 10:11 a.m., she fired off a brief email of her own to her father and brother in Renton.

"Dear Justin and John," she wrote them just past sunrise there. She asked if a noon call—ten their time—would work. "I am so looking forward to speaking with both of you today.

"It is a beautiful day today in Baton Rouge!" Edie opened a paragraph describing our early Louisiana spring. As I combated aggressive weeds plotting to take over the yard, my wife wrote, "It occurs to me that this may also be about the time of year my life began, sometime around late February, early March," adding, "a time for new life, new beginnings, optimism, hope." In closing, she wished that their day was off to a beautiful start. "Talk to you soon!"

Justin replied in five minutes. "Talk to you soon Edie," he returned her smile, "and I love the picture you described for us today."

As mentioned, John sent another long, jumbled message. This would be his fourth email of forty-three that he'd eventually send her through early summer. Their dad's initial unassisted correspondence on Thursday had prompted an already busy Justin to offer his services as his big sister's personal translator.

"I read through John's email," he wrote around the time Beth found Fran, "and I think it exemplifies the difficulty he has communicating. He easily loses track of where his cursor is," Justin explained. "If he doesn't spend time rereading everything, his emails can seem really disjointed." John was able to remain more focused when he was younger, according to his son. "He also tends to ramble, almost constantly, probably more due to his age than his head injuries." Justin also cited their father's "obsessive/compulsive tendencies. He always wants to tell you every little detail about everything!"

It was during this offer to "unpack" John's ramblings that Justin had mentioned the importance of John speaking for himself. "I don't want to be anything more than a translator."

My stubborn wife never bit. She chose to take on the responsibility of getting to know her father firsthand.

I'd later ask how in god's name she managed to navigate the overgrown jungle of words. A somewhat sheepish Edie reminded me that she's the "crazy whisperer," a self-ascribed label inspired by a former *Advocate* colleague with communication issues less severe than John's. His stay in Jackson notwithstanding, John is not insane, but his writings can pass for those of an affected person.

They're frequently streams of consciousness that alter course, sometimes sharply. Things can go from beautiful and inspiring to dark and disturbing in a handful of words, and then back from tumultuous to placid after a few more.

The dramatic course shifts are unpredictable. In Friday's 4,721-word email, "boat" led to "ark," which led to "the president," which led to the "Parkland kids," all in the span of a scant 110 words.

Imagine studying a map zoomed in at street level, and you're able to make out all sorts of fine details about a particular locale. All the street names, the types of homes, and even the flowers blooming in the yards, they're all clearly visible.

And then, right about the time you're digging on the scene, while still zoomed in, the map is suddenly shifted by thousands of miles. You're almost instantaneously transported to a completely different, finely described place.

The only problem is John's lack of context means you have no idea what part of the planet you're looking at. Rather than appreciating the aesthetics of the new scenery, you're too busy trying to figure out where the hell you are.

In short, John's communications can be like getting conversationally *Quantum Leap*ed.

"He often has issues sending emails," Justin later explained, "because he doesn't look at the screen until he is ready to send his manifesto." By that point, however, John "doesn't realize that forty-two minutes ago he fat-fingered the keyboard and switched tabs in his browser."

Like a hoarder's house, John's emails are difficult to navigate. Lots of stuff is stacked up all over the place, apparently in no particular order. As demonstrated in Friday's message, he sometimes initially mentions people without any context about who they are. Or maybe he already did mention them and I still haven't found the reference among the novel-length, 60,000-plus words he'd end up sending to his daughter in only a few months.

And that's counting words separated by actual spaces. Accounting for passages like "iwalked tocampus tried tofind him,Ididn't think to findout where he lived" and "I amnot good withmessages, so i have to-gothroughthe phoneagain," his true word count is at least ten or fifteen percent more than whatever Google Docs thinks it is.

John's latest message Saturday morning was representative of his oeuvre. At 1,387 words (not adjusted for his typing), it was just shy of his average.

His longest email totaled 5,100 words. Another came in at just 176, only twice as long as its subject line, which was apparently a fragment from the message body that he inadvertently inserted there.

Nonetheless, John's admitted difficulty typing would not stop the effusive man from sending dozens of four-digit-word-count emails. Of the forty-three emails he sent by early summer, half of them were over 1,000 words.

That's a lot of herky-jerky navigation and piecing together of mixed-up details that would test the patience of an angel. Fortunately, I married one.

Hours before their initial conversation, John sent his latest email at 4:19 a.m. Seattle time, with the subject line "Tomorrow (actually to-day)." The first paragraph closed with the phrase "glowing energy!"

Where I'm from, "glowing energy" is not a term you normally hear in everyday conversation. I can't remember ever saying it to anyone else, nor ever hearing it said to me. Yet, there it is, in the opening stanza of a message from my wife's biological father, whose image she had first laid eyes on three days ago.

"Whatever, hoe," led the next paragraph.

Did I mention this was an exercise in patience?

It was in reading this email that I realized my wife had inherited from John her ace in another suit.

"Reading with Hadley this afternoon and evening," he mentioned in a brief paragraph, "shared the word 'empathy,'" he said. "The story we read was about friends sharing feelings, needs. Then each of the books we read expressed empathy!"

I've searched John's body of work for the word "empath." It showed up, often in other iterations, fourteen times.

I have watched every episode of *Star Trek: The Next Generation*, and all the subsequent *TNG* movies. Spanning the entirety of its seven seasons AND the franchise's four major motion pictures, I failed to hear "empath," "empathy," "empathic," or "empathize" uttered as much as John typed those same words in just a handful of emails, all despite the fact that Counselor Deanna Troi—a bona fide empath—served as a bridge officer on the *USS Enterprise* the entire time.

And yes, I created a spreadsheet for John's emails. I spent too much time and money on an engineering degree to let it go to waste.

The appointed time approached. Her phone fully charged, Edie sat in our living room, armed with a notepad and reliable pen.

Would he be like many of his emails: both aspirational and unnerving, almost simultaneously at times? John suggested he'd be better on the phone. We were about to find out how true that was.

Edie hummed an anxious dialing melody. We nervously listened to the rings. Justin picked up within two.

At eleven past twelve, he came through on speakerphone as kind and loving as he did in his writing. Brother and sister were finally hearing each other's voices.

The two of them got a little more acquainted for the next few minutes. In introducing myself, I expressed immense gratitude for Justin being that ideal emissary.

We soon spoke with Hadley, arguably the most well-spoken five-year-old I've ever conversed with. She had stepped away from preparing for a gathering of little girls at their house. In the most heart-melting voice, our niece informed us that she was writing a story about her newest auntie.

Minutes later, Justin asked if we were ready for him to hand the phone over to John. An uneasy Edie said yes, prompting her brother to offer us one last caveat. Justin tried to prepare us before engaging with their dad.

We've had our fair share of phone calls with people who can talk your ear off. We thought we were prepared.

We were not.

Nevertheless, we did have enough forethought to keep the extremely loquacious John on speakerphone. As Edie later told Beth about the two of us, "We could help each other with 'Did we hear that?'"

Despite the disparity between father's and daughter's respective inclinations toward verbosity, he did occasionally pause to ask about us. As a listener, John's just as generous and enthusiastic as he is a talker.

Edie and I told him how we met at LSU, and how I followed my soon-to-be-bride as chair of the Union's Pop Entertainment Committee. This led John to share a more colorful story about an incident with a famous person near the LSU Union during his time as a student. It involved a bloody knife and a Nazi.

At 5:14 p.m., we hung up after saying the last of several goodbyes. During those five hours, John did no less than ninety percent of the talking. I missed maybe a couple minutes during the two occasions I had to go pee.

No more than five minutes into the conversation, I realized that my wife's father spoke from a gentle, beautiful soul, not unlike his eldest daughter. John's soothing voice had a lilt, and a little more than a trace of a Mississippi drawl.

Over the ensuing weeks and months, we'd slowly come to realize that you can't converse with John like you would with most folks. To truly understand what he says—just like with what he writes—one must take it in its totality, and then put it all together. You need all the pieces to complete the puzzle.

It's no different than how the CIA learns about those they're surveilling. They listen, and listen, and listen, before piecing together everything to create a more complete picture of the person they're studying. Getting direct answers to specific questions is usually not part of the learning process, which is why Edie's brother sometimes had to remind their dad to allow for queries.

"Your effusiveness can cause confusion," Justin would reply to one of John's later, more disjointed emails. "I know sometimes there is just too much to say," Justin empathized. "Heck, for you, that is probably most of the time. But communication doesn't work so well when there are too many words and your thoughts are jumping from one thing to the next." He reminded John, "Take it easy, Dad, and let us ask you questions to let the story unfold," adding, "kind of like dancing, you know?"

The main difference between email John and phone John is that his vocal streams of consciousness are more congruous. They're no less torrential, however. Nor are their abrupt course changes any less jarring.

"Five-hour phone call," Edie told Fort Worth through a grin within minutes of hanging up.

"Dang," Patrick replied. "I guess it went well?"

"Yes," Edie affirmed. "John did most of the talking."

"You okay?" her brother asked.

"Absolutely," she avowed.

"Phew," he sighed. "Been a little nervous for you. Can't imagine your butterflies."

"Started with Justin," Edie said, mentioning, "got to say 'Hi' to his five-year-old daughter, Hadley, who is writing a story about me coming into their family."

"Wow," Patrick said. "How fucking cool."

"Oh man," an anxious Yvette joined in, "I'm trying to catch my breath."

"So how was he?" Patrick inquired. "Is he the most interesting man in the world?"

"Oh yeah," Edie confirmed, "like the part describing his being a child and giving a massage to a man with a handlebar mustache like Yosemite Sam's, and hair down to the floor."

"That's crazy," Patrick responded. "Where was he raised? Deadwood?"

"Oh," she continued about John's childhood massage recipient, "the guy fought in the Spanish-American War."

"Any awkward silent moments?" Yvette quizzed.

"None," Edie answered. "His dad worked railroad sawmills," she retold. "They moved with the track." John had mentioned time growing up in a pair of Louisiana lumber towns—Kentwood and Bogalusa—each about an hour east of Baton Rouge.

"Oh girl," our hermana said. "I'm crazy in love with all of this."

"Your life is a John Irving novel," Patrick insisted.

"His name is John Irvin," I noted.

"Your life is an Edie White novel!" Yvette fired back. "Once all this settles, maybe think about writing a book!"

I love my sister-in-law, but that's a horrible idea.

"Not sure how far along with *Game of Thrones* y'all are," I prefaced my take on the call, "but I feel like Brandon Stark after the Three-Eyed Raven gave him the entire knowledge of the world at once."

"And we barely skimmed the surface," my wife tacked on.

While the Fort Worth thread was blowing up, Beth was also excited to hear from Edie.

"Five-hour phone call."

"WHOA," Beth reacted. "What'd they say? What happened? Did they holla at Fran? Is it her? Was it weird?"

"I gave them permission to reach out to Fran," Edie responded. "John did most of the talking. It was a historical documentary. The last four-and-a-half hours was mostly John talking," she said, "and me beaming."

Four exclamation points came from Beth. "That's awesome!" quickly followed. She also appreciated both my Three-Eyed Raven reference, as well as Edie's aversion to another phone call that evening.

"All is very good," my wife reassured, promising to phone her friend the next day.

"I am so happy for you, Edie!"

"Thanks in large part to your tremendous efforts."

"It was fun," Beth signed off. "The pleasure's mine."

Back in Fort Worth, the questions kept coming.

"Any plan for a face-to-face meeting?" Yvette inquired.

"At some point," Edie replied. "I think maybe he hasn't even told his wife about me yet."

"This is so great," Patrick declared. "I'm so happy for you."

"What's the word on Rachel?" Yvette wondered.

"I still need to contact her," Edie admitted. "I told Justin I feel bad about that, but I haven't been able to keep up with John."

"It's a lot to keep up with," her older brother sympathized.

Edie then commented on John's remarkable ability to remember tiny details about things that happened decades ago. "He's got seventy-two-plus years of recall better than I could describe the past seven days," she conceded, "hell, hours."

"His thoughts on Fran?" Yvette posed.

"They will reach out to her," Edie answered. "He cannot recall anyone else within the appropriate time frame who could be a candidate. Given his recall of everything else," she said, "I kinda trust that more now than before the call."

Edie and I soon began readying ourselves to join the Cavells in grabbing a final round of drinks at Slinky's, the last real dive bar at the storied LSU North Gates. It was set to close in days.

Alas, life is nothing if not about balance. Yes, we were losing one of the coolest pubs in town, but were gaining some of the coolest people we could ever dream of having suddenly burst into our lives—all with a wild, awesome journey, to boot.

"Thank y'all for sharing this adventure," Edie told Patrick and Yvette. "We're heading out to grab a bite with some friends."

"Thank you for sharing with us," Patrick said. "We are just so happy to know more of you."

"Yes!" Yvette cosigned. "Thank you for letting us be part of your whole new world!"

Not long after the phone call, Justin sent Edie an email. Thankful for the chance to speak with his big sister, he asked, "How did that conversation go?" He hadn't spoken with their father yet. Justin was tied up with "a house full of little girls to feed and assist in adventure."

His message also mentioned details about how they could best contact Fran. "We can make a plan that would work for you," he promised.

As Justin wrote, so did Edie, composing a message for him and their father. She sent it without seeing Justin's newly arrived email. The two were engaged in a correspondence pas de deux of their own.

"John, Justin," Edie greeted. "Thank you both so much for the wonderful opportunity to hear your voices today," she said, "and Hadley's, too! Thank you also for your willingness to reach out to Fran as you see fit. I trust you and agree that it appears to be the most organic, least threatening approach since John and Fran had a relationship.

"If your conversation with her develops to the point of mentioning me, and she is receptive, and you feel it appropriate to share," Edie continued, "I've attached a brief message I composed some time back.

"You are beautiful people," she said with a smile for her brother and father, "and I love that you are in my life!"

11

Gus Tabony

Sunday saw a midday reply to Edie's latest message, in which she had included her composition "If you were my mom."

"Good morning, Edie," Justin greeted, "And what a lovely message. In reading it, I instantly admired your loving, graceful, and grateful words. Perhaps because I had such a troubled, and often difficult, struggle with my own mother," he wrote, "I cried when I read your message. It reminded me of the things I said to my mother when she was dying, and at her improvised eulogy. Sorry," he apologized, "that sounds depressing, and I don't mean it to be. It was certainly a very sad moment, but it was incredibly freeing, restorative, and loving to say, 'I am so grateful,' because yes, of course we are. How could we not be?" said the son of a mom who left her young second husband to raise little Justin and Mason alone. "So thank you for sharing that message with us, and I would be honored to share it, to send it on your behalf."

Justin also promised to send a draft of a brief message for Fran in the next couple days to get Edie's blessing.

"I love that you are in our lives too, Edie!" he continued before his weekend winery shift. "I want to try and plan a time to meet with you." Justin proposed flying down to Austin in April, but work was at its busiest then. Rather than settling for a brief visit due to limited available time off, Justin suggested, "If you are at all thinking about coming out to Seattle, maybe sometime in May/June/July might work?" He added, "beautiful times of the year to be here, by the way.

"Also," their brother reported, "Rachel is so excited to hear that we talked, and hopes to hear from you sometime soon—as soon as you are up for it." Justin closed by sending "big hugs from far away."

While his message to Edie was arriving, its recipient was working on some more words of her own.

"Hi, Justin," his sister answered yesterday's email. "Wow, what a call. It really went well, though I feel like I didn't fully appreciate where we were going, and should have enjoyed more time talking with you before asking to speak to John. I hope at least it gave you more opportunity to prepare for the rest of the day's adventure with the house full of little ones." A grinning Edie beamed, "I could feel Hadley's radiance coming through the phone, and she just filled my heart."

With regard to contacting Fran, Edie wrote, "I am content with whatever works for both of you. I appreciate your willingness to serve as emissary, as Jeremy put it, but also realize all of this has added an unexpected, unscheduled layer into your already full life. Please don't feel rushed on my behalf," she insisted. "I am likely as prepared as I will be any time soon if Fran wishes to make contact, and definitely respectful and accepting if she chooses not to.

"This has been a rush," my wife admitted, "but I'm looking forward to taking the time to get to know each other better, and savor the relationships as they develop. You are surely far more knowledgeable than I am about wine," she noted, "but I appreciate it enough to not want to rush through enjoying the chance to experience a really good one." Edie also mentioned, "I think John may have indicated that he hasn't yet told his wife about me, so that surely would be in order before we arrange a visit in Texas. It's exciting to learn that he may be so close by!"

In answering a question about her name, Edris Ann told Justin Adam about her recently widowed eponym, Aunt Neenie. Doc O'Neal's youthful older sister "lives relatively close to you in Mill Creek," she informed the Renton resident. "Her oldest and youngest daughters live up there, too," a smiling Edie said of cousins she grew up with. "We haven't visited them up there yet, but now there is extra motivation to do so!

"Oh, gee, I'm really on the verge of straying off message," she kept writing, still smiling, "as I warned might happen once I got uncorked." Edie added, "I'm not going to admit how much time I've already spent reorganizing/cutting/pasting/editing this short message.

"OK," she began to wrap up ahead of her weekly hometown trek, "must step away from the computer and go attend to my little old ladies across the river. Hope you have a great day at the winery!"

For the second Sunday in a row, she managed to secure the cork on the erupting matter long enough for a trip to Maringouin.

That weekend, Edie and I resumed our ritual of sharing Sunday evenings with a couple named Rob and Julie, under the pretext of watching *Star Trek: Discovery*. It seemed like a fitting cap to a week of discovering family far more likable than anyone in the show.

A night with old friends provided us some much-needed normalcy and routine before facing another workweek, hopefully one a little less insane than the last. Our collective cork remained secured while visiting. Rob and Julie would later learn about our nascent adventure into the great unknown.

Hours after the epic phone call Saturday, John emailed his daughter a 1,227-word message. It began with a few paragraphs of hippie wisdom about us.

"Edie, you and Jeremy gave me joy," John wrote about our call, "with your sharings, makes me happy that somehow, I may have contributed a tiny bit to the wonderful person you are; and I am happy for, proud of you!"

Anecdotes from his life with Hallie comprised most of the rest. Aside from a sixty-two-word teaser, this was the most lighthearted message from John yet. Nothing too dark or heavy, outside of telling Edie how Hallie once nearly bled out due to gross medical incompetence.

Monday morning was relatively quiet. No emails, chat messages, or texts with or about family, new or old. It was the second consecutive John-email-free day, a nice change of pace to help us catch our breaths.

Even the mightiest of us motor mouths need a respite every now and then, it seemed.

I can't fault John for his hyperverbosity. The man has led an interesting life, to say the least. He's seen a lot. Good. Bad. Ugly.

Lots of ugly, apparently.

John's meandering would frequently bring the reader back to a handful of painful themes in his life, particularly the repeated abuse he suffered at the hands of American men in uniform, abroad as well as at home.

Yet, despite the emotional battering he chronicled—both in his writings and ensuing phone calls—John maintained a baffling ability to regularly find beauty and wonder in the mundane. Nevertheless, given how John's insanely remarkable stories are presented in effusive, less-than-cogent streams of consciousness, it is easy to dismiss them as fantastical tales spun by a gentle soul saddled with a checkered past, filled with trauma affecting his recollections.

"Holy hell," Edie messaged me Monday afternoon. "Just found documentation of the David Duke incident John described."

Yes, *that* David Duke. The former Grand Wizard of the Ku Klux Goddam Klan.

"Oh shit," I replied.

It turns out that while John was earning his PhD in wokeness at LSU, David Duke made his infamous entree. Parading around campus in his Nazi uniform, Duke screamed about the Jewish-Communist conspiracy on Wednesday afternoons at Free Speech Alley, outside the LSU Union.

"Amid the lengthy phone call," Edie explained to Beth, "John described an encounter with David Duke at LSU." She also shared a screenshot from Tyler Bridges's 1994 book *The Rise of David Duke*. The passage read:

> *The largest outcry from the crowd came when Duke said that whites are "the master race. We should have the right to keep the race white."*

Carl Tickles, a black student, challenged Duke's statement. "Look at my hands," Tickles told Duke. "What's the difference?"

"They're black," Duke replied.

Tickles took a knife from a spectator and offered to compare the color of his blood with Duke's.

Duke refused.

A white student joined Tickles. They cut their fingers to show that both bled red.

Twenty minutes into their first conversation on Saturday, John had told Edie that he was the White student.

"Wow" was the best I could manage in response to Edie's discovery Monday.

Meanwhile, her news evoked an "OMG" from Beth, prompting my wife to come back, "ikr?"

Bridges's book wasn't the only one to document the late 1969 encounter.

"There's another book on Google that describes the incident with Carl Tickles," Edie messaged Beth, "but I can't get it to load."

John spoke Saturday for no more than a couple of the call's 300-plus minutes about this incident. The details he offered two days earlier matched Bridges's retelling precisely. Moreover, the other book would eventually load for Edie. Author Michael Zatarain mentioned John Hart by name.

David Duke: Evolution of a Klansman came out in 1990, one year after Duke became the first former KKK grand wizard ever elected to public office in America by winning a seat in the Louisiana state legislature. That was one year before Duke made the runoff against former Gov. Edwin Edwards in our state's infamous 1991 "Vote for the crook: It's important" gubernatorial election.

"On November 13, Duke made headlines on the front page of the *Reveille* in an article entitled 'Jews, blacks lambasted at heated Alley,'"

Zatarain recounted. He then described the 1969 incident in much the same way as Bridges later would.

After the part about Duke refusing to cut his flesh, Zatarain wrote, "But another white student, John Hart, accepted Tickles' offer and cut his hand as well." The author also mentioned that the spectacle "prompted the *Reveille* to print a front-page photograph of a black hand and a white hand, both dripping blood."

The eldest child of that bloody, White hand's owner later retrieved archived copies of the front-page story at LSU's Hill Memorial Library. The fittingly black-and-white, three-column-width photo showed no faces, only a close-up of three hands, two of which were White.

The lone, left Black hand bled from the tip of its index finger, tightly gripped by the White right hand. The sliced middle finger on the other White hand awaited millimeters below the font of the Black man's blood.

"The hands of white student John Hart squeeze a trickle of blood from the finger of black student Carl Tickles in a dramatic demonstration of the fact that a black man's blood is the same as a white man's," the caption stated. "The demonstration took place at yesterday's Free Speech Alley following a barrage of down-grading remarks against Negroes and Jews. The remarks were made by David Duke, who described himself as a member of the National Socialist Party."

A few days after Edie found Bridges's book online, John offered another incredible story about his time as a "communist radical" at LSU, involving another charismatic student leader with further political aspirations. "Art Ensminger, president of the student body," befriended John, who had been banned from campus, hampering his peace activism. Ensminger insisted that Edie's father be part of campus leadership discussions, but only after initially rejecting the pacifist and his opposition to the war. "Art hugged me crying," John wrote. "He said that he had cursed me—called me all sorts of names, considered me the worst person imaginable, the worst of the communist radicals," he recounted, "someone more perverted."

That last part apparently stemmed from rumors fueled by jealous, fantasizing frat boys and cops who were convinced that John was on drugs, thus allowing him to have sex with at least twenty women in one night, he wrote. It was all because John's friend Judy invited him to her apartment to give her and her female friends massages out by the pool, where he also served them drinks.

"I sensed Art was suicidal," John wrote, saying Ensminger was taking on more than he could handle. Sadly, he was unable to find the up-and-coming campus leader to check on him after a group meeting.

"His girlfriend found me," John retold. "She knocked. I answered the door. She told me how Art was saying how much he loved you, how wrong he had been about you, shot himself. He loved you. He would want you to father my child.

"Like with Fran's friend, I could not speak," Edie's father recalled about the young lady insisting he impregnate her, in her moment of immense loss, because her dead boyfriend would want it that way. John said he didn't remember if he "tried to comfort her." He felt somewhat responsible for not "being able to just be with Art, to let him talk.

"Being able to accept accountability is one thing," John followed up. "To feel like you caused someone's death, as I did, is arrogant." It's contradictory to one's image of self, he remarked.

On October 19, 2017, *The Daily Reveille* ran a story titled "Nearly 50 years ago, SG president suicide led to new resource." THE PHONE is "a 24-hour chat line inaugurated for students experiencing a crisis." It was launched just days after the law student became one of six LSU students to take their own lives in a nine-month period, the article detailed.

"Fellow [student government] members described him in a memoriam published by *The Daily Reveille* in 1970 as 'a benevolent dictator,'" the author wrote of Ensminger's legacy. "'He constantly thought about our problems,' former SG member Thomas L. Barnard said. '[Our problems] kept him awake. The last time I saw him he hadn't slept for two days.'

"During his 10-month term as SG president, Ensminger facilitated a 2,000-person Vietnam War protest on the LSU Parade Ground in October of 1969 and established a department of student rights.

"However, Ensminger's magnum opus while SG president is a program that still exists nearly 50 years after its inception," the article said of a resource that tragically kicked off mere days too late for its creator.

Then there's Gus Tabony. In four separate emails, John wrote about the "narc's" purported role as a recruiter for the radical Weather Underground Organization, and the subsequent nightmares that still terrorize John to this day.

"Gus Tabony," he wrote his eldest daughter, "tried to get me to do bombings, political assassinations, steal military ordinance, weapons...have sex with an eleven-year-old he had drugged, used." In another passage, John mentioned "occasional forays into nightmares of the mute eleven-year-old he had drugged, naked on his raised bed mattress." He once described Tabony as "the informant/drug-dealing pilot, child-sex-entrapping one" who "awakened me from a deep sleep," John recalled, "literally asisted me to his downstairs apartment, opening the door and immediate eye contact with the eleven-year-old in a fetal position. I still try to silence his spiel," he shared with Edie. "'I've already had her, she's so good.'"

A still-deeply haunted John said he simply "walked away," rather than taking the incapacitated, mute preteen to a care center, like he wanted to do. "Gee," he added, "I wonder if the law was hiding that night."

When a person who's been in and out of prison repeatedly tells you how a narc set him up and tried to entrap him into horrific crimes—made easier by luring the mark into the same cheap "ghetto" apartment building—your bullshit detector might go off like mine did. Dismissing John's stories about Tabony is so much easier than believing someone like that not only existed, but also worked for law enforcement.

A few days after John's first mention of Tabony, Edie came across an entry in the 1980 *Gumbo* recapping newsworthy items from each year of the preceding decade. The 1974 listing proved significant.

Overseas, a Turkish Airlines DC-10 crashed outside of Paris, killing all 346 passengers. Domestically, Gerald Ford pardoned a newly resigned Richard Nixon, Hank Aaron eclipsed Babe Ruth's home run record, and Patty Hearst robbed banks. And at LSU, Paul Murrill became chancellor, the university mass transit system began, and "Gus Tabony, SGA member, impeached because he served as undercover Baton Rouge police officer."

On the second page of notes Edie took during her first call with John, she wrote, "Gus Tabony—SGA member impeached '74—BRPD informant."

She later found a handful of local newspaper archives of interest.

"August Henry Tabony, 20, of 228 W. Chimes, Apt. 12, sale of marijuana," read the front-page story titled "Drug Roundup" from the September 16, 1970, edition of the *State-Times*. "John Irvin Hart, 28, of 228 W. Chimes, Apt. 2, distributing marijuana," the same report incorrectly stated the twenty-seven-year-old's age, about a column inch below Tabony's inclusion.

John lived in the same building on Chimes Street with a guy who, at the time, no one knew was a narc. Also, getting "busted" with a target seems like a decent strategy for an informant to gain the mark's trust.

In case you're wondering what a former college narc and alleged child sex slaver grew up to become, Edie found a more recent news story from "Belize's Leading Newspaper," *Amandala*. In early 2016, the "Belize businessman" responsible for many of John's persistent terrors ran into some legal issues on the Honduran island of Roatan.

"Hopefully, if he was incarcerated," John would write Edie, "he may have had a taste of the same abuse."

With the exception of David Duke, we had to Google the Baton Rouge names he dropped. Same goes for Dr. Cheddi Jagan in British Guyana, whom John mentioned in his first unassisted email. These were people who each uniquely and significantly affected him; so much so, decades later, their impacts drove him to tell his newly discovered daughter about their interactions.

Any lingering concern about John's mental acuity, or the accuracy of his recollections, vanished when I realized he was actually enlightening us about significant, local events that we—and nearly everyone else in our sphere of influence—were clueless about. In the following weeks and months, Edie would independently corroborate other, even more unbelievable stories randomly volunteered by John.

Also, if there was any remaining doubt about his ability to listen and process new information, three days after their first phone call, John wrote Edie regarding tidbits about our lives that we had revealed during the conversation. He thanked us for sharing those details, in his message, before asking for more.

Throw in the overwhelming evidence screaming that Fran was Edie's mom, and suddenly John didn't seem nearly as discombobulated as he may have at first glance.

Nevertheless, as loudly as the Fran evidence blared, it was merely circumstantial. Edie still needed to confirm.

Two days after their initial phone call, Justin emailed his big sister.

"Thanks for reconfirming your readiness and willingness for us to reach out to Fran," he told Edie. "I have no idea how it will go, but I can't imagine any mother who had given up their child for adoption not wanting to know—at the very least—whether their child had a good life," Justin wrote, "or the most basic information. Perhaps I am saying that because that is what my own mother wanted to know (among other things) when she tried to find her son that she gave up for adoption."

In her late-night reply, Edie failed to mention Monday's discovery of Bridges's book, and how it confirmed one of their dad's wilder stories. She was distracted by previous commitments that she would soon move to the back burner, in light of the past week.

"Yesterday and today have brought their stresses," she wrote back to Justin, "so I am all the more grateful for the uplift of the phone call with you and John on Saturday to help keep me in a more uplifted frame of mind. I brought some of this upon myself," Edie recognized, "but it's easily corrected, and all will be well."

The two siblings also continued their ongoing conversation about recycled monikers.

"I have always thought it beautiful when parents choose family names that repeat throughout their history," Justin wrote Edie. "Hadley is named after my stepfather's family because his only biological son (my brother Mason) is not having any children. My stepfather (Patrick) is really the one who raised me, saved me even, from what could have been a very sad turn in my life," he recalled, "referring to how hurt and angry I was as a youth, and how he helped steer me toward healing. Anyway, Hadley's name honors our connection to the Hadley family, and ties us together that much more closely. It would be cool to meet your aunt someday," he said of Neenie, "and hear about your naming tradition after her."

Edie replied, "It is lovely that you and Cherish found such a beautiful way to tie your family together in the bundle of love that is Hadley. My aunt," she said, "takes great pride and joy in addressing me by our shared name, Edris Ann. It may be one of the few occasions in which a child being referred to by both first and middle names is a sign of love rather than trouble!"

Tuesday afternoon, Justin sent Edie an email with the subject line "draft of message to Fran." It included a proposed message for Edie's presumed mother. He empowered my copy editor to tweak it as she saw fit.

"Let me know what you think," Justin prefaced. "I won't send it until I hear back from you." It read:

> Greetings Fran. You have never met me but I am writing you because I am doing research on my family and it seems you knew my father, John Hart, a long time ago in Baton Rouge, Louisiana. He was a graduate student there in 1970; and as I understand, you two dated briefly in early 1970.
>
> Through my research, including DNA profiles, I have recently gotten in touch with someone who appears to be my half-sister, who was given

up for adoption in Louisiana. Her DNA profile and John's matched, which led her to us.

I realize this is very personal and that my writing to you is out of the blue. But, we are trying to piece together the past. We don't want to disrupt your life, but we wonder if perhaps you are a piece of this puzzle.

John remembers you were dating about the time my sister would have been conceived, so we did some internet searching and found you on Facebook. John told me he lost touch with you sometime soon after you departed for France that year. He was quite surprised to learn about my half-sister and he wants you to know he is ready and happy to talk with you first, if you like.

We are not asking anything of you, except what information you are willing to share, and will completely respect your wishes. We will not contact you again if you don't want us to. But if you think you may be my half-sister's birth mother and would like to communicate with her or want more information in order to confirm, I can provide you with her email address or other details.

Thank you for taking a moment to read this message and, hopefully, to answer. And if I have upset you or caused you pain or concern, I truly and deeply apologize.

Thank you most sincerely,

Justin Hart

Following reassurances from Fort Worth about a giant leap that would make Neil Armstrong antsy, Edie confirmed to Justin that he and Cherish had perfectly captured the tone and tenor she desired for first contact with the woman who ostensibly gave her life. My wife also indicated she'd finally be contacting their little sister that Tuesday evening.

"Hi, Rachel," Edie sent before bed. "It's me, the possible half-sister Justin warned you about!" she opened with a smile. "Please accept my apology for the delay in reaching out to you. This has been such a whirlwind; there was no way I was prepared for the warm reception your brother has given me. But I welcome the opportunity to begin to get to know both of you better, and hope my sudden introduction into your lives hasn't been too unsettling. Please feel free to share as you are comfortable doing so."

Edie offered a couple paragraphs about our lives, supplementing whatever Justin had passed along. Those were followed by a few questions about her new baby sister.

"I truly had no great expectations after submitting the sample to AncestryDNA, but it has been a great joy to learn of these likely family connections, and," Edie wrapped up, "exciting to find out that we live so near each other. I look forward to hearing from you and continuing the discovery!

"Warmly," she signed off her inaugural message, "Edie."

My love also included our Hugo's Cellar pic so Rachel could see what her big sister had settled for.

"Edie," Justin emailed the next afternoon, "I just wanted to let you know that I—just this minute—sent the message to Fran. If I hear anything," he promised, "I will let you know right away."

I would say we then waited to find out if we had found the right woman, but honestly, a bigger concern was whether we had her correct mailing address, in the event her Facebook page had been compromised. "There's no way Fran *can't* be Edie's mom," all of us thought.

Well, almost all of us.

12

Beautiful Journey

"Our conversations have inspired me to heed some of Jeremy's urgings," Edie wrote her father on the final day of February, "to let go of some things that have been draining energy, to focus instead on those things we enjoy together, making more room and time in our lives for the people we love." That led my wife to mention our involvement in "the production of the local Gridiron Show, the one where the current and former Capitol correspondents make fun of the local politicians."

She explained, "We were invited to participate in the show in 2005. I met and instantly bonded with Gloria, the stage manager. She invited me to join her to see Billy Idol perform at the House of Blues in New Orleans later that year, before Katrina. We've participated in the show every year since, me backstage and Jeremy onstage." In fifty years, Gloria had missed only one show, "and this was to be the year she handed over the reins to me."

We were having dinner that Wednesday evening with our Sunday *Star Trek* hosts, who also provide music for the Gridiron Show. "Tonight," she wrote of Rob and Julie, "we are breaking the news to them that they will need to ask someone else to coordinate the myriad pieces and parts of the show. Jeremy will still perform, and I will work backstage," she said of her annual supporting role, "but the other demands are too great at this time, and no longer my priority," Edie told John. "So I want to thank you for helping me embrace this step toward liberation!"

In scheduling the dinner, Edie messaged me, "I'm not sure I'll be able to hold it together." A few tears notwithstanding, she did just fine, and even fielded a few questions from Julie.

"Wait," she interrupted at one point, "you just called him dad," the former journalist sought to clarify. Rob, a former Spanish Town Mardi Gras king, politely asked Julie to hold off on the queries.

At the time, Edie compared herself to a juggler. Bowing out as stage manager meant one less thing she had to worry about dropping as she desperately tried to keep up with correspondence from Justin and John. She also needed to get Rachel into the mix so the sisters could at least begin to get acquainted with each other, all before a potential fourth, unfamiliar ball named Fran got thrown at her at any moment—possibly during the upcoming Gridiron production. Edie knew that could be a real mother to deal with.

Within an hour of our arrival home from dinner Wednesday night, Rachel replied to her big sister's initial message.

"Hi, Edie!" she wrote. "It is so good to hear from you! While talking with Justin over the last week," Rachel explained, "I have said in almost every conversation, 'I hope I hear from Edie soon,' quickly followed by, 'I am glad she is taking her time, feeling comfortable before adding someone else in.'" She added, "As comfortable as something like this can be."

Rachel called her sister "a wonderful surprise to me. I grew up as an only child; Justin and I met when I was nineteen, but I always knew he was out there. Getting to know him was so exciting," she recalled, "full of love and appreciation. I never thought I would experience such a beautiful time again." Rachel said getting to know their brother, "teaching him who I am, helped me know who I am. I am," she continued, "exhilarated to get to know you, but please don't be intimidated," Rachel insisted. "I have no expectations or goals beyond getting to know you. At nineteen," she allayed, "there was a lot more to learn about myself than I think there is now at thirty."

Rachel grew up in an Austin house where her mother, Elizabeth, still lived. With no children, Edie's sister has had her share of cats, including "Tezcat, who is constantly elegant, but somehow eccentric at the same time," Rachel noted. "I am also the person of my roommate's cat, Heru."

"To call me verbose would be an understatement," wrote John Hart's youngest. "I could have a nearly continuous conversation for a whole day if given a chance. This makes me well suited for my current job as a customer service representative for the City of Austin government."

"I self-identify as a nerd or geek," Rachel revealed. "My major hobbies are board games and Dungeons and Dragons." As for family, "my niece, Hadley, and the sons of my cousin," she said, "are the most important people in my life. It aches to be so far from Hadley," Rachel declared, "even more than it does to be separated from Justin.

"I have not traveled much," the Austin resident said. "It didn't seem like an option when I grew up, so I don't have expectations of it, but I greatly enjoy the traveling I have done." After starting in creative writing, "I somehow ended up triple majoring in Social Justice, Environmental Studies, and Elementary Education. I went to school at Antioch College," Rachel mentioned the Youngstown, Ohio, school, "which closed in 2007—the same year I met Justin! We met in Boston, but I was much more cautious than I am now. It took me at least a month or two before I felt comfortable talking to him on the phone, and it was eight or nine months before we met in person." She added, "I ended up transferring to a branch campus in Seattle, and living with Justin after only meeting in person three times!

"Please feel free to ask me anything from my opinions to my history," Rachel maintained. "I am an open person. There is very little I keep to myself or to my closest people. I look forward to learning more about you, but only what you are comfortable with." Prompted by Justin's report that we may get another cat, "What are the things you look for in a cat?" Rachel probed. "What do you look for in people?"

In closing, she mentioned no further DNA testing was required for her sake. The current evidence was sufficient.

"Yours (probably)," she signed off, "Rachel."

Edie would eventually find time to send her baby sister another message. "We have not yet visited your city," she emailed the younger Austinite, "even though it has been on our agenda since two of our best friends moved there several years ago. Now it is definitely moved up on our priority list!"

My wife then mentioned that "there was something going around on Facebook last year about concerts, and we realized how few we had been to, even though music has always been a dominant presence in both of our lives," wrote the woman who introduced me to Kate Bush, after I wooed her with Sade. "So we started doing something about that, and then we had our big twenty-fifth anniversary trip to Vegas that we had been talking about doing for years. That's when we recommitted to each other that we're going to continue doing together things that we love, instead of holding out for everything to be perfect (that had been me).

"So then the AncestryDNA test," she continued, "something else I had talked about for years. And WOW. What a discovery. Like you mentioned getting to know yourself as you got to know Justin," Edie explained, "this process has been not just exciting, but also liberating. Having this opportunity to discover and get to know both of you has also felt like an opportunity to explore who I am, the decisions made along the way, and the decisions on where we go from here."

Edie added, "Like you, I'm content for now with the genetic information we have, which is still a lot to absorb and process. I have been researching the maternal matches on AncestryDNA to see if they lead me to the person we think might be my birth mother. We may or may not get a response from her, but if we do, it could help clarify things.

"As far as our labels for each other," Edie responded to Rachel's query on the issue, "please feel free to call me what you wish as you feel comfortable. I think Justin and I are adapting to bro and sis, but we had a bit more of a head start.

"Thank you for sharing some of your story and your pictures," she wrapped up, "and for being patient with me and reading this far!

"With love," she offered, "Edie."

The sisters' first phone call, originally slated for the weekend of the Gridiron Show, was postponed due to Edie's all-but-gone voice. Baton Rouge allergens and busy schedules conspired to force a week's postponement.

The pace of John's emails dwarfed that of those sent by Rachel. It may sound odd, regarding a grown woman's first communications with her little sister, but they weren't nearly as overwhelming. The two sibs soon shared a connection, namely the cause of their relaxed messaging rate.

"I relate to your feeling," Edie empathized with Rachel, "as I find myself wondering 'who wants to hear about that?'" she wrote, "but then realize how long we've gone without being in touch."

Over the next several weeks, Edie learned a lot about her baby sister. I'll follow Rachel's lead by presenting them in bullet-point fashion.

- Her recently deceased cat Pippin's personality completely blossomed after Rachel's mom's dogs passed away. "We had no idea how much personality she had until she was the only pet!"
- A week after trying regular speed dating, Rachel served as Dungeon Master for a round of Dungeons and Dragons speed dating. "I am going to meet roughly twenty-five players," she said. "Scary! But exciting!"
- It took her some time to call Justin "Big Bro," but only a week or two for Rachel to mention her new sister to friends and family. "I couldn't help but let the cat out of the bag," she told Edie. "If you would like to still keep things small, I will make an effort to pull back."
- Rachel was just past halfway through watching all the *Star Trek* TV series, including *Deep Space Nine*. "I loved *TNG* and much

of *DS9*. *Voyager* is pretty good," she added, "but is fading in season five."

- She admittedly shared a penchant for veering off topic. "Please do not apologize for going on tangents!" she instructed Edie. "Tangents are just shifting the conversation, not ignoring it."
- While in high school, Rachel's mom told her that she regretted her daughter growing up without much family. "She knew dogs and cats and guinea pigs were no replacement for siblings and grandparents," my sister-in-law wrote of her childhood pet menagerie, "but she wanted me to have someone."
- Our newest Texas kin added Edie's name to her work password when she was required to reset it. "I have enjoyed so much our beginnings of knowing each other," Rachel said, "and I am so excited to Skype with you soon!"
- Her abbreviations are sometimes subject to interpretation. "Do you have a regular m-f job?"

The first time Edie read that, largely because she's been married to me for over a quarter of a century, she thought "m-f" stood for a non-radio-friendly gerund instead of "Monday through Friday." For a fleeting moment, Rachel had copped some Samuel L. Jacksonesque attitude with her big sister.

Despite Rachel's invitation to ask her anything, neither of us brought up her noncommunicative status with the elder Austinite. Outside of a satiated morbid sense of curiosity, nothing meaningful could be gained by going there at this point.

Meanwhile, with a second phone call under their belt, Edie and her little brother continued to communicate.

"Hello, Edie!" Justin emailed in early March. "This morning while I was doing some work from my home office, Hadley was sitting on my lap and wanted to see a picture of you. She didn't say anything really, but clearly her interest in you is very tangible." After explaining how their only child was suddenly thinking about the idea of siblings, a smiling Justin added, "I find it beautiful that she really wants to meet you.

"I haven't heard anything from Fran yet," he then reported, "though I took a peek at her Facebook wall to see if she had posted anything recently. She seems to be posting several times a day, but it is all links to articles from Fox News, Breitbart, and the like, which makes me wonder if her account may have been hacked," Justin wrote. "Or maybe it's just my solidly left, tech-savvy brain reading too much into what is on her wall. And I must admit," he said, "I am eager for her to respond."

A reminder to himself to remain patient spurred Justin to discuss their shared OCD. "Obsessive/compulsive is definitely something I associate with John, and to some extent Rachel, too, about as much as I see myself that way," he said.

"Now that you have begun to communicate with Rachel," he wondered, "do you get a sense that our shared DNA is behind some of the attributes we may have in common? I do feel like our genes determine some amount of how our personalities manifest, but maybe not as much as what comes from our experiences in life," Justin noted, "and the things we take from them/add to our sense of self and others. I guess the reason I say that is because I was raised by my stepfather more so than either of my parents," he explained, "and I feel like he has really influenced who I have become. I really look forward to the day when we three siblings can spend a little time together. I think it will be pretty amazing to just sit and talk with you both at the same time."

Moments after their second phone call, Edie and Justin became Facebook friends. For reasons (obliquely) related to discretion, I was restricted from doing the same.

My wife was concerned that if I also became Facebook friends with Justin, then unbriefed members of the O'Neal family might learn we both befriended a handsome man on the West Coast, become curious, and possibly interact with him. In other words, because my wife thinks things through so thoroughly—and because she knows her older sister, Kellie—I was forbidden from befriending my utterly friendship-worthy brother-in-law, all in the interest of ensuring zero surprises involving the people who raised her from birth.

Edie would eventually also connect with both Rachel and Cherish on Facebook, but only after privacy setting issues prevented her from finding my two new sisters-in-law. Ancestry had brought them together; Facebook was trying to keep them apart. Nevertheless, we were bound to come together, whether Zuckerberg liked it or not.

"Good morning, Edie," Justin wrote on March 5, "putting out some dates for a visit." He mentioned Memorial Day weekend. "We could give you guys at least a little tour of the area," he promised, "if there is anything you'd like to see or do besides hanging out with us/your family in the Mill Creek area."

He went on to tell my wife, "You are both welcome to stay with us for as long as you like. We have a comfortable guest bedroom," he said of the Harts' home, only twenty minutes from the airport, "and would be happy to pick you up there."

The two of us were thrilled by their generous offer.

"That sounds great!" Edie replied. "I must warn you that my normal reluctance to impose on anyone by accepting an invitation is far exceeded by my excitement about getting to see you all! Anyone in your household should feel free to kick us to the curb if you feel we are overstaying our welcome!" she added with a wink, as well as a mention that she was perusing flights around the last weekend of May. Edie had also messaged Aunt Neenie "to inquire about her schedule," she told Justin, "but that would be lagniappe, as we say."

Seattle wasn't our only potential late-spring tour stop.

"We've got our sights set on Austin, too!" Edie sent Rachel with a smile. "I want to follow Justin's lead on when all three of us can get together, since he has the farthest to travel and is working on changing jobs. Sometime before July-August is likely the best option on our end," she stated, referencing seasonal officiating obligations, "since that's when football training/practice will begin to heat up (in both temperature and time commitment). But since you are so close," Edie vowed, "we are happy to hit the road if there's a time that works for you."

These wonderful discoveries prompted priority changes. I had parked the podcast, and Edie opted for less involvement in a nearly seventy-year-old show. However, the other gridiron loomed large. Any travel would have to come before the 2018 football season demanded our attention. Mine, mostly.

In our house, football ruled. Literally, football ruled. As vice president of the Baton Rouge Area Football Officials Association, I was charged with training scores of officials in the areas of rules knowledge and application, along with on-field mechanics. This all coincided with my junior college football season in Mississippi, not to mention the dozens of LSU practices I'd be working in my stripes. Our household had a mutually agreed-upon ban on non-game-related travel from August through November.

In her reply to Justin's invitation, Edie also brought up Fran and her seemingly compromised Facebook profile. It had been nearly a week since Justin sent the February 28 message to John's one-time love interest.

"I took the time to check out her Facebook page," Edie told Justin, "and think you may be right about the possibility that it's been taken over, given the big gaps without posts, then onslaughts, and the incongruity of no personal posts, despite all the photos with detailed commentary on her life. Then I realized those were all posted about seven years ago," Edie said, "and most strikingly, there have been no pics of her grandchild in more than five years! Yep," she concluded, "that seems like the biggest tell of an abandoned profile."

This led to the idea of sending letters to the Houston and Georgia addresses Beth had found. "What do you think?" Edie sought Justin's advice. "We could lay off while I try to trace down more from the Ancestry info, or do we try our luck with USPS?" she wondered.

"Regardless," Edie closed, "we are most definitely looking forward to seeing you and sharing a bottle of wine. That's the thought that keeps us smiling!" she sent with love for the Renton Harts trio.

Justin endorsed the postal service idea the next morning, as did my other out-of-state brother-in-law.

"I think a letter is appropriate," Patrick replied when his sister consulted Fort Worth.

On Friday, March 9, Edie asked Justin if he could mail a note to both addresses. "I still think the words you all composed for the initial message to Fran are perfect."

As dusk fell on Baton Rouge, four hours after Edie's understanding boss approved her vacation request, we booked our flights to Seattle. Eight days at the end of May we'd stay. Edie forwarded the airline itinerary to our host.

"Yay! You got your tickets!" an excited Justin replied. With a reiterated offer to pick us up, he sent the address where we'd be staying.

Three weeks earlier, he didn't even know we existed.

As Justin scribed away on a Friday night to the assumed biological mother of a sister he'd yet to meet, Edie and I passed by a friend's birthday party en route to see a New Orleans-based yacht rock band—aptly named Where Y'acht—with our music festin' besties, the Cavells.

It was time to celebrate! We were set to fly 2,500 miles to meet Edie's immediate biological family. Wow, Ducky was going to be so excited!

That is, once she and the rest of the O'Neals learned about these people we'd be staying with, and their potential introduction to Ducky's sister-in-law.

"This is a beautiful journey," Edie wrote John a few days earlier, when Justin first messaged Fran, "and I am so happy to be sharing it with Jeremy, Justin, and you! And also my brother, Patrick, and his wife, Yvette," she explained. "They have been delighting in these discoveries with us. They also look forward to meeting all of you. I've not shared quite as many details yet with my mom, sister, and other brother," Edie said of Ducky, Kellie, and Wade. "They are all intrigued and supportive with various comfort levels, but my mom and sis have a tendency to shift into overdrive before I've even gotten into the car," she confessed. "We want to take time to enjoy the journey and all its twists, turns, adventures."

Over a week after writing that, Edie was still attempting to strap into her new reality. Aside from covering the basics (i.e., she exchanged a few emails with immediate paternal family), my wife had yet to invite the rest of my in-laws to join us on our insane, yet beautiful, journey.

They knew nothing of Edie's little brother's exceeding humanity, nor of his curious five-year-old daughter, the one writing a book about her new auntie. They had no clue how much Red had in common with her baby sister, only a six-hour drive away. And they certainly were not aware that—in the couple weeks that the pair had been communicating—my wife and the man who fathered her had traded more words than Doc O'Neal and I did in the nineteen years I knew him.

If we were going to tell them about our upcoming weeklong trip to practically another country (at least in Louisiana terms), where we were to be housed, fed, entertained, and shuttled around the Pacific Northwest by people we recently met through the internet, a serious crash course was in order.

"Hi. You okay?" Patrick messaged Edie the following Thursday, on the Ides of March. "It's been quiet. You're on my mind," he said after hearing from their older sister. "Just talked to Kellie."

"Tis the day for check-ins," Edie replied. "Wade texted me, too," she said of their eldest brother. "Told him we're still exchanging emails, but haven't positively identified the birth mom yet," she relayed to Patrick. "Didn't want to tell him we booked a flight to Seattle before I told mom."

Patrick suggested getting them all together for a briefing. "It really is fascinating," he assured, "and I think everyone will be thrilled at your progress. But of course," he insisted, "at your own pace and level of comfort."

Edie managed to set up a late lunch for that Sunday, March 18, with Ducky, Wade, and his wife, Cindy, a longtime teacher. Kellie's weekend work schedule wouldn't allow the nurse to attend.

Some forty-eight hours before the Sunday lunch, the two of us treated ourselves to one of Baton Rouge's best sushi places.

That same afternoon, Fran replied.

13

Must Be Wonderful to
Have Made You

Four minutes into Friday evening, the two of us were beginning to unwind in our living room when Justin texted. "Edie," he sent, "check your email. I heard back from Fran. Unfortunately," Justin frowned, "she said she isn't your mom."

We immediately repaired to our office to read his email.

"Hey, John and Edie," Justin wrote, "I just got word from Fran. Here is the entire content of her response copied and pasted below:

> So sorry it has taken so long for a reply, but I only check my mail about once a week. I'm not your sister's mom. So sorry to crash any hopes you had. I remember your dad very fondly and hope that he has had as wonderful a life as I have had, and I hope that you find what you're looking for!
> Sincerely, Fran

"I wrote back to her and thanked her for responding. So," Justin surmised, "the search continues, I guess."

He also addressed his sister and their father individually.

"Edie," Justin continued, "I hope you are not too upset by this news, and that we all take Fran at her word. But you said that one piece of information you have pretty much always known was that your mother was a student at LSU, correct?" he double-checked.

"John, besides Fran," Justin wondered, "do you remember any other students at LSU, or perhaps someone who could have become a student in the fall of 1970, that you dated around the time Edie would have been conceived?" he asked their aging father regarding his hook-ups of yore.

"Thanks," Justin closed with love, "and don't give up!"

At Edie's request, I soon sent word to Ascension Parish. "Justin just emailed," I told Beth. "Fran is not her mom."

"Dang," she replied.

My wife was busy composing a reply for Justin and John, "and resuming her forensic analysis of Ancestry data to find another contender," I informed Beth that Friday night. "Then we can search the *Gumbo* for her," I added, "and maybe jog John's memory with a pic."

"Sounds good," Beth agreed.

Saturday morning, as floats loaded with bros drunk on green beer passed through Baton Rouge, Edie posted in the Fort Worth chat thread.

"So just as we were scheduling a meetup with Mom, Wade, and Cindy tomorrow afternoon," my wife informed the Texas O'Neals, "Justin messaged that he got a response from Fran: She ain't it."

"She ain't it as in not Mom?" Patrick retorted. "There is no way that's true."

"That's her story and she's sticking to it," Red told Cottontop on St. Patty's Day. "With all the info from her Facebook pics, I could trace her lineage, and couldn't find any overlap to my DNA matches. We're looking for someone Eastern European," Edie explained. "John provided the British/Irish."

As Patrick remarked three weeks earlier, it truly was "fortuitous" Fran had all those publicly available photos.

"I'm deep into Lukaczyk searches at this point," Edie elaborated on maternal findings from her AncestryDNA research. "One of my Chicago cousins was a writer for Barack Obama."

"Okay," Patrick conceded. "Keep digging!"

His baby sister had already grabbed her shovel the night before, in the wake of Fran's response.

"No giving up!" a determined Edie had replied to Justin's Friday message, as I sent word to Beth. "This message will be short because JLW and I are back on the case tracking down the DNA matches to see who else might've been at LSU at that time. Justin," she said, "thank you so much for mediating this exchange and letting us know so quickly.

"John," she addressed their father, also included in the email thread, "I hope this isn't upsetting for you, either. I will share with you whatever we harvest from our ongoing research.

"The quest continues! Love you both," she signed off, "Edie."

Ironically enough, she was the only one reasonably dispassionate enough to not be disappointed when the woman said she wasn't Edie's mom. Just two days before Fran's response, my science-minded bride had messaged Beth about doubts prompted by her ongoing maternal research.

"I'm not so sure about Fran," Edie revealed Wednesday during lunch.

"If not her," our Deep Stater wondered, "then who?"

"Fran provided enough info on Facebook for me to trace her lineage beyond five generations in some places," Edie explained. "The maternal DNA links," she countered, "lead me to Lukaczyk/Lukas/Lucas."

Fran's ancestors were almost exclusively French, while many of Edie's DNA matches had Eastern European names. Fran's folks had too many vowels; Edie's maternal peeps, not enough.

"Could there have been another adoption or other alternative family dynamic (ahem) that's muddying the water?" Beth speculated.

"Most likely," Edie said.

Just before bed that same Wednesday evening, following Gridiron rehearsal, Edie expressed to Justin those same doubts regarding Fran, but only after sharing more about her involvement in the show, and our changing priorities. "I have had a long-running tendency to take things on because I don't want to disappoint anyone," she revealed. "But with all the flood of emotion that is pouring in with this wonderful discovery over the past month (has it really been only/already that long?), my heart just is not in the show right now. I went to rehearsal tonight," she said, "but both Jeremy and I might play hooky tomorrow night."

Edie then explained to Justin how, in digging through Ancestry that Wednesday, she had rollercoastered herself into—and out of—a DNA black hole, emerging just in time to depart for rehearsal.

"Not to cast doubt on our Fran theory," Edie continued, forty-two hours before the woman's response, "but John didn't happen to mention anyone named Lucas, or Lukaczyk, did he? That's the abundant domain I'm exploring at the moment on the maternal side," Justin learned late that evening. She'd recently discovered several DNA matches with such names who weren't related to John, according to Ancestry. "I think today gave me a taste of what you mentioned about finding new ancestors. Yikes! I'd best be rejoining Jeremy soon or I might dive back in and get no sleep tonight," she winked.

"I asked John about the names you found," Justin replied hours before hearing back from Fran on Friday, "and he said none of them sounded familiar."

In the wake of Fran's reply, Justin reiterated to John the ostensibly maternal surnames.

"You said none sounded familiar," he emailed their father Friday evening, "but I recall, on the first night we were talking about who Edie's mother might have been, that there were two other women you thought of first," Justin wrote, "but later said couldn't be her mother because of the timing of your relationships.

"Edie's DNA might give a hint at who her mother is," he continued. "I would say her mother was/is at least about fifty percent Eastern European. Since you originally mentioned that woman you dated who was Eastern European or East German, I think she would be a reasonable possibility if you think there was any chance that you were dating in the time frame in which Edie would have been conceived." Justin quizzed their elderly father about his collegiate oat-sowing days, "Do you remember anything about her?"

It was around this time we began to learn two important things about John.

First, while the guy has a savantesque ability to recall names, faces, places, and all sorts of myriad details surrounding past events, timing is elusive for John. He can reliably tell you everything about everyone and everything that happened, except for when it happened. His timeline is severely, and likely irreparably, fractured.

"He has really great recall of details of a lot of relationships and things," Edie would eventually tell the aforementioned Indiana woman about John, "but he also has a great deal of trouble piecing together the timeline, and putting them in the proper frame of reference."

Secondly, when you ask John to probe his memories, the helplessly effusive man will reply in great detail about everything he finds in his ensuing exploration among the vast recesses of his troubled mind. The good. The bad. And the ugly.

"In case you wanted to check them out," Edie emailed John and Justin on Saturday afternoon, "LSU's yearbooks are available online." She included links to a handful of *Gumbos*, including the edition where she found John's Justin-like photo. The hope that St. Patrick's Day was to spur John's memory.

And spur it she did, to the tune of 4,134 words. The majority of them were dark. Exceedingly dark. While Edie represents a delightful addition to John's life in his later years, she was born amid horrific times in his younger days.

"Going back," their father replied to the yearbooks, "trying to make sense out of my very disturbed consciousness, conscience at the time you were conceived, brings up a lot of the pain. The fear I had of women being abused," he recalled, "even killed if police saw me with them. I isolated, even from my best friend, Judy, and her friends."

"Hello, John," an apologetic Edie answered, "I am sorry that these inquiries have brought back painful memories for you; that certainly was not my intent. The main reason I submitted the DNA sample was to make myself available in case my birth mother may have had questions as to whether she had done the right thing," my wife reiterated, "to let her know that her choice was appreciated, to try to bring peace." She insisted, "Please don't feel any pressure to go through a painful mental exercise on my behalf.

"I am so grateful for this opportunity to begin developing relationships with you and Justin. We may or may not be able to piece together the rest of this puzzle," she conceded to their father, "but that's OK with me, too. Since finding you, it has become more urgent for me to help answer questions I created for you.

"I look forward to speaking with you again soon. With love," she closed.

"Edie," John soon assuaged, "you have generated only smiles, inside and out."

Within twenty-four hours, John sent his daughter—and only his daughter, as Justin was not copied—a brief message: 209 words, the last two of which were, "Love, Dad." It marked the first time he signed off in such a manner. In his previous dozen emails, he closed with either "John" or "Me."

If for no one else, I mention this for the sake of our curious friend Julie.

"Hi, Edie," Justin followed up on their dad's dark, 4,134-word email. "I am only responding to you because I am a little bit concerned, and I want to give you some context about the things John says. But first and foremost," he asserted, "you did NOT cause any harm or bother to John. He LIVES to relive and retell the stories of the many hardships and painful memories he has. I don't mean to say that he is in any way taking license," Justin clarified, "but he has been through some terrible things (I can vouch for at least some of them), seen some horrible things, had many terrible things wrought upon him. And yes, he does have real pain and sorrow around some of those things.

"But know that he has some scrambled memories," her brother wrote, "and that, perhaps more significantly, has a tendency to embellish, to relish, to revel in the drama he has known. I don't mean he is telling tall tales," Justin maintained. "It is one part due to head injury and age, one part due to just too much drama/trauma, and one part genuine dramatic flair," he said, adding, "oh, and some genuine OCD, too."

"Thanks, Justin, for the reassurance," Edie answered. She also restated her previously held doubts, in response to Justin's theory that Fran might still be the one, but reticent to admit it, like his mother Shirley once was regarding the existence of her first child. "I think it's best we accept Fran at her word," Edie clarified.

"John said something about wanting to talk to Fran," she continued. If they did correspond further with the former debutante, Edie offered the 8x10 glossy from eBay as "a thank you/peace offering gift," she said, "if you don't think it's too creepy."

"If she happens to reach out again," Justin replied, "I'll mention it. I do think having her confirm whether she remembers the timing of her and John's dating would be helpful," he said, "if she cares to share it."

Beyond her initial reply, none of us ever heard from Fran again.

"Hey, my girl!" Kellie texted her baby sister on the eve of the crash-course lunch with the local O'Neals. The nurse was sad she couldn't make it, but said, "I'm so happy and supportive of you, as I know the whole family is. Mom is so curious and excited for you." Kellie looked forward to learning more from Edie later.

The two of us took a Sunday drive out to Satterfield's Upper Deck restaurant, situated along scenic False River in New Roads. Participants in the local Kiwanis annual fishing tournament dotted the oxbow lake that formerly served as the main channel of the Mississippi.

As Kellie had promised, Ducky was attentive, receptive, and 100 percent supportive. Same went for Wade and Cindy. Once again, just like dinner with Rob and Julie, Edie had lots of food to take home because her mouth was too occupied catching everyone up on details, and providing clarifications for the handful of questions.

We waited till the end of the two-hour-plus gathering to mention Fran, and did so only as an afterthought. The story was plenty complicated enough without throwing in a decoy mom, no matter how convincing—and briefly alluring—she might have been.

With pre-existing family behind us, we continued preparing for our Renton visit.

"Hi, Edie," Justin wrote late Monday evening. "Just wanted to ask you about John being here when you visit. He said he can be here then, too, as long as you would like him to be." Her smiling brother said, "I just don't know if that is too much, so I want to check. And if it feels like it would be too much, it is okay to feel that way."

An enthusiastic Edie answered before work Tuesday morning.

"As long as it's not too much of an imposition on you and Cherish, we'd love for John to be there, too!" she confirmed with multiple grins. "We are excited about the prospect of seeing all the great things you described about the Seattle area," Edie added, "but we are MOST excited about seeing all of YOU! We look forward to spending as much time as we can together," she winked, "but we can also get out of your hair as needed. We don't want you to feel like you need to be a tour guide."

Promising it was "absolutely no imposition," Justin insisted, "it will be wonderful to host this family reunion." He added, "I enjoy being a tour guide."

Meanwhile, only one state away from us, John was also preparing for his partially concurrent trip to Seattle.

"Hoping for a wonderful visit with, for everyone," he emailed Edie and our soon-to-be hosts, before addressing his five-year-old grand-daughter. "Hadley, get your exercise. Grandpa Goat will be exercising, in the swimming pool, gardening, other work. Perhaps I can better run with you on the dirt or grass, and," John wrote, "we can dance more freely, and you'll have more family to dance with!"

Despite nary a mention of my dancing acumen in any previous communications, John also wondered if, while in Renton, I might kick my "choreography career in high gear, teaching us all some of your moves?"

"Let the countdown begin: We get to see you in five weeks!" Edie emailed Justin in mid-April. "Happy dance time!"

A month had passed since our lunch in New Roads. Kellie, an hour east of Baton Rouge in Abita Springs, had yet to be debriefed. This meant I was still forbidden from befriending folks who were inspiring my wife to burst out into spontaneous dancing.

"Yeah, I've waited long enough," Edie responded to my query about finally connecting with our new peeps on social media. "She likes everything on Facebook," my wife joked about Kellie and their inability to connect in the past month, "so maybe that's more efficient."

"Just requested all three," I replied. Nearly two months after Edie and Beth found them, my new in-laws were Facebook official.

Following a twenty-minute phone conversation later that same afternoon, Kellie received pics of Justin and Rachel.

"Edie," she soon replied, "I'm so overwhelmed! Looking at these strangers who are your people. Your blood! Tearing up," Kellie added. "All attractive people. Justin's kinda really cute! I'm looking at their faces, or pieces of your face in theirs! They must be wonderful to have made you is all I know!" Big Sis insisted. "So happy for you to explore this!" She topped off her text with four hearts, one shy of a flush.

"Justin's name popped up," Kel came back about a minute later, "so I sent a friend request. Is that ok?"

"Sure," my justified wife affirmed, "they are all very open people, and Justin has been super helpful."

Edie had already begun composing an email to Justin, Cherish, and Rachel to prepare them for the anticipated barrage of friend requests from people they didn't yet know. My wife offered another crash course, this time to her new folks about her lifelong ones, "since Kellie has already started the next wave of friend requests."

Rachel responded with her own mini crash course about her peeps. "When I met Justin and Cherish," she wrote, "their side doubled the small family I grew up with; now it looks like it's doubling again!"

It didn't take long for Edie and Rachel to embrace the inherent bullet-point-like nature of both Facebook Messenger and texting.

- Rachel found another Edie White in Baton Rouge, prompting her to message my wife that there was another Austin resident named Elizabeth Sears, who also had a daughter named Rachel Sears.
- During Thursday night bar trivia with the Cavells, Edie texted Rachel to say that she thought about her baby sister when our team settled on an answer by dropping a ten-sided die, to which a smiling Rachel replied, "Fun! I like trivia and ten-sided die."
- When Rachel expressed regret via text about not being able to join us in Seattle because she was going with some friends on her first-ever cruise, Edie insisted she go relax and have a great time on the previously booked trip.
- On the evening of April 20, Edie chatted up Rachel: "So if Justin is our brother from another mother, does that mean you are my sis from another miss?"

That same evening, Edie and I had an overdue phone call with the Texas O'Neals, starting en route to dinner, and ending in our vehicle several minutes after parking outside the restaurant. It had been over a month since we last spoke or chatted online. After dinner, I managed to forget our leftovers on the table as we left to catch a local comedy show. It was 4/20.

Around that same time, Justin informed Edie that the letter he mailed to the Houston address had come back marked "no longer lives at this address."

I've since gone back to Fran's Facebook profile, out of morbid curiosity, to discover she's posted even more far-right nonsense, along with more recent, personal things only she could have posted. She hadn't been hijacked. That was all her.

I'd be lying if I said I didn't feel like we had dodged a bullet.

14

Grandma Mary Was a Sklarczyk

A month from our upcoming trip, Edie copied Justin in a reply to their father's latest (2,179-word) email. "What a delight to wake up and see your message, John!" she wrote on the last Tuesday of April. "I was just telling Jeremy last night that it's been too long since I had been in touch with you. And now it's only four weeks until we get to Seattle!

"I spoke to my aunt who lives near Justin," Edie referenced her eponym. "She also wants to meet everyone and is so excited." My Edris Ann added, "Perhaps we'll get to introduce Hadley to four cousins about her age." After reporting that she was "fading fast," she closed the late-night message, "We are counting the days, and so looking forward to our time together."

She also asked John about planning another phone call, because phone calls with John require advanced planning. For a while, he and Edie spoke most Tuesdays, before dinner, so she'd have a reason to end the call. My wife's meekness was often no match for her father's verbosity. Once, in an effort to halt John's talking long enough so his daughter could try to say goodbye, I feigned a kitchen emergency by yelling and banging cookware.

"I would love to meet your family here, Edie," Justin replied to his sister, "but my number one goal is to spend time with you and Jeremy (and John when he arrives)." He'd let Edie take the lead on time with Aunt Neenie and her area brood, whom Justin offered to host in Renton, or join us in visiting.

In that same email thread, John also discussed potential activities during our time together. Edie apparently had inspired one idea by bragging about this zebra's athletic prowess, as recently exhibited in Tiger Stadium during LSU's Spring Game. "If you & Jeremy would enjoy," her father wrote, "I can do massage, feet only, or any/all u wish. While talking, listening," he added, "teach some playful to professional stuff simple to use if you like."

This was going to be an interesting trip.

We were two weeks and two days shy of meeting Edie's paternal folks when she received an alert from AncestryDNA. A message from a new match, a close one on her maternal side, awaited her.

"You must be from the Novak side of our family," the message said. It came on the first Sunday in May from a user named John Lukas. His mother's maiden name was Novak, he said. He had yet to upload a profile picture on his AncestryDNA account.

"Eek!" Edie messaged Fort Worth. "New maternal match," she reported, "closest yet, just messaged me."

"How close?" Patrick asked.

"First-second cousin," she cited Ancestry's estimation, based on their shared DNA (465 cM across twenty-two segments, whatever that means). "He's probably about John's age," Edie noted, "based on parents born in the 1910s."

Later that Sunday afternoon, after her weekly river crossing, she messaged Justin about John Lukas.

"Wow!" her younger brother texted back. "That is awesome." A smiling Justin hoped the man might know about her birth mother.

"Lots of deep breaths," she replied. "Patience." Edie said she was "grateful that he initiated contact," and "trying to respond in the least shocking manner."

She elaborated in the Fort Worth thread.

"So I'm trying to come up with a response," Edie shared, "in case he hasn't looked at my biological tree and seen that I don't know who gave birth to me." She then shared what she had drafted for her initial communication to a maternal relative.

"I think that's perfect," Patrick assured.

"Hi, John," Edie replied to Mr. Lukas that same Sunday. "Thank you for contacting me. I'm just starting to explore my lineage, and I'm grateful for your suggestion." She added, "I'm happy to share information as you see fit."

That same Sunday evening, Edie exchanged texts with Rachel.

"Hi, sis!" she wrote after being surprised by an additional, mysterious ball to juggle. "I miss talking to you. I'm obviously not as good a multitasker as I once thought I was," Edie apologized. "Just want to let you know I think of you way more often than I reach out in writing."

"Hi!" Rachel answered. "I miss talking to you, too! I had meant to email you this weekend," she admitted, "but I went from one thing to another all weekend."

The newest John in my wife's life sent a second Ancestry message Tuesday morning. In it, Mr. Lukas briefly noted that the Novak brothers ran a sawmill in the Michigan City area, and that his grandfather, Mike Novak, worked for Amoco Oil. He also said he had a number of wedding pictures from the house of his Grandmother Mary, who died in 1961.

"So I got a second message from the maternal match," she messaged Patrick and Yvette after work Tuesday, moments before sharing John Lukas's latest. "I think that may be my lead-in to suggest that his Grandma Mary and her husband are how we are connected," she explained, "since I have matches from at least two of their children's descendants." Thanks to tons of online research, my bride knew Mary was John Lukas's paternal grandmother, which meant he and Edie were not related on his mother's side.

"Fascinating," Patrick said.

"Sounds like a great lead-in," I advised.

"Novak?" Patrick asked. "That's Eastern European?" he guessed.

"Nowicki," Edie replied with a family name belonging to deceased relatives in the Novak branch of her growing, yet no less puzzling, maternal tree. The Americanization of surnames would only add to the confusion.

"Lukaczyk," Edie soon offered as a context-free, one-word post. "Grandma Mary was a Sklarczyk," she added seconds later.

"That name is vowel-deprived," Patrick observed.

"I've always loved the letters Z and Y," my wife said of her adorable linguistic peculiarities.

"Then you should be happy," Patrick said. "Also, somewhere deep inside, you can make a mean borscht."

That same Tuesday evening, Edie updated Justin about her maternal kin's latest message. "A theory I'm keeping to myself," she revealed, "is that one of his brothers (unknowingly) sired a child who would later meet John at LSU." Edie added, "I'm treading carefully, and not asking too many questions yet, since his messages are just one or two sentences apiece. But his mom's uncles ran a sawmill up north," she related. "His name is Lukas, shortened from Lukaczyk." Edie also informed Justin, "Grandma Mary was a Sklarczyk."

"That is the title of your first album!" he shot back, evoking laughter from his now-Ancestry-savvy sister. Prompted by the Novaks' sawmill, Justin made mention of the logging industry.

"In the past two days," Edie said, offering him a peek at her maternal research process, "I've created two trees with 138 people—and that's just who I had already pieced together between four DNA matches. They're from two big branches that I haven't linked up yet. When we do," she cried, "timber!"

Back over in the Fort Worth thread, Edie proposed a reply to John Lukas's most recent message.

"Gentle enough?" Edie prefaced. "I think your grandma Mary and her husband may be how we are connected," she shared, "because some of my other cousins descend from their daughter Anna Jean."

After confirming Grandma Mary's been gone since 1961, Patrick confirmed, "I think your approach is going to be fine."

"I'm not going to drop my theory that one of his brothers sired a child who would later give birth to me," she shared. "I've got another big trunk of the tree to scale before committing to that one." Patrick soon received a sprawling genealogy chart Edie had built out around her nearest maternal DNA matches.

That Tuesday evening also included another text exchange with Austin. Rachel and Edie planned on having a Thursday phone call. Before that would happen, though, the Fort Worth thread again crackled with more news of Edie's maternal peeps.

"So after I suggested his grandparents are our link," my wife reported early Wednesday evening, "the new cousin John replied with a total non sequitur last night: 'My mom had an Aunt Edith that lived on a farm. I don't remember her last name, and she raised Great Danes,'" Edie quoted Mr. Lukas, "'the damn things were big like a horse.'"

A little later, Mrs. White followed up on the Fort Worth thread.

"I just sent one more subtle response to see what he comes back with before going the fully direct route: 'Wow,'" she had written back to John Lukas. "'I grew up in the country, down in Louisiana, but not exactly on a farm. We had dogs and cats, and a horse and some cattle and rabbits for a while. Do you remember anyone in the family who lived down in Louisiana,'" she inquired, "'or who still does?'" With a wink, Edie told Patrick and Yvette, "and that's the only Ancestrying I've done all day."

"That's a great way to raise the subject. Also," Patrick ribbed, "so crazy that Edith loved animals."

"I did tweak that chart after I sent it to you last night," she said of her ongoing research, "had to stretch it out to add a bunch more folks."

Edie explained to her big brother how she had started with a dozen or so maternal DNA matches provided by Ancestry. She then connected them—mostly distant cousins—by working up to their common ancestors. The burgeoning family tree had been fleshed out after many weeks of my Molly Marine's reconnaissance on esoteric websites, where she found all sorts of illuminating documentation—obituaries, gravestone markers, death records, birth records, birth announcements, wedding announcements, just to name a few. Her flourishing creation was impressive, to say the least.

"Didn't know we had relatives in Louisiana," read John Lukas's fourth message in five days, "but we have a big family," he wrote Thursday. "My Grampa Mike Novak had six brothers."

After channeling Beth by doing a bit more online research, Edie updated Fort Worth at lunch.

"OK, so the guy I'm corresponding with is only sixty-four," she shared, casting doubt on her theory that Edie's bio mom was John Lukas's secret niece, "a decade younger than I had guessed." She also mentioned, "He's still stuck on me coming from his mom's people, which isn't what the DNA shows. Looks like I have to come out and make it clear that he doesn't know about me based on adoption," my subtle wife said, "and that it's his siblings or his dad's side where we're connected."

"Yeah, I think so," Patrick concurred, as did I with a thumbs-up.

"Too much? Not enough?" Edie asked ahead of her proposed response: "Hi John, based on the DNA results, it appears that we are related through the Lukas side of your family, not the Novaks. The reason I am unfamiliar to you is because I was adopted at birth in 1970. I do not know the identity of my biological mother, but my biological father was a graduate student at LSU at the time. It's possible that my biological mother, like me, was a child born out of wedlock (maybe sometime around 1948-52) whose biological father did not know about her.

"Please know that I don't wish to cause any turmoil," she promised, "but I am receptive if you would like to continue sharing information.

"Respectfully," she closed, "Edris White."

Patrick and I again approved.

"Sent!" she reported.

"Fingers crossed," Patrick promised.

"That second cup of coffee may have just become unnecessary," his sister confessed near midday.

Patrick chuckled. Moments later, he and Yvette would learn of John Lukas's freshly sent fifth message.

"Why would I not help you," he asked, explaining, "I have acquired a brother who was adopted at birth, my father's child," John Lukas wrote, "dad was married."

"I'm not entirely sure what that means," Edie added, "except that it's good."

"No, that's great!" Patrick agreed. "He's already had a big shock."

Edie answered her maternal relative a little later in the day.

"Wow, John, thank you," she expressed, "and how exciting for you! Did you find your brother through AncestryDNA? That's how I found my biological dad, brother, and sister earlier this year."

"You're still missing your mom," John Lukas soon messaged back, "or do you know anything about her?" he wrote, continuing the Thursday afternoon volley.

"We think she was a student at LSU in Baton Rouge, LA, in 1970, but that's about it," my wife answered in the early evening. "She saw an OB/GYN doctor here in Baton Rouge who helped a local firm arrange the adoption."

That same night, Edie phoned Rachel for their previously planned call. Two minutes shy of an hour it lasted.

"I am glad you said, 'I love you!'" Lil Sis soon texted. "I wanted to say it," Rachel offered with a heart, "but I didn't know if you were there yet."

On Friday morning, Edie messaged me after finding John Lukas's Facebook profile. We now knew her closest known maternal relative had a warm smile and a full head of graying hair.

"Right off the bat," my wife updated me on the puzzle, "I see he's Facebook friends with his brother's ex," she messaged me, "and someone in the branch of another match through his aunt."

We would not hear from John Lukas again for over a month, several days after returning from our approaching Washington trip.

As the departure date drew closer, so did Edie, Justin, and Rachel. They explored their new relationships with one another, all while my wife continued searching for her bio mom.

"Happy Siblings Day," she initiated the trio's group text thread with three hearts representing traditional Carnival colors (purple, green, and gold). Edie's younger brother and sister echoed her wishes with various emojis on a day marked for celebrating their relationships.

"Edie, I am so happy that you have joined us," Rachel added that evening, "which is funny to say since you are the oldest."

"I second that," Justin quickly followed. "As the one who was always the oldest sibling before, it is fascinating to now have an older sibling. Nevermind the lack of memories from years prior," he noted, "we will now get to make many years of new ones. So looking forward to spending time with both of you together," Justin told his sisters. "A whole new dynamic for all of us!"

"As the former 'baby' of the family," Edie winked, "I can relate! Looking forward to our time together," she shared with a heart before bed.

Days later, in the three-sibling thread, my wife shared the side-by-side shot of Patches and school-aged Edie next to her sister's image. "Rachel, I had to compare these pics of us." She asked, "What do you think?"

"Beautiful! I had a calico cat as a young kid," Rachel responded. "Do we have the same smile? Yours looks like a reflection of mine."

To Justin's delight, the two sisters continued comparing smiles amid an exchange of pictures, including one from when their cousin Erica, daughter of John's older sister LeMerle, visited Rachel in Austin. Another showed the two of us at our first Bacchus Mardi Gras Parade with the Cavells in New Orleans a couple months before.

"Y'all take great pictures!" Rachel remarked.

"He makes me smile," my easily entertained wife replied, "and so do y'all."

Justin later suggested, "We should organize a Skype session with Rachel when you are here, Edie." The two sisters were down with the idea.

Justin later shared a picture of a pink-pajama-clad Hadley sitting erect in a large cardboard box laying on its side near a dining table. "Hadley says this is her apartment in New York City," he explained. "One day, we will probably see her in a real one, and it might actually be slightly larger!" The pic prompted hearts—red from Texas, purple from Louisiana.

"Hadley says she loves you both," Justin soon passed along to Baton Rouge, "and thank you for coming to visit her."

Just over a week before our flight to SEA-TAC, the two of us spent Mother's Day at Wade and Cindy's New Roads home along False River. Edie had a picturesque venue to finally tell Wade's two daughters and their sister-in-law—all young, nurturing moms—about where we were going, and why.

She told Justin about the family get-together in an email the following evening.

"It was the first time I've had the chance to talk to my oldest niece, in person," Edie wrote, "and I really needed to talk to her first, and in person, based on her personal struggles prior to her adoption of her son. She is much stronger now, but still harbors some fears related to what questions he may have and what might possibly happen with his biological parents at some point in the future," my wife said, "so I needed to be able to look her in the eyes, hold her hands, hug her, and let her know how much I love her, and that it's all going to be OK. It's like a wedding," Edie retold, "we're just bringing more people into the family! So now," she added with a smile, "I'm trying to reach out to my older sister's far-flung offspring to do the same.

"Because in eight days," she continued that Monday, "this is happening: I get to hug my younger brother and youngest niece! Yay yay yay!"

An emotional Justin replied, "You have an incredible story to share, and I am blessed to be a part of it. And you are so right," he said, "it is like a wedding, the adding on, the uniting of family far flung and lost/found, new and old, chosen and born with. It is all going to be okay—something my mother used to tell me, something I couldn't actually believe when I was a kid and I was angry and alone (or felt

that way, abandoned), but now," Justin continued, "I understand. It can
be so difficult when you are so young, and maybe feeling that horrible
question of why, why didn't my mother, father, family want me? Why
didn't they stay? Why are they not here for me when I want or need
them to be?"

He then asked Edie, "Did you ever feel abandoned, or unwanted, by
your biological parents when you were growing up?"

"I can't say that I ever felt unwanted or abandoned," his sister wrote
back, "but there was a period of loneliness given the age differences
between me and my older siblings," she explained, "and the isolation
of where I grew up." Edie recalled, "I spent a lot of time with the
TV, Atari, and solitaire (with actual cards). Whereas Jeremy thrived
on entertaining everyone around him, I entertained myself in my head,
interacting with characters from books or TV, and didn't really develop
strong social skills. I'm still working on that one," she smiled.

Covering three states and two continents, Kellie's five photogenic
kids replied to their aunt's news with excitement. Edie also ensured
Patrick informed his daughter about our upcoming trip.

"I didn't want her to be surprised if stuff shows up online next
week," she told him. With regard to her Mother's Day talk with their
oldest niece—Patrick's godchild with an adopted son—Edie "was glad
she was OK about it."

"I think everyone is either okay, or will get there," Patrick reassured.
"It's a wonderful thing."

Edie messaged me Tuesday afternoon. "This time next week," she
screamed, "we'll be at SEA-TAC!"

Within the hour, Edie got an email from our ride. While curbside
pickup was an option, Justin was leaning toward meeting us inside the
airport. "I feel like we might need the luxury of a few moments to just
hug and greet each other for the first time."

"It was seriously hard not to bounce around like a giddy fool at work
today," Edie wrote back Friday night, "knowing there's only one workday left before we get to see you." She said, "Today was like Friday on

steroids with all of the anticipation. Ninety-two hours to go!" my heart exclaimed. "Yay!"

She and I spent a mild Sunday in late May with the Cavells in New Orleans. Eponymous cocktails at the Roosevelt Hotel's Sazerac Bar followed ZZ Top at the Saenger Theatre.

In the middle of the afternoon, John sent an 1,857-word email with the subject line "exploration."

"There is a high probability that Debbie/Deborah Abrams is your birth mother," he dropped on his daughter within forty-eight hours of our arrival in Renton.

Between tangents about a Marine door-gunner reluctantly complying with an order "to machine-gun fifty or sixty women and children," and how John "was homeless for days" before getting arrested, he described how he met Edie's latest potential birth mother with the help of "Rosedale, the infamously handsome Cajun Narc."

Her father then told Edie about the steps he took in trying to out the newest narc in his life, the one who allegedly sexually exploited John's latest bio-mom candidate. "I mimeographed a description of Rosedale," John recalled, "put them up on campus."

In the span of a few paragraphs, John eventually realized that he had led Edie down a dead end. His time dating Debbie was interrupted for ten and a half months by John's 1972 prison sentence, two years after Edie's birth. "Debbie did not mention having a child, especially with me," he said. "Just thought of that, so again," John asked, "is the trail cold?"

John had copied his son on the message.

"He seems to be struggling with things, reaching for stuff," Justin wrote Edie. "Not that I don't trust he is remembering real people and feelings and experiences he had," the younger Hart maintained, "but his memory is sometimes not reliable." For their father, "one of the most difficult things to accept is that of being a parent. And by this, I just mean that he is very much like a kid. I don't mean this in a diminutive way," Justin explained. "His heart is youthful, he's a little bit like Peter Pan. He has a wonderful innocence and sincerity, but he just never seemed to see himself as capable of making a lifelong commitment to raising a child. Perhaps to his credit, that is because he knew he wasn't capable of doing so," Edie read. "His mind and body are too fractured and discombobulated.

"I am not complaining and criticizing him, really; it was just that both of my parents were, in a way, children." Justin added, "I also think John is dealing with emotions he has about circumstances with Rachel and her mother (all very negative stuff in his memory), and your appearance in our lives has intensified those emotions for him." John's son noted, "He may feel some guilt, he may feel regret, and much more."

Incidentally, when coming from the interstate, Rosedale is the name of the last town one drives through before reaching Edie's hometown of Maringouin.

We were hours from our flight's early-Tuesday-morning departure when Justin checked in with Edie on Monday night. "Any last-minute questions?" he texted. In the ensuing exchange, they discussed the Debbie Abrams fallout.

"All is well," a smiling Edie ensured. "We are getting on a plane in the morning, so we will be great!"

"Feel free to ask us to dial it back," Justin reminded, "especially John." He winked, "Did I tell you we have a penchant for drama?"

"Don't you worry," Big Sis insisted. "We all have occasional drama; it might just help confirm that DNA thing. I am so thankful to have the best husband and brothers in the world." Edie warned, "You might be kinda stuck with me for a while."

"Deal," Justin accepted with a smile.

15

Touchdown Seattle

"About to head to the airport for our flight to Seattle," I messaged my podcast partners just after awakening early Tuesday morning. "We'll be meeting and staying with Edie's newly discovered bio family," I told Knick and Sunny in our group thread. "Also gonna visit her aunt and a couple cousins who happen to live up there," I added. "Coming back Wednesday next week."

"Buckle up for a surreal experience," Knick responded.

"Yeah," I agreed, "it's gonna get extra surreal over the weekend and Memorial Day. The dad is flying in Saturday," I expounded.

Thanks to an eighty-seventh birthday party for Aunt Neenie, Monday would mark the first time members of Edie's lifelong family would meet folks from her new one.

With the help of another friend from Edie's days at the newspaper, we booked a 5 a.m. rideshare with her husband. He gave us a listening ear en route to Baton Rouge Metropolitan Airport for our 6:36 a.m. departure.

We quickly made it through security—ten minutes tops—leaving us plenty of time at the gate to think about what we were about to do. As we waited for the call to board, the scenario began to more fully permeate my consciousness. I soon heard a familiar voice.

"Surreeeeeeeal," Knick resonated in my mind.

"Yes, I know. It's surreal as fuck," I projected back to my friend's echo. "Now shut up; I have a plane to catch."

A couple hours later, we grabbed breakfast during our layover at Dallas/Fort Worth. With full tummies before our four-hour-plus connection to Seattle-Tacoma, I snapped a pic to help Justin recognize us.

Edie wore a big smile and an olive cotton blouse. Kellie's recent gift of a modest fleur-de-lis pendant necklace highlighted her sister's gentle brown eyes. Wavy auburn locks framed my wife's beaming visage, illuminated by sunshine pouring through the window near our gate. We sat in view of the plane set to take us to meet people who shared a significant portion of her genes.

A freshly shaven dome topped my resting-bitch-face mug in the same selfie. My sunglasses hung from the collar of a tee featuring the word UNBROKEN across the state of Louisiana. The Sunny-designed shirt meant all three podcast members were making the trip in one way or another, be they on my chest or in my head.

About that same time, Justin was also taking a selfie. "So you will know what I am wearing to the airport," he texted Edie. Justin wore a black "Bubba's Burgers in Hawaii" T-shirt, nicely coiffed wavy hair, and a respectable pair of sideburns.

"I was just thinking the same thing!" his sister replied with the photo I had taken moments before.

Our boarding time eventually arrived. It passed without an announcement. We grew slightly more antsy than giddy.

A voice crackled over the P.A. system. The crew was inspecting our aircraft for damage. It had struck a bird en route to DFW.

Edie alerted Justin about a potential delay.

"Yikes, bird strike!?" he shot back. "Well, if I were a bird near the airport, I would go on a strike too," he winked. That's when any lingering worry about the plane's airworthiness gave way to concern I might end up fighting my wife for more time with Justin to trade corny comedy bits.

"Boarding commencing," Edie soon texted him after another announcement.

"Have a safe flight and see you in a few hours!" Justin sent with a heart. "Wave to Cherish as you take off; she's at work in Dallas until this evening." Our sister-in-law and cohost would depart for SEA-TAC a few hours after us.

With Cherish's late-night arrival two time zones later, we were set to be awake for nearly twenty-four hours, on just a handful of winks. A sensible plan would have been to relax and get some sleep on the flight.

Then again, "sensible" is not a word most people would use to describe what we were doing. Any midair snoozing by either of us was negligible.

I attempted to keep Knick's voice at bay by trying to identify geographical markers from my window seat. Edie tried to keep herself grounded with puzzles that had zero to do with Ancestry research.

After a brief game of chicken with Mount Rainier, our flight crew initiated final descent through the cloudless sky. We landed in the middle of a glorious late-spring day in the Pacific Northwest.

"Touchdown Seattle!" I messaged Fort Worth with a photo. Sun lit Edie's face as she rested her right cheek against my chest. My heart peered wide-eyed out the window, past the wingtip, at the approaching terminal building.

"Woo hoo!" Patrick rejoiced.

"That's the only time we celebrate that call," my fellow Saints fan clarified with a wink.

"Right," Patrick chuckled in agreement.

Yvette soon sent us six smoochy-face emojis, a hand signaling "peace," and a purple heart.

Two minutes after our scheduled arrival time, Justin texted that he was walking into the terminal.

"Just pulling up to gate D9," Edie updated him from her seat.

"Yay!" he exclaimed.

"YES!" she agreed.

With the entire length of the D terminal separating the two of them, the two of us made a "quick pit stop" after the lengthy flight. We were about to engage in some vigorous hugging with an incredible human being who also happened to be my wife's long-lost brother. Neither of us wanted to risk treating him like the cops had treated their dad.

Pit stop made, we each slung our carry-on bags onto our shoulders. She grabbed my left hand with her right. I soon started videoing my typically demure wife pulling me forward through the terminal. Her free arm swung emphatically as she strode with a bouncy determination.

I significantly outweighed her, and was occasionally expected to beat some of the nation's best college football players to the goal line. For a few minutes, though, I felt like a jockey holding on for dear life as Secretariat came down the stretch at Belmont Park.

With a firm grasp on her husband's hand, this notoriously defensive driver was zooming past slower traffic, veering into oncoming travelers—with me and our bags in tow—before cutting off the people we had just sped past. It's a small miracle we didn't take out at least a couple of older folks.

We approached the point where the terminal connected to the rest of the sprawling complex. Mostly looking past the phone, I continued recording while trying to locate Justin in the distance. About a dozen steps after our left turn into the main terminal, I knew she had spotted him.

The former ballet student broke her grip and bolted forward, performing an extended jeté while bounding past an armed TSA agent. For about twenty yards, her arms were flung wide in preparation to hug her brother.

She rounded one last corner, barely clearing a freestanding sign to her left. Justin walked toward his quickly approaching sister. With a straight left arm at eight o'clock, and her hoisted right at two, she aped our plane, banking hard as the distance between them vanished.

Two paces later, the former Marine OCS candidate threw those surprisingly strong, freckled arms around Justin's neck. He wrapped his around her upper back, pulling her in closer. Their chins buried against each other's right shoulders, brother and sister tightly embraced without a word. I continued videoing, walking up to them.

With my wife's head tilted slightly toward the ceiling, due to nearly a foot worth of height difference between the siblings, I couldn't see her face. After twenty-five years of marriage, I didn't need to. I knew.

Her brother stooped slightly for accommodation. His head was tilted down enough for me to see the entirety of his sunglasses resting atop his head. Justin's eyes were closed, and Edie's hair covered most of his right cheek. His smiling face exuded a loving warmth and, to some extent, a sense of relief. After more than forty-seven years, my wife had made physical first contact with her blood.

Edie eventually relaxed her headlock, came down from her tippy toes, and faced her kin.

"HI!!!" she squealed through tears, prompting them both to giggle as they maintained eye contact, almost like they had taken a moment from dancing to admire each other at arm's length.

Justin eventually broke his gaze to face my way. With the widest grin I'd ever seen, Edie quickly turned toward me, swinging her right arm open. "This is Jeremy," she managed between gasps punctuated with nervous laughter.

"How are you?" I asked, hugging Justin. My still-recording phone got a nice shot of SEA-TAC's ceiling.

Two seconds later, his sister went in for another embrace. "HI!" she chirped again as they engaged once more. Edie hummed her exuberance. Justin gently passed his right palm up and down against her back. The encore lasted three times longer than the first.

"HI!" she greeted him face-to-face once more, this time in a slightly lower tone.

"Great to meet you," he replied with a smile, seemingly trying to keep himself together in front of us, and everyone else going by at one of America's busiest airports.

I stopped recording that same second.

Following a stop at baggage claim, our trio made our way to the top level of the open-air parking garage. Justin's brand-new black Tesla shone in the bright, early afternoon sun.

"Our chariot," I sent with a photo to Fort Worth.

"Is it worthy of a cargasm?" Yvette asked me.

"Oh yeah," I confirmed in the back seat.

Edie rode shotgun, aside her brother, whom we literally had just met. I lost count of how many times I reminded myself of that fact during our trip.

About fifteen minutes from the airport, we arrived in Renton, known for 737s and Jimi Hendrix's grave. Justin pulled up to a two-story house with a daylight basement on a quiet neighborhood street. Towering trees and verdant brush bordered two sides of the lot, which sloped significantly downward leading away from the street, toward the west.

The two of us exited the Tesla before Justin pulled into the right bay of their snug double garage. As he eased the vehicle into its tight quarters, I marveled at the sound of nothing but the crunch of pavement against four rolling tires carrying two and a half tons of an otherwise silent, electric car.

Once inside, Justin showed us upstairs to our room. The west-facing window offered a view of the impressive back patio below, including the Japanese tea house that Justin and his stepdad, Patrick, had built for the latter's namesake. Hadley would sleep in her room across from ours, at least when she didn't crawl into bed with her folks at the opposite end of the hall. We'd have to wait until the next day to meet the light of their lives. Our niece was staying the night with Cherish's parents.

Next to our room was Justin's office, equipped with a bed. John would sleep there days later.

The three of us settled downstairs in the kitchen, where Justin occasionally checked his laptop. He was technically working from home the day he met his older sister. The rest of the week was officially vacation time for him.

We grazed on light snacks while my wife and her brother slowly began to get to know each other better. I spent a good bit of that afternoon comparing their faces. For her part, Edie has since told me that she doesn't remember that much from those same couple hours.

She was her typically reserved self, not offering a lot or asking many questions. Following her lead, Justin wasn't saying much, either. Meanwhile, in that moment, my dumb ass knew better than to assume the role of conversation carrier.

While there were moments of silence, I wouldn't characterize them as awkward. Rather, they were more like opportunities for our brains to get a better grasp of this stark new reality, one literally staring each of us right in the face.

Justin eventually took the lead. Silences were displaced by the back and forth between a brother and sister finally bridging thousands of miles and several decades of separation.

Also, there was Sebastian, the partially shaved, thirteen-year-old tabby basking in the sun pouring through the sliding glass door. Justin soon led us through it to an elevated deck outside, then down the stairs to see their vibrant, terraced garden, descending away from the house. The wide array of greenery framed most of the bricked patio, which abutted another sliding glass door.

This one, directly below the door we had exited, led to the quarters of the Harts' housemate, Jenny. Her mother had helped look after Hadley when she was too little for school, earning Jenny's mom the moniker "Nannie Sue."

Justin continued our tour of their home. Topped with solar panels, it also housed a surprisingly large wine cellar. We'd end up inflicting our fair share of damage on that sucker over the next week. Justin would serve as sommelier and enabler.

A couple hours into our visit, we were comfortable enough with one another for Justin to take out a custom-made Christmas card that John had sent Shirley when their son was six.

To the right of one side was a simple illustration depicting two people walking away, arm-in-arm, through knee-deep snow. The person on the right held up a candle. "Peace on Earth" read the message below.

The rest of that side was occupied by a photograph depicting some sort of wooden table. Or maybe it was a small bench. And it wasn't in the foreground, but it was definitely in focus, because I could clearly see that sitting atop that bench, or table, was the better part of a brick of cocaine. A cocaine mound, if you will. Like an ant mound, except it was cocaine, with a 1979 street value around a quarter million dollars. A red mango peeking over the white mound provided scale and festive coloring.

On the back was John's handwriting. It delivered an obviously appropriate message.

"And, may all your Christmases be White!" Edie and Justin's father offered in black ink. To the right, he had translated the sentiment into Spanish, writing it with at least four different-colored crayons (red, yellow, green, and blue).

"Con toto mi Amor, John," he wrote in ink, with all his love below. The note on the bottom left said "XMAS '79."

My wife's father made god-knows-how-many of these cocaine Christmas cards. He then mailed god-knows-how-many of these— again, cocaine Christmas cards—in the U.S. Fucking Mail.

I've never done coke before, but based on everything I've seen and heard, nothing says "Peace on Earth" like Scarface amounts of powder.

There's no way to confirm if John packaged this particular batch of powdery product—maybe along with some weed, and perhaps clothing for a young Justin—and mailed it to Shirley in lieu of more traditional forms of child support. Nevertheless, Justin said John would occasionally do that sort of thing, because he figured Shirley could move the enclosed substances.

I asked Justin if I could photograph the card. He said sure. That's when I knew, barely three hours after landing, there was no way this was not going to be an awesome trip.

We spent the last several hours of daylight on the elevated deck. The sun began to hide behind neighboring trees, descending from the busy sky above. Air traffic from SEA-TAC and a smaller nearby airport frequently drew the attention of this former Naval avionics technician with an urge to identify low-flying aircraft. I found it oddly therapeutic, looking at all the planes floating above in the majestic Pacific Northwest. It gave me an excuse to kind of zone out from time to time, allowing my brain to divert the energy it needed to process everything we'd end up experiencing in those eight days.

We took our first sips from Justin's wine collection while he grilled chicken for supper. I gradually shifted my seat toward the heat as cooler air set in. I'd soon realize that all three of Edie's brothers know how to cook. If they're making it, no matter what it is, it's going to be awesome.

The clock read ten. Our bodies were feeling midnight. Not long after that, Cherish arrived.

She was as lovely and sweet as one would expect from a woman sharing a life with Justin. Her warm eyes were tired, just like ours. Nevertheless, we all stayed up a little longer, chatting, laughing, at least until the yawns got too frequent to ignore.

Laying there in bed with plenty of silence to contemplate where we were, and why we were there, exhaustion was our ally. Mercifully, we fell asleep quickly.

Cherish was already awake in the kitchen downstairs by the time we woke up. Justin took advantage of his first true vacation day by sleeping in, something they could rarely do with a five-year-old. Between sips of Cherish's French-pressed goodness, Edie and I began to bond with the household's only hardcore coffee drinker.

Her husband soon descended the stairs, joining us in the kitchen to discuss our first full day together. The plan called for a hike, something we love doing whenever we visit Fort Worth.

"How we doing?" Patrick checked in with his sister as we finished a light breakfast.

"Doing great," Edie replied, "getting ready for a hike."

"Is it so beautiful?" he asked. "Is everyone so nice?"

"Yes and yes!" she answered.

"Good deal. Can't wait to hear all about it. Y'all be safe," Patrick implored.

"We're debating about going to the trail where a big cat killed someone recently," Edie informed her big brother.

"Odds are in your favor now," he argued.

"Exactly," she agreed.

"Eat a bunch of edibles," Patrick instructed his baby sister on the first morning of our visit to a state that had recently legalized recreational marijuana. "That way if you get eaten," he explained, "you're passing the buzz on to the kitty. That cat will develop a taste for THC and eat every hippy that comes along."

"Po," Yvette addressed her husband. "I'm a hippie," Yo reminded Po.

"For purposes of this conversation," the attorney clarified, "so am I."

"Blaze it forward," I remarked.

"Exactly," Patrick laughed.

From the kitchen area, I stepped outside onto the elevated deck to begin my weeklong scenic respite from the oppressive heat and humidity back home. Area cottonwood trees were in full bloom, much to Justin's chagrin. Their snowlike seed pods gathered on everything like oversized dust bunnies. I had noticed them whooshing around the Tesla during yesterday's arrival.

With coffee and phone in hand on the driveway, I videoed the abundant white tufts floating under a clear blue sky on a quiet Wednesday. Bright midmorning sun highlighted the tiny wafting wads against the verdant landscape surrounding neighborhood homes.

It felt like I was living out a scene from *Edward Scissorhands*. We had woken up inside a giant, refreshingly comfortable snowglobe.

Back in the kitchen, while Justin packed for our hike, Cherish was kicking off her workday from home. Her parents and child would arrive later.

As we began our hourlong drive to Rattlesnake Ridge, I was amazed by the stop-and-go Seattle metro traffic. Not because of the volume, mind you, but the prevailing attitude. Everyone was so goddam nice to one another. It was about as unnerving as their ridiculously smooth roads.

Everyone seemed to know—for the traffic to be just as smooth—they needed to cooperate with one another, instead of repeatedly cutting off other vehicles that were "in the way." It was as if they realized that, rather than being "stuck in traffic," they *were* the traffic. During our entire stay, I witnessed nary an asshole who thought he was a genius.

We pulled into the well-maintained park and began our ascent up the clearly marked trail's modest grade. Abundant timber shaded us and our lush surroundings. I soon realized why Washington is the Evergreen State.

I also began to realize how perfect this excursion was for Edie and Justin's first full day together. Fortunately, the photographer brought a camera that allowed this ill-equipped iPhone user to take proper first photos of brother and sister posing in the shade of abundant canopy, with a brightly lit landscape in the distance.

As someone raised to quickly find fault, I began to wonder if Justin had any.

We were approaching a hairpin turn in the climb when I heard music. Childish Gambino's then-new anthem "This Is America" blared from a boombox carried by one of about a half-dozen teenagers jogging down the trail above us. Rather than being annoyed, I thought, "How cool." As those kids shortcutted the hairpin turn by jumping down to the trail below, they unknowingly reminded me of a recent hike with Patrick and Yvette, during which we passed a couple discussing Childish Gambino.

We reached the east-facing rock ledge overlooking the shimmering azure Rattlesnake Lake at the foot of the ridge, hundreds of feet below. A crystal clear blue sky with unlimited visibility framed majestic peaks in the distance. Nothing in our home state even approaches the awe-inspiring beauty of our vista under the midday sun in the Pacific Northwest.

"Is it pretty?" a nearby hiker asked the gentleman taking her picture atop the same rock ledge, with the same incredible view.

Just as I began to imagine the snark I wished I could say to this attractive young lady, her boyfriend flatly fired back, "No, it's horrible."

That's when I knew this place was special.

We took a few steps to begin our descent when another woman on the ledge, urged on by her friends, performed a marvelous little aria.

We halted in our tracks to enjoy the impromptu operatic solo. And yes, it was pretty.

After wading shin-deep into cool, clear Rattlesnake Lake, Justin drove us to Snoqualmie Falls. Unseasonably high water thundered over the 268-foot waterfall featured on David Lynch's *Twin Peaks*. Brother and sister posed in the midst and mist of a natural wonder associated with the master of surrealism.

The two chatted most of the way back to Renton, at least in part about the family Justin had yet to connect with. As beautiful as the moment was, I tuned in and out, captivated by the scenery going by outside the Tesla, particularly since there were no billboards to detract from the view.

Louisiana, on the other hand, has such a glut of billboards occupying the flat landscape, multiple state lawmakers would end up proposing measures seeking to restrict them the following year.

Everywhere I looked were these things that Edie and I (and everyone else back home) called mountains. Justin insisted they were hills. The real mountains, he said, were further east.

Whatever they were, they dominated the horizon. All sorts of huge trees covered their slopes. Various shades of green tickled fluffy white clouds above.

Honest to god, it was like living in a goddam Bob Ross painting.

Hadley was back from her grandparents' home in Toledo, about thirty-five miles west of Mount St. Helens, when we arrived in Renton. The self-described vegetarian enjoyed a late lunch involving chicken nuggets, served by Cherish's folks, Jack and Marsha.

Hadley also appreciated the gifts Auntie Edie had recently shipped to her. After learning of the young author's fondness for our Mardi Gras parade's mascot, my wife correctly figured our niece would appreciate a book about a flamingo. *If I Knew a Flamingo* arrived that week with a plush stuffed flamingo named Mingo.

In one of his emails, John described his granddaughter as "an ebullient little delight." By the end of the weekend, she and I would become BFFs.

Jack and Marsha joined Jenny and the rest of us for a tapas-style dinner on the mostly shaded patio. Multiple bottles from Justin's cellar would end up losing their collectible status that night.

"Look," someone whispered, gesturing toward a small adult rabbit that had joined us for dinner. The brown-and-white bunny barely paid us any mind, sitting just a few yards away from several wine-drinking adults and one occasionally exuberant five-year-old. I snapped a handful of pics before he casually scampered off, presumably in search of Justin's strawberries growing near the driveway.

Back inside, a giggly Hadley played with Auntie Edie and Uncle Jeremy until the pre-K student relented to her parents' wishes and went to bed. Marsha and Jack soon followed suit. Jenny and Cherish stayed up a little longer, until the wine and a pending workday demanded some shuteye. After polishing off another bottle, Justin, Edie, and I followed their lead.

We had another day of hiking ahead of us. This time, in downtown Seattle.

"I hope y'all are having a nice day," Rachel messaged her sibs Thursday morning. "Can't wait to see y'all tomorrow!" she said ahead of their scheduled Skype session. "I know y'all have been used to the plural use of siblings," she added, "but I was really excited when I said that to my roommate last night."

In the Harts' kitchen, Cherish attempted to feed Hadley before school with an audience of four visiting adult relatives to distract her. Between bites, the five-year-old—who had drawn remarkably accurate world maps hanging on the pantry door—further impressed us with her knowledge of foreign languages.

Even more impressive, Justin's sister ate one of his freshly picked strawberries. Edie held it between her teeth as I recorded the rarity. Disgusted by their texture, my wife hadn't eaten a strawberry since our first date in 1991.

Like Justin, I was ignorant to her aversion when I offered her some of the strawberry pastry I got for us at Highland Coffees after watching *Russia House* at the old dollar theater near campus. She said nothing before eating a couple bites. The way my bride tells it, that's the moment she knew she was in trouble. Twenty-seven years later, Justin managed to become the second member of an exclusive club.

On their way home after breakfast, Jack and Marsha drove Justin, Edie, and me to the Mercer Island Park & Ride. I learned that morning how, from their backyard in Toledo, five-year-old Cherish had watched Mount St. Helens erupt.

A bus ride later, Justin was showing us around Seattle's Central Business District. Our first stop was the Amazon community banana stand, at the foot of several skyscrapers comprising the tech giant's headquarters campus. As much as she despises strawberries, my wife loves bananas, especially free ones. In one photo I snapped, the attendant held a banana in front of her mouth like a giant smile, resembling the upturned arrow pointing from "A" to "Z" in the ubiquitous etailer's logo.

As we shoved Bezos's bananas into our mouths, Justin led us to the billionaire's giant balls. They're formally known as the Amazon Spheres: conservatories made of concrete, steel, and glass. Most people refer to them, our guide told us, as Bezos's balls. We beheld them at the base of a rigid, 521-foot steel erection looming over the downtown area.

After selfies below the Space Needle, our trio took in the Museum of Pop Culture, including its exhibit *"Star Trek*: Exploring New Worlds." It would close in four days to tour the country indefinitely. None of us Trekkers knew that then. Timing is everything.

When one of your earliest communications with your adult brother includes Starfleet's Prime Directive, it seems fitting that one of the first pictures of y'all together would involve crawling through a bona fide Jefferies Tube, like a pair of redshirts desperately trying to save the USS *Enterprise.*

"We fit in the Jefferies tube!" Edie texted Rachel.

"AHHH!" she reacted. "Awesome!!"

There was also a Picardigan, a Starfleet uniform sweater for when Captain Jean Luc Picard felt like rocking a sexy-bald-Kurt Cobain look.

A short walk down a couple halls was MoPop's "Nirvana: Taking Punk to the Masses" exhibition, featuring rare artifacts from the emergence of the groundbreaking band led by the young man from Aberdeen, Washington. The neighboring permanent exhibit "Wild Blue Angel: Hendrix Abroad" covered Jimi Hendrix's meteoric rise to fame through the late '60s.

Incidentally, I've never understood why "meteoric" connotes "rapid ascent" when meteors so rarely go up.

After checking out MoPop's horror showcase, we strolled in the warm afternoon sun to Pike Place Market. Along a shimmering Puget Sound, we walked by the first Starbucks, as well as the fish-throwing mongers, made famous by every Seahawks home game TV broadcast.

Justin led us through an alleyway to experience Seattle's Gum Wall. Our passage through the cave of dried-out wads was apparently Justin's attempt to whet our appetite for a late sushi lunch at Japonessa with Jenny.

She and Cherish became good friends when they worked together at Mrs. Hart's employer, the American Heart Association. This anecdote led to me learning about aptonyms.

A bus took the four of us back to the Mercer Island Park & Ride. While walking to the Chevy Volt that Jenny would drive us home in, Edie found an iPhone on the pavement.

Back at the house, we left the phone on the counter in the chronically occupied kitchen. After a bowl of Jen's tasty udon noodles, Hadley gave Auntie Edie a tableside makeover with her handy, shiny, pink lip gloss.

"She continues to be fascinated by the idea of you," Justin wrote Edie a couple months earlier. Hadley apparently hadn't changed much in the interim.

In that same email, Justin mentioned he was reading to his girl a book about a pair of penpals, something Rachel and her niece were considering becoming. "The book is honestly way above Hadley's head right now, though I don't mind." Justin explained to Edie, "It exposes her to a lot of wonderful vocabulary, and gives us many opportunities to talk about what words mean."

It's little wonder the little wonder was so well spoken and sharp as a whip. Trust me, as someone without kids, I know a thing or two about parenting.

Once Hadley's active brain finally settled down for the night, Justin broke out their edition of Joking Hazard, an illustrated iteration of Cards Against Humanity. The game gave the five of us—the Harts, the Whites, and Jenny—a chance to learn how sick of a sense of humor each of us has. Let's just say Edie wasn't the only guest who felt to be amongst one's people that evening.

Once again, alcohol and a looming workday forced Jen and Cherish to hit the sack before the rest of us. Justin, Edie, and I didn't stay up too much longer. We faced an arduous day of drinking wine in Woodinville before the first-ever face-to-face conversation between John Hart's three (known) children.

He'd arrive within forty-eight hours. Four days remained before John and the rest were set to meet the family of my late father-in-law.

16

You Can't Fake That

Friday was the first overcast day of our still-rain-free trip. Sometime midmorning, I heard a ring from the phone Edie had found at the Park & Ride.

"Hello," I cautiously answered.

"Hello?" a bewildered female voice replied.

As I began to explain that we had her phone in Renton, it became apparent that she was expecting to hear it ring somewhere in her home. When some strange man from Louisiana answered, however, she started to wonder who was in her house.

The grateful lady soon started listing potential meeting spots for the handoff that day, so I handed her off to our good—no, great—Samaritan host. We'd connect in Woodinville that afternoon.

A little later, as Justin got ready upstairs, Cherish worked at her bedroom computer after dropping off Hadley at school. Meanwhile, Edie and I were downstairs in the kitchen when we heard a ruckus outside. Something was agitating the birds into making a racket.

I sat at the kitchen table while Edie stood by the sink. Per her instructions, I looked outside in the trees, through the sliding glass door, past the elevated deck; the grove stood guard over the tea house. I saw nothing, I informed my wife.

She called me over. I complied.

Looking out that window over the kitchen sink, where my wife had been standing, I realized the open umbrella on the deck had blocked my view of what was causing the trouble: a bald eagle perched on a tree branch at eye level, maybe twenty feet above the property line.

Thankfully, the neighbors' Jack Russell terrier was safe inside their house. Hopefully, Wednesday's cotton-tailed dinner guest didn't become breakfast.

The drive up to Woodinville and its collection of winery tasting rooms was, of course, spectacular. The sun occasionally joined our lunch trio on the Heritage Restaurant patio.

Justin wore one of his personally designed vinophile T-shirts, popular with winery staff and customers alike. A horizontal, silhouetted wine bottle poured into a glass on the front of the red-and-black shirt with baseball-length sleeves. The message above on Justin's chest read "POUR'N STAR!" He was saving his "I Make Pour Decisions" shirt for another day.

After lunch, we walked a few steps to a tasting room run by a winery that shall remain nameless. Upon exiting, Edie and I learned how they had not duly treated Justin like an industry member, and that the indiscretion had been noted for future reference.

Finally, the angel had briefly, and ever-so civilly, flashed his "fuck those guys" side. I liked what I saw.

Next was Patterson Cellars across the street. Before strolling in front of stopped traffic, each of us grabbed one of the brightly colored flags available at either end of the crosswalk. I wasn't yet lit enough to wave mine at the cars like a total ass. The day was still young, though.

The aroma of brick-oven pizzas wafted around Patterson's open-air setting. We debated what vintage to sample next when the lost phone's owner arrived with a gift of gratitude: a bottle of cabernet from Chateau Ste. Michelle Winery, one of the largest growers in the Columbia Valley.

Justin taught us a bit about the valley to the east, like the variety of grapes grown in the different types of soil offered by the region. My brother-in-law knows it's much easier to justify downing fine wine all afternoon if it comes with legitimate tutorials.

Patterson's red wall of wine behind the bar highlighted both Justin's shirt and his sister's hair. They sat across from each other at a rustic woodblock table. Elbows resting on the high-top propped up beaming faces lounging in nearside hands as they gazed in my direction.

While I was partially prompted by the scenery to capture the moment, I also wasn't sure how photogenic everyone would be after more day drinking.

We ambled over to a couple more tasting rooms, including Justin's part-time employer, Dusted Valley. Since the Great State of Louisiana restricted shipments from the winery, we made sure to enjoy lots of their outstanding offerings while there.

A short jaunt away was a visit to the Woodinville Whiskey Company. We headed for home after dinner next door at the Hollywood Tavern.

Justin drove carefully, at least until I asked him to gun the quietly powerful Tesla. Days earlier, he and his right foot inadvertently threw me into the back of the seat. The G forces had made my stomach feel like I was on a roller coaster, something I never experienced in a car, and I wanted him to do it again. This time, though, I videoed the car's computer display as the velocity climbed to seventy miles per hour in seconds, all while the electric motor made no audible protestations about the owner's penis size.

Back at the house, we helped Cherish and Jen put away groceries while Justin set up his laptop for the first gathering with his two sisters. We soon had a good connection with Austin, where Rachel had taken a break from preparing for her cruise, departing from the Texas coast Sunday. Tezcat occasionally made her presence known in their kitchen.

The video conference allowed me to more fully appreciate the similarities between my wife and Baby Girl. Mannerisms, facial expressions, hair, freckles, and that nose all confirmed that these two were sisters as they finally interacted eye-to-eye, albeit virtually.

"Hi, Auntie Rachel!" Hadley trilled as she jumped in front of her father's computer.

"Hi, Hadley," Rachel replied, quizzing her niece about the latest fun things happening at school.

The two had last spent time together when Rachel visited Renton the previous summer. After Hadley had done her hair, Rachel snapped a selfie that she shared with Edie in March. "I am not a bow person," Rachel remarked, "but she made it work."

Hadley had fun further demonstrating her cosmetological skills on Auntie Edie, with more pink lip gloss, as Auntie Rachel looked on with joy.

By the time we said goodbye, over an hour after saying hello, I gained a better appreciation for tidbits Rachel shared about herself in her first email, particularly, "I could have a nearly continuous conversation for a whole day if given a chance."

With Jen gone to a wedding, Hadley in bed, and no workday looming, Cherish, Justin, Edie, and I eventually repaired to the tea house, squeezing in around a table of traditional Japanese height. We either reclined or sat on floor cushions inside the custom-made structure long enough to finish off another bottle of wine or two. I let out an audible grunt upon rising for bed.

On Saturday morning, we visited the Seattle Museum of Flight, where I took a selfie with D.B. Cooper's life-size likeness—complete with parachute and cash bag—under the tail of a 727. We both wore sunglasses.

Even cooler, however, was riding in the back seat with Hadley, teaching her about the Godfather of Soul and his preoccupation with "the one." Justin cued up some classic James Brown to help me demonstrate the foundation of funk to my fellow outspoken only child with a penchant for dramatics. There in her car seat—two days after the two of us played around on her Casio keyboard—she was jammin' on "the one."

Following a couple of fun hours checking out all the neat air and spacecraft exhibits, Edie and I swapped places on our return to Renton. I had made my wife jealous, and she demanded equal Hadley time.

Riding shotgun back to the house, I snapped a group selfie of everyone in the Volt. We all wore Buddy Poppies, pinned on us at the museum in observance of Memorial Day. Everyone also wore sunglasses, including Hadley's plush flamingo, sitting next to her in Edie's lap. The girls in the back seat looked amazing, as did Mingo.

At some point during the weekend, I pulled Cherish and Justin aside to let them in on something. In this online age of catfishing and scams, I said in so many words, it's hard not to retain a smidgen of skepticism about recent strangers you've met through the internet, no matter how awesome they seem.

From the moment we landed—when my wife hugged her brother like they knew of each other their whole lives, but had been separated the entire time—whatever picayune reservations remained in the recesses of my mind had all but vanished over the next couple days.

By the weekend, I straight up told them about my stubborn, infinitesimal trace of doubt, only to let them know it was obliterated by the "ebullient little delight" they nurtured.

"You can't fake that," I informed them about Hadley and her impact on me, desperately trying to hold my shit together. "That can only come from a home truly filled with love." It deeply touched them.

To this day, I can't believe I doubted the authenticity of a couple who met in Americorps.

Among the endless hours we had with Hadley, not once did I hear that girl whine or complain about anything. She'd let you know what she thought about something, but her opinions were typically stated matter-of-factly, with an almost lyrical delivery, usually between fits of what Auntie Edie called the "best laugh ever."

No crying. No gratuitous screams. Just a bright, happy kid who communicates like a bright, happy adult, who happens to have an impossibly cute voice. She even wore sensible, yet fashionable, glasses.

Upon returning from the museum, I joined Justin in tending to the garden by the driveway. Close by grew a small version of a lush, purple tree populating the area. It was one of three Japanese maples he and John had planted together. This particular tree was in what John described as "the Shrine," where Justin had spread Shirley's ashes.

Back when we were cyberstalking the newly discovered siblings, Edie shared a public post from her brother's Facebook page.

"It's been two years since my mother passed," Justin wrote. "It is strange, but I still feel like she is with me in a way. Maybe like the way she always was, an echo, a song sung by the wind in the trees. Hers is a voice in the shadowy corners," he added, "and it reminds me that everything will work itself out, somehow. I miss you, Mom."

His words framed the reshared public post he'd composed two years earlier.

"Shirley Hadley, my sweet, soulful, weird, beautiful, loving hermit of a mother," Justin told the world, "is dead. Mom and I never had much normalcy in our relationship. She was a true hippy, free-spirit artist, a rebel, a deeply wounded person who may not have been able to succeed in many aspects of life some might deem important. In fact, she did a lot of things that were deeply disappointing, hurtful to say the least, to her family in particular. But these are not ugly things, they are not bad, disparaging things to dwell on—they are simply the grittier side of a profoundly complex and wonderful person.

"More than any other, perhaps, my mother taught me about love, what it means to accept someone unconditionally, what it means to forgive and let go. She was a mirror for me," her son said, "and she helped me understand my own shortcomings and problems, taught me to own those things and try to mend the hurt they wrought in the world.

"You may want to know if there is something you can do," Justin told the reader. "If it doesn't seem too weird, I would like you to take a moment and think about how you and I know each other, and what our relationship means to you, whether or not you knew my mother. Think about significant or touching moments you and I shared; think about painful ones, too, maybe. Know that I wish I could take back any hurt or disappointment I ever caused, and work it into something more beautiful and radiant. Know that I love you unconditionally. Now let your family and friends, the people you depend on, let them know you love them, too. Now let yourself know.

"Goodbye, Mom," he closed. "I love you, and I will see you in my dreams..."

Later that Saturday afternoon in Renton, I learned this family's acquaintances were no less open about themselves. Within minutes of meeting Alex, a friend visiting with his family, the gregarious father of three young girls explained to us—upon Hadley's prompting—how he had come to have only six digits on his two hands. With a pair on his right and four on his left, Alex truly is the six-fingered man, just like in *Princess Bride*. Justin later told me that they enjoy joking about this whenever they all visit a vineyard in Walla Walla (so nice they named it twice) that makes a wine dubbed in honor of Mandy Patinkin's character Inigo Montoya.

Alex drove his family back to Snohomish while Justin got busy working on his signature, personal-sized pizzas, each baked in his wood pellet grill/smoker outside. As he managed to toss the dough just shy of their kitchen's eight-foot ceiling, I prepped for the gumbo I promised to make on Sunday. Everything was locally sourced except for a can of Tony Chachere's Creole Seasoning brought from home.

The culinary cultural exchange with my brother-in-law prompted me to make a second musical request of him that day. Bounce music is a uniquely New Orleans genre featuring call-and-response lyrics against an energetic, electronic drumbeat. It's perfect for getting stuff done in the kitchen when you're dragging from day drinking.

Nighttime slowly encroached after dinner. Hadley eventually went to bed and fell asleep around sunset. John's flight was scheduled to arrive less than an hour later, just before ten. I looked at the time more frequently, wondering when we'd leave to go meet him at SEA-TAC.

Given the reception there just days earlier, I was somewhat surprised when I was told I'd be staying at the house, moments before Edie and Justin departed to go pick up their father.

I soon got it, though: It wasn't about me. This was her journey, not mine.

Plus, at the time, I had hardly read a couple hundred words of John's emails. I was woefully ill-equipped to comprehend how much darkness he had effusively expressed to my wife over the past couple months, particularly within the last week.

Outside of that first phone call, I sparingly listened in on their conversations, and only when Edie wanted to share something light or funny he was saying. Things like trash-talking the forty-fifth president in wildly imaginative ways, and gems such as "Compost tea sounds awful."

I knew about Vietnam, the fragging, and being left for dead. I knew about BRPD harassing and abusing him, locking him in a cell with a bunch of killers. I knew about all that. Or at least I thought I did.

Turns out I had no idea that "all of that" was not in the past, at least not in John's mind. I was in the dark about the darkness, and its all-too-frequent presence in John's consciousness.

Edie, on the other hand, had become intimately acquainted with her father's seemingly ever-present ghosts. Given her ostensible concern about how things might go down between the airport and the house, I ultimately assumed she sought to minimize collateral damage from a potential emotional episode in the car.

I've since asked my wife about her mindset at this moment during the trip. She reminded me that Hadley's car seat was still strapped in the Volt, conveniently parked on the driveway. As Justin told her, there'd be room for three adults, including the driver, once all of John's things were loaded.

In any case, I stayed in Renton, where there was chatter about John's pending arrival. This was going to be interesting.

17

Bothell

Just over an hour after leaving for the airport, Justin and Edie returned with their father. John entered the house after his son, followed by his eldest. Justin helped wrangle their dad's luggage and its owner into the house. Within seconds of walking inside, our host was already repeating himself, because Justin had spoken to his father while John was looking down at his bags.

Sensing my involvement would only complicate matters, I stayed out of the way. Edie, still barely inside the door, stood by silently. The look on her face caused me a bit of concern. Her lack of eye contact with me across the room did nothing to allay my worry.

Justin eventually managed to introduce me to John, who greeted me with an enthusiastic hug that felt much bigger than his build would suggest. If the nearly seventy-five-year-old man riddled with health issues was tired from the four-hour flight, he sure didn't show it.

John wore a boonie hat that suggested it provided him shade during many warm growing seasons in Austin. Over the next couple days, his stooped, humble frame shuffled about, often energetically, and occasionally with the aid of a walker, though I hardly recall him using it indoors.

I soon realized that John is the kind of person who noticeably focuses on whatever he's doing, including speaking to another person.

The stream of consciousness pours out directly at the listener, with John's eyes trained that way. He closes them briefly sometimes, amid the torrent, to ostensibly search for even more words. Only someone inside that tight periphery could visually signal for him to kindly close the valve for a bit. If the listener is either unwilling or too timid to assertively alert John that they'd like him to shut it off, the stream continues until someone willing and able comes along to rescue the drowning.

As midnight approached, John was seated at the kitchen table after a nosh. Naturally, he had been talking for a while when Justin steered the conversation, for my wife's benefit, toward their dad's 1970 sex life. My brother-in-law knew him well enough to know we couldn't afford to squander too much time together if we were going to learn with whom John had sired Edie.

I was soon struck by the familiarity of Justin repeatedly reaching out toward John, placing his hand on their dad's arm or hand, and gently arresting his attention, before graciously attempting to bring John back to the topic of Edie's birth mother.

To his credit, the man welcomes being told when he's going on and on. However, Southern social norms make it difficult to sufficiently communicate "Please stop talking" to anyone you've just met, particularly when that person who won't stop talking is your wife's biological father.

Justin served us whiskey as John offered scant leads. We hit the hay sometime early Sunday morning.

A couple hours past sunup, I awoke in an otherwise empty bed. Edie was sitting on the floor past my feet. I could see the back of her head, slung low between her shoulders. That's when I realized I had been awakened by a disturbing sound: my wife's sobbing.

She had woken up crying an hour earlier, and had yet to stop. Rather than rouse me to talk about it, she messaged Patrick about his granddaughter's birthday.

"Are y'all celebrating today?" she asked.

"It's tomorrow," Patrick clarified. "How are y'all doing? Did John make it in?"

"Yes," replied a sobbing Edie, feet away from my snoring. "It's been great getting to be up here with Justin and Cherish and Hadley."

"I bet," he told his sister, unaware of her emotional state. "Were you nervous?" he asked about John's arrival. "Was it overwhelming? I bet he was tired."

"He was," Edie confirmed, "but he talked nonstop until Justin made it clear that the rest of us needed to get to bed."

Patrick chuckled. "Edie," he said, "I'm so very happy for you. Thanks for sharing this with us. I know that this is an intensely personal experience you are having," he conceded. "I imagine it's more than a bit surreal. I just want this to be joyous for you."

Abstaining from the recently legalized, Pat-prescribed substances available nearby, a tearful Edie explained to her still-unaware brother, "It was kinda weird how at ease I've been here all week. The worst I've felt is that it has been too one-sided because I wasn't saying or asking enough."

"That's great: a testament to Justin and his family." Patrick also noted, "It's pretty consistent Edie behavior to be listening rather than talking."

That's when she finally mentioned waking up a bit of a mess.

"I imagine your emotions are going to be on a bit of a roller coaster for a while," Patrick responded. "I'm so very happy y'all are going to get together with Neenie and crew," he said of tomorrow's gathering. "That should really be fun."

"I hope so," she answered. "I'm a little nervous about how overwhelming it might be for Justin, Cherish, and Hadley," Edie explained, "and how much John will share details of Baton Rouge experiences with people who trapped minors in awful situations."

"I think less overwhelming than if it were Ducky et al," her brother supposed.

"Oh my, yes," Red said with a wink.

No other details about her worries were discussed.

More so than me at the time, Patrick had no clue about Gus Tabony, not to mention all the other insane things that John shared with his daughter, some of which came after her enthusiastic approval of his presence in Renton. Neither of us had any idea what was racing through her mind regarding her father and Monday's get-together, featuring a portion of Doc O'Neal's family.

My wife woke up freaking out, worried the Florida native might, like a gator, ensnare someone into a conversation and take them down to one of his many dark places. Will he drag Aunt Neenie to see Tabony's eleven-year-old sex slave in a fetal position after, once again, being ravaged by a guy secretly working for the police, she wondered, or will he only slightly creep out someone by extolling the curative powers of "nurturing touch" among sexual abuse victims? Perhaps he'd end up recalling how, during his youth, his family accused him of being a "'N... lover,' studying to be a prostitute."

Just before exiting the bedroom, my love informed me that she needed me with her that Sunday. I was still just waking up, trying to make sense of everything. If she was going to survive the day, Edie later told me, she knew she needed to leave the room at that moment.

Hadley and Cherish were already gathered downstairs in the kitchen. Despite her best efforts to hide it, Edie's face reflected her emotional turmoil.

Cherish fixed the horrible actress a cup of coffee, just the way she likes it. She handed it to Edie, all without a word, almost like she knew all too well what was distressing my wife. If anyone could relate to introducing John to one's family, and all that that encompasses, it was our sister-in-law.

Hadley sat on a stool at the kitchen's island, coloring drawings. She handed her auntie a sheet to follow suit with the many crayons on the counter. Edie joined our niece in the artistry while sipping Cherish's French-pressed goodness.

As daylight more permeated the house, the other two men upstairs arose. Justin descended first, and soon realized Edie was vexed.

He asked his sister if she would prefer their father stay in Renton the next day.

Feeling instant relief at the suggestion, she verbalized that it might be a good idea. No sooner than the words had come out of her mouth, Edie was slammed by a massive wave of guilt. The sudden rush of rejection that John experienced throughout his life—in Vietnam, in Baton Rouge, in his own family, and that all but defined who he is—hit her. Hard.

"Oh my God, I can't do that to him, after all he's been through," she realized in that moment. "Tell him to stay here alone with the cat while the rest of us go see my family?"

John was coming with us to Bothell, the Seattle suburb where Aunt Neenie's youngest would host Monday's gathering.

Since she wasn't awake when he flew in, Hadley was the first to greet her Poppa John downstairs on Sunday morning. Before I knew it, the two of them were playing together. It's the only time I've ever seen a man his age crawl around on the floor, roll over on his back, and pretend to be a kitten in desperate need of attention.

Inspired by the comedy duo of Hart and Hart, I paid a visit to Hadley's "New York City apartment." I managed to fit entirely inside the cardboard box in the Harts' sitting room by, of course, sitting, specifically with crossed legs and a tucked chin. I was enjoying my tour of Hadley's magnificent Manhattan residence when she capriciously locked me in by closing the tabs and holding them shut. She found my captive state absolutely hilarious. Fortunately, Hadley's folks convinced her to let me out before I called the cops for false imprisonment.

As the day drew on, my love grew more at ease with the next day's gathering.

By midafternoon, I was making roux for that evening's gumbo. Justin had me sample some links he grilled outside. I told him it was OK spicy sausage. He then informed me that it was the alleged boudin we bought at the fish-throwing market on Thursday. A tiny version of my home state's flag planted next to the links in the meat case moved me to get some out of morbid curiosity.

As the roux darkened, I told Justin why—in no uncertain terms—no one back home would ever mistake this mediocre, spicy imposter for anything close to boudin. Apparently, for folks not from South Louisiana, the only thing harder than pronouncing boudin is producing it.

For the record, it's pronounced "boo dan," so long as you throw away the last two-thirds of the N.

Moments later, I witnessed John composing an email. He types exactly as his son had described. Like Schroeder at the piano, the visibly focused man's head and eyes remained trained down toward the keyboard, while his hands banged away at the same.

Whatever he types stays in there. He might as well be using an old-school typewriter. There's no going back and editing or deleting. Clicking "send" for him is the digital equivalent of ripping the final page from the Underwood.

The gumbo took a little bit longer to finish than his message did. Justin, who still eats small portions after living in Japan for five years, went back for seconds. His dad did the same, devouring both bowls, raving about my creation between spoonfuls. John's default line of conversation the rest of the night involved Louisiana food he's enjoyed over the years.

A bit later, Justin paid me a huge compliment by dozing off for about fifteen minutes while getting Hadley to sleep. Gumbo is like sex. Rendering someone unconscious with it, after they insisted on more, is a reasonable metric for quality.

After supper, we all retired to the TV room to watch some of Justin's YouTube videos. One was from their 2015 Kauai vacation; Rachel had joined the Harts, including three-year-old Hadley, and Cherish's family at their timeshare. The six-minute soundtrack featured Ini Kamoze's "Here Comes the Hotstepper," and "Easy Skanking" by Bob Marley, two songs I never previously imagined ever hearing at my in-laws'.

Justin had also made annual one-minute montages of still images chronicling Hadley Lorine Hart's progression from baby bump to ebullient little delight. These videos were set to Buddy Holly's "Everyday."

The whole reason Edie's father and brother were on Ancestry in the first place was to help Justin learn more about his family. His search for his older half-brother—the one Shirley gave up for adoption, the one who'd be around Edie's age—had been all but thwarted because the orphanage fire destroyed all records. Decades later, Hadley's father was documenting her family and her upbringing, and then uploading it to the cloud, which lasts forever, or so I'm told.

Memorial Day started off much more chill than the day before. After breakfast, we all gathered to watch a touching 2014 documentary titled *Snow Day*, written and directed by the siblings' cousin Erica. Her mom, John's sister LeMerle, made a brief appearance alongside Erica's dad, Clark, one of the spry octogenarian skiers featured in the film.

It marked the first time Edie or I had seen an image of her aunt. After it finished, Justin backed up the video to that moment and paused it. He became the first of several people to note a strong resemblance between LeMerle and her newest niece.

Hadley joined us intermittently during the screening. She had already seen her award-winning cousin's work, even though Hadley didn't watch movies because—as we learned—all movies are scary. All of them.

Two weeks earlier, Justin had mentioned to Edie that they "dressed up Hadley in a Darth Vader costume for Halloween," adding that she still loves the costume and wants the entire family to dress like the dark Sith Lord. Because movies are scary. All of them.

After the screening, Justin introduced Edie to their cousin in the San Francisco Bay area. "I'd love to meet up sometime this year and hang out," Erica messaged the two sibs on the new thread. "I'm super curious who and where you've been in life," the documentarian later told Edie.

Justin also chimed in to say the Harts were considering visiting us during Mardi Gras early the following year.

Walking past Justin's office upstairs, I saw John and Edie with him in front of his computer, looking at old family pictures. One showed Justin with his parents in the sun, months after his birth. A much younger John wore a mustache-adorned grin while simultaneously holding his son and a much taller Shirley's left breast.

The collection also showed Justin and his hairstyles through the years. The guy has never been anything short of photogenic. A handful of the pics seemed to have been taken when he was mainlining The Smiths.

Seeing John with freshly combed, wavy hair, standing between his two eldest kids—all looking at old family pictures, no less—I realized that the three of them had not yet been photographed together.

"Is that John?" Patrick soon asked me on the Fort Worth thread. "That's a great picture."

After delivering on a promise to let me take the Tesla for a quick spin, Justin drove Edie and me to Bothell. Cherish ferried Hadley and John in the Volt.

Aunt Neenie and her youngest daughter, Jennifer, greeted us at the door with giant hugs. The Gluecks were celebrating the eighty-seventh birthday of their remarkably youthful matriarch this Memorial Day.

Jennifer's husband, Dave, manned the grill on the sizable wooden deck overlooking their inviting backyard, equipped with a large trampoline surrounded by a safety net. Their Hadley-aged twins, Ellie and Lincoln, soon invited our niece to bounce with them and other kids close in age. Neenie's oldest, Jami, was there with her two adult daughters and their young children.

Back inside, Justin presented our hostess with a special bottle from Dusted Valley. ENO's a Rhône-style red blend, he explained, and is available only via winery employees or a visit to the Chicago steakhouse it's specifically made for. He barely finished his spiel before Jennifer opened the bottle and filled several glasses with pours at least twice as generous as anything we'd experienced on Friday in Woodinville.

Years before he passed away the previous July, Neenie's beloved husband, Dee, suffered a heart attack at the age of fifty-nine. The renowned architect lived his remaining twenty-eight years with a pacemaker, and by a philosophy that says, "Life's too short: Eat dessert first."

Staying true to their late patriarch's mantra for squeezing the most out of one's time on this ball of mud, the Gluecks glug-glugged the gift. It was empty in an hour, to Justin's somewhat muted surprise, that sunny afternoon.

Out on the deck, Edie called Patrick with John by her side. She placed her brother on speakerphone. John leaned in to hear Patrick's welcoming first words. Neenie joined them moments later. She flanked a gleeful Edie, as did John, all having a smile-filled conversation with Patrick in Texas.

Following the phone call, Jennifer visited with Edie and John, getting to know the man we had met less than forty-eight hours earlier. Moments later, the school principal ceded her seat to her mom, while Justin grabbed a chair next to Edie across the table.

John, sitting next to Neenie, soon began giving her an impromptu birthday gift: a massage, one unlike any I'd ever seen or received. It looked more like he was teaching her tai chi by gently guiding her hands, arms, and shoulders. In his tie-dyed tee, John cooed gentle instructions for a seated Edris to visualize calm, flowing imagery. I recall hearing the words "clouds," "water," and "wind" as my wife's aunt experienced, up close and personal, John's hippie wisdom.

I made sure to capture the moment in which the sister of my late father-in-law, who never would have approved of this adventure, got massaged by Edie's biological father, all while that man's son and daughter held hands and looked on with broad grins.

"Surreeeeeal," Knick's voice whispered.

My wife's worst fears were happily unfounded. Nevertheless, at least one person expressed surprise when she learned that John was married. I honestly can't blame her.

Over a year later, John would still talk about the gathering. It was such an honor for him. He knows he's a bit much, and deeply appreciates those who are patient with him. He wants to listen better, but can't help but fill the quiet with the things in his head.

Before we left Renton for Bothell, a reluctant Hadley insisted that she wouldn't have fun with the other children there. A few hours later, when her folks told her it was time to go home, she again expressed reluctance, without getting upset. This time it was because she was having so much fun with the other children there. Her new friend Ellie was also disappointed, telling Jennifer that she was just about to show Hadley some more cool stuff.

Edie and I walked with the Harts to their vehicles and hugged her new family goodbye until the next afternoon. We were spending the night at Aunt Neenie's place.

After thanking our hosts and saying our goodbyes, I rode in the back seat to Mill Creek with the two Edris Anns. Given how young she is in every other aspect of life, I suppose I shouldn't have been surprised to learn Neenie's still a good driver.

At her charming condo, next to Snohomish County's North Creek Trail, Edie gave our newest hostess a 1948 newspaper clipping Ducky had mailed to us a few weeks earlier. "Edris Ann O'Neal Is Picked Queen for Homecoming" the headline read next to a full-length photo of a dazzling teenage Aunt Neenie in a calf-length dress. The caption below said Edris was a "Port Allen High School cheerleader, who was selected to reign as queen over the school's first Homecoming festivity Sunday," because you can never squeeze too many firsts into one day.

Also, it's strange reading the full name of the woman you married in a headline written decades before she was born.

After walking along a woodsy path lined with cottonwood "snow" on a chilly Tuesday morning in a Bob Ross painting, Edie and I returned to the condo. We investigated Uncle Dee's office, apparently left as is since his passing. His widow spent another morning with her grandchildren in Bothell.

Aunt Neenie had been trying to sell the rest of the family on the Pacific Northwest since the Gluecks originally moved there in the 1980s after Uncle Dee accepted a position as associate athletic director at the University of Washington. He was brought in between similar stints at LSU and Auburn, where he became known for his stadium renovation acumen. The way Aunt Neenie described it, her husband came in one day and asked how she'd feel about moving as far away from Baton Rouge as possible. She obviously, and understandably, granted her blessing.

Among the many displayed artifacts in Dee's office was an itinerary for a football game in Nashville between the LSU Fighting Tigers and the Vanderbilt Commodores. The date on the front cover: October 24-27, 1935. This particular timetable belonged to future Chicago Cardinal Pat Coffee, and listed multiple train rides both ways. LSU players were to be in their rooms at the Hermitage Hotel by 9 a.m. after breakfast on game day for "taping by Mr. Mike," as in team trainer Chellis "Mike" Chambers, the namesake of LSU's live tiger mascot.

Most importantly, though, was a teamwide imperative: "Drink only Baton Rouge Water on entire trip." Personally, I'd love to know the backstory that necessitated that caveat, as well as how many gallons they hauled for the seventy-two-hour excursion involving dozens of young men and a regulation college football contest.

After brunch with Neenie, we snapped a selfie together in front of the Saw Mill Cafe, Uncle Dee's favorite place. Moments earlier, in recapping our trip so far, I offered a receptive Neenie a primer on Bounce music. Port Allen's first homecoming queen promised to bring up the topic with Jennifer to impress her youngest with her mom's hipness.

Neenie later drove us to an Everett high school, where Jami was wrapping up a day of passionately teaching literature to teenagers. We transferred our bags to her vehicle, hugged Aunt Neenie, and vowed to return soon.

An hour later, Jami pulled over in downtown Seattle across the street from Justin's high-rise office, not far from her place. We bid Edie's cousin goodbye, and soon saw Justin in his building's lobby. This sibling reunion was somewhat less emotional than the one at SEA-TAC a week earlier.

Reunited with the rest of the Harts in Renton, the six of us enjoyed our trip's final meal together at Red House Beer & Wine Shoppe. Justin brought along a magnum of JM Cellars' Longevity red Bordeaux blend from his panoply. A smattering of raindrops sprinkled the cars outside, representing almost all the precipitation we saw in rainy Seattle.

Our ride back to the house was my last chance to hang with my new BFF in the back seat. Hadley rocked a red-white-and-blue wool cap reminiscent of *South Park*'s Stan Marsh. As her auntie took pics from the front seat, Hadley began to pull the cap around, and then over, her own face.

I stepped in and offered my usual brown tweed paperboy hat in exchange for her cap. She accepted and donned my standard lid. Hadley looked like a Peaky Blinder, if the notorious fictional gang killed people with cuteness. One of Edie's pics on our fridge shows our niece enjoying my hat, smiling at me wearing hers. It still wrecks me to look at it sometimes.

Back at the house, I was exiting the vehicle when she said something that truly touched my heart. "Uncle Jeremy," Hadley announced, "you're one weird dude." Her dad and auntie commenced cracking the fuck up.

In all honesty, it's one of the greatest compliments anyone's ever paid me.

We were gathered around the kitchen table, just a couple days after Sunday's morning freakout, when John decided to give my wife a scalp massage. It was not so much relaxing as it was hilarious. Edie winced and giggled as her father wildly tousled her curly locks into a fantastic, red mess.

Meanwhile, his granddaughter thanked me for reading a pop-up book to her by crowning my stubbly dome with a jeweled, silver tiara, complete with a pink-and-white orchid over my right ear. Although the crown was upside-down, in Auntie Rachel's words, Hadley made it work. Justin's lens captured me, chin in hand, channeling equal parts Paul Lynde and Madeline Kahn's Lili Von Shtupp, like some creepy, Hawaii-terrorizing cupid who's tired of being admired.

Edie and I eventually said goodnight and goodbye to the new ebullient little delight in our lives. We were leaving for the airport before she'd awaken. Again citing Rachel, who declared the ache she feels when leaving her niece, this farewell was so much more difficult for me than I ever would've imagined, namely because this cynic never fathomed a five-year-old flat-out stealing his heart.

We soon bid adieu to Cherish and her wry sense of humor. In a week of unprecedented surreal craziness, I deeply appreciated the coffee lover's persistently laid-back demeanor and calming energy.

After staying up a bit more with Justin and John, it was time to pack our bags, including booze from Woodinville. In bed around midnight before a 5:30 flight, we set our alarm for 3 a.m.

"It's not even 6:00 a.m.," a phone alert from back home taunted me shortly after awakening, "and already 'feels like' the 80°s!" Someone at WAFB-TV had managed to make our departure for Baton Rouge even more regretful.

John woke up to fix us coffee and a quick breakfast as we shuffled about the house in the wee hours of the moonlit Wednesday morning. We hugged Edie's father goodbye, taking solace in knowing he lived six hours away in Austin, where he'd return home a week later. That's when he planned to break the news about Edie to Hallie in person.

We arrived at SEA-TAC around 4:15 with bags to check. Our tardiness and a bustling unloading zone forced abbreviated, less sorrowful farewells with Justin. We had other stresses to deal with.

Standing at the end of the soul-crushingly long line of travelers waiting to be screened by a partially staffed TSA in the predawn hours, I was sure we'd see Justin again before we'd see the inside of a plane. Knick's voice was silent as the words of another friend, who repeatedly pimped TSA PreCheck to me, rang in my head.

Our boarding time came and went with scores of unscreened passengers in front of us. Moments after more agents clocked in, I grabbed Edie's hard-shell suitcase from the conveyor belt, slung my gym bag across my torso, and began running with my bride for Gate D10 at the far end of the terminal. It had been a while since I worked out at that ungodly hour with alcohol likely on my breath. After a short walking spell about halfway, we resumed hoofing it upon hearing our name announced, along with news that the aircraft door would soon be closing.

Seated in the half-empty plane with seconds to spare, we struggled to catch our breaths as the door closed behind us. The arid onboard air, pressurized to the equivalent of an 8,000-foot altitude, exacerbated our respiratory distress. Coughing for nearly an hour before beverage service, I seriously considered buying a slightly used bottle of water from the young lady in the aisle seat.

Between coughing fits, I snapped dawn-lit Cascade peaks above the broken cloud deck, including Mount St. Helens's mostly missing north face. An onboard showing of *Black Panther* lifted our melancholy spirits at cruising altitude.

Outside of Starbucks, sports teams, and Frasier Crane (sorry, Macklemore—maybe next time), I didn't know much about Seattle when we first landed there. Days later, Edie and I decided we'd ultimately move to Washington before Canada annexes the state.

During our stay, Patrick indicated they were game to follow our escape plan to the Pacific Northwest. "Maybe we'll tag along next time," he said on Sunday morning. "I'm afraid we might just stay."

"That's how I've felt all week," Edie revealed. "If only I had a couple mil for a house and a marketable resume," she winked with teary eyes.

"You and me both," Patrick replied.

We could all move there and make a killing selling something that's at least in the same area code as boudin. The market's wide-ass open.

I fell in love with the area's vibe. Despite an abundance of economic wealth—the Emerald City led the nation in construction cranes dotting its skyline for three straight years—I failed to sense any notable pretension there. Incidentally, Justin proves it's possible to be a vinophile without being a dick about it.

I'm not saying there aren't pretentious people who live there. I'm just saying my radar wasn't sensitive enough to detect any after being bombarded with the stuff for decades in Baton Rouge.

On Thursday at MoPop, in their Nirvana exhibit, I saw a map of the Pacific Northwest showing the hometowns of many legendary grunge bands, all part of a cultural rebellion against the blatant pretension of glam rock and corporate manufactured music. The genre was, if nothing else, a demand to be real, a rebellion against all that sought to airbrush away our humanity for the sake of profit. It only makes sense that such an incubator for an anti-pretension revolution would be populated with people who are, in fact, real.

Around the same time Seattle's culture was becoming synonymous with the human authenticity of grunge, Baton Rouge produced a rapper named Kyper, whose first hit was titled "Conceited." Popular during my days as a teen dance club DJ in the late '80s, it's a super-cheesy techno ode to insufferable snobbery, intermittently delivered in a horrible British accent.

Days after our trip, during my weekly talk radio gig, I trashed Seattle's boudin, prompting the host to ask me what one thing I would've brought back from there if given the chance. "A less individualistic attitude toward one's community," I told my buddy's conservative listeners.

There's a reason we don't have HOV lanes in Louisiana. They require an inherent trust that drivers won't chronically fuck it up nine ways to Sunday. It took a whole week in Washington to almost quit expecting some asshole stuck in the adjacent, non-HOV lane to cut in front of us every time we whizzed past slower traffic.

We touched down at BTR during the early afternoon, peak jungle heat hours in the Red Stick. The now-unfamiliar, moisture-laden air welcomed us back home in the jetway with a sweltering bitch slap. Later that evening, I noticed my laptop still hadn't changed back from Pacific Time.

"It didn't want to leave, either," a smiling Justin explained.

"Nope," I said, "I ain't mad."

It's impossible to overstate how remarkable of a human being Justin is. Sometime during our stay, he told us how, as a kid, he had essentially been taken hostage by a man who "looked after" him while John moved a certain amount of cocaine.

Before meeting my new brother-in-law, I always thought I had a troubled upbringing. It didn't take long for me to realize, however, that

whatever bullshit I might have encountered as the child of acrimoni-
ously divorced parents wasn't dick compared to what he experienced.

As much as we longed to be back with the Harts, though, after being
away from the yet-unsolved maternal puzzle for so long, Edie was
ready to chase down the leads John had provided over the weekend.

18

Five Hippies in a Ford Pinto

"LIFE LESSON," I prefaced a message to Edie the day after we returned. "You put yourself at risk, mentally and emotionally, for self-less reasons for someone you had never met, and who may not have even been alive. It's turned out to be arguably (I might argue)," I teased, "the most rewarding experience in your life."

"You and Justin give me way too much credit for not fully thinking things through," a humble Edie returned my wink. She then alluded to Justin's comment about an awe-inspiring pic of her sitting on the ledge on Rattlesnake Ridge, overlooking the eponymous lake hundreds of feet below. "'You're brave sitting so close to the edge like that,'" she projected, "versus 'I hadn't considered that I was about to sit on loose gravel at the edge of a cliff.'"

My self-effacing bride alerted Justin the next day that she had contacted human resources at WBRZ, the TV station where John worked as a camera operator circa Edie's conception, in hopes of chronologically cementing a few shards of John's fractured recollections.

"They will check their records next week," she messaged her kid brother, "and get back to me to see if they may be able to confirm when John worked there."

Later that Friday night, Edie also told him that she'd be calling the daughter of a couple, Joe and Judy Dreyer, whom their father had mentioned several times in accounts of his Baton Rouge days.

"Well, tomorrow morning ought to be interesting," she informed Justin. "Jodie Dreyer just provided her phone number via a common Facebook friend." Jodie was also Facebook friends with Vikki, a contemporary of John Hart and Debbie Abrams, "who took Fran's spot as his primary suspect."

My wife speaking to someone who knows someone who dated John? That does sound like an interesting Saturday.

Justin answered Edie, "I will tell him this; we are drinking whiskey now and talking about electric cars. Maybe I made John's drink too strong," he added. "He is very interested in hearing about what you learn, but for now, he just wants to tell stories about what happened when he knew these people."

The idea of a drunk John rambling on about his time as a super-woke pot saint in the Red Stick prompted me to respond with a shocked emoji.

"And he wanted me to warn you about Vikki (being unstable)," Justin continued that evening. "Jodie and her mom," he learned from John, "are better contacts. Vikki, he says, is volatile."

True to form, John sent a 1,722-word email with the subject line "contacts/debbie abrams" a few hours later. About a third of the typo-riddled, early morning message pertained to the matter at hand.

"I think you can empathize strongly with Jodie, Judy, and Debbie," he wrote. "I think if you say that you are most likely my daughter, just got back from a family visit, encouraged to seek J & J, find Debbie, they would help you with their hearts, minds, spirits."

"Have you seen the email yet?" Edie asked Justin by midmorning Saturday.

"No, but will check now," he replied. "I think John stayed up all night. What the hell did I put in his drink?!"

Edie then alerted Renton, "I hope I left a voicemail for Jodie Dreyer this morning: It was a generic greeting. I will probably follow up with a text later today if I don't hear from her." She closed, "Continually seeking context...and missing my Harts out in the PNW. Please give Hadley a big ol' hug for me!"

Eleven minutes later, on the first Saturday of June, Jodie called back. Edie emailed Justin and their father about the nine-minute conversation.

"I just had a short but great call with Jodie. She is vivacious and excited about helping us," Edie reported. "Jodie instantly remembered John's name and said she's heard a million stories about him but couldn't put them into context off the top of her head.

"Her mom, Judy, is in France for the next two weeks teaching meditation, so contact with her is on hold," the Harts learned. "But Jodie mentioned that Vikki is her mom's best friend, and Jodie is reaching out to her.

"Jodie was born in 1972, in between me and Justin," Edie wrote. "At age sixteen, she had a daughter whom she put up for adoption. They met in 2012, and Jodie describes her daughter as an unbroken version of herself, exactly what she wanted when she made the decision that she was too young to raise a child.

"Wow," Edie closed. "This day is looking better already. So much love and awe." She promised, "I will continue to share info as Jodie provides it."

"That is just truly awesome!" Justin replied. "So happy for a positive development," he smiled.

The following afternoon, around the time Justin shared a video of Hadley kicking ass on the soccer pitch, Jodie began texting Edie.

"Well, I gave you a tiny mention of the drug stories I thought would be coming," her first message read. "But are you ready for a firsthand account?" Jodie asked. "Look, I grew up on this stuff, and what seems normal to me shocks a lot of people. This one isn't too bad, but God knows what will eventually come out."

"Yes," Edie replied, "I quickly learned that in my first few emails/phone calls with John. It's cool," she insisted, as Jodie copied and pasted an incoming message from Vikki.

"Vikki's answer to who was John Hart," she texted moments later that Sunday, forwarding a story that precisely matched one told by John back in Renton.

"Oh, very long story," Vikki said of John. "He was Debbie's friend, a Vietnam vet who came back with issues. He was with us in San Francisco. We all drove back together, five hippies in a Ford Pinto, one of them black. It was brutal. We were holding a LOT of drugs, mostly LSD that John bought to sell in Baton Rouge. We got lost in the desert at night, too. In Texas, John peeled out of a gas station at 2 a.m. and we got stopped. He told the cop he was hurrying back at the mental hospital on Monday (true). They got the judge out of bed, searched the car, found some wine in a Coke bottle, and fined us $72 because me and Debbie were under twenty-one. It was all the money we had. Thank the gods, we had thrown stashes out the window as we crossed a bridge. They came REALLY close to finding the acid but didn't. I was SO pissed at John that I didn't want to see him anymore after that. He and your mom went back to SF to get our stuff. That's her story to tell."

This "unstable," possibly "volatile" woman signed off her account of this harrowing, now-fully corroborated story to Jodie with three emojis: peace, love, and flower.

"She hasn't seen or heard from him since 1973," Jodie added about Vikki. "I assume my mom and dad lost touch with him, too. I'll find out what my mom knows next," Judy's daughter offered.

"Thanks," Edie answered. "Looking forward to what light your mom may be able to shine, but definitely appreciate your help!"

A couple hours later, Jodie called Edie back. She answered in our office. There was a conversation going on at the other end of the line. Jodie had apparently butt-dialed her.

With a wide grin, my wife danced in place. She made a shushing gesture to her nose with the hand holding her cell phone while frantically motioning me over from the kitchen with the other. "It sounds like they're talking about John!" she whispered emphatically. Two minutes is how long the call lasted. Nothing further was learned.

A few hours later, Edie's father sent her a 917-word email, just past midnight. Justin must've fixed him an even stronger drink Sunday night because John fell asleep toward the end of typing his message.

Immediately after writing "and a brian stiem injury form anidiot dance," he closed his third-to-last paragraph with thirty-five consecutive e's, immediately followed by 347 w's, then by another 137 space-free e's, and finally ten back-to-back hyphens. The next paragraph started with "woke u againso muchlov, caringand goodnight..."

Later in the week, Edie found a half-dozen newspaper archives mentioning John, nailing down the timing of some of his legal woes in Baton Rouge. She also shared with her brother a slew of historic photos of the capital city from the public library's archive. Before John flew home to Austin, Justin showed them to their dad in hopes of stimulating a memory or two, and perhaps gleaning some previously unrecalled details circa the mystery hookup.

"When I was talking with him Sunday," Justin said, "we stopped at about March 1970. I will try picking up from where we left off to get through the point where he went to jail."

"You're definitely getting first shot at that Four Roses Special Reserve." I promised my brother-in-law dibs on an unopened bottle of bourbon won as a door prize, with a reported street value of several hundred dollars.

"Perhaps if I give John some bourbon, the memories will flow more freely," he laughed, "but in measured form, so I don't ignite my keyboard from trying to keep up."

While Justin did what he could with John and his memories, Edie turned her focus to someone with whom she hadn't interacted in some time, someone who had also just returned from traveling.

"So we were thinking about a road trip to Austin in June," she messaged Rachel, "if there's a good weekend for us to visit you?" Edie suggested the 15th through 17th, but only after checking with Patrick and Yvette about joining us in Austin amid their jam-packed June.

"YES!! THAT WOULD BE AWESOME!!" Rachel replied to Edie about the proposed visit, two weekends away.

"Yay!!" Edie mentioned Patrick and Yvette possibly joining us, "but we can postpone that til next time if you prefer."

"I would like to meet them, too! I would like to meet them, too!" Rachel parroted herself. "I may introduce you to the family I grew up with," she said. "I AM SO EXCITED."

"We are all excited to see you!" my partner informed her kid sister.

Rachel followed up with advice on what to pack. She also mentioned their brother's forty-fifth birthday, falling within a week of our upcoming Austin trip.

"I want to discreetly share that Rachel is very nervous about meeting you," Justin told us. "Who wouldn't have some nervous energy in such a circumstance," he conceded, "but I think she feels like she has to somehow impress or entertain you. I told her to relax, be herself, that you guys weren't looking to be impressed." Our trip was strictly about getting to know her, Justin assured his little sister. "I am sure it will all be grand, but just know she will be worried about meeting whatever it is she imagines you might expect from her." Justin grinned, "I'll remind her to expect to be welcomed and appreciated."

"Appreciate the heads up," I replied. "I'm sure by Sunday, she'll be well beyond that."

"I would sure think so," he agreed.

He also sanctioned Edie's plan calling for just the two of us to meet their sister on Friday, before the O'Neals would arrive from Fort Worth on Saturday.

"I think that sounds good," Justin said. "Give Rachel a chance to meet you and start getting to know you two by herself first. I think that would be important to her."

On the same day Edie reached out to Rachel about the road trip, I published a Facebook album of photos and videos from the Seattle trip. It was visible only to people we specifically shared it with, including Rachel.

"I am so happy y'all had a good trip!" she sent from South Central Texas. "Even though I feel all three of us have felt connected since the beginning, it is still a very anxious thing. Have you seen my 'brother and me' album on Facebook?" she wondered about the collection of 2007 images from her first meeting with Justin in Boston. "It seems to have similar emotions in the pictures."

My wife spent almost a week paying overdue attention to her new sister. It was a nearly weeklong respite from a frequently frustrating four-month-old DNA puzzle; nearly a week of not chasing down leads from John's LSD-dealing days, leads that were seemingly exhausted.

"I just got a voicemail from WBRZ indicating their records don't go back that far," Edie shared with Justin.

The trail also went cold regarding John's previous second-best bio-mom guess, Debbie, the woman he said was sexually exploited by Rosedale, "the infamously handsome Cajun Narc." Outside of a voice-mail-free missed call at 4:30 the morning after Edie's nine-minute chat with Jodie, we never heard back from her, Judy, nor Vikki after the butt dial.

It's not like I didn't think about giving them a ring, though. Without hope of help from John's specious suggestions, the maternal search was almost entirely on his daughter's shoulders. If Edie's birth mother was going to be found, it would only happen because of my wife's ability to demystify an ancestral perplexity flummoxing her for months.

"Aw fucking hell," she messaged me about the time she "Ancestry-DNA'd" herself into "a black fucking hole."

"Ah shit," she sent two weeks earlier. "This is the second time I've been tracing what I presume to be maternal matches, only to have them lead back to John," she wrote on the last day of the shortest month. "I start with someone close to me, but not a match to John; I trace back our common matches about ten people and find someone linked to John," she explained, "but not connected to the person I started with."

In the interim between those frustrating episodes, back when we were waiting for Fran's reply in early March, Edie revealed something about her husband to John and Justin. "I'm grateful for his energy and dedication to keeping me on a productive track, balancing neces-sary chores with time nurturing relationships, not letting me get too consumed with exploring/wondering about the questions we don't yet have answers to."

She was bragging about me distracting her from the DNA search by regularly dragging her out of the house to go fart around with some friends. Nevertheless, there's much to be said for stepping away from something chronically perplexing, at least for long enough to clear your head and come back with a fresh set of eyes.

The time she spent focused on her sister was effectively a reset. Getting to know more about Rachel, and arranging a trip to meet her 430 miles away, sufficiently cleared Edie's mind to see a tree through the forest. She had alleviated much of the self-imposed pressure before turning her attention back toward the puzzle.

If not for being "distracted" by their upcoming meeting, my wife would have likely gotten only more consumed, more obsessed by the quest to solve the maternal quandary online. God only knows how much longer she would have continued to overlook a previously established link that would drastically change the course of our journey.

19

Hey Sherlock

The weekend before our trip to Austin, Justin sent his sisters a selfie with his brother.

"Even though Mason isn't related to you two," he messaged from the Hadleys' Olympia home, "we all want to hang out together some-day. Likely that would be on some future trip here. Have a great visit next weekend," he smiled, "and send me a few photos when you have a chance."

On Monday, June 11, Edie emailed Beth, four days ahead of our departure for Austin.

"If you don't mind," she sent with the maternal tree she'd been composing, "I'd appreciate another perspective on this. Before Seattle," Edie explained, "I was tracing two clusters of maternal DNA matches to figure out how they're related to each other: the Lukaczyks on the left, Weis family on the right."

In the lead-up to our trip, after identifying around five dozen con-firmed maternal DNA matches (i.e., not related to John), Edie sought to figure out who was most closely related to whom on her mother's side. This was before Ancestry offered users tools to help group their rela-tives. However, with a trick she found online, my spreadsheet-fluent wife managed to identify the two large clumps of interrelated maternal kin after painstakingly entering the data she'd uncovered. As my wife would tell me, "You can't say tedious without Edie."

By virtue of being related to two large, distinct groups—with no connection to John Hart—Edie deduced that, somewhere along the way, these two clusters intermingled to produce the woman who produced her. Back when we were learning of the Novaks' sawmill, Edie's cry of "timber" alluded to this potential linking of "two big branches."

After searching through the DNA forest for so long, she apparently discovered the previously established connection she'd been searching for, but had overlooked.

"I just had a new match pop up who led me to the marriage linking these two groups," Edie emailed Beth on Monday morning: "Michael Lukaczyk and Nancy Jane Weis." After explaining the maternal tree's colors and selective bolding, she asked, "Am I off base in thinking they could be my maternal grandparents?"

Could this be how, in Chinese menu parlance, something from column A got paired with something from column B?

"It kinda looks like it, doesn't it," Beth replied.

Back in mid-March, my wife revealed something about herself to Justin. "With Pi Day (3.14) earlier this week," she shared, "it reminds me of a self-inflicted project back in high school where I spent my down time in class manually calculating the cube root of nine just because I got curious after a teacher had listed it as one of the wrong answers on a multiple choice test."

If anyone was capable and tenacious enough to solve this puzzle, it's my Edie, who's also wise enough to know when a task requires an equally capable and tenacious Deep State ninja.

"I have questions re: Michael Lukaczyk," Beth soon messaged with queries about his obituary. "How the fuck did he get down here?"

"Well, not him, but his daughter," Edie clarified. "So far, no one has left Indiana."

"Yeah," her partner replied, "but there's no mention of her in the obit. Maybe he and Jane split early and weren't on good terms?" Beth would sometimes refer to Nancy Jane, Edie's ostensible grandmother, as "Jane," although Nancy Jane's mother was also Nancy Jane.

"Anything is possible at this point," Edie conceded.

"I'm going to find Jane," Beth vowed.

Within a half hour, Beth messaged, "In which Nancy Jane has a birthday party," along with an old newspaper clipping.

"Children's Party," the heading stated about an event hosted by Edie's apparent granny when she was still single in Munster, Indiana. "Nancy Jane Weis, daughter of Dr. and Mrs. W. D. Weis of Ridge Road, entertained a group of fourteen neighborhood children at a Halloween party Monday evening," the article reported, next to an advertisement announcing, "RUPTURE EXPERT COMING HERE AGAIN."

A few minutes later, Beth shared a 1948 death announcement.

"Daughter Nancy Jane," Edie observed, "got married the same year mom Nancy Jane died."

"To Michael Lucas," Beth added, citing the Americanized surname of Edie's yet unconfirmed grandfather, because Nancy Jane Squared wasn't confusing enough.

"Yep," Edie acknowledged.

"And Papa Weis is the health commissioner," Beth learned about Edie's ostensible great-grandfather. "I bet there's a wedding announcement. Hold please."

Moments later, Beth delivered a screenshot.

"Announce Daughter's Troth," the headline read. "The engagement of Miss Nancy Jane Weis and Michael Lukaczyk, son of Mr. and Mrs. Andrew Lukaczyk," the article reported with their addresses, "was recently announced at a dinner party by Dr. and Mrs. William D. Weis."

Seconds after her friend shared evidence of how columns A and B met up, Edie found a divorce decree from a neighboring state that may or may not have involved the same couple. It said Nancy J. Weis married Michael L. Weis in 1948, and that the couple lived together in Sandusky, Ohio, where they had one child and dissolved the marriage within a year. The decree was dated March 20, 1986.

"There's definite weirdness," Beth declared. Moments later, she managed to dismiss the coincidence.

"Back to the Nancy Jane whose daughter we seek," Edie said about her apparent grandmother, who seemed to be around from 1928 to 1990.

"I don't get any obits from 1990 for Nancy Jane Lucas or Nancy Jane Weis," Beth informed Edie. "Need. That. Obit."

"WAIT," Edie interjected before copying and pasting bold type from a document she had just come across on Ancestry. A record showed Nancy Jane Weis became Nancy Jane Lukaczyk, before settling on Nancy Jane Karpova.

"She's buried in TEXAS," Edie followed up with a link to a gravesite marker.

Meanwhile, Beth's detective work led her to Nancy Jane's daughters, Susan and Sharon, one of whom could possibly be Edie's mom.

"I've seen Susan," the researcher said. "Sharon is more interesting. We know that's our Nancy?" Beth wondered.

"No," Edie replied, "just did a Google search to see if I could find Nancy Karpova in Baton Rouge."

"Because I get Mr. and Mrs. John Karpova all over the place in the 1960s, with their daughter Susan," Beth reported. "Baytown/Galveston area," she added. "She was president of the Plumwood Garden Club."

Our ninja soon found another 1948 announcement. "Nancy Weis Is Bride" detailed how the "colorful bouquets of red roses carried by the bridal party accented the otherwise all white wedding of Miss Nancy Jane Weis, daughter of Dr. William D. Weis, Lake county health commissioner, and the late Mrs. Weis of Munster, when she repeated her nuptial vows with Michael Lukaczyk in St. Joseph church on June 19." Inset on the right was a full-length photo of Edie's apparent grandmother in her bridal gown and horn-rimmed glasses, representing the first discovered image of anyone from this new potential line of maternal ancestors.

On July 15, 1951, *The Times* in Munster published a photograph of a woman in horn-rimmed glasses leading a group of four young ladies sitting on the grass, crafting together sticks. "Mrs. Michael Lukaczyk supervises senior Girl Scouts in the art of lashing," the caption read.

Moments after confirming Edie's apparent grandparents were still together in 1951, her friend found a Nancy Jane-free obituary for Michael's father. "Andrew dies in 1953, and she's not listed," Beth said. "Just Michael."

"Aha," my wife replied. By late May 1953, after no more than five years of marriage, Nancy Jane was out of the picture. Thirteen years later, she was still gone, as evidenced by the death notice for Andrew's widow, Mary, the one who was a Sklarczyk.

In 1946, Michael's family threw the World War II vet a surprise Christmas party—complete with a tree, candles, and gifts—in the middle of March. "Mike has recently returned after two years of active duty in the south Pacific," an article stated, "and three months in a San Diego, Calif., hospital, where he spent his last Christmas."

Michael was also mugged in 1942.

Neither Andrew's nor Mary's obit listed their dozens of grandchildren's names, thwarting Edie's wish to identify Michael's nieces and nephews. "They only had like thirteen kids," she only somewhat exaggerated.

"Who is Stephanie Lukaczyk?" Beth wondered about another 1948 bride, from nearby Gary, Indiana. "She's a foster daughter in a different family," the archivist added, "which is most interesting."

"Andrew and Mary had a daughter named Mary Stephanie," Edie replied, "1914-82."

Neither Stephanie pertained to their search.

"Just what we need," Edie commented, "MORE Lukaczyks."

"Fucking everywhere," Beth agreed.

The first part of her response was definitely accurate. However, while the old folks were indeed getting busy in the cornfields back in the day, they were doing it exclusively in the northwest corner of the Hoosier State.

"It certainly looks like you spring from this particular union," Beth told Edie.

Moments later, she followed up with more findings.

"AH-HA!" Beth announced. "By 1952, Michael was living back on Kennedy Street with his folks."

On January 27, 1950, "Baby gifts were presented to three new mothers in the group," an area paper reported. "Mrs. Michael Lukaczyk" was one of them.

"A girl," elaborated Beth, hot on the trail, "born November 26, 1949."

Our ninja asked for a refresher on which *Gumbo* edition contained John Hart.

"Got it," Beth soon announced. "Susan Karpova went to LSU," she told her dear friend. "In 1969."

"Hello," my love replied.

"If she's the right one, she'd be sixty-eight." Beth quickly confirmed, "And she is."

Edie noted Susan would've been old enough to give birth in 1970.

"Lives in Metairie," Beth discovered.

"Oh shit," Edie responded to news about the New Orleans suburb, an hour's drive from the Red Stick.

"Picture, or do you need a minute?" Beth asked.

"Pic," Edie requested.

Her friend drew a circle around Susan standing on the back row of a co-ed group's somewhat fuzzy official photo. Her face was partially obscured by the front row, almost as though she was shying away from the camera.

"So the one hiding in back," my wife remarked on the less-than-satisfying first photo of her apparent mother, "(as I would be, not that that's relevant)."

Beth found Susan in no other *Gumbos*.

"Grr," my Tiger growled.

Our friend soon found Susan's Facebook profile. The cover photo showed a family of five dressed in dated, European ethnic garb and headgear, posing like folks from the old country. A woman resembling Nancy Jane sat next to a spinning wheel. A young lady, possibly a teenager, stood next to a man, her right hand on his left shoulder, the other on her hip. A much younger boy and even younger girl flanked the trio.

About the time Beth noted Susan's inactivity on social media, Edie found one last decoy. "There was a Susan Lukacik engaged to a West Point cadet in their 1969 yearbook." Throwing out a wild theory, she added, "I'm grasping, I realize."

"Susan Karpova was confirmed by a bishop in 1961," Beth soon sent, along with word that a married John Karpova lived in Munster in 1955, "which is about the time we lose track of Nancy Jane Lukaczyk." She noted, "Mrs. Karpova is miraculously active in all of Nancy Jane's clubs."

The subject line of an email from Beth asked Edie "Is this the same person?" The body contained only two grayscale images of what appeared to be the same woman wearing seemingly identical horn-rimmed glasses.

"First is Mrs. John Karpova," the sender clarified in their chat thread. "Second is Mrs. Michael Lukaczyk. Both of Hammond, Indiana." Beth added, "In the same damn clubz."

"Enough for me," Edie said, satisfied they'd positively identified her maternal grandmother, and, more importantly, the woman who gave her life.

Susan Karpova was her name.

By hovering her mouse over Susan's Facebook cover photo, Edie soon confirmed that her mother was the teenager in old-country garb. The image offered a much better look than the *Gumbo* at the girl who would become Red's mother. Moments later, Beth found her in the same high school yearbook as Fran.

"You rock," Edie grinned, moments before discovering Susan was divorced in 1983, nineteen years before buying property with her current husband in Metairie. Neither Edie nor Beth, however, could find any evidence of Susan having any other children.

"I think I'm all out of steam," Beth admitted.

"This has been above and beyond awesome," her grateful friend averred.

About an hour earlier, when the pair found the first photos of Susan, Edie shot me a message.

"Busy?" she wondered.

"Whatcha got?" I asked.

"Beth may have found mom."

"Uh oh."

She told me of the "one awful pic" from the 1969 *Gumbo*.

"Can I see?"

"The one hiding in the back, of course," my wife acknowledged.

Around that same time, Edie also brought Justin up to speed on the day's revelations.

"Interesting," he responded to details of how a new DNA match provided breadcrumbs leading to Susan. "So is it okay for me to ask John about her?" Their dad was back in Renton for more medical treatment.

"Definitely," she responded.

A few minutes later, Justin answered, "John isn't sure and said 'maybe' he remembers her. We are going to discuss more this evening." Edie's brother also noted a strong resemblance to her in Susan's sophomore class photo.

"Susan was two years behind Fran in high school," Justin learned.

"John has been focused on people he had a particularly intense experience with," he said, suggesting perhaps Susan was a "casual encounter." Justin added, "Maybe the East German woman is just the wrong lead."

While Beth was chasing down photos, Justin and I theorized how John and Susan may have connected at LSU to bring my soul mate into the world.

"There were plenty of drugs," I said.

"Yes, I never know whether to trust John's claims that he really didn't do many drugs at all," his son winked, "but we all saw that Xmas card from 1979." Noting that a younger John would drink heavily at times, Justin said, "All it takes is one time."

The screenshot of Susan's high school yearbook showed a grid of six sophomores, three of whom were girls. "For your consideration," was all Edie told Fort Worth about it.

"I see likenesses in two," Pat replied that afternoon. "Most in Karpova."

Edie filled him in on the rest about Susan, before beginning to ponder what to include in a message to John Lukas, Susan's all-but-confirmed first cousin. How much should she reveal? Is the tone measured without sounding cold? What if this opens an unpleasant can of worms for a large Eastern European family?

"Hi Edie!!" Rachel popped up on Facebook Messenger early Monday evening. "WE WILL SEE EACH OTHER THIS WEEK!"

Imagine honestly needing a reminder from your adult sister about your upcoming first-ever meeting in four days because you're in the middle of messaging a man, whom you only know through the internet, mere hours after discovering the identity of your birth mother, who just happens to live an hour away.

"Hi sis!" my wife soon replied. "Less than 100 hours! I love the idea of seeing the area where you grew up!"

There was no mention of that day's discoveries. The upcoming trip was all about Rachel.

"Hi John," Edie began her Ancestry message to her first cousin once removed, "I hope you are doing well. I wanted to share a discovery we may have made with a new DNA match that has shown up. It looks like my biological mother may be the daughter of Michael Lukaczyk and Nancy Jane Weis. I was wondering if you might have any insight that could be helpful? Thanks, Edie," she signed off, and joined me in the living room for dinner and needed distraction via TV.

Back in the office, an Ancestry email alert arrived. John Lukas had replied to his cousin's message, which did not mention her mother's name.

"Wow, I knew of Susan," he shared with his phone number, around a quarter past eight. "It's a big story." He asked her to call. "I can't type that much," John Lukas explained, "that's my dad's brother."

"Wow," Edie sent back a bit later, around 9 p.m. "What's a good time to call you?" she asked, seeking to confirm they shared the Central Time Zone.

Afterward, she revived that day's chat thread with Beth.

"I messaged the maternal cousin," she said. "He asked me to call him."

"WHOA," Beth answered. "Are you?"

Edie told her she was awaiting his reply to do so. During that time, Justin popped up on Facebook chat.

"So John remembers a friend of Fran's," he wrote of their father's decades-old recollections about his sexual relationships. "He hardly remembers what this friend looked like (other than she wasn't as physically fit as Fran and she was perhaps a little shorter, for what that is worth)."

As Edie began telling Justin about the exchange with John Lukas, she realized the Hoosier had replied again, just after 10:30 p.m. The lag time in seeing her cousin's messages that night was consistent.

"I missed another message forty minutes ago," Edie told Justin. "He said he's up at 7 a.m. our time."

In his latest dispatch, John Lukas informed my wife, "You have been a hot topic to all your cousins, you are sort of a missing person. Your mom's first name was Susan." He also said Edie's grandparents were deceased. "I'm glad you found me," he closed. "Thanks, cousin."

It was 11:15 p.m.; too late to call, we agreed.

"WOW!" Justin remarked. "That seems pretty likely then. OMG! Are you nervous?"

So nervous was my wife that we were already in bed before my brother-in-law asked the question.

"And by the way," he continued writing, shifting to Susan, "after looking at the picture, John doesn't recognize her. His only comment," Justin added, was that "maybe she was the woman who said she was East German. I find this kind of doubtful."

So did we, since John repeatedly claimed his Soviet Bloc girlfriend was likely twice the age of the twenty-year-old Baton Rouge high school grad—originally from Indiana—whom he obviously impregnated.

"John seriously thinks Susan was the East German woman," his son followed up moments later. "He is as certain as he was that your mother was Fran," Justin reported. "He gets fixated on ideas of concepts and can't let go."

Around two in the morning, his time, John Hart sent his first text to Edie. The series of messages read like one of his emails, but with emojis (butterfly and rainbow) near the top. Per Justin's heads-up, John asserted that Susan was the East German woman. Of the message thread's remaining ninety percent, a small portion essentially admitted that his daughter was more capable of figuring out the puzzle than her father was of accurately remembering how she was conceived.

At sunup, Edie replied to Justin. "She appears pretty youthful," my wife noted about Susan. "Passing herself off as forty would have been quite a trick."

After discovering the fate of the young boy in Susan's Facebook cover photo, Edie soon offered a qualifier.

"However," she said, "Susan was apparently well-traveled. This is from the obit of her half-brother," Edie prefaced citing the death notice of her apparent uncle, "who was seven years younger. 'Growing up, John was well traveled. He lived in Boston, Indiana, Baton Rouge, New Orleans, Houston, Holland, London, Bahamas, Turkey, Miami, and Spring, TX, among others." Edie's late uncle John Karpova, Jr. "was also able to speak French, Dutch, Turkish, and English.'"

It's not often you come across an obit that reads like lyrics from "The Heart of Rock & Roll."

Joking that such worldly experience could mean Susan was "a spy after all," Justin offered, "I hope you have a great conversation with the cousin today. I'll be thinking of you."

Before leaving for work on Tuesday, Edie messaged John Lukas. She apologized for not seeing her cousin's latest message sooner, and asked if they could talk during her lunch break.

"You've inspired me," Beth messaged her midmorning. "I bought a month of Ancestry."

"I'm going to try to call the maternal cousin," Edie answered, moments before an initial talk with her maternal blood.

"Let me know what they say!" insisted Beth, who had just solved a decades-old mystery in her own family. "Meanwhile, I found my great-grandmother! Charity Elizabeth Williamson Robbins."

"Yay!" my wife rejoiced. After learning more about her friend's new familial discovery, Edie forwarded John Lukas's "hot topic" message.

"So it IS Metairie Susan!" the Google Fu black belt exclaimed. "YAAASSS. How do you feel?"

"Like I need to make a call," Edie replied, "but I need to eat something first."

Minutes later, after a quick snack, her phone rang. Area code 219 led the number calling. She took copious notes since her plan to record the conversation didn't work out.

"Awesome thirty-four-minute call," Edie messaged me.

"Awesome!" I replied with an animated GIF of two giddy young women.

"My Grandpa Mike 'would've sold his arms to know he had a grand-daughter,'" she reported, "and bought me the circus if I'd wanted it."

"Wow," was all I could muster.

"The belief is that Susan was told he was dead," she learned from her cousin. "After Nancy ran away with Susan, Mike never saw them again." Edie's grandfather remained unmarried "and doted on nieces and nephews."

"That is crazy," I wrote. "More chapters being added each day."

Cousin John had told her about a photo of Edie's grandfather and his ten siblings "with their parents, and my mom and grandmother."

"Sounds like you stirred up a very large family," I observed.

"Twenty-six first cousins," she came back. "Second cousins numbering in the seventies."

"Sweet Jesus."

"Last night," Edie told me, "Cousin John was on the phone with cousins, telling them to round up pictures."

"Lots of people contributing to a common goal," I messaged my wife. "You're more influential than you thought."

"He said there were two females in the window of childbearing age in 1970," Edie reported, "and he had assumed it was the other one."

"It's always the quiet ones," I quoted my late stepdad, evoking a devilish emoji from Red.

"They love to cook and have parties, and we are welcome to visit and get introduced to everyone," Edie briefed me about her long-lost family, and the woman they'd fruitlessly searched for since the early 1950s. A couple of them even "went to Atlanta to look for Susan in the phone book; they thought she was using the name Susan Weis."

"Wow," I mustered again. "Does he think they'll be able to contact her?"

"We didn't go that far yet. Oh," she led an interesting tidbit, "so Nancy's father was a doctor; Mike's father was a garbageman and bootlegger for Al Capone."

"Kinda like O'Neals vs. Harts."

Edie humored me with a laugh, and added, "Mike's parents are Ukrainian." They "met on the ship to the new world at the turn of the century, got married here, and built a house in East Chicago that they lived in for the rest of their lives."

"An excuse to visit Chicago," I told my wife.

"Cousin John also has a brother in Victoria, Texas," she said. "Two hours south of Austin."

Three days before meeting Rachel, the idea of making a combined road trip—possibly with her in tow—was quickly quashed. Victoria was too far away, the O'Neals were arriving Saturday, and our upcoming visit was to be all about Baby Girl.

Edie soon updated Beth about the call with Indiana.

"So they knew about Susan and Nancy," our favorite Deep Stater observed, "but Susan didn't know about them."

"Cousin John thinks she was about five when Nancy took off," Edie said. "I didn't tell him it's probably more like two or three."

North Texas soon received an alert.

"So I have inherited a horde of Ukrainian cousins."

"Borscht!" Patrick responded. "Is that what they eat? And sausage?"

"It would seem," I shared in the thread, "Edie has been a red-hot topic amongst a large Eastern European family in northwest Indiana."

Red then explained her maternal ancestry, including how the nineteen-year-old child of a county health commissioner wed Grandpa Mike.

"So your presumed bio mom Susan was the product of a bootlegger," noted Pat, who appreciates poetic contrasts, "and the young daughter of a doctor."

Our red-hot topic soon informed her younger brother about the maternal Ukrainian horde, and their theories about what happened to Edie's mother. "They thought she was a teacher or baker going by the name Susan Weis," she told Justin.

"Wow! It sounds like she has some tribulations with her own family, too. As did my mother," he responded. "Maybe John had a thing for women that were estranged from their families," his son supposed. "That was essentially his condition, too, and the main reason I did the AncestryDNA test in the first place."

During their call, John Lukas told Edie that she needed to talk with their cousin Paula. The eldest daughter of Michael's older sister Julia, Paula served as primary caregiver for Edie's grandfather in his latter years, before Grandpa Mike passed away in 2003.

At 6:34 Tuesday evening, Edie received her second call of the day from the 219. She put Paula on speakerphone. Since the earlier call with an Indiana cousin wasn't recorded, I fired up my phone's voice memo app.

The audio file opens with Paula telling Edie about her grandfather having "a slight nervous breakdown" after the war. He had been looking for a "good buddy" after their ship was attacked, Paula said, when he came across a disembodied arm. The ring on a finger told him who the limb previously belonged to. It's why he spent Christmas of 1945 in a San Diego hospital.

The voice on the other end told the story in an unmistakable Chicago accent.

"He loved decorating all the graves around here," we learned. "His other favorite pastime was garage sales." Paula made her cousin laugh. "I swear to God, he would go out and buy things just to sell them again."

"We have a friend who does that!" Edie shot back, both of them cracking up. "I can be a sucker for a garage sale, but I don't get rid of anything. That's one of my problems."

"Mmm-hmm," I can be heard concurring as my wife laughed some more.

Paula then reported, "John said you had a wonderful life growing up."

"I did," Edie confirmed. "I was really blessed."

"You have any children?"

"No kids for us," my wife said. "We're the end of our line."

"Well, no," Paula snickered, "now you have an extension of your line."

"That's right!" Edie exclaimed. "I've got enough cousins and nieces and nephews to meet now!"

"You got that right!" an enthusiastic Paula agreed. She then posed a question that would further shift our already altered priorities. "Do you think there would be any way you guys would come here?"

"Oh," my wife asserted, "we'll make it happen."

"Mmm-hmm," I again hummed my agreement, less than two weeks away from the first of numerous weekly football meetings.

"Ok, good," Paula said. She then learned about her Louisiana cousin's paternal discoveries, our recent life-altering trip to Washington, and our quickly approaching trip to meet Rachel in Texas. "OH, WAAAOWWW," the Hammond resident exclaimed.

"So yeah," Edie vowed, "we will definitely work Indiana into the mix."

"Oh my goodness," Paula remarked, "this DNA stuff could either be a blessing or a curse, and in our case—believe me—it's a blessing. It breaks my heart, though, that your grandfather—my uncle—isn't here."

After learning how Edie and Beth solved a mystery plaguing their family for some sixty-five years, Paula told us how the nearby Weis family "wouldn't say a thing" about Susan or her whereabouts. When members of both families were in the hospital, the Lukaczyks begged for any information. For two-thirds of a century, not a soul cracked in the Weis clan, which included at least one priest.

"With the divorce," Paula conceded, "I have no idea what happened. That part he never talked about," she said of her beloved Uncle Mike.

"If you can save someone from heartbreak," Edie responded to the Weis family's silence, "that's the whole reason I did this. I had a great life. My life is full," she added. "And now it's just better because now I get to meet all these new cousins!"

"Of course," Paula replied, "you may change your mind after you meet 'em!" The pair guffawed like old pals.

The two Lukaczyk sons, Michael and his older brother, John, had Americanized their names to ensure that the payroll folks at the mills would cut their checks. "None of this was done legally, either," Paula said of a bootlegger's sons' actions. "Legally, it's Lukaczyk." Why the two brothers, Michael Lucas and John Lukas, would assume different iterations was not explained.

Paula soon drew a deep breath before another confession.

"Oh my God!" she stammered. "My heart is still pounding. This is just so amazing. I guess better late than never, huh?"

"Exactly," Edie agreed.

During the gastronomical portion of their call, Paula implored us to attend nearby Whiting's annual Pierogi Festival in late July; if not the next month, then in 2019. "We gotta get you back to your roots, girl!"

Moments later, Paula said she was anxious to go through her photo albums. "Oh my God, Edie, it's so wonderful to talk to you!"

"It's great to talk to you, too, Paula."

"Welcome to the family."

"Oooh," my wife whimpered.

With thirteen minutes left on the recording, we began saying our goodbyes.

Discovering Uncle Mike's granddaughter was like having a part of him back in Paula's life again. She wasn't alone.

"The phone lines have been buzzing all over the place," the recording continued. "'Oh my god!'" Paula mimicked. "'Guess what! Guess what!'"

Seconds later, she brought up a still unknown aspect of the mystery: What, if anything, did Susan know about her birth father?

"Personally," Paula stated, "I'd like to know what Susan was told."

"Right," my bride said. "That's what Jeremy and I were talking about before you called: When and how to approach her, because it was one thing for me to reach out to John because he was already in AncestryDNA," she explained. "Susan isn't in that same place right now," Edie countered. "I don't want to push her away," she added. "We don't know what she was told."

As far as we knew, Susan may have been brought up believing she was fathered by John Karpova, whose family had migrated from the Ukraine to Canada.

"In 1964," Edie told Paula, "she and the family were in Baton Rouge." Monday's discoveries had included local newspaper clippings.

In October that year, the *Morning Advocate* published an entry titled "Newcomers Club Hostesses Coffee." Mrs. John Karpova was the second "honored guest" listed. Five months later, a *State-Times* photo caption indicated Nancy, with her horn-rimmed glasses, had become the group's recording secretary. She ascended to program chairman by early 1966. Nancy's half-smile in the latest *Morning Advocate* photo offered a softer option to her previous, more stern expressions.

Another photograph captured Mr. and Mrs. Karpova with the president of the hoity-toity City Club and his wife. "The Karpovas are newcomers to Baton Rouge," the 1965 caption read, "having moved here last fall from The Hague, Netherlands."

Susan's younger half-sister had two daughters, and lived in Houston, Paula learned. Edie's late uncle, John Karpova, Jr., died on Christmas Eve 2016, and was survived by three children.

"I got a lot of the information from his obituary," Edie revealed. While some documents suggested Susan might still be in Atlanta, "There's a chance Susan might actually live in Louisiana," she said on the phone.

"Oh, waaaaow," we heard on the other end.

I chimed in, noting that Hurricane Katrina in 2005 may have sent my wife's mother back to Atlanta.

As Edie recited the cities in her late uncle's obit, I realized the Karpovas' movements almost seemed like they were trying to throw someone off their trail.

"Well, you've gone this far," Paula told Edie, interrupting my thought. "You'll finish."

Paula closed with a pair of stories about my wife's grandfather. They involved hospital stints, one for a procedure that took longer than expected. She was worried the anesthesia, given Mike's age, might accelerate his dementia.

"I went to visit him," she recalled, "and I'm standing outside the door. I see he's talking to somebody, and he's shaking his finger. And all I heard was, 'And don't bullshit me. You're no virgin.'" As Edie and I chortled, Paula continued, "And all I could think of was, 'Oh, please God, don't be the Blessed Mother! Please don't be the Blessed Mother!'"

Edie soon filled in Fort Worth and Renton about the forty-three-minute phone call. She also emailed our Hugo's Cellar photo to Indiana.

"More to come!" Edie promised Paula. "But your call made my night tonight," she said. "Thank you again!"

"Cousin!" an enthusiastic Paula soon sent back. "You are gorgeous! Hubby's not too bad, either," she threw in. "Told my girls about you," she reciprocated with photos of herself and her three adult daughters. "They are so excited and can't wait to meet you!"

Just before 1 a.m. Wednesday, Paula sent two images of a middle-aged Grandpa Mike in a tuxedo at a wedding. Dark brown hair swept across his forehead toward 1970s-length sideburns. A familiar, wry, closed-mouth smile rested between high cheekbones. His warm, brown eyes were the same, unmistakable peepers looking back at me since 1991.

Shortly after awakening Wednesday morning, Edie saw her handsome grandfather for the first time.

Coincidentally, John Hart had sent a 2,748-word overnight email sans subject. In asking about Susan, he greeted their daughter, "Hey Sherlock."

That afternoon, Paula messaged her newest Facebook friend.

"I never went to sleep last night! I still can't believe it! I hope you didn't think I was crazy when we spoke," Paula said. "We've spent a lifetime wondering."

"Aw, Paula, we loved talking to you," Edie replied, "and my heart just melted this morning when I saw the picture of my Grandpa Mike! I hope you don't think I'm crazy, because I'd be looking to get up to that Pierogi Festival next month if we weren't already committed." She added, "The closest experience I had to a set of grandparents are a couple I kind of refer to as my 'other parents,'" she said of the Wagleys.

"If your Grandfather would have known you," Paula claimed, "you would have gone to Notre Dame!"

That evening, Edie brought her investigative partner up to speed about Grandpa Mike, including some details Paula divulged before I began recording.

"An 'idiot aunt' told him a girl belongs with her mother when he wanted to hire a private investigator to track down Nancy and Susan," Edie wrote. Mike was also "a maniacal Cubs fan."

"I love these people," Beth replied.

"You have helped make a whole bunch of Ukrainians up in Indiana very happy," my wife smiled.

"Awwwww," Beth followed up, "они очень приветствуются," which Google translates as "you are very welcome."

Two days earlier, after seeing Susan's photo, Justin had asked Edie how she found her.

"So I got a new AncestryDNA match," she explained, "who led me to a marriage that linked up the two clusters of maternal DNA matches."

The new match was Nancy Gouch, who fell on the two Nancy Janes' side of the family. The stunning lack of creativity in naming children contributed to Edie not recognizing the connection before.

In researching available records connected to Nancy Gouch, Edie came across a document confirming her grandparents' marriage. She had previously linked Mike and Nancy Jane in the Lucaczyk tree, drawn out separately from the Weis cluster's tree. It just hadn't clicked that this was where the two clans came together.

In salty Marine parlance, too damn many Nancys were fouling things up. Half the family seemed to bear the same moniker, or a close facsimile, as that of a near relative.

"John Lucas is one of six Lucases named John," my wife messaged me after her Tuesday phone call with John Lukas. My award-winning copy editor wife had typed the wrong Lukas/Lucas in that exchange, which only further confirms my theory that some of these people did not want their progeny to find them.

This whole journey may resemble a soap opera, but it is lacking in one critical qualification: not every character has a uniquely recognizable one-word name. Of all the silly melodrama that soaps offer, none of it involves two characters having the same first name.

Edie realized that her newest match, Nancy Gouch, led her to a subset of the Weis clan, where she had previously found a document linking Mike and Nancy as husband and wife. Maybe she previously overlooked it because she was so focused on finding her ancestral line through one of eight Lukaczyk daughters. Not unlike John Lukas, she failed to recognize a link involving one of the two sons. If she had initially come across the document during one of her late-night/early-morning research sessions, it's understandable that she could've missed it, especially considering all the Nancys and Johns.

But the third Nancy was the charm. Mrs. Gouch led Edie back to ground she had previously trodden. On this return trip, though, she recognized a critical piece of the puzzle she hadn't noticed laying there before.

After turning her attention to Rachel, and arranging a visit to Austin that would include her adopted family, Edie's mind was cleared enough for her to see what she had previously overlooked. By the end of the weekend, she had it figured out. That Sunday night, though, she managed to resist siccing Beth on the trail. She patiently waited until Monday morning to message her friend.

Four days before meeting her sister.

20

Baby Girl

"OK," Edie messaged Rachel on Thursday morning, "I've got a silly idea. I don't know if Austin has one of those sculptures where it's the letters spelling out the name of the city, but since Justin and Austin are spelled the same except for the first letter," my wife proposed, "we could maybe play off that to take a picture for him."

"Cool!" Rachel approved. "I bet there is one somewhere."

"We are so looking forward to hanging out with you this weekend!" Edie sent.

"I am looking forward to it, too," the Austinite replied. "Last night going to bed, my thought was, 'Tomorrow, I can tell Edie: See you tomorrow!' I am so excited to meet y'all. I'm not a very religious person," Rachel revealed, "but I feel blessed that we've found each other." That drew a love reaction from her sister.

"Given our sitter stop along the way," Edie said of weekly Maringouin responsibilities, "and Houston traffic potential, I think 5 p.m. arrival is an optimistic estimate." She offered for us to stop at Rachel's favorite kolache place, ninety minutes outside of Austin, in a city made famous by ZZ Top for its whorehouse. "We can swing thru Lagrange and pick up an order from Weikel's if you let me know what you'd like," Edie smiled again.

201

"I like the cream cheese kolaches the best," Rachel responded with a review of the bakery. "The only thing I would vote as average are the cookies."

There would be no shortage of carbs this upcoming weekend.

"We will be together this time tomorrow!" Rachel alerted Edie some twelve hours later. "I can't wait to give you a big hug," she added Thursday evening, evoking another love reaction from Big Sis.

"Have a great visit today/this weekend!" Justin texted the two of them as the two of us headed out the door Friday morning. "Big hugs to you all!"

"So excited!" Edie sent back. "Just wrapped up business and on the road. Can't wait to see you, Rachel! Love you both."

"Edie," Rachel soon said, "I can't wait to see y'all! It is hard to care about work today!"

"I know the feeling," her sis sympathized. "Less than eight hours to go," Edie reminded Rachel. "Hang in there!"

Weather was as nice as one could reasonably expect from south Louisiana and southeast Texas in the middle of June. Warm and sunny with a chance of afternoon showers was the order of the day.

This was our first real road trip in the new Nissan Rogue we bought a couple months before Edie mailed off her kit. The SUV proved to be a timely purchase for this venture and future road trips.

"Are you already on your way to Austin?" Patrick asked at 1:39 p.m.

"Yep," his sister confirmed as the Rogue got closer to empty while driving through Houston, "trying to make it to Buc-ee's in Katy since Waze decided we didn't really want to stop in Baytown."

Before reaching the state line, Edie had programmed the navigation app to route us to the giant gas station with a cult following—and every roadside snack known to man under one roof—on the east side of Houston. However, Waze apparently called an audible we didn't hear. We never got the command to exit I-10 for the Baytown location.

So we laid a course for the next one on the way, in Katy, west of Houston. The Rogue indicated we had enough in the tank to make it. Barely. This was a chance to use my engineering degree.

To conserve fuel, I drove through incorporated Houston mostly tailgating a tractor-trailer hauling a wide load. Edie's phone showed how many miles remained to our destination. The Rogue showed how many were left before we ran out of fuel. We constantly compared the two as they both ticked down.

In other words, our anxieties were focused on something besides meeting her little sister.

"Be safe," Patrick implored. "We plan on leaving early mañana."

He also said he was "jelly" of our plan to see over a million winged mammals emerging at sunset from the undergirding of the Ann W. Richards Congress Avenue Bridge. Patrick confirmed that the world's largest urban bat colony taking flight was a must-see.

A week after telling Edie she loved the bats, Rachel checked in on our travels on Friday afternoon.

"Just exited toward Lagrange," Edie replied at 3:18 p.m.

Back when she and Beth were finding Susan, Edie came across a Lukas Bakery in the legendary town. "This is probably my new people," she soon messaged me with their Facebook page, indicating they closed at 1 p.m. However, Paula would confirm that Lagrange's Lukas Bakery was not affiliated with my wife's new people, allaying any regret for lack of opportunity to stop in and stare at strangers.

Back on the road for the last leg, we headed for the parking lot at the *Austin-American Statesman*, located along Lady Bird Lake, near the base of the bridge where the bats hang out all day. Rachel worked only a few blocks from the city's largest newspaper.

Before arriving, my passenger put me through my paces to ensure I knew the names and interrelatedness of the people we'd later meet, the only family Rachel grew up with. Edie also sent her some information about parking.

"*Austin-American Statesman* says parking is $6," the former *Advocate* employee messaged less than an hour out, "which is fine with us if it helps delay a journalist's layoff."

We parked, paid at the kiosk, and scoped out the grounds on the east side of the bridge's south end while waiting for Rachel to arrive.

"I am here," she messaged at 5:19 p.m., "trying to find the place to pay."

We made our way back to the kiosk. Within seconds, we spotted Red's little sister walking toward us, a dozen or so parking spots away.

Edie bolted toward Baby Girl. She began running as well.

In the middle of a newspaper parking lot, under partly cloudy skies, the two sisters embraced for the first time after living in neighboring states for thirty-one years. Moments later, once they finally released each other, Rachel and I enjoyed a lengthy hug, too.

The three of us eventually made our way out of the path of vehicles arriving for the nightly spectacle, which didn't occur for another two hours. That left plenty of time for walking and taking photos.

Trees along Lady Bird Lake's southern bank shaded our trio's path as we walked off some of the snacks we'd bought along the way. Edie and I both noted snowlike cottonwood seedlings on the ground. She wondered if Rachel and her estranged father ever unknowingly passed each other in the city they shared. My wife did not verbalize this thought. Neither did we have to worry about such an occurrence, since John was still in Renton.

As we spoke, I realized Rachel would change her speaking voice, to represent someone or something else, more frequently than I did. As an only child, I could totally relate to growing up doing funny voices to entertain oneself, if no one else.

We made our way toward a crosswalk to see a bat sculpture across the highway from the newspaper, but stopped to watch a shirtless young man riding a bicycle he was sitting on backwards. After a couple laps around the parking lot, the fit fellow pedaled northbound heel-first, across the bridge along six-laned South Congress Avenue. He occasionally peeked over his shoulders at the Friday rush-hour traffic, his hands resting behind his back on the handlebars. Because keep Austin weird.

With a reach of around fifteen feet, the purple metal bat sculpture known as "Night Wing" offered a fitting backdrop for the first photos of our newly acquainted siblings. Although they couldn't play off their brother's name with this Austin sculpture, it would more than suffice. The trick was getting the breeze to simultaneously cooperate with their hair and the freely rotating sculpture.

We started with shots of the pair standing side by side, each facing me with an arm around the other. That soon turned into another lengthy hug. I continued snapping away.

Back on the other side of the highway, we saw the prime bat-watching area getting more crowded. As the sun crept toward the horizon beyond the bridge, the three of us staked out a spot on the grassy hill sloping down like natural theater seating toward the bats' summer home.

I grabbed a selfie with the three of us sitting on the ground before realizing that my scruffy mug had no business being in the first up-close image of my wife and her sister. I followed up with a pic of just them, heads leaning against each other. Their side-by-side smiling faces—complete with matching freckles, hairstyles, and slightly up-turned noses—looked at me and my phone as trees and folks on the hill provided the background.

"Surreeeeal," I faintly heard Knick comment.

A crowd of hundreds began to gather above on the bridge. An apparent local walked back and forth along the railing, dressed for the occasion in a propeller-topped fedora, sunglasses, and a black T-shirt with a gold Batman silhouette. He occasionally stopped to lean against the railing to look down at the growing throng of onlookers below. We were thankful that his kilt fell below his knees.

As the sun started to set, boats passed to and fro under the bridge. Aboard some were patrons who paid to see the show with the aid of a tour guide. Rachel told us how, one time, she and a friend had a bit too much to drink before partaking in one such cruise. They openly commented on the guide's bat acumen, she said, probably to his displeasure.

A handful of Mexican free-tail bats suddenly started darting around the concrete structure. Their squeaky chirping increased as more and more of their fellow colonists joined them in serpentining under the nearly thousand-foot-long span. I joined others in raising my phone to document the ritual. Some held small children on their shoulders.

The crowd of thousands stood collectively amazed by the million-plus swarming mammals known as the "jets" of the bat world, fluttering en masse across the downtown Austin skyline, into the clear Texas twilight. A nearby table manned by members of a local bat enthusiast club showed live radar imagery tracking this colony—and several others—taking flight for the night across the south-central portion of the Lone Star State.

Once the bridge's nocturnal inhabitants had departed, our trio repaired to Phil's Icehouse for cold beer, quality burgers, and even better ice cream. The conversation wasn't bad, either.

The booze and food inevitably reminded the two of us of our long day. We said our first-ever goodbyes with Rachel outside in a parking lot, hours after first meeting in another.

Edie and I checked into our hotel as Rachel drove home nearby, where we'd meet her for breakfast.

She asked us the next morning to stop for eggs and H-E-B's fresh-made butter tortillas. That's when Patrick alerted us that they had "hit the first traffic snafu" thirty minutes into their planned three-hour drive, just past 9 a.m.

"But of course," Edie remarked.

Rachel shared a house with a roommate we never met, in a quiet residential area anchored by a middle school. After big hugs at the door, she introduced us to the nearly solid-black Tezcat, who indeed proved to be "constantly elegant, but somehow eccentric at the same time."

We settled at the same kitchen table from which Rachel had Skyped with us in Seattle; she stood by the stove making French toast. I had fun watching Tez do backflips while chasing the feather plume wand in my hand.

After breakfast, we hung out for a while, talking and playing with Tez. I learned that my new sister-in-law owned lots of boxed games, enough to make another only child jealous. I also learned that she's a vegetarian who isn't too keen on veggies.

"Hola!" Yvette popped up to let us know they were about a half-hour from Austin. The five of us decided to meet up at Conans on the north side of the city. Like Phil's the night before, the pizza place is one of Rachel's favorite spots.

She and Edie rode in the Rogue's back seat on the way there around noon. The entire glass storefront of the funky joint was plastered with colorful bills promoting upcoming shows at area venues. We waited under knotty pine beams for some of our favorite people to arrive from Fort Worth.

"Let's get this one behind you," Patrick had promised on that emotional Sunday morning in Renton, "and then maybe we'll tag along next time."

Two of the best people you'll ever meet walked in a little past noon after a nearly four-hour drive. Edie and I embraced them at the door. We finally released Patrick and Yvette to introduce them to their newest kin. An emotional Rachel hugged her newest family members, both exuding abundant warmth and tenderness, in the entranceway of Conans Pizza on West Anderson.

I marked the joyous occasion with a photo of the three smiling siblings. Like Night Wing, the tapestry of show bills behind them offered a uniquely Austin backdrop, while conveniently muting the daylight outside.

A smidge past six-foot, Patrick towered over the ladies flanking him, with Edie to his right. His wingspan pulled both of them in against his plain black tee. My bearded, cottontop brother-in-law resembles a taller, slimmer, much-more-alive version of Philip Seymour Hoffman.

My wife rocked her version of the shirt I had worn when we met Justin, Sunny's "UnBRoken" Louisiana design. Rachel's black tee featured a colorful peace symbol circle. All three grinned broadly.

Someone over Patrick's left shoulder, above Rachel's curly locks, managed to photobomb them. She was Sexy Future Space Lady, or at least that's what the bill featuring her photo—complete with futuristic toy gun and knee-high boots—was titled.

The five of us grabbed a rectangular table in an unoccupied section of the restaurant. On one side, Patrick joined our lovely hermana, with her big brown eyes, rich olive complexion, and black Beto O'Rourke T-shirt. Edie sat opposite them, between Rachel and me, providing the O'Neals prime side-by-side viewing of Patrick's two younger sisters over sodas, teas, and pizza.

Rachel's admittedly small family continued to grow before our very eyes as the couple connected with her for the next two hours at one of her favorite places. They made her feel like she had known them for years. Rachel reciprocated by sharing more about her life; so much so, that at one point, she brought up a topic the rest of us had been instructed to steer clear of.

As Rachel began talking about John, though, Edie noticed her sister seemed to pull back, ostensibly concerned that we might have preconceived notions on the matter after already meeting Justin and her estranged father. My wife reassured Rachel that we weren't interested in third-party interactions, explaining it was why we drove from Baton Rouge—and why the O'Neals drove from Tarrant County—to meet her.

Edie informed her tearful sister that none of us had any sort of opinion on the John matter, as with most other aspects of her life, because we knew nothing about it. John had said nothing. Justin told us the bare minimum. We were there to get to know Rachel and her perspective, Edie avowed, insisting that we wanted to learn her story firsthand.

Before departing Conans, I photographed the sisters sharing an emotional hug in the middle of the eatery. No one else was in the photo, taken from behind Rachel. The back of her black shirt provided a contrasting canvas for Edie's fair arms and dainty hands, pressed against her sister's back. Unmuted sunlight through a glass door illuminated the left side of the elder's countenance, emerging from Baby Girl's curls with eyes closed. My glowing bride's calm, comforting look in that moment of raw joy remains beyond words.

We soon relocated to Thunderbird Coffee on West Koenig. This time, I joined the O'Neals in side-by-side gawking from their side of the booth. Sitting across from Edie and Rachel, I realized that even wilder than their identical noses and weirdly similar hairdos (that they'd each been sporting for some time) were their arms.

The skin tone. The countless freckles. The tiny, wispy, practically color-free, sad excuses for hair. No DNA testing was needed to tell these two were sisters. I snapped exactly half a dozen pictures of their right arms laying next to each other on the table in a crowded coffee shop.

I was doing my part to keep Austin weird.

Around 4:30 p.m., the O'Neals invited Rachel to visit them whenever she was in the Fort Worth area. They also let us know they needed to head home, where Father's Day festivities were planned for the following day. We sent the couple off with many hugs and thanks for giving up an entire day, including nearly eight hours on the road, to join us in our wonderful discoveries.

Once again, the sisters were in the Rogue's back seat. The two frequently giggled as I chauffeured my fair pair fare around Austin. Among other things, they discussed catching Pokemon, which Rachel shared with a severely disabled young cousin, making it more than just a game for her.

As afternoon gave way to a sunlit evening, we arrived at Lake Austin for dinner with Rachel's mother, Elizabeth, and her family. The rest of our party was already at Hula Hut, a waterside Tex-Mex place with Hawaiian flair. Rachel greeted her mother with a hug before introducing her to us. As much as Baby Girl resembled Edie, her likeness to Elizabeth seemed to surpass it.

We soon met Elizabeth's older brother, Tom; his equally youthful wife, Candy; and their son Mike. A few years younger than me, Mike and I quickly found common ground with humor and awful hairlines.

Rachel's mom, uncle, aunt, and cousin were cordial and engaging. I ended up talking with them mostly about college football, particularly LSU and Texas.

Sorry, Texas A&M. Maybe next time.

The fun meal was the family's way to finally celebrate Rachel's thirty-first birthday, which officially happened two weeks earlier, while she was on a cruise. The relaxed venue also helped mitigate any inherent awkwardness that might accompany meeting people whose only connection to us is a man who's been largely absent from all of our lives.

Rachel's small family was an easygoing bunch. Elizabeth had worked in elementary education for three decades. Tom was a retired pediatrician.

After dinner, we were all to muster at the home of Tom and Candy's other son, Chris, and his wife, Jenny. Our trio's arrival would be delayed by a stop at Rachel's house, where we had the rare privilege of meeting someone special in Rachel's life.

"I am also the person of my roommate's cat, Heru," our hostess had mentioned in her initial email to Edie. She was right. I could tell that Rachel belonged to the one-eyed Heru. He came out because of her, and in spite of us. And yes, I am ascribing thoughts to cats, not unlike a couple of Austinites we'd recently met.

Our second visit to Rachel's place prompted Elizabeth to call her daughter and let her know that everyone was wondering where we were. There was a cake awaiting its birthday girl, after all.

I quickly drove us to the newer neighborhood where Tom, Candy, and their kids' families all live. Inside their home, Chris and Jenny greeted us, and introduced us to their clever dog, Izzy. With the rest of the Hula Hut gang already there, I soon realized that Chris shared his brother Mike's fun attitude, but not his forehead.

Our hosts had named their oldest son Michael, after Chris's hairline-challenged brother. The well-spoken preteen was Facetiming from Dallas. Sadly, circumstances prevented us from meeting Michael's younger, disabled brother, Ben. Rachel's fellow Pokemon enthusiast was being cared for in a nearby room.

It was soon time to make a wish, so Rachel donned a tiara. A small chocolate cake held a decorative candle brightly glowing under the dimmed lights.

The guest of honor stood facing the round table where the cake was placed as the flames awaited. Rachel turned to her left to tightly hug her sister, with her entire being, it seemed.

Unlike the previously photographed hug at Conans, our birthday princess's face was completely visible. Her left cheek pressed against my wife's left shoulder, framed by a birthday crown above and ridiculously similar, intertwined arms below. A bespectacled Rachel squeezed her eyes shut in an apparent attempt to hold back a torrent.

Seconds later, I snapped a blurry pair of sisters diving toward the cake in unison to blow out the twin-flame candle.

Around 10:30 p.m, Tom led the women in imploring his sons to sing. By then, Mike's wife, Kathy, a realtor, had joined us after a busy Saturday of open houses.

Chris and Mike soon sat next to each other holding acoustic guitars. The sisters did the same, opposite the brothers, sans six-strings. It was an enjoyable, siblings-on-siblings serenade with an intimate audience. The talented duo harmonized late into the night as their dad fed them requests.

With Sunday morning approaching, we let the bard bros rest their lovely voices. It was time for us to say goodbye. Sleep was needed ahead of our drive home Sunday.

Despite the hour, our hostess remained gracious. You wouldn't have known Jenny was dealing with issues involving caregivers just down the hallway.

Edie and I hugged Rachel's lifelong family goodbye and dropped her off at her place, with plans to meet up for breakfast the following morning.

"It was great to see y'all even for a short while," Patrick shared in the thread upon returning to Fort Worth earlier Saturday evening. "I'm so thrilled to have Rachel in the family," he wrote. "She's so smart and funny. And she looks like you, E," Patrick noted, "so much I thought my heart would burst." He asked us to give Rachel their best, and to be safe on the road the next day.

After Sunday breakfast at Torchy's Tacos, Rachel again joined Edie in the back of the Rogue. The Father's Day tour included her mom's neighborhood and at least one now-shuttered restaurant where she and Elizabeth used to enjoy visiting.

Rachel retrieved her vehicle at Torchy's, and led us to the Austin Nature & Science Center, where she had recently worked part-time. Like gangsters entering a restaurant through the kitchen, we pulled around back, and met some of her friends working there.

Inside, Rachel showed us a couple dozen reptiles, including snakes and colorful iguanas. The scene reminded me of Edie's first workplace as a married woman, at the Baton Rouge Zoo.

Outside, Rachel introduced us to the menagerie of rescued birds in a nature center where former first lady Lady Bird Johnson once accidentally got locked inside. Among the residents was Pogo, the smart raven. He and Rachel would regularly converse in caw, she recalled.

Morning turned into early afternoon. It was time to hit the road.

The three of us gradually ambled over to our parking spot for our final goodbye hugs of the trip. Amid tears, we shared promises of meeting up again soon.

Edie and I climbed into the Rogue and slowly shut the doors. We sat there for a moment or two in silence, looking at each other, elated that we had experienced this chapter in our lives, yet sad to see it give way to another. Nevertheless, we took solace in knowing there would be many more involving both Rachel and Justin.

Baby Girl wiped tears from her face in the mirror as we drove away for Baton Rouge.

21

Golden Child

"I had such a great time," Rachel messaged a couple hours into our drive home. "Thank you so much for coming! Tez agrees," she said, "we already miss you!"

"Aw," Edie answered from the passenger seat, "we had a great time and love and miss y'all, too!"

"Please send me a picture or three when you get a chance! I am so focused on being in the moment," Rachel told her, "I never took pictures this weekend!"

During our time in Austin, the sole mention of our recent maternal discoveries came Friday while waiting for the bats. Neither Edie nor I brought up the topic. The discussion about finding Susan was both brief and downplayed.

"Happy Father's Day," my passenger wished her baby brother as we approached Katy. "Don't want to interrupt anything y'all have going on, but we'll be on the road another four-plus hours if you're up for a call?"

"Just gotta fill up the kiddie pool (with bourbon, it's that kind of holiday)," Justin winked.

"Damn, that sounds awfully good," Edie responded moments before she endured me driving through Houston traffic.

After their hourlong call, she sent Justin some of my recent photos. "I think it was great that Rachel got a firsthand welcome and invitation from Patrick and Yvette," Edie gushed.

"She got to meet them first. In some small way," Justin smiled. "I am sure that helps her feel like she wasn't missing out."

After spending the weekend with her Baby Girl, Edie dialed Abita Springs so Kellie could talk to hers. The two sisters spoke for nearly twenty minutes around the state line.

Moments later that Father's Day, I phoned my dad from behind the wheel as Edie composed an email to John, still in Renton. We traversed a bridge along I-10 known for crossed derringers depicted along its guardrails.

"Greetings from 'the pistol bridge' as we cross Lake Charles on our way home from a quick weekend trip to Austin! I'm sorry we couldn't be together today," she wrote John, "but I wanted to let you know that we love and are thinking of you. We were happy to see the pictures from Hadley's graduation yesterday and hope you are enjoying lots of joyful time together!" Citing trouble typing in a moving vehicle, she closed, "Updates to come soon as we learn more about the rest of our DNA puzzle!"

He replied a little later with fewer than 500 words. "Mr. Sherlock would be envious," John said of our "beautiful efforts." For most of the rest, he wrote about his granddaughter, whom he got to see graduate from kindergarten, complete with a royal blue cap and gown.

Later that week, Edie would wish John a happy seventy-fifth birthday. He'd reply to her email at 5:37 a.m. with 3,729 words, the first four being "Love is a rainbow," followed by "spanning the distance, coloring between the edges of being, softly holding, and sharing all between, lightly, colorfully."

Along the way back from Austin, Edie also reached out to a third member of the Ukrainian horde. Cousin Paula's sister, Carole, lived in South Carolina. The two cat lovers connected for more than half an hour over three separate calls because the reception around Smithville,

Texas, was crap. Cousin Carole spoke of many things that Paula had mentioned, and some she hadn't.

"How did I forget this," Carole followed up in a text. Cousin Drea, the "family historian who knows everything," could offer more light on the Lukaczyks' numerous futile attempts to learn anything from the Weis family about Nancy and Susan. As young girls, she added, cousins Arlene and Lois would have known Edie's mom and grandmother. "Thanks for talking with me today, Edie."

"Thank you for sharing that info, Carole," my passenger messaged back that Father's Day. "We enjoyed our conversation with you."

The next day, Edie updated her new "Biological Family Tree" on her AncestryDNA account to show Michael Lukaczyk and Nancy Jane Weis as her maternal grandparents. She began building it out from there, starting with Susan's closest relatives. Edie made the tree public to provide a trail, in case someone was out there looking for her. She left out all the peripheral puzzle pieces that led her to Susan, for fear of seeming like a lurker to total strangers/distant cousins.

Sunday after Father's Day was the eve of the Baton Rouge Area Football Officials Association's first meeting of the season. That final Monday of June would herald my five-month eschewment of travel unrelated to football officiating.

John Lukas called us as we finished supper close to 9 p.m. on Sunday. Edie put him on speakerphone so I could join in.

He was at a steel mill in Gary, and—like his cousin in Hammond—definitely from Chicagoland. We paused the conversation a few times when announcements blared over the PA system with a sense of urgency. He reassured me that the place wasn't about to blow up.

We spoke for over two hours. Cousin John was no less jovial and engaging than Paula.

He was also equally heartbroken about his Uncle Mike spending the final half-century of his life not knowing where his only child was, or if she was even alive. Just as tragically, Mike lived his last thirty-three years completely ignorant that, 900 miles away, he had a granddaughter being raised by a loving and generous family.

216 | JEREMY WHITE

"He'd have cut off his right arm just to hold you in his left," I heard.

That completely fucking slayed me. Seriously, sitting there on our sofa late Sunday night, I was done.

Edie had quoted essentially the same thing from her first phone call with John Lukas nearly two weeks earlier. Getting it secondhand, however, is no match for hearing it straight from Mike's nephew who grew up knowing the tragedy of the horde's favorite uncle. My wife's first contact with her mother's side was all but begging me to share her with them, in an effort to reclaim a part of their family that had been mysteriously deprived from them since the Korean War.

John Lukas then told us about his older brother Gene, a former Marine in Victoria, Texas. Like cousins Lois and Arlene, he was old enough to remember growing up with little Susan before Nancy Jane took off with Mike's daughter. Gene received dialysis treatments three days a week, we learned, and would kill to meet his new cousin, little Susan's little girl.

Football or not, we planned on visiting Victoria as part of a future weekend in Austin. What was I supposed to tell the seventy-nine-year-old Devil Dog with bad kidneys? "Sorry, pops. You waited sixty-five years, I'm sure you can wait a few more months"?

Moreover, what about his brother, John, and all their cousins in Indiana, practically pleading with us to go see them? Do we tell them that we can't go there until December? Do I tell my wife, born and raised in South Louisiana, that we'll go see her family near Chicago in the heart of winter?

After hanging up around 11:30, an emotional conversation ensued about our priorities, which the call had further shaken up. Family now came before football, especially new family who'd been waiting for this moment since folks were still getting used to saying "President Eisenhower."

We agreed that I'd talk to the rest of the board after Monday's meeting to let them know I wasn't sure how much I'd be available for the upcoming season. I fully intended to offer my resignation as vice president if our uncertain schedule proved too big of an issue.

The day after returning from Austin, I had touched bases with our president, Jody Lavigne, a witty writer who came up through the ranks as part of my high school officiating crew. I gave him a heads-up about our journey thus far, including the clamoring Lukaczyks, a week before the insanity of football season started.

"Oh," Jody said, "so Edie's like the Golden Child."

Yes, a redheaded one at that, I agreed as we mimicked lines from the Eddie Murphy film.

The following Monday morning, hours after the late-night call from John Lukas, I alerted Edie about my latest conversation with Jody. "Told him I planned on giving the board the Cliff's Notes version about our situation tonight."

Edie wondered if she should attend.

"Come to the meeting," I replied. "You provide the face for our quest."

"Wait, BRAFOA quest?" my confused crewmate asked. "My quest?"

"Our quest," I clarified, citing *The Golden Child's* plot. "That's the word Jody used to describe it."

The entire board was completely understanding and willing to work with us as our situation continued to evolve—at times, day-to-day. I only broke down like twice as I let them in on the incredible story we were living out. I also explained that, after decades of Edie supporting me in my wacky endeavors—including (but not limited to) football officiating, stand-up comedy, and satirical publications—it was time for me to have her back, and be by her side during this incredible journey.

Later that week, I also contacted my junior college league supervisor, Thomas Miller, as well as my juco and high school officiating crews. All of them were supportive, understanding, and willing to accommodate me and my unsettled calendar during the upcoming season.

Before the Monday meeting, Edie managed to squeeze in an eighty-minute first phone call with cousin Gene, a fun, gregarious sort, just like his kid brother back in the Hoosier State. He certainly didn't sound like a dialysis-dependent near-octogenarian in a wheelchair after undergoing hip replacement surgery in February, who had also suffered subsequent strokes. The two cousins mainly talked about two topics: the Corps and Susan.

There was no way we were not going to go see Gene ASAP. We were on a quest.

That same day, our efforts to acquire TSA PreCheck kicked into high gear. If we were flying around on a crazy reunion tour, the Golden Child and I were not sprinting with luggage through airports after waiting in ridiculous lines with the unwashed masses again.

There was something else we had to do before embarking on the tour: plan it. And before we could plan a tour, this nerd helped his wife prioritize the expansive list of family members longing for her presence.

"I'm setting up a map of all the relatives (all four major time zones covered) who have requested an audience with Edie," I told Knick and Sunny on Monday evening. "Then we'll prioritize who we go see when based on age, health, distance, number of relatives within the geographic area, etc."

In the Fort Worth thread the next day, I dubbed it "familial triage."

"Man," Patrick chuckled, "future Christmases are going to require a spreadsheet and a flow chart."

"I feel like we're getting ready to book a rock tour or something," I said.

"A good warm-up for the book tour," the lawyer remarked.

"We met with the football board last night to let them know why my participation this season may be very limited," I noted. "One of them said we should write a book."

Okay, maybe I'll think about it.

That same Tuesday, Edie discovered that the woman she still hadn't reached out to apparently would travel to the Red Stick on occasion. "Susan reviewed the Pastime restaurant last year," she messaged me around midday regarding a seventy-plus-year-old institution not far from LSU.

A little later, she let Yvette and Patrick in on an earlier discovery.

"So I've been sitting on a possible address and phone number for Susan for two weeks," Edie revealed. "I'm thinking maybe a hand-written note. A phone call seems like too much instant pressure, as does Messenger. What do y'all think?"

"I totally agree about the note," Patrick insisted. "Much more per-sonal," her big brother concurred, "and less imposing and demanding."

"And maybe include my email address but not necessarily phone number," Edie suggested, "in case I don't have the right person?"

"Yes," he approved. "That's a good plan."

"Or get a burner phone?" Edie joked.

"Burner phone!" Yvette endorsed.

Edie then noted that, while stalking her bio mom on social media, she noticed Susan "wished at least two people 'happy birthday' on Facebook this month."

"So she's way more technologically astute than Ducky," Patrick observed, drawing LOLs from both of us.

That led Edie to bring up cousin Gene and their phone call.

"Crap," Patrick responded to news of Gene's ailments. "You better see him soon."

"He used to work in Hollywood," Edie reported, "but about fifteen years ago, he could no longer stand having to get along with the liberals."

"Oh shit," Patrick laughed. Yvette replied with a digital facepalm.

"He almost went AWOL on the Corps to stay in Mexico with his first wife," my jarhead said.

"Sounds like a rugged individualist," Patrick noted.

"He joined in 1958," she added, "after abandoning the family farm."

I rounded off the Gene conversation with some empathy. "Holly-wood is often the worst advertising for progressivism."

"It's a power structure of white men controlling everything for money," Patrick explained.

"Exactly," I concurred.

While my brother-in-law and I were fixing the world, Edie was figuring out what to include in her initial correspondence with the woman who gave her life. She ordered two prints of the selfie from our DFW layover (only because she couldn't find our Hugo's Cellar pic), and picked them up on the way home from work Tuesday.

Later that evening, less than twenty-four hours after addressing the BRAFOA board in the same building, the two of us went back to the main library to see if we could confirm Susan's address in the most recent New Orleans area phone book. Within minutes, we found a Susan Karpova at the same Metairie address Edie and Beth had uncovered. The listed phone number also matched online findings.

We reached back out to Fort Worth one last time that evening before dropping something in the mail Wednesday morning. "It was basically to reaffirm messaging from lunchtime," according to my wife.

"Edie," Patrick informed his sister, "you don't have a disingenuous bone in your body. Be your sweet self. Be clear and to the point. And hope for the best."

"Love you!" she declared.

"I love you, too," he reciprocated.

"Love you guys," Yvette shared with a smoochy face, peace fingers, and purple heart emojis.

Edie wasted no time in letting Beth know about her plans after confirming the address they'd found. "Mailing a note tomorrow," she said.

"WHAT?" Beth fired back. "That's awesome! Fingers crossed!"

"Thank you!" Edie winked, "Yay, libraries!"

"Yay!" her friend rejoiced.

While the women were touting how well-spent tax dollars can benefit the community in unimaginable ways, I updated Sunny and Knick.

"This is all so awesome!" Sunny gushed.

"Surreal," Knick said.

Like, actually in the thread. Not just in my head.

Edie dropped a pair of letters in the mail on the morning of Wednesday, June 27. One was addressed to Susan. Her envelope contained a print of the month-old pic I took of us waiting for a plane. It also held a pair of handwritten notes.

"Dear Susan," read the first one, date atop on the right. "We have not met, but I have been led to you through family research on AncestryDNA.

"I was born Nov. 30, 1970, in Baton Rouge and adopted by a wonderful family. Dr. Anthony Leggio may have helped facilitate the adoption. I now live in Baton Rouge with my husband of twenty-five years, Jeremy.

"We realize this correspondence is a surprise. We do not wish to disrupt your life, but are wondering if you may be part of the puzzle we are piecing together. We are not asking anything of you except whatever information you are willing to share.

"We completely respect your wishes and will not contact you again if you don't want us to," she continued on the second page. "But if you would like to correspond," Edie offered with her email address.

"Thank you for taking the time to read this message and, hopefully, to answer. I truly apologize if I have upset you or caused you any pain or concern.

"I wish you love and peace." She signed off, "Edie White."

On the other note for Susan, Edie transcribed the three heartfelt stanzas she had composed some time ago, specifically for this gravity-laden moment.

If you were my mom, I hope you are well.

I hope you are happy and healthy and at peace.

I hope you have people in your life who you love and who love you back.

I hope you have no regrets about the separate paths our lives have taken.

I want you to know that I am well.

I want you to know that I am happy and healthy and at peace.

I have people in my life who I love and who love me back.

I have no regrets about the separate paths our lives have taken.

I am so grateful to you.

You selflessly and generously gave me unlimited opportunities.

In my mind, you are perpetually young and beautiful.

I want you to know that you are loved.

The other envelope dropped in the mail Wednesday was addressed to Gene. It contained the other DFW selfie print, along with a personalized, handwritten letter.

By midmorning, I learned from its sender that there are "407 miles from our door to his."

"A little closer than Austin," I said.

"Yep," she replied. "About 130 miles" separated Gene Lukas and John Hart.

"Did you wanna maybe see about this weekend?"

"Maybe," she responded, "but if we go to Austin, we kinda have to see both John and Rachel to avoid hurt feelings—and part of me doesn't want to rule out Susan getting the note tomorrow, sending a positive email response."

"We can wait," I said. "Might as well do a twofer if we go back to South Central Texas."

My ever-deliberative bride messaged me again a little later near midday that same Wednesday.

"So now part of me is thinking we should just go to Texas this weekend, while another is thinking that if we do have positive contact with Susan," Edie said, "we might end up going right back since she has all those people in Houston."

"True dat. Let's hang tight this week. Maybe the following weekend," I suggested. "We can play week by week as it hopefully completely develops. Then we can start setting more hard dates."

We could have gone to the library to confirm Susan's address much sooner than two weeks after Edie first learned of it; the thought did occur well before we actually did it. My ruminative wife probably would have delayed sending initial correspondence to Susan even longer, if not for concern someone else might beat her to the punch.

"The other reason I needed to drop that card in the mail," she conceded to me, "is because I already gave her name to one of the cousins, who could easily type it into Facebook and message her if she thought about it."

Edie also reached out to her paternal folks on the West Coast later that Wednesday evening.

"Greetings!" she posted in the chat thread with Justin and cousin Erica. "Hope you both are doing well. Jeremy and I were excited to visit Rachel in Austin in mid-June, and now that we have with near certainty determined who my biological mother is, and shared that revelation with her paternal cousins," Edie said of the horde, "the 'newly discovered family meet-and-greet tour' plans have been kicked into high gear. We still welcome y'all to Baton Rouge, but we would also like to try to coordinate some time to come out to meet the Milsoms if possible? We don't want to interfere with your schedule," she insisted, "but we're opening up ours to any opportunities."

"We would love to join you all," sent back Justin, who'd recently started his new project manager job at a tech firm.

"I'm super into it," Erica announced from Northern California.

Edie then contacted John about possibly visiting him and his wife, Hallie, either the upcoming weekend (because there was still a tiny chance we'd jump in the Rogue and go) or the second Saturday in July. In either case, we wanted to save Sunday for Rachel and Gene. "We anticipate making more trips in the future if these weekends don't look good for you," Edie emailed her father Wednesday night.

He replied during lunch the next day.

"We can stay at John Hart's either Saturday," his daughter updated me Thursday. "He wants to know if we prefer ribeye or lamb chops."

Among the 628 words he sent, John mentioned they'd have "cold brew and regular coladora drip coffee." He also offered to pick us up at the airport and/or rent us a car with his AARP and Costco discounts if we were flying in, which we weren't.

In the midst of all this uncertainty about whether we were making a road trip in the next forty-eight hours to visit her biological father and half-sister for the second time each—and before making the first face-to-face contact with someone from her birth mother's family—Edie was worried if she properly addressed Susan's envelope.

"Google Street View from May 2014 shows a 'House for Sale by Owner' sign in front of Susan's house that I mailed the note to," she messaged me Thursday afternoon. "That doesn't mean it actually sold."

A 2017 Jefferson Parish property tax record soon confirmed she indeed had Susan's current address. However, she still fretted.

"I just hope I wrote the correct address on the envelope," Edie told me, "because I keep typing the wrong one into the map search."

By noon Friday, it was readily apparent that Texas would have to wait until after Independence Day. The end of June was upon us, and we still hadn't nailed down anything yet with Gene. By early evening, my wife emailed her father to confirm that we would not make it the next day.

"We are gradually trying to establish contact with the other relatives," she updated John. "Susan has about thirty first cousins! And I have not made contact with her yet, but I did mail a note two days ago to the address we found for her. My GI tract has been a bit devastated since then," she revealed. "So I'm just trying to be patient, work on contacting others and catching up on overdue chores around the house. There's more than enough of both to keep me occupied if I allow it!"

John, who was twenty-six when he obviously had relations with a twenty-year-old Susan, replied from Austin two hours later with 1,152 words. Many were used to argue for the case that he fathered Edie with a fraulein fling that fell out of a bad spy novel.

"Justin said he can't believe that it would be the woman who told me she was from East Germany, married to a philandering nuclear scientist, who would have her deported if he ever found out she was having an affair for herself. Possibly," he said, "she might be the one who was concealing her identity. Justin wants to fit things neatly into his thinking, and said, 'because she seemed (older than I), she couldn't be,' but when he mentioned that she was difficult to relate with family, used different identities, it might be that person," John argued. "East Germany/Poland genetics are not that precise, with all the shifting boundaries. The woman was intelligent, she just slipped in when she wanted to, and never revealed anything more of herself."

Twenty-four hours later, Edie kicked off her Saturday night with a thirty-seven-minute, second conversation with her newest favorite Marine.

Gene had gotten the letter. Susan was effectively on the clock.

Sunday morning saw the two of us preparing to walk out the door to do things for important women in our lives. I headed to my mom's place to handle some chores as Edie prepared for her weekly Maringouin trek.

She checked her email beforehand. There was a new message from an unknown address. The subject line simply read "Surprise."

22

The Bravest Person
I Know

"I got an email from Susan," Edie texted me from home on Sunday, July 1. "I knew I should not have checked before leaving for Maringouin."

"Oh shit," I replied from my mom's living room near midday.

"Yes," my wife confirmed. "She is confused but curious," Edie explained, "and didn't want to keep me in limbo."

"Still at the house?" I asked. "Want me to head back?"

"I better go now or I won't," she maintained. "We can talk when I get back."

As I was relaying the breaking news about her presumed mother to my own (quite confirmed) mom, Edie also updated Fort Worth.

"This is why I don't check email when I am already late leaving for Maringouin," she led. "Surprise," Edie cited the subject line, before sharing the rest of Susan's message.

"Edie," Susan greeted her, "after receiving your wonderfully sensitive letter and beautiful picture, I didn't want to leave you in limbo wondering about whether or not you'd get a response. Unfortunately, it's taking me a while to catch my breath after the tsunami that hit me when I opened your envelope.

226

"I'm an analytical person," she continued, "and I was instantly drawn in by your 'puzzle' reference. At this point, however, I think you've got more of the pieces than I do. You might get asked a lot of questions. Are you up for that?

"Sorry this is short. I'm having a bit of trouble with thoughts and words right now," Susan wrote. "I didn't want you to think yours weren't read and appreciated. I'm just very confused, but curious.

"Love," she closed, "Susan."

Patrick responded first.

"What. The. Fuck."

I was next.

"OMG."

"IKR," Edie replied. "OK, Susan is off the clock." My wife conceded, "Ball's back in my court."

"Well, this day just got a lot more interesting," I noted.

"So is she Mom or not?" Patrick asked. "Wouldn't she know? Sorry, it's a stupid question."

"Well, apparently not," Edie answered his last query. "I even mentioned Dr. Leggio in the note, and birth date," she said, "for what it's worth."

"Oh," he responded. "So wtf?" Patrick asked again.

"WTH?!" an emphatic Yvette inquired.

"As little info as is traceable about her," Edie shared our belief, "maybe she's wondering how I put this together, especially if she doesn't know the history of her birth parents."

"That's what I said. She's analytical and wants to know how the hell you found her," I theorized. "You have the pieces of the puzzle."

"OK, so I guess I'm happy I appealed to her analytical side," Edie remarked. "I did see that she was a *Jeopardy!* fan. And now I'm going to calmly drive to Maringouin, take care of business, and come back to craft a response," she wrote, countering, "or I could answer now (she sent her message an hour ago) and see what's waiting when I get back."

"My two cents: Go to Maringouin and consider your thoughts," I suggested. "Let the adrenaline settle down."

Patrick was "gobsmacked again."

"You know, if she is my mom," Edie observed, "there's no way this could NOT be a convoluted process." Her brother and I each agreed.

A couple hours later, before returning home from across the river, Edie alerted her younger siblings about Susan's email. "I am on my way back home to craft a response."

"Wow!" Rachel gushed. "Oh Edie, this is exciting! I hope you both get, at the very least, some peace of mind and answers."

"Wow!" Justin joined the exchange. "That is awesome! Her trepidation seems like it is appropriate, considering a whole range of possibilities. I hope it goes well, Edie." He added, "Let me know if there is anything I can help you with or if you need me. Full of love and hope for you both."

Edie thanked her younger siblings, and told Justin she'd "borrowed heavily" from his original note to Fran.

By mid-afternoon, Edie alerted me that she was headed home.

"Oh thank god," I responded.

"I hope that's only because of Susan," she texted, "or did something else happen?"

"Susan," I clarified. "Trying to distract myself."

"OK, good," Edie replied, "because I don't think I'm prepared to deal with anything else."

My love made it home within the hour. At 4:22 p.m., she replied to that morning's "Surprise."

"Hello, Susan," Edie began her first email to the woman she'd been searching for. "Thank you so much for responding. It's certainly understandable that you'd want to take some time to process this, especially coming out of the blue as it has. Please accept my apologies for the tectonic shift and resulting tsunami. Jeremy has sometimes described me as an earthquake type of person," she winked, "and apparently that applies in this case, as well. But I certainly don't want to upset you or cause any distress.

"I am happy to answer any questions that I can," my wife promised, "share the information we have, or work with you to resolve unanswered questions, if you wish. Please know that you control the tempo, and we can pause or proceed at the pace you are comfortable with. I don't want to push, so please ask whatever you would like as you are comfortable doing so, and please don't hesitate to pull the reins if I overstep," Edie insisted, "or ask me to back up and clarify details if I get ahead of myself.

"And I am so, so happy to hear from you. Your note has me smiling," she told Susan. "I hope I can return the favor!

"Love, Edie," she signed off.

For the record, an earthquake person is someone who holds things in, building subsurface strain, until stresses evoke a sudden release of stored emotion. Hurricane people, like myself, on the other hand, howl and bluster as emotion boils up.

"OK," Edie promptly updated Fort Worth, "now we hold our breath again—or not."

When she began composing her reply to Susan, their cousin in Texas called. Edie spoke with Gene for seven minutes. Had she revealed that day's "Surprise," it would've undoubtedly lasted far longer, not to mention the ensuing avalanche of excitement and questions from the rest of the horde. She would've been too distracted to be completely emotionally available for Susan in their now-hours-old relationship.

That evening, Edie "slept about three nonconsecutive hours," Justin and Rachel learned the next day. "Running on three cups of coffee today," my wife reported Monday. "No nap before football meeting this evening; hope to get some sleep tonight."

As I drove us to the nearby meeting, Edie checked her phone to learn Susan had sent a new message. My wife opted against risking an emotional scene in the public library by opening it there.

"On our way home to read a new message from Susan," she updated the Texas O'Neals following the meeting. Edie sent a similar message to her newer siblings.

"So excited for you!" Rachel responded in their group thread. "Good news, bad news, idk what to do with this news," she vowed, "we are here for you!"

"Best email yet," Edie followed up. "Will be working on a reply for a while. Love you so much!"

"Love you, too!" Justin texted. "So happy for you!!"

"Best email yet," I echoed in the Fort Worth thread.

"What's going on?" Patrick popped up moments later, from the family camp on the Louisiana coast. "Sorry, we are down in Grand Isle," he said. "We've been gorging on shrimp."

"Susan replied," I said. "It's very good. Edie is composing a response now."

Susan's email was very good.

"I've spent more than a little of the past few days trying to learn what I could based on some of the things in your letter," she wrote back. "I hate to start this way, because the questions are tough and I'd much rather concentrate on the joy I'm feeling. Maybe getting the tough stuff out of the way early will clear the way for all of the really important things we want to know. So...

"As far as I know, you and I are unique in that both of us have siblings, but neither of us have the same pair of birth parents as any-body else in the world. That being said, one of the things that confused me was how any connection between us could be found through AncestryDNA. I've never submitted a sample for testing. How did that part of your research lead you to me? What else did it tell you?

"You mentioned Dr. Anthony Leggio. It looks like he left this world way too early, and that's a sad thing, because he was so very good to me. He led me to believe that he was helping me at the same time as he was helping friends of his. Is that true?" she wondered. "Were your parents friends of his?

"I also learned of the passing of your Dad, Dr. O'Neal," Susan re-ported on her research. "He sounds like a wonderful man who was the head of a large, loving family. I pray that's true, but I know it makes losing him even harder. Reading about him brings me to the hardest part of this puzzle section—Ducky. Is she aware of your quest? How does she feel about it?

"Since I'm asking hard questions here, it's only fair to share a little piece of my past life with you that kind of parallels where we are now. My mother and I spent a few years on our own after she and my birth father divorced. She married again when I was four, and I became part of another family. I was never allowed to see or even mention my birth father again. I was officially adopted by my dad when I was seven," she said of Mr. Karpova. "My mother passed away just after I turned forty. Dad died eight years later. It was only then that I felt that I could search for my birth father without disrespecting my parents. Unfortunately, by the time I found him, it was too late. He had passed shortly after my dad.

"I tell you this because I want you to know there are things I truly can understand about what you're trying to do. I really want this to work for you, but I just can't be responsible for hurting anybody. Can you understand that?

"Whew, none of that was easy to get through. I hope you still have some of that smile left. It's gorgeous, by the way!

"Looking forward to hearing from you. Hoping I haven't scared you away. Praying the rest of the questions, answers, and puzzle pieces are way easier, lighter, happier, and maybe even fun.

"Love," she closed, "Susan."

While Edie composed a response, I reached out to Beth.

"Hope I'm not disturbing your awesome vacation," I messaged, "but I felt it would be wrong not to let you know today is even more magical than you could have imagined."

"DID IT HAPPEN?" she inquired.

"Oh, it's happening," I said.

"OMG, OMG, I'm Jessie Spano excited!" She asked, "Is it happening right now?"

I soon got her up to speed. "Susan was confused but curious," I passed along. "She had lots of questions, if Edie was ready."

"Wow."

"Edie replied late yesterday afternoon," I informed Beth, "telling her to fire away."

"Because she's the bravest person I know," my wife's hero proclaimed.

"IKR?" I agreed about the self-effacing woman who sat so close to the edge while hiking in Washington.

"I'd need pharmaceutical support out the wazoo," Beth shot back.

"So basically," I said of Susan, "Edie is allaying her fears and telling her how we got here."

"I don't suppose there's a template for this kind of thing," the archivist noted, "but I didn't expect Edie to be the one allaying fear in this situation."

"As she's doing this," I shared from our office, "I'm starting to more fully realize how crazy it is y'all determined Mrs. Michael Lukaczyk is also Mrs. Karpova with pictures from the '50s you found on the internet."

"Same social circles, same clubs, same cat-eye glasses," Beth noted.

"Yep."

"If you edit enough 'Pam's Party Line,'" she wrote, citing *The Advocate's* social feature, "you get real good at picking out the pattern."

"BTW," I told her, "Susan said she was never allowed to even speak about her birth father."

"That's fucked up," the mother of two concurred.

"Edie will hold off on telling her about the horde of cousins who have been looking for her since the Truman administration."

"They are…enthusiastic," she deadpanned.

"Yep," I posted at 9:52 p.m. "BTW, she's been up since 1:30 this morning and we haven't eaten supper yet."

"Get that woman a taco," Beth demanded.

"Email sent," I messaged the ninja at 10:35 p.m. One minute later, I sent the same alert to Yvette and Patrick.

"Dear, dear Susan," Edie wrote, "I wish I could hug you right now—I hope that doesn't scare you away! I am definitely still smiling and happy to hear that you are joyful that we have made contact with each other. Your words are beautiful, and I thank you for also sharing the sorrow related to not having the opportunity to reconnect with your birth father, which could not have been easy to write.

"If I fail to address any of your concerns," she continued, "please let me know—I'm striving to answer each of your questions, although not necessarily in order.

"I certainly appreciate your desire to avoid hurting anyone. As you mentioned the parallels in our story," Edie explained, "that's part of the reason I didn't embark upon this journey until after my forty-seventh birthday.

"It's true that Dr. Leggio and his wife were friends of my parents, in addition to Ducky being one of his patients," she confirmed. "Mom and Dad had a son (1956) and a daughter (1957) soon after getting married (1955), then went through the agony of multiple miscarriages and realized they would not be able to have any more biological children. They adopted my other brother in 1964, and Mom was overjoyed at the opportunity to bring me home in 1970.

"Apparently, it was Dad's decision not to learn anything about my birth parents, aside from possibly being told they were LSU students. Mom told me from a young age that she was open to answering any questions I might have," Red allayed, "and as I got older, she would often reiterate that she was willing to do whatever it took to help me find out about you if that's what I wanted to do.

"I was blessed with a loving family and wanted for nothing. I did not want to risk the possibility of opening an old wound that someone may have tried to leave in their past and move beyond. However, as I got older, I began to wonder more often if maybe I was preventing a wound from fully healing by keeping to myself, rather than making myself available to be discovered by someone who might have a lingering question as to whether they had made the right decision.

"My adopted brother, Patrick, submitted his sample to Ancestry-DNA about a year before I did. I resisted the urge to ask him about any results, wanting to allow him to share as he was comfortable.

"All four siblings were together at Mom's house for Christmas 2017," Edie recalled. "Patrick, his wife, Jeremy, and I stayed with Mom that night after everyone else had gone their separate directions, and that's when Patrick shared with me some of his findings. Mom was so excited both for him," Susan learned, "and also when I decided to go ahead and submit a sample, too; she dug out the few records she had related to my adoption in case they could help us learn anything. I think she's really been wanting us to seek out our stories for fifty years, but has shown remarkable restraint in not pushing us to do so until we were ready.

"So please know that Ducky is not only overjoyed about this journey of discovery," Edie informed Susan, "but also at least as eager to meet you as I am, if that is something you would like to do at some point. (If it is, I would selfishly prefer for the two of us to meet first, but please don't feel pressured to move at a pace that is uncomfortable for you.)

"I also have discussed this with my two older siblings and their children so that everyone is aware, especially my oldest niece, who blessed us with the opportunity to be a part of her adoption of her son. Everyone is supportive of our endeavors and realizes that the opportunity to expand our circle and bring more joy and love into our world is a beautiful thing," my bride assured before returning to the puzzle.

"So, to get back to the DNA: I ordered my kit on Christmas night, received and submitted it just after New Year's, and the results became available in early February. At first glance, I saw that there were hundreds of close matches, far exceeding what Patrick had found. It seemed so daunting that it took me a while to look at anything beyond the ethnicity estimates.

"And that's when I was struck with my own tsunami, which I hesitate to bring up at the risk of causing you any pain," Edie warned. "The first time I looked at my DNA matches, it revealed the identity of my birth father. He and his son were in the system already.

"Not knowing your feelings in that regard, I do not want to expound upon those details without your blessing. I hope that you may continue to read on to how I found you without distress. I realize that was your first question," Susan's daughter conceded, "but I hoped to alleviate some of your concerns up front, and I didn't want to lead off with a bombshell that plays a significant part in the discovery process.

"AncestryDNA presented me with an extensive list of people in their system with whom I share DNA," Edie explained. "It orders them based on how much DNA we share, indicating how closely we are related. It also allows me to see shared matches: I can select any individual and see who we both share DNA with.

"Because my biological father was identified, I inferred that anyone who did not share DNA with him was likely a maternal match, so I focused on those people. I started with the closest maternal relatives and mapped out clusters of individuals who shared DNA. Two distinct groups emerged, both on the maternal side.

"Within each of those two groups," Edie wrote of her methodology, "I compared the family trees that were publicly available and used Ancestry's search tools, as well as online obituary searches, to work out how the individuals within each group were related to each other. It took several months to build out two family trees to determine the couple that formed the common ancestors in each group, but I still didn't know how the two groups were connected to each other.

"A new DNA match appeared in June that led me to discover a marriage that united the two groups: Michael Lukaczyk and Nancy Jane Weis. I turned to a dear friend who is a trained archivist, and she helped me look for information on those individuals. She found newspaper clippings that indicated they had a daughter in November 1949, another that suggested they were together in 1951, then another that indicated Michael was living with his parents again in 1952, and no more mentions of Mrs. Michael Lukaczyk.

"So I reverted to searching the Ancestry records for Nancy Jane Weis/Lukaczyk," Edie shared, "and found a record that introduced a new surname: Karpova. My friend was able to determine that John Karpova was married by 1955, and that Mrs. Karpova was active in the same clubs in Hammond, Indiana, that Mrs. Lukaczyk had been in, then found a photo of her that helped confirm she was the same person.

"She also began finding information about you and your sister," Susan read. "And then she found you in LSU's 1969 *Gumbo* yearbook, the same one we had previously found my biological father in. She also found your LinkedIn profile, indicating you had been in Metairie. So Jeremy and I went to the library to check the New Orleans area phonebook, found your address there, and decided to reach out.

"And here we are," Edie began wrapping up. "I hope you are still happy that we did reach out, and that I didn't overwhelm you with this explanation, and that we can continue on this journey and get to know each other better. Emails are great, but if you might want to schedule a phone call sometime," she offered, "I'm open to that, too. Regardless, I am looking forward to continuing our conversations!

"Love," she closed that Monday night, "Edie."

Before work Tuesday, she emailed John, alerting her father about the past two days. "I wanted to check in to let you know that we still want to come out to visit you," she wrote. "This Saturday, July 7, is still available for us."

Later that afternoon, Justin asked, "Things still going well with your bio mom?"

"Hope so!" she winked. "Took me about three hours to draft a response, sent late last night. I had Jeremy help, read over my shoulder since I was working on about that much sleep. Crashed hard after we ate." Following a sleepy emoji, Edie told him about Susan's near-lifelong forced estrangement from her father.

"Wow!" Justin replied. "So there is some common experience (the distance/separation from parents) that just ripples through all our lives. You, her, Rachel, me," he noted, "a familiar pattern, shared history, though unique to each, too. It sounds like things are going well with her."

"Another excerpt from her letter that also applies to Jeremy, you, Rachel, Mason, Hadley," Edie quoted: "'As far as I know, you and I are unique in that both of us have siblings, but neither of us have the same pair of birth parents as anybody else in the world.'"

"Wow, this is just kind of surreal," Justin channeled me channeling Knick. "I am so glad you made contact with her. And she is confirming she is your bio mom, right?"

"Not in such precise terms," my oft coy wife said, "but she acknowledged it was Dr. Leggio who helped her, and also led her to believe that he was simultaneously helping his friends, my parents, Dr. O'Neal & Ducky." Red winked, "She did some of her own research."

"How are you feeling?" Justin asked. "Any sense of concern on your part?"

"No," Edie insisted. "I may be projecting, but she just sounds like we have the same heart. Or at least the heart I hope I have," my love shared. "We both keep repeating how concerned we are about the possibility of hurting someone to the point of not wanting to take that risk."

"Sounds familiar," Justin replied.

Later that Tuesday, we managed to distract ourselves at the Cavells' home along the route of the annual Kenilworth neighborhood Independence Day Parade, which rolls on the third of July because it's Baton Rouge. Guests enjoyed my acclaimed bourbon mint slush punch, as well as some bullhorn-aided heckling of Congressman Garret Graves. I couldn't think of a better way to honor our Founding Fathers.

It was already early Wednesday morning when we got home. We went to bed without reading the two emails Susan had sent while I loudly and repeatedly asked Graves if it was true that he sold his spine for beer money as a college student at the University of Alabama.

"Having a lot to process after the past few days," Susan wrote in the first message, "I thought we both might need a bit of a break from questions." She'd found links to the 1968 and 1970 editions of the *Gumbo*, but not 1969. "I wasn't able to see the pictures you found. Did you happen to copy them in a shareable format? (Oops, that was a question, but at least it wasn't a tough one.)

"You and your friend found things about my Mom being in clubs that I'm not even sure about," she added. "The one organization that was near and dear to her heart that I fully embraced was Girl Scouts. We can go into a lot of that later," Susan wrote.

"In case you don't already have them," she continued, "I'm attaching a couple of VERY old pictures. One is my Mom's father, Grandpa Weis," the mostly bald county health commissioner whose image we'd seen during all the sleuthing. "Everybody called him 'Doctor' but me, I think. The other is my family in costume from the first time we moved to The Netherlands. (The costumes were provided by the photographer at the 'tourist' place where we had the picture made. We definitely didn't dress like that every day!) In case you can't tell, I'm the one standing next to my dad," she wrote, confirming her identity in her Facebook cover photo.

"Happy fourth of July Eve!" She closed, "Love, Susan."

"Happy Independence Day!" Edie replied on Wednesday morning. "And thank you for the pictures! They are much sharper than the images we came across during our quest. And," she added with a smile, "it is nice to have a lighter exchange for the holiday.

"Wow, the FIRST time you lived in The Netherlands," Edie joked. "I was the only one of the O'Neal siblings who lived in the same home from Day One until 'leaving' for college (LSU wasn't much of a getaway, but it was across the river)." She also provided the proper link to the 1969 *Gumbo*, and the photograph of Susan therein. "You are somewhat obscured from view in the only picture we found you in."

Susan's initial, nearly question-free message of the evening came with the subject line "Easy Day." "Big Mistake" soon followed. Both sound like great horses to bet on.

"I just realized that I haven't mentioned the two other most important people in our lives," Susan confessed in the second message. "It wasn't intentional, and I sincerely apologize for the inadvertent omission.

"Your picture with Jeremy sent me a message that you are very happy together. His look also clearly reads, 'Don't you dare hurt my lady.' Jeremy," she addressed me, "let me tell you straight out that that's the furthest thing from my mind. We may not know where this journey will lead us, but I'm not in it for anything that doesn't work for all of us.

"Speaking of 'all of us,'" Susan wrote, "my Jeremy (actually Emery) goes by the name of 'Skip.' We've been together for thirty-three years —married for almost thirty-one. He's my best friend, partner, and the only other person in the world who comes anywhere close to knowing everything about me. That includes the rest of my immediate family.

"I hope that makes up for incomplete introductions for now." She signed off, "L, S."

In her reply to Susan's "Big Mistake," Edie allayed her mother's apprehension about my resting bitch face.

"Good morning!" my wife started with a smile. "We got a kick out of your interpretation of Jeremy's look! He says he's OK with that. And we are very happy to learn that you and Skip share such a special relationship." She told Susan, "Today we are off to my oldest brother's house on False River, where there is a boat parade—and an even more spirited water balloon fight—each year." She grinned, "I think we're going to hang back and stay onshore this time around, however.

"I hope you have a wonderful day, and I look forward to our next exchange!" She closed with, "Love, Edie."

Email sent, we drove for New Roads to enjoy a gorgeous Wednesday with the O'Neals and their families. Nothing was said about our recent revelations. The popular Fourth of July bash was neither the time nor the venue for a remedial course on an unfolding, emotionally complex situation still early in the developmental stage.

In addition to Wade and Cindy hosting a ton of people coming and going all day, Red's brother was responsible for captaining their party barge around False River amid an armada of watercraft filled with alcohol-drinking, water-balloon-hurling revelers. We didn't have the requisite hour or so of uninterrupted time with just the O'Neals. They'd have to learn about Susan later.

Moreover, even if we did have some downtime, we likely wouldn't have broached the topic, anyway. When listing people who tend to steal others' thunder, I'd be in the top third. Edie, on the other hand, would be dead last. My Molly Marine ain't stealing nobody's thunder, especially America's on her birthday.

23

You Are So Loved

Susan offered more insight into her nomadic upbringing in a Thursday email to her daughter.

"You picked right up on a subject that highlights one big difference between the ways we grew up." She admitted, "I always envied the people who lived in the same place and grew up around the same people. That certainly was not the case for me. I'm not complaining (much), but there were challenges in living the way we did.

"My dad was a civil engineer responsible for the construction of chemical and oil refineries," she explained. "Because of what he did, we moved—a LOT! I changed schools about twenty times before I hit college. There were a few schools that I went to twice," Susan added, "but the breaks in between made them seem like starting over some-place new.

"The moves between the northern and southern parts of the USA and into Canada were some of the most challenging," Edie learned. "Children, being children, could pick up on any little difference in accents and make a newcomer's life difficult. I got skilled at picking up new accents very quickly.

"I always told myself that I'd never move again once I was on my own. That didn't work!" The communications company Susan worked for moved her four times before her "first retirement."

"I trust you had a good time playing with family at False River." Susan recounted, "We used to go there with family friends during the summer when we lived in Baton Rouge.

"I know you're busy with work and other things," she continued, "so don't ever think you have to answer right away. It's just that I think of things and want to share them with you." Susan conceded, "I'm horrible on the phone, but we can work up to that.

"Have a great rest of the week!" She closed, "Love, Susan."

Four days after first contact with her, we were getting ready for that weekend's return trip to Austin, several hours in the opposite direction from Susan.

"Hi sis!" Edie messaged Rachel on Thursday, about an hour after Susan's latest email. The two sisters soon settled on meeting for breakfast Sunday, before our trip to Victoria. Saturday's plan called for travel from Baton Rouge to Austin, where we'd spend the evening with John and Hallie.

"Best summer ever!" Rachel declared with three celebration emojis. "Full of the best surprises ever!"

I threw our bags into the Rogue on Friday afternoon, and picked up Edie at work on the way to Maringouin for her weekly business. Ducky, an incredible cook, offered us supper, a place to stay the night, and lots of love and support for our upcoming Texas weekend.

That same afternoon, John sent an email to five people, including his eldest. The subject for this assemblage of 749 words was "Emergency room."

Justin soon popped up on Facebook Messenger.

"John went to the ER early this morning," he reported. "He is home now and fine." Justin explained that their dad "had a fall in the bathroom and banged his head. Likely he fell asleep on the toilet, or just stayed too long on it, and his legs came out from under him. He has bruises, a scrape, and a neck strain/ache."

"Oh no!" Edie replied. "I talked to him this morning and he told me he had fallen, but didn't mention the ER."

"I think the ER was just a precaution because of his history of head injuries," Justin offered. "I am certain he will be very pleased to see you. Give him a hug for us, and maybe indulge his descriptions just a little extra."

As the two of us conversed on Friday evening in Ducky's kitchen with my previously known mother-in-law, my newly discovered one sent Edie another email. The name of our satirical publication, *The Red Shtick*, was the subject.

"I remember a news magazine from way back when I lived in Baton Rouge called *Gris Gris*," Susan wrote. "I loved the subtitle that read something like 'Covers Baton Rouge Like the Dieux.' I was a regular subscriber."

Susan mentioned how as a young communications consultant, one of her favorite customers was the man in charge of the newspaper where Edie used to work. "I was new in marketing at the time," she recalled, "and there were only about five females doing what I was doing in the state. He did absolutely everything to make me feel comfortable, and agreed with/purchased everything I recommended, to boot. There were times that we would actually sit in his office and just talk. Such a special man!"

Susan's memories of her time in Baton Rouge were proving far more pleasant than John's recollections.

"If my constant messages are starting to feel like spam," she continued, "I'm sorry. Maybe you can just stick them in a folder for when you're bored and want to be reminded about how wonderful the path you got to follow really was.

"Believe it or not," Susan revealed, "I'm a very private person. There's a reason I'm throwing all of this information out," she explained, "to try to let you know who I am. It's mostly because I want to know everything you want to tell me about you. It's also because," she added, "being a private person, I'm absolutely the only person who can answer some of the questions you might have. I mentioned the fact that Skip knows more about me than anybody else. The problem there is that he's ten years older than I am. That may not sound like a big deal, but 'I can't remember,' 'I don't know anything about that,' and facial expressions that look like he's trying to interpret sounds made by an alien are becoming more prevalent.

"I'm sure you have questions that have absolutely nothing to do with what I'm sharing," Susan closed. "I think it may be a good time for me to just wait for questions and answer them as best I can."

She signed off with a kiss and a capital S.

Edie replied from the road on Saturday, after Ducky saw us off with a hearty breakfast, heartier hugs, and more well wishes. For the sake of discretion, we departed Maringouin without ever mentioning that week's email exchanges.

"Please don't feel that you need to hold back on my account!" Edie sent Susan. "I wanted to give you space to not feel like I was pouncing on your every message and in need of an immediate reply. But I love them." She added, "I may not get too far in this one because I'm not so great at typing on the road (it's OK; Jeremy's driving). We visited Ducky in Maringouin last night to get a head start on a quick road trip to Texas to catch up with other family."

That led to Edie telling Susan about her "other parents," the Wagleys. "According to Earle, when I entered the picture," she explained, "Ducky brought me over and told her they were sharing me with them." Red added, "They have always been loving and extremely generous to all of my family.

"Well, this message certainly hasn't been much of a response (to your inquiries) yet, but I'm sharing an important part of who I am," she admitted, "which is not a skill of mine, either. Jeremy is the only one whom I've shared most of myself with. I've not asked many questions of you yet out of respect for your privacy, and my wish to avoid asking anything painful. And I'm also not really good on the phone," Edie smiled, "so we can both work toward that.

"To get back to your message," she continued, "I'm happy to hear that you were a *Gris Gris* fan! We take it as a great compliment whenever anyone likens us to that icon." Edie also explained to her private mother how I parked the podcast "since this AncestryDNA discovery, in order to avoid bringing it into the public conversation.

"Which brings me to another heavy question," she warned, "but it's based on respect for your privacy. One of our cousins contacted me through AncestryDNA to ask how I fit in." Edie mentioned John Lukas. "I do not want to overshare, so I would like to ask your comfort level in that regard. He is a Lukas, a nephew of your birth father, apparently one of many cousins who has wondered what became of you. If you would like to contact any of them," Susan read, "I am happy to ask for their email/mailing addresses. They have many fond memories of their Uncle Mike, who apparently never remarried but doted on them.

"Sorry, I did not mean to get so heavy," Edie apologized, "but even *The Red Shtick* tackles hard issues sometimes. I'll try to stay lighter next time around.

"We will be heading home Monday," she mentioned. "I hope you have a lovely weekend. Peace," she closed, "Edie."

Three weeks after first meeting Rachel, we made a second trip to Austin, the city Baton Rouge once tried to become. Both are southern state capitals with flagship universities, folks in a civic group called Austin 6 argued. How did Austin become known for its music, while Baton Rouge became known as the Big Raggedy? How did two seemingly similar cities end up so different, they wondered, fact-finding trip after fact-finding trip.

In short, Austin cherishes and nurtures its local creative talent, while Baton Rouge is the ultimate cover band town with a pervasive "if it's local, it's crap" attitude. It only took me one trip—and four years of producing shows with talented folks back home—to figure that out.

In the interim since our first road trip there, I had discovered the Rogue's ECO mode. We again made it to the Buc-ee's in Katy, minus the drafting, plus fuel to spare.

Around 4:30 p.m., we drove up in front of the Harts' home, largely obscured by front-yard greenery. The neighborhood dated back almost as far as Edie's father did. John was shopping for supper down the street. A youthful, gray-haired Hallie came out to greet us.

Like Susan, she was about a decade her partner's junior. Like her husband, Hallie was small-statured, and more than a bit energetic. The elementary educator proved just as active as John, but with far fewer health issues.

He soon walked in, after removing his shoes and leaving them on the stoop. Edie and I hugged John, assuring her father we had a good drive. He joined us at the table where we'd been catching up with Hallie.

As evening approached, we led John to the Rogue to help him finish his remaining errands for dinner. Walking out to the vehicle, I snapped my first pic of our return trip to Austin. On a glass-top table in the postcard-worthy front yard was what I believe to be a ceramic planter, one that strongly resembled pipes found at every American head shop. While it was small for a planter (about the size of a coffee mug), it would've taken a 1970s-John amount of weed to fill the bowl. Nevertheless, it was no cocaine Christmas card.

Our first stop was Sunshine Community Gardens, where John spends lots of time helping others by tending to their gardens when they're too busy. Among other things he picked were several handfuls of sweet potato greens he cut for a salad to accompany Hallie's ribeyes. His plot was along the perimeter, near a pair of large composting piles drawing a Hitchcockian number of birds. We also saw an enormous, alpha-male rooster who never skipped leg day at the gym.

Over at Central Market, John mounted a motorized shopping cart. Things got a bit dicey in the store as he tried to converse with us, which requires him to look at the speaker rather than where he's going. He damn near knocked down an endcap of stacked beer cans. We're not sure if that would've happened before his recent bathroom fall, but the latest bonk on the head certainly didn't help.

Back at the house, John showed us the backyard. Their cat, Dusty, was allegedly somewhere in there. It was so jungle-like, I'm surprised it didn't give John 'Nam flashbacks. He walked around barefoot, hunched over in the same boonie hat he wore to Seattle.

We went inside as the sun started to go down. Hallie steadily did her thing in the quaint kitchen, with John as sous chef. She's a talented cook, as advertised in his emails.

A few weeks before, back in Bothell, someone was visibly (and justifiably) surprised to learn that John was married. After spending a couple hours with the two of them, however, he and Hallie appeared happy together. They seemed to love and care for each other.

We all went to bed before it got too late. Rest was needed after that day's travels, and before those of the next. We crashed in the same room where Hallie's son slept whenever he visited.

Edie and I arose not long after sunup to prepare for that Sunday. John began stirring about the same time we did. He fixed us coffee and offered us a bit of breakfast in the form of a bowl of fresh, homegrown figs. I enjoyed the tasty sugar rush as John learned his eldest child is no fan of their texture. Justin's strawberry was one thing, but a fig was a bridge too far.

Hallie soon joined us as we slowly became more awake. We finished the rest of our coffee in the company of our hosts before hugging them goodbye, without mentioning that we were on the way to meet John's other daughter.

"Couldn't help but be early," Rachel messaged us from Cafe 290, in nearby Manor. "Just got here," she said with a grin.

"On our way!" Edie replied as I turned right off John and Hallie's street. While waiting to turn onto West Koenig Lane, I pointed out Thunderbird Coffee on the corner.

"Leaving John's to meet Rachel for breakfast," she messaged Patrick and Yvette. "His house is two blocks from the cafe we went to." She also reported, "John's wife, Hallie, is super nice, petite."

After driving fifteen minutes into the sunrise, we parked under a clear blue sky. I opened the door of the roadside diner for my wife to enter. Seconds later, Rachel was embracing her. My hug soon followed.

During the hour or so we enjoyed together, my sister-in-law told us about her looming move. Though such events are never fun, it was going to be especially difficult for her to lose her housemate, the one-eyed Heru.

"It will be very hard to leave him behind when I eventually move," Heru's person had stated in her initial email to Edie.

While we didn't discuss where the two of us had just been, we did talk about where we were going and who we were visiting on the final leg of the new Texas family tour. On multiple occasions during our conversation, I became acutely aware of how unaccustomed I was to seeing so much of my wife in another person.

Before our midmorning farewells, Edie brought up the ongoing email thread between the three of us and their West Coast kin. Justin had suggested a possible gathering with the Milsoms in Northern California in late September, when Cherish had a work-related event in the Bay Area. Edie told her younger sister that the two of us were strongly considering making the trip, and even more strongly hoping Rachel could come along. Another trip to Texas likely wouldn't happen before then, we explained.

Edie and I hugged Rachel goodbye. She headed to a gathering of gamer friends for a virtual experience, while we were destined for a surreal one in Victoria.

The Texas hills flattened out as we neared the coast. Our two-and-a-half-hour drive ended in front of an attractive prefabricated home partially obscured by large trees on an acre-plus lot. It featured a pond and a storm-damaged metal shed.

Gene's demure wife, Lynn, met us at the door. Inside, she introduced us to someone far too invigorated to be an almost-eighty-year-old stroke victim recovering from his third dialysis treatment of the week. To borrow Beth's description, Gene was...enthusiastic.

He practically leapt out of his wheelchair to throw his arms around Edie. It was like he was finally able to embrace a cousin who'd vanished when he was a kid.

An excited Gene led us to a desk in their hallway where he kept his collection of family photos dating back to when his Uncle Mike and Nancy Jane were still married. One picture showed his mother's family, the Novaks, dressed in their Sunday finest circa 1950. On the back were names and corresponding birth dates, marriage dates, and dates of passing.

An envelope accompanied another pair of black-and-white eight-by-tens. "May 6th, 1952, Helen & Ken Shell's 25th Anniversary & Mother's Day," the handwritten note read.

One photo was taken inside a home in East Chicago, Indiana, not far from Hammond. Thirteen adults—most smiling, one hamming it up a bit—either sat upon or stood around a white-draped sofa. Among those pictured were Edie's Grandpa Mike, his eight sisters (including Helen), his one brother (Gene's dad, the elder John Lukas), and their parents, Andrew and Mary. Making it a baker's dozen was Helen's hubby of twenty-five years, Ken. It was wall-to-wall high cheekbones.

In the other eight-by-ten, the patriarchal garbage truck driver/Capone bootlegger joined the former Sklarczyk on the porch with the rest of the Lukaczyks. Edie's great-grandparents sat atop the steps, surrounded by thirty-one people, one of whom was a priest. The rest represented the family they'd raised in America.

Sunday, July 8, 2018, marked the day we began to appreciate how, among the Lukaczyks, this photo was much more infamous than Andrew's extra-legal "business associate."

His daughter-in-law Nancy Jane, in those same glasses, stood behind Andrew, next to the priest. Her husband, Mike, and his brother stood in front of the porch, to the right of the steps. Like the Novak family photo, everyone was dressed up.

The dozen kids from Gene's generation were either flanking the steps or sitting on them. Preteen Gene looked like he wanted to be anywhere but in that suit.

Sitting on the top step in front of her parents, Paula's mom, Julie, was one of three people photographed looking at something off-camera to the right. The other two distracted Lukaczyks were a toddler in the lap of Julie's sister Anna Jean, and a slightly older child on the lowest row of kids seated on the steps, all the way to the right.

Julie seemed to be gasping in surprise at something out of view, while the toddler didn't have a clue what was going on. The two-and-a-half-year-old girl at the bottom, meanwhile, wore a look of terror; her pose suggested she was cowering from whatever was drawing her gaze. Upon closer inspection, however, the slightly older cousin seated next to the little girl had his left arm around her and was squeezing her in.

Edie and I recognized that look. She wasn't cowering from something off-camera. Paula and Carole's older brother Ron was keeping Susan from bolting out of the photograph.

Not long after this moment was captured, Nancy Jane took off with Mike's only child. As far as the Lukaczyks were concerned, it's the last known image of Susan. For the next half-century, it would have to suffice for Edie's grandfather in lieu of ever seeing his daughter again.

Almost immediately, Gene began trying to determine which aunt looked most like his Louisiana cousin. It was a toss-up between Helen and Theresa. I noted some resemblance in Katie, as well.

During our drive to Texas, John Lukas promised that Gene "will tell you Hollywood stories forever." Edie's cousin did not disappoint.

He talked about owning and driving a truck hired out by movie studios. With minimal backstory for context, Gene began regaling us with stories about his unorthodox, yet profitable, enterprises.

My wife's kin practically had a gleam in his eye as he told us how, as a union member, he never loaded or unloaded the truck. His job was to drive the vehicle where it was supposed to go, and nothing more. With surprising force, Gene asked, "Why work? That's stupid." His face remained as lit up as it'd been since our arrival.

Instead of waiting around during that day's film shoot, Gene told us how he'd use his unloaded truck to buy large quantities of auto parts, to later sell them at a profit to his fellow motor enthusiasts, all while on the studio's dime. The dude was a straight-up hustler, and proud of it.

In his early teen years in East Chicago, Gene and an equally ambitious partner bought a railcar full of peaches for fifty cents a pallet, and sold them door-to-door to the old-country buscias in their neighborhoods for $1.25 a pallet. The two moved every pallet by hand, which likely explains why he later refused to unload his truck.

Around that same time, Gene said, he got taken into police custody in Chicago for driving without a license on account of the fact he was fourteen. He was such a smooth talker, the cop was ready to let him go—until our host mouthed off to him. For his one phone call, he dialed a woman connected to the leadership of an area organization. The matriarch of this particular "family," for whom he had done work, went straightway to the precinct and got that good boy out of jail.

One of the few members of the horde to have exploits outside the Hoosier State, Gene said he got tired of living on the farm with his father, so he left to join the Marines because he knew it would piss off his old man.

There are worse reasons for joining the military, especially the Corps, but not many.

Gene told us how he sort of stumbled into his Hollywood career after hearing there was money to be made there. He recalled trying to help Paul Newman's son in his battle against drug addiction. After Scott Newman lost that struggle in 1978, Gene said, the legendary actor let him know that his efforts did not go unappreciated.

One of his best stories involved Gene driving Shelley Winters and some men in a crowded luxury car owned by a studio. The actress sat next to Gene, in the middle of the front seat. In the back was a man letting everyone know that he was in gastrointestinal distress.

Tired of his bellyaching, the two-time Oscar winner emphatically advised, "You'd feel a lot better if you just let rip a big old fart."

Gene laughed so hard, he crashed the car. When he called the studio with the news, the fellow told Gene not to worry about it. It may have been the same guy he referenced in his otherwise most memorable line of the day.

"I used to work for [so-and-so]. He was a pedophile. Good guy. Good guy."

"Oh, Gene," a meek Lynn lamented. From across the room, she looked on in a bit of horror, reminiscent of young Susan's face, as though she was helplessly watching her husband fall off the wagon.

Gene also entertained us with a tale about whipping the ass of a close relative. Or maybe they whipped his ass. I'm not sure who whipped whom's ass, but it seemed like ass whippings were not all that rare during Gene's upbringing.

"Such a violent family," Lynn directed our way.

I likely can't recall whose ass was being whipped because I was trying so damn hard not to bust out laughing at the dichotomy before us. To our left was Gene, waxing enthusiastic; to the right was his wife, shaking her head with disapproval.

Edie's cousin also made it clear that Al Capone was a beloved figure among Chicago's working class. Other than a little incident on February 14, 1929, he was practically a saint.

Of my wife's two maternal great-grandfathers, one was the county health commissioner. The other was affiliated with the guy who orchestrated the Valentine's Day Massacre. I don't understand how the marriage didn't last.

Around 4 p.m., we followed our hosts to a nearby hibachi place, where we enjoyed the culinary show with Lynn's daughter, her husband, and his brother. Afterward, we helped Gene into their BMW's passenger seat. He bid us farewell with big hugs and some colorful descriptions of where he'd like to eat if given the chance to visit us in Baton Rouge.

As with Ducky, we never mentioned communicating with Susan.

From our hotel room a little later, Edie called Paula, following an earlier text from Indiana. During the ensuing forty-six-minute call, Paula asked if her cousin had made contact with Susan yet. Edie said no.

Turns out, Susan had contacted Paula on Facebook Messenger.

"I'm sorry if you're not the person I was looking for, but I found the name Paula Teibel listed as niece on the copy of a death certificate I requested from the State of Indiana for Michael Lukaczyk," she wrote. "If I found the right person, I believe that would make us cousins."

Susan added, "You can certainly unfriend me if none of this makes sense, and I do apologize if I've contacted you in error."

"OMG!" Paula replied with her phone number. "We've been looking for you for years!"

"This is all so crazy," Susan answered her long-lost cousin. "I had believed the door to that part of my past was locked when I found out he was gone." She said she needed to catch her breath before a phone call. "I never dreamed this could really happen—and so quickly!"

"Better late than never," Paula sent back.

Once Edie realized that the two cousins were already chatting and swapping phone numbers, my wife admitted to being in contact with Susan. She explained to Paula how she vowed not to reveal that tidbit to the horde yet.

"Great visit with cousin Gene," Edie updated Patrick and Yvette as they drove home from Grand Isle, "then phone call with cousin Paula, who received a Facebook friend request from Susan!"

As that chat session wound down, Susan sent her daughter an email with the subject "Family Ties."

"The tsunami has broken apart and is sending earthquakes, wildfires, and tornadoes in different directions," she led off. "I'm trying to keep up and find myself laughing, crying, and shaking my head in amazement at the same time.

"Your mention of contacting the other side of my family (Michael's) led me to look back (just today!) at the copy of his death certificate," Susan said. "I found the name of a niece named Paula on it and took a chance on finding her on Facebook." Seeing Edie was also friends, "I took a chance that she might respond to a friend request from me, too. Bingo," she reported, "and thanks for the push!

"Since you're so far ahead of me on all of this," Susan mentioned, "I need to know whether you've reached out to any of the people in my life now. I have to ask, because my family is VERY complicated," she explained, "and I'm not good at handling drama.

"Hope you had a good trip," Susan closed, "and have a good week ahead.

"Love you! S."

Her child replied on our way home Monday.

"Oh wow! I am so happy that you reached out to Paula!" Edie wrote back. "And I have not attempted any contact with anyone who has been in your life. That's a boundary I won't cross," she promised. "I don't like drama, either, and certainly don't want to create more disturbances than I already have."

Edie explained how John Lukas thought our Victoria visit "would be a good pick-me-up for Gene, who has had some health issues recently that kept him from attending a gathering to meet the brother they just discovered in January through AncestryDNA." She added, "Gene had some family photos that we took pictures of." Edie attached them, and listed all the names from the indoor photo taken on the couch. "Spouses and children join them in the other pic," she said. "Jeremy spotted your mom in the center, top row, and we are guessing you may be the toddler up front."

She was.

"We are now driving back home in the rain," Edie noted, "but see hope of blue skies ahead. I hope you are able to weather these storms of emotion well, too." She closed, "Love, Edie."

That same Monday morning, she learned that Susan and her cousin had actually done more than just converse online.

"Talked to Susan last night," Paula texted Edie. "I accidentally butt dialed her. I thought I hung up fast enough," she said, "but she called me back!"

Edie replied with three exclamation points.

"I told her she didn't have to talk to me if she wasn't ready," the Hoosier insisted. "She wanted to! Just like we thought," Paula relayed, "she was lied to. Nancy also didn't tell the judge the truth when her husband adopted Susan."

Edie did not bring up the butt dial in her email to Susan. Nor did she show the slightest bit of jealousy about Paula talking to Susan before she did. After all, Paula had been waiting to talk to her cousin much longer than Edie had been waiting to speak with her mother.

Later that Monday afternoon, another cousin texted.

"I talked to Paula this morning," Carole sent from South Carolina, "and she shared your/Susan's/our Great News! This story, and how it's unfolding," she wrote, "is amazing and exciting! You are so loved! Here's to love, healing, and heart connections! Cheers!"

"This is so awesome," my navigator replied. "I am so happy for all of us!"

Edie also spent part of the day updating her little sister, who was curious how things went.

"You didn't talk about Susan," Rachel said of our time with Gene, "but did you feel a connection to him?"

"He is a character, for sure," Edie replied. "He pulled me in for a big hug right off the bat. I think we hit it off better than I had hoped," she remarked. "He has an abundance of stories to tell, and I am a good listener."

"Wonderful!" Rachel enthused. "I'm so happy it is going well!"

Edie also sent Justin an update on Monday. In addition to all the Lukaczyk news—including Susan finally beginning decades' worth of catching up with the horde—Edie told Justin about our separate meetings with their father and sister.

"Had a great breakfast visit with Rachel yesterday morning," she shared, "when we learned she's moving probably a block away from him." Edie added that we "did not take bait with either to discuss the other."

Later, I shared with Fort Worth some of the Gene-isms learned in Victoria.

"I've been thinking about starting doing drugs again," the Marine told us. "A little cocaine never hurt anyone." At the time, I didn't think to tell him Edie's father probably still knows a guy or two.

During our drive home Monday, my passenger spied the greenery along the roadside, featuring a plant both she and our hermana are fond of.

"John's yard is full of wild Texas sunflowers," she messaged Yvette and Patrick. "It was all I could do to resist trying to bring some home."

The first of several photos I took on the trip showed a planter in John's lush yard that looked like it could get the whole street high. The final pic snapped featured a funnel cloud, loitering on the north side of the interstate around Beaumont as we drove past that afternoon. Given all the crazy twists and turns in the past few days—and the fact that we certainly weren't in Kansas anymore, Toto—it seemed like a fitting closing image.

24

The Hub

Tuesday, July 10, began with an overnight email from an excited cousin Erica in California about the proposed gathering in late September. "We can make that happen!" she wrote in the group thread on behalf of herself and her husband, Ben Choi.

"We also are looking forward to the opportunity to meet our California family," Edie messaged everyone, including her new sibs, "and see our Seattle family again!"

A week and a dozen emails later, Cherish booked a Sonoma County home, in the heart of California wine country, just over an hour north of the Milsom-Chois in Richmond. We'd stay in the rental three nights before checking out on the last Sunday of September.

"Woohoo!" Edie raved, "Cherish is awesome! The AirBNB looks fabulous," she said of accommodations for the first-ever gathering of John Hart's three (known) kids, "and we are so looking forward to this weekend together!"

By the following evening, all travelers—including Rachel—had booked their flights to the Bay Area.

"Excited excited excited!" is how Edie described herself to Justin in the midst of planning the trip a couple days before. "Football is definitely taking a back seat this fall," she said, "or getting benched."

Edie's little brother received that message just after she hung up with Crown Point, Indiana, where eight cousins from Susan's generation were gathered at John Lukas's home in mid-July. Paula sent Edie a pic of them before the call, allowing us to put faces to the voices we heard as the phone got passed around cousin John's backyard. One of them belonged to Lois, a young girl in the 1952 Mother's Day photo, sitting in plaid just behind Susan.

We also got the chance to talk to John's wife, Mira, during the twenty-one-minute Sunday afternoon call. As the photographer, she was not in the backyard photo of the gathering. My brain had a hard time not associating her voice with a famous Chicago native who unsuccessfully ran for president.

The next day, Edie created a Facebook Messenger thread with Paula and John Lukas to discuss potential dates for a weeklong visit with them in September or October. "We figured we'd need at least that long to give us a reasonable shot of catching up with folks," she explained Monday.

"And to check out the area," Paula added.

"You better believe it," John Lukas confirmed.

Edie said she'd run the proposed dates by Susan.

"YEA!" Paula exclaimed.

Moments later, Edie sent me screenshots of direct flights from New Orleans to Chicago. She also sent an email to Susan about possibly joining us.

"We are just so happy about the prospect of getting to know you and our extended family," Edie wrote on Monday. "That's the source of our smiles. I hope your day may be filled with them, too."

"Flying into which airport up there?" Susan replied the next day. "We've got a bunch of Delta skymiles. I've got some Southwest ones, too, I think."

"Omg omg omg," Edie soon messaged me on Tuesday, "I think Indiana with Susan might be happening!"

I responded with a love reaction and an animated GIF of a surprised Jessica Jones from *The Daily Show.*

Two days later came an email from Susan. The subject line was "Timing."

"I really want to go to Indiana as soon as I can," she lamented on Thursday, "but I've already got a commitment here that I can't abandon." In a separate email, Susan explained how she was the only nearby kin of a Texas cousin who was in New Orleans for an extended stay at Ochsner Hospital, including stretches in ICU. "If I thought we could make plans—and that that would magically ensure that my cousin would get better—I'd do it. Life just doesn't work that way, though," she noted. "I just have to be here right now. We can talk more about why when we get together.

"Things could change for the better tomorrow or next week," Susan countered with optimism, "and maybe they'll get everything working right so she can go back to Texas. If/when that happens," she said, "I'll be elated for her, and be ready to look at schedules to get away, too.

"I hope this doesn't disappoint you too much, because I don't want you to feel disappointed at all. It's not a never," she insisted. "It's just a later.

"Love," she closed, "Susan."

By sundown Thursday, Edie had booked our flights to Chicago's Midway Airport. She also passed along Susan's news to Indiana.

"I would love it if Susan were able to come with us this time around," Edie reported to her Hoosier cousins, "but she is committed to taking care of a family member in the hospital right now." She added, "But we can't wait to see y'all!"

Forty-eight hours after slating an essentially five-day trip to the West Coast in late September, we scheduled a week in northwest Indiana just after Labor Day. The two of us would be out of state for nearly half the first full month of the regular football season. Edie was quickly blowing through her allotment of vacation days at work.

The previous weekend began with Edie freaking out over an incoming call on her iPhone.

"Omg," Edie messaged me that Friday, "I just got a call from a 504 New Orleans number."

"Oh shit," I reacted. "Does it match hers?"

"I answered just in case it might be; I haven't put hers in my contacts," Edie explained. "And as I answered, I was like, 'WTH am I doing taking this call in my office while my phone is plugged into the charger?'"

"So it wasn't her," I surmised.

"Thank god it was a bot."

I LOL'd and sent my wife Susan's number from the phone book.

The next evening, almost two weeks since her first email, Susan sent Edie another.

"It's been a crazy week," she wrote that Saturday. "I kept getting ahead of myself trying to plan meeting you. I'd talked myself into believing that you wouldn't be totally disappointed to find that I'm not 'young and beautiful' as you'd pictured me. You've got enough of that for both of us," Susan told her daughter. "We might be able to find some old pictures of me that would show me in a far better light. You're creative, and you have a good imagination. I just know that." She winked, "It's one of those things I learned when I played with handwriting analysis.

"I'd even thought about a place we could meet that I could actually find in Baton Rouge," Susan passed along, asking if we knew of the Pastime Restaurant. "But then I realized that I have no idea what your schedule looks like," she followed up. "From what I've been reading, it might be tough getting a spot on your calendar!"

Following an update on her cousin in ICU, Susan closed with a query. "So, how was your week?" She signed off, "Love and happy thoughts, S."

Edie replied that same Saturday night before bed.

"I am so happy to hear from you," she led, "and had hoped that 'young and beautiful' line wouldn't be a hangup. There I go again," my apologetic wife wrote, "creating pressure despite my best intentions. Compliments aren't an easy thing for me to accept, and I also should know better, given the weight of expectations I felt I had to live up to in earlier days; but I wrote that a couple years ago, and refused to let my editorial instincts overwrite my heart. As far as I am concerned," Edie maintained, "you are a lovely person with a beautiful heart and youthful spirit, and I will make time to meet you anywhere! But certainly, please take the time you need right now to attend to your cousin."

She told Susan how Doc O'Neal introduced her to Pastime after an LSU football game when she was around ten years old. "And we are happy to come your way," my wife added. "We will be in New Orleans the last weekend of July, so perhaps we could meet up that Sunday, July 29? (Not saying we need to wait until then; just wanted to mention that option.)

"As far as this past week, I was so excited about you getting to connect with your cousin," Edie said of the returned butt dial, "but also a bit concerned that I had not been thoughtful enough in my handling of this whole situation. I still felt guilty about fibbing to Paula early in our phone conversation by not admitting that you and I had corresponded, even though I came clean after she revealed that she had connected with you."

Turning to work, she told Susan, "My boss is fabulous, by the way. She is aware of this family discovery adventure we are on, and has told me that I can take time off whenever necessary to make these connections."

Following an update on our trivia team's Thursday night performance, Edie reported, "Today has been the best day by far: a phone call with a brother this morning, a movie and dinner with Jeremy, then emails from you this evening—smiles all around!

"I hope that your cousin's situation improves soon," she offered. "Both of you are in our thoughts. Love," she closed Saturday, "Edie."

The next afternoon, on the way back from her Sunday Maringouin visit, my wife texted me. Because Edie didn't yet have Susan's cell number, she explained, "I had an excuse to not call and make a lunch date for Mom."

Edie visited Ducky, who'd recently submitted her DNA, to deliver Ancestry's pie chart breaking down my mother-in-law's ethnicity. She also delivered news about discovering and communicating with her birth mother. Ducky responded by telling her youngest to set up a "girls lunch" at Ruth's Chris Steakhouse in Metairie for the two of them, plus Susan and Kellie.

"Eek!" she later messaged Justin about the encounter that same afternoon. "It was all I could do to escape my mom's house," Edie retold, "to get home to a 5,000-word email from John with the subject line 'please call.'" An emoji expressed her shock at John's longest email. "I walked into the house and grabbed a beer instead of my meal replacement shake," she winked.

"Please work with me, guide me to YOUR focus," were some of John's 5,100 words. "My mind has a kaleidoscope of fascination from art to physics, from childhood, it easily tries to relate the infinite possibilities in each moment."

That same Sunday, she also read and sent messages to coordinate multiple trips across the country with a dozen people we'd known for as little as a few weeks, some of whom would be serving as our hosts and chauffeurs. There was also that twenty-one-minute phone call with some of those hosts and chauffeurs, gathered in John Lukas's backyard. You know, the ones who had been looking for Edie's mother decades before my wife was even born.

There were all these people in all these cities. If, like an airline, you drew out the connections between them—Seattle, Austin (John), Austin (Rachel), San Francisco Bay Area, Chicago Metro, Victoria, Maringouin, Metairie—Baton Rouge would be the hub connecting them all; and airspace was getting perilously crowded. Nevertheless, my wife did a bang-up job ensuring nobody had a bad day because of her.

She would have been perfectly justified in telling her adoptive mother that we had no idea how much remaining baggage needed to be unpacked before Edie could even think of setting up a meeting between Ducky and Susan. But she didn't. With only a few hours remaining on her "day off," she still needed to get back to the hub. There were birds aloft waiting to hear back from the tower. She did what was needed to avert potential disaster.

In a Tuesday email to Susan a couple days later, Edie frowned that we couldn't make Paula's beloved Pierogi Fest in Whiting, Indiana, because we'd be attending a football officiating convention in New Orleans that weekend. "My frown will turn upside down if we get to catch up with you that weekend, however," she smiled.

"What does your schedule look like for your event here next weekend?" Susan emailed two days later. "We're still good with coming up there any time that's good for you." She had mentioned Pastime because she wanted to meet "where we could have a bit of privacy."

Susan then admitted, "I don't know how to move forward. I want to find some way to connect," she wrote, "but this is something I'd given up on happening. I'm so glad it has, but I want it to be right for you.

"Help!?" she signed off Thursday, "L, S."

In her response the next evening, Edie promised to share whatever she and Beth had uncovered, and allayed Susan's concerns about reciprocating with photographs and other family memorabilia.

"I am happy to see anything you are willing to share," Edie emailed Friday. "Please don't feel stressed to pull together everything for this first meeting! I am hopeful that it is just that: a first, not an only," she explained, "a chance for us just to be together and alleviate any anxiety over that first meeting. I'm sorry if my initial correspondence raised the stress level," she again apologized. "I wrote that poem out of a feeling of 'What would I most want to say if I only had one chance?' But I'm also trying to keep in check that part of me that's a little anxious that I don't have much interesting about myself to contribute, aside from the research. Please know that I really just want to meet you," she wrote, "even if I don't know what to say or ask, and love you regardless, and hope that you won't think I'm too horrible."

My wife also informed Susan that our football officiating convention the following weekend would leave open that Sunday, the last of July.

"Let's get this straight from the get-go," Susan replied later that same Friday night, "we don't know each other, but we both want to. We both have obligations that keep us from being able to do everything we want to do as soon as we think of doing them. We're both very determined to work past obstacles and make things happen—maybe not as soon as we want them to, but when we can work past the obstacles.

"As I mentioned to you before," she continued, "there are several things/people in my life that are 'complicated.' I may tell you about some of them over time, but none of them are anything for you to be concerned about. Nothing scary, nothing that you have to worry about healthwise, just 'complicated.'" Susan also noted, "There are some things you've told me about yourself that sound similar to traits that I have."

She vowed to her apologetic daughter, "There's nothing for you to be sorry about. I want you in my life and hope we can get past all of the scary parts that might challenge us in making that happen."

Edie's mother also mentioned, "Skip and I go to Gator's Den in Manchac," between Baton Rouge and New Orleans, "sometimes on Sundays. We usually go early and are back in Metairie by about 2 p.m. Could that be a possibility on your way back home next weekend?" Susan proposed. "Evenings are a little tough for us any day of the week, because we turn into pumpkins and have to be home by about six," she sent on Friday at 9:30 p.m., well past Skip's bedtime.

"The Gator's Den sounds like fun!" Edie sent back on Saturday afternoon. "We can definitely do that next Sunday." She also mentioned finding an album that Ducky had composed of photos from Edie's infancy into her college days.

"We are so excited to see you," my wife continued, "and thank you for the reassurance about getting past all the scary parts. I don't know how much support you had when I first came into the picture, and I don't want to create stress by complicating things now." Edie smiled, "I am just so grateful that we have this opportunity to get to know each other now, with the love and support of Skip and Jeremy." She signed off with "Love, Edie."

"This is actually happening," Susan wrote back that same Saturday night. "I'm so excited!" She also requested we meet at Gator's Den's opening time of 11 a.m. the following weekend to maximize time together before that afternoon's band began their sound check.

"My mom put together a picture book that sounds like Ducky's," Susan reported. "Sharing them should be a great icebreaker." She also gave us a heads-up about Gator's Den's typical clientele: "a bunch of older guys" and "some bikers" passing through. "All easy-going banter," she promised. "I hope Jeremy is okay with that. Just warn him about Skip's jokes. They're sometimes very old, and sometimes he gets the punchlines messed up," she winked.

"Have a great week!" Susan closed with love, and a postscript that most of her post-retirement wardrobe "consists of jeans and T-shirts. They fit in just fine at Gator's Den. L, S."

Shortly after nightfall Sunday, her daughter responded to confirm their first meeting in one week.

"Yes! This sounds great!" Edie enthused. "Jeremy is well-versed in awful jokes," she smiled, "and even the host at last night's show had trouble delivering punchlines after a year of practice."

That same Sunday, John Lukas messaged. "Every minute is going to feel like an hour until you're here with us." After setting up the long-awaited meeting with Susan, we completely empathized with Edie's Indiana kin.

"Busy?" she asked me during lunch Monday.

"Whatcha got?" I messaged back.

"Just got off the phone with cousin Paula," Edie reported. "She just texted me a pic of Susan that I haven't looked at yet because I'm not with you," she explained. "And because Susan hasn't sent it to me yet, because I didn't push like Paula did," she winked.

"You can call me if it's too much," I insisted.

While she didn't call me, she did admit, "Not sure if I can ignore my phone for the next four hours."

At home after work, she finally opened Paula's text. We looked at the picture together.

It was taken in an establishment worthy of the moniker Gator's Den. Susan and Skip were cozied up together at the corner of a table with a few drinks on it. Behind them, horizontal blinds partially occluded bright daylight.

Susan wore a plain olive-colored T-shirt, a decorative vest, and a set of glasses reminiscent of Nancy Jane's spectacles. The eyes. The chin. The jawline. The cheekbones. The eyebrows. The forehead. The smile. Jesus Christ, that all-too-familiar "I'd really rather not take this picture" smile. They all screamed "Edie's mother."

Skip had a vibrant smile, equally vibrant blue eyes, and a visor corralling his white hair. He wore a white sports-themed sweatshirt with his right arm around Susan.

"Thank you!" Edie texted Paula on Monday afternoon. "I somehow managed to wait until I got home from work before looking."

"This will sound weird," Paula replied, "but she was kind of reluctant to send it to me. I don't know how she would feel about me sending it to you."

Actually, no, it didn't sound weird at all, because I know my wife. I also know that apples, especially beautiful red ones, often don't fall far from the tree.

"Yeah," Edie gently answered her cousin, "I was thinking about that, too."

"I don't want her mad before we've even all met," Paula said.

"I think we'll be ok," Edie reassured. "We're planning to meet Sunday." My wife promised to call Indiana afterwards.

Paula later texted a photo of Grandpa Mike sticking his tongue out at the camera with a plate of food before him. "This is what happened when you tried to take a picture of your grandfather!" she laughed. "It's one of my favorite pictures."

The Fort Worth thread soon came to life that same Monday.

"Uh, is that Susan?" Patrick asked after seeing the new photo. "Because now I know what you're going to look like in a few decades minus the curl."

"Can confirm Sunday," Edie answered. "Sssssshhh."

"Meeting?" he asked. "Yay. I can stay shhhhh."

"Gator's Den in Manchac," she confirmed.

"I'm nervous," Patrick admitted.

"All will be well," Edie reassured her big brother. "Doesn't she look nice? Though I am a bit nervous that I have a nonpublic photo that she didn't give me. I almost didn't look at it," she shared. "I waited five hours till I got home. She and her dad apparently both hate(d) taking pictures as much as I do," my wife winked.

"Well, I think she's beautiful," Patrick wrote back, "and I think you're beautiful, and it's amazing to see the similarities."

"Justin, Rachel, and I all got John's hair," Red said, "and nose."

"Honestly," he told his little sister, "from a distance, I thought it was you in that picture. It's the smile," Patrick noted. "Yours all the way."

The next day, five before Manchac, John sent a 177-word email message. The subject line had eighty-three words, all of which were seemingly intended for the body of the message.

Four minutes later, his daughter called him. They spoke for just over an hour that Tuesday night.

The following afternoon, Edie messaged Justin about the call. She finished by mentioning that John was still "doubting the DNA."

Moments later, before Justin had a chance to respond in our three-person chat thread, Edie sent me a separate message about including that comment. "Guess I shouldn't have typed that last bit," she told me, "just lost my shit again."

"I wouldn't worry about it too much," I attempted to console her. "His brain is all screwed up. He means well."

"Yeah, he does," Edie agreed. "And it makes me realize more that I kinda need to figure out what I do/don't want to ask Susan."

"He just can't get over not remembering someone he impregnated," I added.

"He has so much respect for women who don't abuse him," she shared. "Also gaining more appreciation for Rachel's perspective."

Some fifteen minutes later that Wednesday, Justin responded to John doubting the science.

"He has a lot of emotional baggage about being an absent father," John's son explained. "I wish he would just accept the realities of each of our situations and not dwell on the way any of us, his children, have come into this world or made our way through it." Justin also shared that "John's family has always judged him harshly."

"Thank you again for the helpful perspective," Edie answered. "Love you!"

Justin closed the chat session with a Father's Day picture of him and Hadley, like an adorable salve to soothe his sister's angst. By Wednesday evening, both Justin and Rachel knew about our upcoming trips to Manchac and Indiana.

Their father kicked off our three-day weekend—set to culminate in a reunion with the woman he cannot remember impregnating—with a predawn email.

"The sun rises and sets, the world turns, and new beginnings," was a standalone paragraph at the start of the 808-word message sent at 5:03 a.m. Friday. "I am still alive," was another in the middle. "Be safe, and do a better job of taking care of yourself than I have," he began to wrap up with a smile. "YES!" he shouted in one line. "You and Susan," was the next. "Much love, appreciation, and support," followed before he signed off, "John."

En route by midmorning to the largest-ever gathering of zebras outside of Africa, Edie received an email from Susan. The subject indicated a "Possible Problem."

"In ER with Skip," she wrote from the hospital. Susan's husband was set to momentarily receive a pacemaker following a routine checkup. "Will keep you posted," she wrote, "but we may need to postpone our Sunday plans." Susan added, "Don't be worried. Everything is going to be fine." She threw in a thumbs-up with her now customary sign-off, "L, S."

"Oh no!" Edie answered before midday Friday. "That's definitely all you need to focus on now," she assured. "Don't worry about us. We'll be thinking about you," Edie sent with her love.

"Should be coming out shortly," Susan soon messaged back. "Doctor said he should be able to go home tomorrow. Told you not to worry," she said. "He's a tough old guy."

That evening, Edie and I walked around the French Quarter, where my wife's ear caught a quality rendition of Guns N' Roses coming from The Famous Door, on Bourbon and Conti. As we began walking toward the entrance, I realized that the drummer with his back to Bourbon Street in the plate-glass window was my cousin Sammy, whom I grew up with down the bayou, and hadn't seen in over a decade.

If nothing else, at least one family reunion would happen that weekend.

"I hope everything goes well with your mom tomorrow," Justin messaged Edie the following afternoon. "You have the perfect approach to this very emotional experience." He also offered, "Hugs!"

Edie thanked her brother and explained that the meeting was in doubt due to Skip's recovery. "That's priority for now."

By sundown Saturday, mother and daughter had traded lighthearted emails, including one from Susan claiming Skip was already driving her nuts after being released that afternoon. His need for pain medication would determine whether tomorrow's meeting would happen or not.

"Selfishly," Susan admitted, "I just really want to meet you. I actually had some 'good' news to share about my cousin." Her ailing kin was recently back in Texas. "I was going to surprise you with the news," she revealed, "because I thought it might make my going north with you possible. Surprise!"

The woman with a flair for employing the word "surprise" said she'd give us a heads-up in the morning.

Storms rolling through the city on Saturday evening kept us from venturing out into the Quarter again. Hoping it might clear up, we waited in the hotel lobby, where we ran into Bradford, a fellow football official who helped my career for years. Edie then helped him with his AncestryDNA research project to learn about the father he never knew.

She also fielded a text from Paula, who was celebrating the glorious pierogi that weekend in Whiting, Indiana. "Are you anxious about tomorrow?" she asked.

Edie told her that it may be on hold for Skip's health. "Hope y'all are having a great festival!" she added.

A little after 9:30 on Sunday morning, Fort Worth learned about Skip's procedure. "We are no go for Susan today," Edie reported. "Good news is they're home," she followed up, "and her cousin that was in ICU here was sent back to Texas, so just a delay."

"Oh, dang," Patrick reacted. "Well, I'm glad he's okay."

"Yeah," his sister shared. "Also glad I didn't widely disclose meeting plans."

"Oh, yeah," he concurred. "No kidding."

About an hour earlier, Susan emailed Edie why she and Skip couldn't make it.

"The most impatient patient in the world!" is how she described her husband of over three decades. "He did have to take something for pain," Susan wrote, "which means he can't drink, which means he'll be cranky and moody. Moody is not his best trait," she warned, "and I'm not ready to expose you and Jeremy." Susan added, "The good news is that he's excited about how much better he feels, so he should be 200% soon, and we can start a new plan."

"I'm glad he's feeling better," Edie soon wrote back. "We are available to work on plan B as he continues to improve. Rest easy today!"

The next day, she emailed Susan that we'd be available to meet at Gator's Den the next few weekends. "And since you mentioned that fabulous surprise," Edie added about Susan's Texas kin, "if things work out, we also wanted to let you know that we booked the trip to meet the cousins for September 5-11. Again, no pressure," she ensured on Monday. "We're looking forward to seeing you when we all can enjoy our time together. You make the call!" my crewmate told her.

"Our favorite bartender at Gator's usually works every other Sunday," Susan replied on Tuesday. "She could help keep the guys entertained while we were in the other room," she explained. "I'll start checking flights after we see what the doctors say," she promised with an update on her impatient patient. A heart emoji helped reassure her only child, "YOU are not pressuring or stressing me about anything.

Hearing from you was a miracle I thought God was saving for another life. I'm glad He changed his mind."

Susan also alerted Edie to look out for a separate email thread regarding "Faith."

"Just wanted to let you know in advance that I'm not any kind of zealot," Susan explained, expressing views on spiritual matters that had evolved to the point of meshing well with those of my wife. "I'm far from being agnostic. I've just gotten to a point where I don't need anybody else to tell me what to believe or how to think about religion," she revealed.

"In the meantime," she closed, "just know I'm happy you found me, I'm relieved that my choice was right, and I can't wait to see you in person for the first time! L, S."

By lunch Thursday, Plan B had been set. Edie was set to finally meet Susan a week from Sunday, on August 12.

In the immediate wake of the postponed Manchac meeting, Edie and her father traded a trio of emails. She later texted Justin about him while tuned in to National Public Radio. "I can't help but think about John, listening to this episode of *Radio Lab* about how a memory becomes less reliable every time you think of it."

"I bet," Justin agreed. "The more he relives them, the more he commingles stuff. That and his general litany of head injuries makes for quite a mess sometimes. But," Justin closed with an NPR reference, "he is still doing well, I think, all things considered."

That same afternoon, Rachel made an admission.

"I am looking at my office board," she shared with a photo of her work desk, "and realize I didn't update with pictures from Edie and Jeremy's visit! We will need to take family pictures at the reunion visit!"

"Absolutely!" Edie agreed.

"Guaranteed!" Justin promised.

Earlier that week, Facebook reminded Rachel about her reunion with Justin in Boston eleven years earlier, a time span both she and her brother couldn't believe. "And we're going to have a big reunion in less than two months!" she reminded us in the group thread.

"The comments from my mother brought a tear to my eye," Justin said of Rachel's photo album of their 2007 reunion. "She was very inspired by you and I finally meeting, Rachel," he noted. "It led to her doing research into her family on Ancestry, which in turn led to me doing it; so we could say," he closed with a heart quartet, "this photo memory captures the impetus of all our knowing each other today."

"I am glad I got to meet your mom," Rachel shared. "I am glad we piqued her curiosity!"

Within thirty-eight hours of another reunion, Edie emailed Susan in her "Faith" thread.

"I can't believe these two weeks have passed so quickly," she opened a message that included details about her Catholic upbringing, in response to Susan's description of hers. "So I hope we are still on for Sunday," my wife wrote that Friday. "We are so looking forward to getting to meet you and Skip! I promise," she winked, "I'll really try to be able to talk. And how do you feel about hugs? Those come a little more naturally for me," Edie smiled, "but that's not everyone's thing."

Before signing off with love, the high school valedictorian alluded to a picture taken on the final day of her senior year. She wrote that it "somewhat conveys my sentiments after thirteen years in its uniform."

Attached was an image of a striking seventeen-year-old, red-headed Edris Ann in light blue socks and spray-painted sneakers. Along with a school-issued cross that could've been from the Billy Idol collection, she also wore a less-than-knee-length Catholic school girl dress uniform. With a genuine smile, she's pulling the bottom taut to each side, showing off the Class-of-1988-themed graffiti adorning the garment, just below the better-than-fist-sized hole cut out in the midriff.

It's the only pic of my wife that makes me feel like a total creep every time I look at it.

Susan replied Saturday afternoon with a list of topics she wanted to definitely cover with Edie the next day in Manchac. "Yes," she reaffirmed. "Plan B is still the plan."

25

Glad I'm Not Adrian Monk

"We are on the way to meet Susan," Edie alerted Justin and Rachel, as well as the Texas O'Neals, at 10:23 a.m. on Sunday. "Of course we left late, but Jeremy will make up the time. I will not panic," she promised, "but will be going off the grid for a while."

Five weeks after first contact with Susan via email, we were passing up an initial phone conversation and proceeding instead to a much-anticipated, face-to-face meeting between my love and the woman who brought her into this world. I couldn't wait to thank Susan for doing so.

"Awesome!" Rachel hollered back. "I hope it goes well!" She offered with a heart-topped-cat sticker, "Love you!"

"Will be thinking of you all day," Justin answered. He added his love with a half-dozen hearts.

"Oh shit," Patrick replied. "I didn't realize this was on. Love vibes flowing your way!"

"After last time," Edie answered from the passenger seat, "I wasn't going to telegraph it so soon. Yesterday, Duck invited us for lunch today," she revealed. "I told her we had a meeting."

"Let us know how it goes," Patrick said.

"Will do," she vowed. "Love you!"

Yvette also sent "Big Love" with a trio of emojis—kissy-face, peace fingers, and a heart.

We drove east on I-12 for nearly forty minutes to Hammond (Louisiana, not Indiana) before heading south for about fifteen on I-55. I had tuned the radio to 91.1 FM for Zia the Cat's weekly jazz and blues show to help distract us from freaking out. When we got too far from KLSU's tower, I changed the station to keep the music going. I also made offbeat observations, like the number of powder-blue vehicles we passed along the way. Even if Edie didn't need it, I sure as hell did to keep Knick's voice at bay.

I took Exit 15 off the north-south highway following the tangent line of Lakes Maurepas and Pontchartrain, down to the thin strip of land, fringed with marsh grass and cypress trees, that hurricanes sometimes inundate with storm surge. Next was a left to Old Highway 51, paralleling 55 just a few dozen yards to the east. We passed Middendorf's, renowned for its thin-cut catfish, before traversing the pass connecting the two large lakes. A left at the far foot of the bridge led to the Gator's Den parking lot, where I pulled our black vehicle into a spot under a tree opposite the front door in hopes of catching afternoon shade from the brutal South Louisiana sun. After stepping out of the car a few minutes past eleven, I began recording video.

The two of us can be heard mouthing a kiss at each other as we approached the wooden building, topped with a metal roof and green sign. It read: "GATOR'S DEN: OPEN DAILY—STEAK NIGHT THURSDAY—LIVE MUSIC."

About halfway across the paved, sundrenched parking lot, my wife began giggling when she realized I was recording. She let out a sigh as we walked between the saplings in the planter boxes flanking the entrance. Stopping short of opening the door, I panned left to her smiling face, just as she started laughing again. I opened the door. Still laughing, Edie took three steps in before we stopped to allow our still-adjusting eyes to look around the establishment.

A smattering of patrons surrounded a bar to the left. An empty stage sat to the right. A handful of vacant tables and chairs lay in between, while a trio of video poker machines occupied part of the back wall.

Seconds later, Edie was on the move again, walking slowly past a nearby table, toward the middle of the room. She had already made eye contact with Susan, who was soon seen emerging from the far side of the bar, wearing jeans and a blue, striped, half-sleeved shirt. After nearly half a century, the woman who brought my soul mate into the world was about to finally meet her handiwork.

"We get to hug! We get to hug," Susan gleefully sang while walking across the hardwood floor toward the sunlight.

With a bag on her shoulder, Edie threw her right arm up as the two drew near. Susan extended both of hers. She continued melodically expressing her joy as mother finally embraced daughter.

Three seconds into their mutual clinch, Susan referenced Tony Shaloub's award-winning portrayal of a hug-averse germaphobe. "Boy, I'm glad I'm not Adrian Monk."

The image of the two embracing in the wooden interior of Gator's Den is remarkably similar to the photo I took of Edie hugging her sister at Conans Pizza. They're identically framed, with Susan facing the sunlight pouring through the door this time. Her fair arms and flat hands lay across her daughter's back exactly like Edie's did across Rachel's in Austin—same orientation, spacing, angles of elbows and wrists, everything.

Susan and Edie had the same hug.

After nearly ten seconds of embracing, the laughing pair disengaged and stood smiling face to smiling face. "Hi," they said to each other.

Susan began to fan herself when Edie introduced her to me and my phone. A giggly Susan and I shook hands.

"Hope you don't mind me documenting this," I said as we pulled together for a hug involving two audible slaps on the back. As we separated, her eyes went from mine to those of her daughter, and her beaming face. A mere second was all Susan could handle. She gasped, reaching for her chest, and turned away in shocked disbelief.

"I'm not breathing yet," she said. A broadly grinning Edie gently placed her right hand on her mother's left shoulder. Susan reciprocated with her left and a big ol' smile of her own. The pair single-handedly held each other at arm's length, trading gazes into eyes that had never met before, yet were intimately familiar.

"You're gorgeous," Susan purred like a Cheshire cat seconds later, their eyes still mutually transfixed. "I don't know where you got all that," Susan chuckled, dismissively waving her hand, "but I'm so glad you did."

"And we're the same height," Edie observed. "This is awesome."

"I used to be taller," Susan revealed. "Just wait till you start shrinking."

It wasn't just the eyes they had in common. It was also that smile. And it wasn't just the smile. It was the laugh emanating from that smile. I knew it well.

After a few more chuckles, it was time to meet Skip, still seated at the bar, watching TV. Susan approached her husband from behind, tapped him on his right shoulder, and said, "Skip."

"What?" he turned toward her.

"I'd like you to meet Edie," she replied with a smile and a gesture toward her daughter.

"Oh, hey!" he exclaimed, turning a little more to his right to shake hands with the two of us.

"How are you doing?" a joyful Edie asked him.

"I'm doing," an emphatic Skip replied.

"We had a little setback," Edie said in the video's closing moments, "but I'm glad you're up and feeling better."

The two of us soon settled down at the bar next to Skip and Susan. She introduced us to Joanna, who promptly served us drinks in large styrofoam cups: a Sunday morning mimosa for me, bourbon and Diet Coke for Edie.

Susan then reached into the canvas bag she had stowed next to her seat. She pulled out a copy of the *Culinary Arts Institute Polish Cookbook* and a plastic pierogi-making device. They were for me. She had previously emailed Edie a mini-cookbook, which Susan had put together for guests at one of their annual Ukrainian Christmas dinners.

After some light conversation, and free food prepared by the bar's resident chef, Susan politely asked me if she could take her little girl into the back room for privacy. She also asked me to keep Skip out of trouble. I agreed to both.

For the next three hours, I hung out with the former sailor. We talked about our wives and the Navy.

"Skip is crazy all the time," is how his wife described him in one email. Hours after receiving his pacemaker, he was trying to convince her that he could drive, despite doctor's orders to the contrary.

Some might describe Susan's husband of over thirty years as a jovial contrarian. He disdains football in a state where the sport is king. Skip especially hates the Saints, despite frequenting havens for passionate fans of the beloved New Orleans franchise. At nearly eighty years of age, he prefers soccer, as evidenced by his T-shirt promoting the German pro soccer league Bundesliga.

I asked him about Susan and her reaction to Edie's letter, with the Baton Rouge return address. He said she opened it and looked at the photograph. "That's my daughter!" he quoted his wife's immediate reaction, pointing to an imaginary photo in his hand.

After over an hour of our wives' sequestration, I grew slightly antsy, wondering how it was going. Mercifully, Edie emerged to retrieve something from the laptop bag at my feet. She smiled, and reassured me with a kiss that it was going well in there, before returning to Susan and closing the door behind her.

Just as mercifully, the TV behind the bar was switched from the Food Network to Fox News later—rather than sooner—during our stay. Susan had forewarned us about this. "I'm sure Jeremy knows how to deal with that kind of situation," she'd written.

Yes, I am well versed in that.

By the time mother and daughter exited the room to rejoin their husbands at the bar, members of that afternoon's band had started to muster and haul their equipment inside. Conversation became increasingly difficult as the musicians warmed up and the crowd grew more cacophonous.

Susan insisted on grabbing the tab, so we grabbed our bags. We followed them to their van, where we grabbed even more bags. These were filled with beads and trinkets to add to our already ample collection of future Mardi Gras throws. They also included a stack of vintage T-shirts, including one promoting *Gris Gris* magazine. Susan and her daughter shared the trait of saving things that might be needed—by them or others—one day in the future.

We hugged the two as they got in their van, and watched as Skip drove south toward Metairie. Edie and I got in our vehicle, where we agreed we needed to eat. Beau's dirty rice and potato salad had worn off.

Decompression and messages to loved ones soon commenced at Middendorf's, but only after receiving a text from the woman we'd just said goodbye to.

"Thank you for being you!" Susan sent Edie.

"Thank you for making me," my heart replied.

"I'm so glad you have somebody like Jeremy to share life with."

"I am so thrilled to finally meet you," Edie enthused, "and looking forward to more time together. We have some great fellas."

"Ditto, and yes, we do!" Susan winked. "Please ask Jeremy to send copies of our pictures together. I was going to take some to send to Paula and didn't," she added. "I can't imagine how I could have been so distracted by any of what was happening."

While she and Edie traded texts, I did the same with Beth from our table.

"Just had five hours with Susan," I reported to the archivist, along with news that Edie thought her great-grandpa Dr. Weis looked like *The West Wing's* Richard Schieff, whose silhouette was on Beth's water bottle.

"I can see it," she said.

Edie sent updates to Fort Worth and her younger siblings in their two respective threads.

"Great five-hour visit, first of many," she messaged Yvette and Patrick. "Today was the first time she saw me in person. None of her family knows I exist. I want to give her time to sort that out. Not ready to bring Ducky and Kellie into the picture yet," Edie conceded, "so I want to keep our meeting between us, if that's cool with you?"

"Of course," her older brother insisted. "This must always be at your pace. I'm so happy for you."

"It was great," Edie gushed. "I know babies look like babies, but we had the same skull. We're the same height," she added, "but she says she used to be taller."

"I'm just crazy about your story," an excited Yvette posted with a host of kisses and hearts. "Edie, 2018 has definitely been a good year! Is she as beautiful and kind as you?"

"She is wonderful," Red shared with a carnival-themed heart trio. "She had a heart attack and flatlined last year, was in hospital two weeks. She has already outlived her mother by eight years, but her dad lived to seventy-eight," Edie said of Mike. A seventeen-minute phone call with Fort Worth followed later that evening.

"AWESOME!" is how Rachel responded to Edie's tableside news that afternoon. "I am so happy for you! HUGE HUG!"

"Yay!" Justin posted with seven exclamation marks and three hearts. "I am so happy about this."

"Did you and Susan get together?" Paula texted early that same evening.

"Yes!" Edie affirmed. "We had a great first visit. Jeremy sent her pics to share with you."

"Oh yay!" Grandpa Mike's caretaker cheered. "I'm so happy to hear that!"

While they were in the back room, she and Susan showed each other old photos of themselves and their families. Susan also revealed how she not only had never seen Edie in person before that Sunday, but she had no idea if her child had even survived the birthing process.

Susan said she had every intention of keeping her baby. That changed, though, after she overheard some women at the downtown

Baton Rouge communications firm—where she still walked to work six months into her pregnancy—discussing the cost of child care. Even in 1970, it was enough to arrest her attention and force her to question whether she could do it on her own.

As for John, his name did not come up. She simply said that she knew a family with the father was not an option.

Susan would've been seven months along with Edie when John was arrested with Gus Tabony in September that year. My wife's father was too busy not getting killed by BRPD to help raise an unexpected daughter.

Around that same time, Susan's avoidance of an apartment complex pool prompted her roommate to ask if she was "hiding" something. Her discreet friend soon introduced Edie's mother to Dr. Leggio. He made her feel that, by allowing his friends to adopt her child, Susan was doing as big a favor for them as he was doing for her.

He also told her that, one year after giving birth, she'd have to come back to sign some forms to make everything official. Susan was never contacted to complete that paperwork, however.

She was also out cold when she delivered Edie at Our Lady of the Lake. The nuns wouldn't even tell Susan if she had a boy or a girl, at least not until she insisted she wouldn't leave the hospital without that information. For nearly half a century, until she saw that DFW selfie, Susan had no idea whether her only child was alive or not.

Along with that burden, Susan had also carried an even bigger secret: my wife.

Turns out, Nancy Jane and her husband, John Karpova, were in Europe the entire time their daughter was pregnant. Susan's younger siblings were with them, as well. They had moved across the Atlantic from Baton Rouge following Susan's junior year of high school.

"After much moping and sighing on my part," Susan would write, "my parents broke down and let me come back to BR to finish the second half of my senior year." She lived next door to a high school friend and his family, led by a single working mom of an eight-year-old, for whom Susan "played au pair."

Following graduation, she stayed in town to attend LSU, where her path would somehow cross John's.

Thirteen years before Mike Lukaczyk died without knowing Susan had born him a granddaughter, Nancy Jane went to her grave ignorant of the same. Edie's grandmother never knew Susan gave birth. Neither did Mr. Karpova, nor the siblings.

She wore loose clothing to disguise the bump as nothing more than a few pounds picked up by a twenty-year-old female college student. Like a pregnant Gates McFadden portraying Dr. Beverly Crusher in the fourth season of *Star Trek: The Next Generation*, she hid it well.

My wife's mother missed an entire day of work to deliver her. Susan was back at the office—on foot—one day after Ducky and Jimmy took Edie home.

That doesn't mean coworkers didn't suspect something. Company officials did phone her parents to let them know she was depressed—about being away from her family during the holidays.

They gave her some time off so she could be with her folks in Europe. The closest Nancy Jane came to realizing the truth was when she told Susan that she looked fat again. Susan, in her head, replied, "You should have seen me a month ago."

When we met, the only person in Susan's life to know she ever had a child was Skip.

I'm not a woman, but I know some. I've told this story to a handful of them, like my mom. This is the part that they have the most trouble fathoming. Such a secret would be unbearable, I've been told, and I have no reason to doubt it.

In the interest of further demonstrating how out-of-the-box this story is, remember when Beth and Edie were chasing down Fran? Beth said, "I think another good assumption is that, pregnant and spurned, she wouldn't venture far from family." Turns out, during the entire pregnancy, Edie's mother and her family weren't even on the same continent.

By Monday afternoon, I had managed to rotate the video of Edie and Susan's first meeting to its proper orientation. I shared it with Fort Worth.

"I'm not crying," her brother feigned. "Uh, I could pick her out as Edie's mom in a crowd. The smile, the laugh," Patrick gushed. "Oh, Edie, I can only imagine the emotions. You seemed so cool and collected. I guess you've had a little practice, but still. Gobsmacked again."

"I was overcome with the best feelings for y'all," Yvette shared with a smattering of emojis. "Edie, I just can't imagine what you and Susan are feeling! So beautiful to watch you; you had a beautiful air of confidence. You moved with such purpose and ease," she observed, "it was like this is the way it's supposed to happen." Grateful to be part of the beautiful journey, our hermana proclaimed, "Yours, John's, and Susan's stars have finally aligned."

"Tis a lovely day," Edie noted. "I need to share a text from earlier," she alerted the two of them about an exchange she had that Sunday, August 12, with Susan.

My wife loves daylilies. We have all sorts of varieties planted in our yard, many she bought at a plant sale not long after we moved into our house nearly two decades before. Edie often takes time to appreciate their fleeting beauty when they bloom, occasionally capturing it by camera.

"When we got home," Edie explained to Fort Worth, "I sent her a pic." It showed an eye-catching crimson and gold flower along our driveway, greeting us upon our return from Manchac.

"One new daylily for our special day," accompanied her photo to Susan that Sunday afternoon. "Love you!"

Susan replied with an etymological tidbit neither of us were aware of. "Beautiful flower, and doubly symbolic. In case you didn't already know, 'Susan' comes from the ancient names for lily," she sent with a heart. "Have a great week!"

"That's beautiful," Patrick said of Susan's response.

Susan also emailed Edie with concerns she had about the musty smell in the back room where they met. "It's never been that way before," she apologized. "They must have had some major issues with the latest flooding. I'm so sorry we were exposed to that, and highly recommend some kind of nasal spray." Burning scented candles at home that Sunday evening because she could still smell the odor, Susan wrote, "Sorry today's choice didn't work out to be as perfect as I had hoped. The place, I mean, not the company," she clarified with a hearts-for-eyes emoji. "That part was perfect."

"Well, that's the upside to my not having much of a sense of smell," Edie answered. "It didn't really register that much for me. And we could have met in a box, with a fox, in a house, with a mouse," she maintained, "and I might not have noticed any of that, either." With a heart, she shared, "I am just so happy to finally get to see and be with you!"

Edie soon alerted Susan that we were available the remaining Sundays in August, reminding her, "We only have two left until September and Labor Day weekend!" Our Golden Child shared our Indiana itinerary, which kicked off two days after the upcoming holiday. "My priority is getting to share more time with you, so I hope the next two Sundays are good for you," Edie added, "wherever we may choose to meet! There may be time down the road when we invite Ducky and Kellie, but for now, it's more important for me to get to be with you. We still have lots of catching up to do! Yesterday was awesome," my wife raved. "I want more!"

"Your turn to pick the place and time," Susan wrote back. "We can absolutely come up there," she said.

One possible Baton Rouge meeting place Susan mentioned, Edie informed me, was Pinetta's, a European restaurant dating back to 1962. "Nope," my wife promptly clarified about the venerable eatery, "closed on Sundays."

"Pinetta's is definitely quiet," I remarked on its romantic atmosphere.

The two eventually settled on our Thursday night trivia spot. We'd meet Susan and Skip for the second time the ensuing Sunday when The Bulldog opened at 11 a.m., precisely one week after Manchac.

Two days after her maternal reunion, Edie emailed Justin about it. "Susan and John" was the subject.

"We did not talk (significantly) about John," she wrote. "When we were together, I mentioned meeting my half-brother and half-sister, and she asked about that. I told her that we went to Seattle to meet you, and went to Austin to meet Rachel, but I didn't use your names. I explained that the three of us have the same father, but different mothers," Edie reported. "She asked where the father lives, and that was the extent of our conversation regarding my paternity.

"I'm so relieved that Susan is glad I found her. I am, too," she admitted, "but I had also gotten to the point where I wasn't really sure about whether I was doing the right thing. For me, this all started because I wanted to make myself available in case someone was looking for answers. When it led me to you and John," Edie explained, "I felt like I needed to answer the questions I created for him. Then I got back to thinking I had violated the prime directive by reaching out to someone who was trying to stay private. (Yep, I now know whence I inherited that.)

"John has asked me on each of our recent calls if Susan has talked about him and their relationship," Justin learned, "if she has specifically stated that she is my mother and he is my father, because he thinks my quest must continue in the absence of that. I trust the DNA, my eyes, our research, and our hearts. I do not need to know the details that led to my conception," Edie asserted, "and I'm not going to ask about them. I'm hoping I can gently but adequately convey that to John.

"I want to develop a relationship with both of my birth parents (and you and Rachel) while respecting the needs of each of them. We have a lot of catching up to do, and hopefully a good bit of time to do it. We're off to a good start, and after the frenzy of research to find Susan, it seems like a good time to ease back and take some time to enjoy getting to know each other and see where the path leads from here.

"This isn't meant to be a request for you to be the arbitrator yet again," Edie qualified. "I want to let you know where I'm coming from, and find out your comfort level, before I let my excitement take over and I go nuts telling you all about Susan. I don't want to put you in the middle." She acknowledged, "I've kinda already done that with Patrick and Yvette. They're the only ones in the family besides you, John, Rachel, and Jeremy who know Susan and I set up a meeting. Some of the Louisiana family is so eager to meet her," Red said, "that it's over-riding her and my need to have more time to ourselves right now. Plus, I feel somewhat guilty about sharing things she's telling me that no one else knows," she added. "I know I wouldn't appreciate that.

"I am looking forward to seeing you in September!" She closed with love, "Edie."

"Wow! Just wow!" Justin wrote back. "Your statement about not needing to know the details of your conception are so powerful, and resonate so strongly in my mind. And you are absolutely right!" he concurred about John. "His family has judged him so harshly," he reiterated about their father, "but do NOT let him convince you of anything you don't want to do or are not comfortable doing. He has really messy filters or boundaries. He doesn't really get what saying such means for you. He kind of assumes you are just like him, that most people see things the way he does," Justin explained. "It is a kind of self-centeredness born of his psychological and emotional need to explain why or how he is 'innocent.'

"What matters is you and what you want," he insisted. "So I suggest either simply telling John that it isn't your responsibility to find this out for him, or to just kind of ignore/say 'no' it hasn't come up yet, if you feel like you need to protect his sensitive ego." Justin added, "A simple request to please not bring that up in your talks should be something he can accept (though it could take him multiple tries)." With a smile, he also told his sister, "Don't worry about me being in the middle. I have never NOT been in the middle."

In a follow-up message, Justin assured Edie, "You actually don't owe any of us answers." He wrote, "I know you know this already, but as someone who is (also) very sensitive about his impact and intrusion into other people's lives, I hear something that sounds like you aren't sure if you can or should be present. YES," he reconfirmed, "you are always welcome, and your role in our lives is something you should feel certain that we love and appreciate wholeheartedly. I don't know if you ever struggled with these feelings," Justin wondered, "since you did have a very different experience growing up."

He advised his big sister, "Please take all the time you want and need just to get to know Susan on your (and her) own terms. The rest of the family can all wait. I mean they have waited forty-seven years already," Justin reminded Edie with a smile, "what is a few more months?"

He also shared a video of his talented five-year-old singing "Tomorrow" as the lead in her school's production of *Annie*. I've been through some warm Louisiana Augusts, but I've never had my heart melt like that before. Hadley nailed her solo number far better than most of the adults in the Gridiron Show.

Sunday the 19th came. Edie and I made our way to The Bulldog, about twice the size of Gator's Den. Susan and Skip had just arrived. Besides a few employees opening up, we were the first ones there. The four of us sat at the bar, where we introduced our guests to an occasional trivia teammate. Celeste took great care of us during our four-hour-plus visit.

Before they left, Susan spoke of an incident involving a school genealogy project, for which she'd approached her mother for information about her father.

"There he is right there," Nancy Jane insisted, directing her child to Mr. Karpova. When Susan clarified that she needed to know about her birth father, Nancy Jane's ensuing reaction practically took the paint off the walls. A grounding was also involved. Susan said she never brought up the verboten topic with her mother ever again.

That's why she didn't begin her quest to learn about Mike until Mr. Karpova died in 1998, eight years after Edie's grandmother passed. Five years of searching later, Susan eventually learned of Michael Lukaczyk and his role in this insane story—four months after her estranged father died in 2003.

Susan recalled seeing Paula Teibel listed on the death certificate. Since the name meant nothing to her at the time, she didn't bother contacting a complete stranger.

She also confirmed at The Bulldog that she and Skip were driving up to Indiana to coincide with our trip in just over two weeks. Mother and daughter agreed to keep that juicy development on the down-low to surprise the Ukrainian horde.

Later that Sunday evening, Susan emailed Edie more information about a heart condition that demanded she limit the amount of stress in her life. "Broken heart syndrome—Symptoms and causes—Mayo Clinic" was the subject line. "This is the condition I was trying to explain," she wrote. "The Japanese-sounding part is takotsubo cardiomyopathy. It's not something you have to worry about heredity-wise."

Susan also said, "Thanks for your time and hospitality today. The venue was really great and made me miss my first 'hometown,' Baton Rouge. I lived there longer than anywhere before Georgia and the combined years spent here in Metairie."

Two nights later, Edie sent her newest Facebook friend a photograph of herself holding one of our beloved cats, Grady. "This was right after the hairdresser gave me straight hair," she messaged Susan. "I see a lot of resemblance in this one."

"I can see our physical resemblance when I look back at pictures of me at my best," Susan's reply greeted her daughter Wednesday morning. "I just love looking at you and seeing you look at Jeremy. It makes me so happy to see that you found that kind of life partner."

As for Ducky, "If/when you think it's right for the three of us to get together," Susan wrote, "I'm good with that. If not, I'll try to come up with a note for you to pass on to her thanking her for exceeding my hopes for you. I don't want anybody to think I'm trying to insert myself into your family. I just feel blessed that we can explore our special bond. I thank God that he remembered that we hadn't met yet," she told Edie, "and let me stick around last year."

Susan also mentioned that she should be getting her AncestryDNA results after the trip to Indiana, where she hoped they could "slip away with Paula for an all-girls chat."

Edie liked the idea, and suggested it might be best to have it before the big gathering that their cousins were planning to celebrate Uncle

Mike's granddaughter's return to the fold. Additionally, in an effort to give Susan a "head start on sorting out all the Lukaczyks," Edie shared the family trees she had built out in Ancestry. Between consonants and kids, I'm not sure which they had more of.

That same Wednesday, Paula created a Facebook event titled "Lukaczyk Welcome Home Edie," and invited her two Louisiana cousins. "Please join us in welcoming Uncle Mike's granddaughter, Edie, and her husband, Jeremy, into our crazy, loving, and fiercely loyal family," the email notification read. "Bring your favorite Uncle Mike story, pictures to share, and a dish," Paula requested. "Edie is so excited to meet her family, we hope you can make it!"

"I replied with 'can't attend' after talking to Paula," Susan reported to her daughter. "It's your party, but we're going to be surprise guests."

"Will keep the surprise," Edie promised. "I'm most excited about us getting to spend more time together," she smiled.

"Ditto," Susan replied.

A few days later, Edie mentioned our approaching trip to Beth. "Susan and her husband are driving up to surprise them," she said.

"Yay!" Beth exclaimed. "I demand pics!"

That led to Edie sharing the video from Manchac.

"OMG," Beth responded with four large heart emojis. "So much dust in my eyes!" Commenting on a couple still shots of Susan and Edie, our ninja noted, "That's crazy how much y'all favor." She followed up, "So Susan doesn't know these cousins at all. They haven't seen her since her mama run off."

"Right," Edie confirmed.

A couple days later, she alerted Patrick how the gathering would feature some of our South Louisiana favorites. "Susan is picking up boudin and hog's head cheese for the cousins reunion," she wrote. (No, there isn't an actual hog head involved, at least not anymore.)

"Wait," he wondered, "Susan is going, too?"

"Yes, she and her husband are driving up," Edie explained. "To surprise the cousins."

"Wow. How much fun is that?!" Patrick reacted. "I was going to say how blown away I am about Susan's sweetness, then I realized you are she," he told his sister, "and so I'm not surprised at all."

"She is so awesome," Edie proclaimed.

Patrick mentioned showing the Manchac video to his adult daughter. "We all cried."

Around this time, Paula, John Lukas, and his wife, Mira, learned of Susan's pending arrival. Meanwhile, we learned how they'd be treating us like royalty. Transportation, lodging, food, and entertainment for the Golden Child and her husband were all covered, with backup plans.

Paula sent Edie and Susan a seven-year-old photo of fifty-one people gathered outdoors. "Only 'some' of your cousins!" she wrote.

"Wow!" Edie reacted.

"Can you imagine how we've multiplied since then?" Paula wondered.

"OMG!" Susan shot back. "I thought the porch picture was a crowd!"

Susan also told Edie that her and Skip's travel itinerary had grown to include their annual Oktoberfest tour of America. "Just wanted to let you know I'm thinking about you," she added, "and missing your smile."

"I was really missing you, too," Edie answered, "despite realizing we're only ten days away from Indiana. I can't believe it's only been a week since our last hug. Love you," she finished with a single heart emoji, "and so looking forward to our next time together."

"Ditto!" Susan signed off with twin hearts.

"We leave for a week in Indiana to meet the bio-mom cousins," she informed Justin three days before our flight, "assuming there isn't a tropical storm development in the gulf that prevents our departure." Potential Tropical Cyclone Seven's forecast track that Sunday brought it toward our neck of the woods right around scheduled take-off from New Orleans. On Labor Day, the system intensified into Tropical Storm Gordon.

"The countdown begins!" Paula texted her Louisiana cousins on Monday morning. "Wheeeee!"

"I'm just so excited about everything," Susan texted Edie. "God has really been throwing wonderful surprises down to me for the past several weeks! You were the first!" She added, "And best!"

"I'm so glad y'all are heading up ahead of the storm!" Edie answered with love.

"I'd say 'what storm,'" Susan conceded, "but last time I did that, we woke up to Katrina."

"It's getting closer!" Paula texted Edie late Tuesday afternoon.

"Fingers crossed!" my wife replied.

"Made it to our inn in West Memphis," Susan updated her daughter on Tuesday evening.

"So glad you're done with today's leg of your road trip," my giddy wife replied, "and so excited to see you tomorrow!"

"Any flight issues, Edie?" her mother asked about the storm.

"Not that we know of," she answered. "Looks like we'll miss the worst."

"Edie," Susan demanded, "just make sure you get to Yankee-land! I'm not planning to drive back to bring y'all up," she said, "but I will!"

"I picked an early flight on purpose," Edie noted, "plenty of backups! We will get there!"

"Family traits must be foresight and determination," Red's mother observed.

Scarce rainfall met us on the hourlong drive to the hotel Tuesday night. We checked in and hoped to sleep a few hours before the 4 a.m. wake-up call.

"Edie and I are at the Comfort Suites in Kenner," I opened a lengthy message to Knick and Sunny after their bedtimes. "Flying out in the a.m. to Chicago to meet her maternal grandfather's family in northwest Indiana, as in the assload of cousins who had been looking for Edie's mother (Susan, their first cousin) for sixty-five years." A few hundred words later, I wrapped up: "So here we are, getting ready to share Edie over the next week with a huge group of Ukrainians dying to meet her because she's the granddaughter of their favorite uncle, who doted on them for fifty years because he never remarried or had another child, who would've sent Edie to Notre Dame had he knew about her, who would've cut off his right arm just to hold her in his left. And they have no idea Susan is driving up there."

Though Edie had met her birth mother—twice—the quest was far from complete.

26

I Know You

Over an hour before first light, Edie and I grabbed a couple of the hotel's go bags and their earliest airport shuttle. We quickly went through security thanks to PreCheck. Before boarding, Edie bought candied pecans in the terminal for Paula and Mira, who'd both be hostessing us during this weeklong trip.

At cruising altitude over northern Mississippi, I could see Tropical Storm Gordon continue to churn away as we passed him. The forecast called for his wet remnants to follow us.

In my window seat, with a torrential cyclone over my right shoulder, I jotted down my first notes for this insane story. I already knew how it would open, on another Wednesday morning, six and a half months earlier. As we approached what felt like the summit of our journey, involving Edie's maternal family, I knew that the predawn moment of paternal discovery—and our early ascendancy into the surreal—was where we'd begin.

Our Southwest pilot gave us a view of downtown Chicago, including the interior of Soldier Field, as we banked toward Midway, away from a brilliant sun rising over Lake Michigan. On final approach, I began videoing our plane's shadow traversing below. Thirty-one seconds later, our steadily growing partner gently met us on the ground for a gorgeous Midwest midmorning.

Our phones connected us to the rest of the world as we bypassed baggage claim and headed toward Midway's passenger pickup area outside. We had arrived during major renovations.

"This is so fucking awesome," Sunny replied to my late-night message from the hotel. "I'm not crying," the notorious cynic added. "You're crying."

Edie soon alerted her cousin, "I've got a big pink scarf!" Paula had advised wearing one to catch her eye. Unfortunately, Edie sent the message to cousin Carole in South Carolina instead of cousin Paula in Midway's cell phone lot.

"Hello, Chicago!" Carole replied.

"We are so excited!" Edie texted back.

"Me, tooooooooooooooo!" Carole exuded.

"On the way," Paula answered Edie's properly addressed text, prompting a trio of grins from my one and only.

Paula excitedly waved at us from several car lengths away. Her head was stooped forward to see us under the deployed sun visor. Paula peered above the steering wheel through sunglasses as she pulled over her brand-new, red Kia Sportage. Its frantic driver immediately unbuckled herself as Edie made her way around the rear of the SUV toward the driver's side. My wife dropped her bags near the hatchback, freeing her arms to assume the identical pre-hug, left-banking-airplane pose she employed at SEA-TAC.

You know it's a quality hug when you can clearly hear the impact from around the corner of a vehicle in the middle of an active construction zone on a workday outside a Chicago airport, all over the joyous screams from a pair of Ukrainian cousins meeting for the first time. The embrace lasted twelve seconds, according to my video. They backed off just enough to face each other, hands firmly grasping each other's shoulders.

"OH," Paula yelled at full throat, "THIS IS THE BEST!" She immediately pulled Edie in for another, briefer hug.

We were standing near the only passable traffic lane. Paula's door was still open toward it.

"I gotta get you in the car before the cops come," the bootlegger's granddaughter said as she released Edie and dove in my direction for a hug, screaming with her arms extended toward me on her approach.

"How are you?" I responded with my now-standard greeting for such occasions.

"Wonderful now!" Paula shot back.

We disengaged to load our bags, and got on the road toward Hammond, Indiana, nearly an hour away.

"He made this happen," Paula said about her Uncle Mike. "I wish he was here for this," she rued before adding, "but we've come full circle. We're all together."

Edie's grandfather had outlived everyone in his generation except for his sister-in-law, Aunt Bernice. She was John and Gene Lukas's mother. Grandpa Mike tended to the graves of his deceased relatives twice a year, planting hostas in the spring, we learned, and mums in the fall.

As a young kid, Paula said, she and her cousins were always instructed to be extra nice to their Uncle Mike, without explanation, especially during Thanksgiving. She later realized Susan's birthday is in late November.

Grandpa Mike was a great storyteller and loved to laugh, Paula reminded us as she retold a story from our first phone call. Intubated and unable to speak, a hospitalized Mike motioned for pen and paper to communicate. After scribbling gibberish in his semi-lucid state, he handed the paper to his niece Drea, the family historian. She shook her head before handing the indecipherable writing to our driver, who was also there visiting.

"I can read it," Paula said, taking the note from Drea to study it for a bit. "Uncle Mike," she told him, laid up in ICU with a breathing tube down his gullet, "that wasn't very nice."

When Drea asked what it said, Paula turned to her cousin and said, "That you're a ho."

"And that's when," Paula recalled behind the wheel, "I learned it's not a good idea to make a joke when somebody's intubated, because he wanted to laugh so bad."

At ten past ten, we approached the "Welcome to Indiana: Crossroads of America" sign spanning I-94. I met the occasion in Paula's back seat with a rendition of "Back Home Again in Indiana," à la Jim Nabors before many Indianapolis 500 races.

Our first stop came within minutes of crossing the state line. We strode on lush summer grass at St. Mary's Cemetery, past about a dozen rows of gravestones, to a marker near the center of the lawn. Edie squatted down in her denim shorts and "UnBRoken" T-shirt. She pushed aside a yucca plant just as tall as the headstone behind it. Sunlight invigorated my bride's auburn curls as she read the family name at her now-assumed eye level, near the slab's slightly rounded top.

"LUKACZYK" read the engraving. At the bottom corners were the names Andrew and Mary, as well as the years marking their time on Earth. An inscribed three-barred Russian Orthodox (aka Byzantine) cross laid between the names of the great-grandparents of a red-headed O'Neal who had always heard how Irish she was.

"Surreeeeal," I heard.

"Dammit, Knick," I silently replied, "show some respect for the dead."

I later updated Beth with an image of the moment when her dear friend came face to face—if only metaphorically—with the ancestors whom she helped Edie find.

"Whoa!" she replied. "That's a lot for the first stop. How's she holding up?" Beth asked.

"She's great," I reported, drawing a thumbs-up.

Edie stood up after regarding the patriarch and matriarch's final resting place for some time. Paula showed us one more grave of another relative buried there before making our way to her home nearby. That's where we'd stay through Saturday, before spending Sunday and Monday nights with John and Mira in Crown Point, about forty-five minutes south.

"There may be cousin competition over who gets us," Edie had alerted me in July while making lodging arrangements. The Golden Child was in demand.

Paula fed us lunch at her place around midday. We had been chatting for a couple hours when she insisted Edie and I take the twenty-minute drive to Lake Michigan in her new Sportage, still sporting temporary tags.

The two of us strolled along the water in Whiting, two miles east of the state line. Through the midafternoon summer haze, we could make out the skyline we'd flown over that Wednesday morning.

Back at Paula's, I updated Beth. "I've spent so much time thinking about how I'll write this book," I revealed.

"Lifetime movie, yo," the editor answered. "Like, you could not make this shit up. COULD NOT."

That's when I mentioned another movie. "Hammond is the town in *A Christmas Story*." While the Chinese restaurant from the holiday classic was no longer around, much to Beth's chagrin, Ralphie's cinematic childhood home would blend right into Paula's neighborhood.

"Susan and Skip are coming over tonight," I informed Beth, "as are John and Mira Lukas. The rest of the gang will (hopefully) be surprised Friday." Edie had come to realize that she may have inadvertently spilled the borscht to Gene about Susan coming back home.

Mira and her calm demeanor arrived first. John came by shortly afterward with his unique brand of chaos after knocking off at the mill in Gary, a few miles to the east along the lakeshore. Both are wonderful souls who balance each other out.

John's hug reminded us of his older brother's, when Gene all but leapt from his wheelchair to embrace Edie. Johnny Mark, as he's known in the John-filled family, lifted my wife up off the ground. While he's built like what I assume to be a typical steel mill worker—neither a ninety-pound weakling nor Mr. Olympia—he suffered from a bad back. After putting my wife down, he realized he had let his abundant enthusiasm override his instinct to not cripple himself.

It didn't take long for him to start comparing notes with Paula as to which of their relatives Edie most reminded them of. They pointed out the same aunts in the Mother's Day photo as Gene, who phoned his little brother not long after Johnny Mark got to Paula's.

John swiped the screen to answer the call from Victoria and immediately handed me the phone. He proceeded to tell me to pretend to be him. I proceeded to butcher the proud Chicago accent.

Like Susan, with some immersion time, I can mimic dialects, but this was unexpectedly hoisted upon me. I've seen plenty of *Saturday Night Live* "Bob Swerski's Superfans" skits, but I knew I couldn't just say "Dah Bearsss" and "polish saah-sauge" over and over again. I was suddenly called upon to pass myself off as someone I literally just met, to his older brother. My accent was nowhere near the Midwest. I'm not really sure how to describe my rendition—likely because my mind's all but blocked it out—but with a gun to my head, I'd go with Bugs Bunny after a stroke.

Gene and I spoke for ten minutes without him even questioning my voice or identity. John finally, and mercifully, took the phone. "You had no idea that wasn't me, huh?"

I'd be lying if I said I didn't have visions of coming to Chicago and reenacting scenes from *Ferris Bueller's Day Off*, but I didn't think it would involve one with Cameron or Grace pretending to be someone else on the phone.

Near a quarter to seven, following a second travel day that lasted much longer than expected, Skip and Susan drove in. Paula and Mira met them at the home's main entranceway, two rooms away from Edie, John, and me in the living room. Mira escorted the latest pair of Louisiana arrivals through the kitchen and toward the arched opening leading to us.

An excited Edie waved her arms to her sides as she and her mother made eye contact for their third meeting. "I know you," they said to each other just before embracing in the archway. Edie led in with her now-patented left-banking approach.

Still hugging her girl with her right arm, Susan extended her left, pointing to John, just past Edie. "And I know you," she said with a lilt. My wife's mother did the same toward me, twirling her index finger in my direction like a magician's wand, before her hand rejoined its partner, firmly pressing against her daughter's back.

"That's gotta be Susan," John said softly as the two women released each other, his newly arrived cousin gasping in agreement with his observation. "That little girl" was all he could continue to get out before Susan abruptly halted him.

"No, no," she chuckled, wiggling her body in a manner to suggest she no longer fit that description. Three steps and a "There's John" later, Susan was embracing the cousin who had made first contact with her child exactly four months earlier. "OK, y'all can go," she told the rest of us during their twelve-second, gasp-accented hug. "We'll just stay right here." They parted with a kiss on the cheek from John.

Skip greeted me amid the abundant laughter. I stopped the video after asking him about the drive, which he didn't find all that pleasant.

The seven of us eventually made our way into the dining area, where Paula served up homemade lasagna. She and John noted Susan's resemblance to certain aunts and cousins, like they had done earlier with Edie. The two Hoosiers also asked Susan if she remembered ever visiting the house, the same one where Paula's mother, Julie, raised our hostess.

In addition to her mom, a young Paula had two aunts (Helen and Rosie) nearby to deal with. With each living no more than a door or two away, she became adept at sneaking out of (and back into) the back door to avoid the block's watchful eyes, especially Rosie's. She was a narc.

Susan didn't remember Paula's house, but she did recall living with her mom in the upstairs portion of a house in Hammond. Another family lived downstairs, she said.

After dinner, around nine, I captured the first group photo of the cousins, gathered in the living room: Indiana represented on the left, Louisiana on the right. Like the Night Wing pics with Rachel,

I continued snapping away as their four smiles in my direction gave way to a group hug. I shared one of each pose with Beth, as well as Fort Worth.

"So wonderful that y'all are there," Patrick replied. "You look so happy," he told Edie.

Given Skip's usual bedtime and their long day on the road, he and Susan soon departed for their nearby hotel. We'd see them in the morning for Paula's tour of the area.

Later that Wednesday evening, just before eleven, Susan texted her child.

"They were all so wonderful," she remarked, "and I feel like we didn't even get started with sharing. I didn't want to leave, but we really needed to get some rest tonight. That drive was way more than what we thought it was going to be. Was Paula too disappointed?" Susan wondered. "I'm just so happy and so angry at the same time. I just hope you're not feeling the second half of that pair of emotions about us," she added. "I want this trip to be really good for everybody."

"No disappointment over here," Edie answered the following morning. "We can't change what brought us to this point," she reminded Susan, "but I am happy we are here and together now. Love you, and see you soon!"

Edie and I slept about as well as we did that first evening in Renton. Our brains were processing similar weirdness about our situation in the quiet of the night. Once again, exhaustion was our friend.

As for Paula, the insomnia sufferer insisted we never leave because she hadn't slept that well in forever. While drinking coffee with us on Thursday morning, she described experiencing "spasms" the previous evening, undulating between "Oh my god" and "What the hell is happening?!" Paula said, "This is a miracle," and described Wednesday night's reunion as "crazy."

She also couldn't fathom how the Weis family could maintain such cruel silence all those years. We learned that following Nancy Jane's divorce from Mike, her first cousin—the priest in their family—excommunicated her from the Catholic Church.

After his wife took off with his only child, Mike would "stake out" the cemetery whenever a Weis family member passed, in hopes of seeing them, Paula explained. Following years without a glimpse of either one, Edie's grandfather ended his reconnaissance so as to avoid disrupting his daughter's life.

Susan and Skip arrived near 10 a.m. The five of us piled into Paula's SUV, with Skip riding shotgun for the needed legroom. Edie sat in the back between her husband and mother as Paula drove us around old neighborhoods in East Chicago and Hammond.

As forecasted, Gordon had followed us. We stopped in front of a few notable places amid the cool intermittent rain.

The first was a white house with siding and an A-framed roof. Susan rolled down her drizzle-splattered window for pictures of the structure, which stood only a few feet from the curb. It was Andrew and Mary's formerly brick-faced home, Paula informed us, where the infamous 1952 Mother's Day pic was taken.

The front porch had been closed in, and the front steps descended against the side of the house. No longer coming straight out toward the street, they'd been turned ninety degrees.

Making it even more unrecognizable was the size. It looked much tinier, narrower, in person. The photograph seemed to give the impression that the house stretched beyond the image's boundaries. It did not.

A short drive away was a religious bookstore, housed in the former St. Basil the Great Byzantine Church. Across the street was the church's former rectory, a brick residence with a full-sized upper level. There, a despondent Mike resided for a stretch in the early 1950s.

Back in Hammond a few minutes later, Susan had her window down again, this time to photograph a brick home trimmed in burnt orange. A green lawn led to where Susan and Nancy had once lived upstairs, while Mike did the same one town over, also amongst nonfamily.

A few turns later, we pulled in at a cemetery. The five of us made the short walk to the hosta-obscured grave of Michael Lukaczyk. As he had demanded for previously deceased kin, his plot was well-kept and beautifully appointed.

The women stopped a few paces from the headstone. Skip and I stood behind our respective spouses. All eyes were trained on the grave. I snapped a sole pic of Mike's final resting place, flanked by the daughter he lost, and the granddaughter he never knew.

Susan was suddenly overcome and turned toward Skip, who was there to embrace and comfort her. The two walked toward the car for a bit. She asked Skip to take her back to the cemetery "when it's not raining."

The weight of that moment was immeasurable. Finally, Susan saw the grave of the father whom she was forbidden from knowing, and whom she finally learned about four tragic months after his passing. I can't begin to imagine the torrent of emotions that washed over her in a drizzly St. John's Cemetery.

Back in the vehicle, we headed to Madvek's Dog House for lunch. Our driver ensured we followed Mike's tradition of chili dogs for his nieces and nephews after visiting the graveyard with him.

Around noon, we dropped off Skip at their hotel so he could rest up from Wednesday's drive. I jumped in the front seat to afford mother and daughter more customary personal space as they bonded in the back.

As Mike's primary caregiver, Paula ended up with lots of his stuff. His menagerie contained drinkware, Notre Dame paraphernalia, and whatever else caught his fancy. Nearly every item had his name or initials on them.

Paula opened cabinets at her place. With a simple gesture in an Indiana kitchen, my wife soon became caretaker of some of her grandfather's prized personal belongings. First were a pair of champagne flutes with the name "Lucas" etched on them.

There are theories amongst the horde as to why Michael Lukaczyk and his older brother, the late John Lukas, went with different Americanized spellings. However, I'm the only one who believes it was to save on engraving, etching, and embroidering.

Along with his Social Security card, Paula also gave Mike's granddaughter his Notre Dame stein. She explained how, when her uncle was considering such a purchase, he would ask and answer himself thusly: "Do I NEEEEED it? No. Do I WAAAANT it? Yes."

A grin overcame my wife's face as she realized she had asked and answered those same two questions in her mind in the same manner innumerable times. One such case of internal pre-purchase banter occurred the summer before the two of us met, Edie explained. It just so happened to involve a stein bought in a Midwest state. At the time, she was in Wisconsin before her junior year, for a study involving LSU and—well, whaddaya know—Notre Dame.

Paula also bestowed a number of Mike's personal things to the daughter he lost. "She has nothing," our hostess later told us about passing these down to Susan. "We have everything."

I soon took Paula's Kia to make copies of some old family pictures. I also needed to buy a frame for a crackling, curled-up photograph of Company 1154 from the U.S. Naval Training Center in Great Lakes (aka "Great Mistakes"), Illinois, on June 8, 1944. While I was gone, Susan tried to identify which of the 150 newly graduated seamen in the faded and creased document was her father. The best she could do was narrow it down to three.

Edie would later tell me that, while the three of them were talking in the living room about Mike and his things, "some heavy stuff happened." She also said, right around the time of maximum gravity, an area transformer tripped, causing the power to go out for about a minute. The resulting nervous laughter about the outage's timing, and its potential supernatural origins, lifted much of the weight from the moment.

Later that Thursday afternoon, Edie helped Paula make the Eastern European version of ravioli, celebrated annually in Whiting. Handling flour in a black T-shirt sans apron, she wore a proud smile.

"Look who's helping make pierogies." Fort Worth received a photo showing my bride's hands in a bowl. Paula's near arm hung over her younger cousin's shoulders.

"Fantastic!" Patrick responded.

I resisted sending the pic of Edie sticking her tongue out at me, à la Grandpa Mike, in Paula's kitchen after our household's cook teased her for being in a foreign setting.

Susan was soon back from their hotel after fetching an invigorated Skip and their iPad. When he wasn't using the device to buy lederhosen for their upcoming Oktoberfest tour of America, he was getting down to some solid oom-pa-pa music blasting on it. Skip said he was playing his favorite German band. He showed me their video just before he traipsed through the house like a little kid, iPad swinging in his hand to and fro. I swear, I saw Skip and his new pacemaker high-stepping out of the living room.

Since he loves old-fashioned German music, I've been tempted to get him a Kraftwerk album or two.

Paula's two youngest daughters, Jamie and Jodie, came over from nearby Schererville to help assemble the pierogies. Their older sister, Julie (named after her grandmother), lived in Boston with her husband.

Jodie brought her youngest, June, a sweet, olive-skinned brunette, set to turn four the following week. Jamie had her two precious blond kids in tow, as well: fellow three-year-old Jocelyn (aka Joss) and a rambunctious Declan, age two.

Moments later, I was urged—and subsequently instructed—to drive Skip to the Schererville Lounge, about twenty minutes away. We were the ones who would "slip away" so Susan and Edie could have that all-girls chat with Paula, her daughters, and Mira, who also had come over. I partially understood verbal driving directions from multiple people. They also said who we'd be meeting there.

I led off down the road in the Kia with Skip. The only thing he gleaned from the exchange was that we were going to grab a drink somewhere.

Steering with my left hand some distance down the highway, I finally managed to find the place on my phone with my right, after figuring out how Schererville is spelled. By this time, though, Skip was pointing out every bar along the way, insisting we stop at each one, since he believed we'd simply been instructed to go to a drinking establishment for a spell. I tried explaining to him that we were going to a particular bar where Paula's sons-in-law were expecting us. He didn't seem too keen on passing up watering holes, where we knew not a soul, to go to another place, where we knew no one else, farther away.

Relieved to finally arrive safely with my ward at our intended destination, we walked in. I scanned the place for the two hubbies. One was to be a handsome Hispanic gentleman named Joe, as shown in a pic by Jodie. The other looked like a swole, bald Matt Damon, Jamie told me. That would be Gavin.

I continued toward the dining area, past the bar, when I heard Skip holler at me from behind. He had stopped just a couple steps into the place, where he stood pointing out the two empty seats at the end of the bar near the door. In hopes he would resume following me, I reminded him that we were there to meet some folks who were not at the bar.

A few steps later, I saw a table full of people, two of whom matched the descriptions provided. Joe and Gavin had been briefed on our appearances, as well, and welcomed us over.

After greeting the two of us, they introduced their father-in-law, Paula's former husband, Bob. The Arizona resident was in town visiting his grandkids. Also at the table was an old acquaintance of Bob's, who just happened to be at the restaurant that night. The gentleman and his female companion had joined the three men for dinner while we were on the way.

My ass had yet to warm my chair when Bob grabbed my attention and insisted I explain what the hell was going on. Gavin immediately seconded his father-in-law's motion. They and Joe had married into the Lukaczyk family, which meant they weren't raised hearing the details of its insane, sixty-five-year-old mystery. Like their directions to the Schererville Lounge, the explanations from Paula and her girls hadn't fully sunk in.

Skip and I did our best to lay out our tale to that point. There were, of course, a few questions; but Gavin said, after three attempts by his in-laws to explain it to him, he finally understood why he was talking to a fellow bald guy from the swamps of Louisiana. Joe, Bob, and his old acquaintance verbally indicated that they were wowed by the account. Seconds of silence later, the woman with Bob's friend rasped, "I don't get it."

She'd have to rely on her companion for a retelling. I was too busy feeding my face with some legit fried chicken. Skip drank a couple of beers and eschewed supper.

Back at Paula's, I was debriefed. I soon learned that, among the instructions given to me by nearly a half-dozen people a couple hours earlier, was a directive to ensure that Skip—a grown-ass man who just drove across the country—ate supper. I told my wife that we were lucky to just meet up with the gang in Schererville. Had I been aware of the nourishment directive, I'm confident it would've devolved into a horse-and-water scenario at the table.

Before Jodie left her mother's, she invited Edie and me to dinner with her and Joe on Friday night in Crown Point. Paula's youngest thought we'd appreciate a night with (in her words) people closer to our age.

As the ladies made pierogies that Thursday night, three kids under four roved around their grandmother's house. Susan turned to her daughter and joked, "Don't you wish you had six of those running around?"

She also used the words "cruel" and "insecure" in describing Nancy Jane to the red-headed granddaughter Mrs. Karpova never knew about.

During dinner, Bob confirmed what we'd heard about Grandpa Mike. "Eccentric," "colorful," and "great to the kids" were among the words he ascribed to his three daughters' great-uncle. Aside from the few items he splurged on, Mike pretty much lived a spartan life for himself, Bob said. In Susan's absence, he preferred spending dough doting on his myriad nieces and nephews.

Paula's mom, Julie, was Nancy's matron of honor in 1948. Mike's sister Theresa was a bridesmaid. Our hostess suspected her Uncle Mike's sisters may have embellished the wedding announcement in an attempt to raise the groom's perceived status, to ostensibly be more on par with his new in-laws.

"Why is Dr. Weis's nineteen-year-old girl marrying a clerk at Goldblatt's?" was wondered by many reading the society pages back then, particularly since the groom came from a self-described "family of thieves." Paula explained how, if one of Mike's sisters couldn't afford something at the store, she'd bring it to him and give him a $20 bill to "buy" it. He'd then bag the item and give her $20 "in change."

Speaking of bags, Paula also told us about the time Mike's older sister Mary (aka Auntie Matza) and a young friend hitched a ride with a couple of fellas to a big dance hall in Chicago. The two gentlemen safely dropped them off at their desired destination. On the way there, however, the friend did something Andrew's daughter likely knew was unwise.

"What's in the bag?" Matza's naive friend asked.

"Little girls shouldn't ask so many questions," was the reply from the front seat.

Later, after looking at pictures, the girls recognized one of those two nice men as Al Capone.

Rather than a "family of thieves," a descriptor Paula passed down from Mike, I prefer to think of the Lukaczyks as "gangster-adjacent." John Hart's cartel connections notwithstanding, that would make my wife gangster-adjacent, twice-removed, I believe. Or is it third-removed? Those relationship charts are complicated.

Before driving us to Jodie and Joe's place on Friday, Paula told us one more family story, this one involving Aunt Katie and America's first Public Enemy Number One.

At the age of nine, in the depths of the Great Depression, Mike's sister Katie had been sent off to stay with a nearby family to serve as their nanny. They operated a drinking establishment downstairs from the living area, during the Prohibition era. When the family departed for an outing one day, Katie stayed behind.

She was in the home alone as a teenager, Paula said, when Katie heard someone breaking into the place downstairs. She hid upstairs under a bed. Moments later, after the handful of men entered the same room, Katie heard them say they never saw her leave with the rest of the family. As fortune would have it, one of the men made contact with the bed's large comforter, creasing it in such a way to give a still-concealed Katie a clear view of a man who, at that point, had become the most wanted person in the country. John Dillinger and his gang of murderous bank robbers had busted in to grab whatever they could, and were looking to wrap up any loose ends, the story goes.

It concludes with Katie telling police what and whom she saw. When the cops told her that was impossible—because (according to their sources) her guy was in California—she doubled down on Dillinger. This apparently prompted an increased law enforcement presence in the area, not long before the notorious criminal was killed by police.

We arrived at Jodie and Joe's in Schererville on Friday afternoon, one day before they'd host a family reunion sixty-five years in the making. While plumbers and an exterminator did their part to ready the Guzmans' home for Saturday's gathering, Edie and I hung out with Jodie and her cool family. This native of South Louisiana—where we bury our dead above ground for a reason—geeked out over their playroom basement, appointed with a pool table, TV, and giant sofa.

Their teenage son, Jack, headed to a friend's house down the street as the rest of us piled into Joe and Jodie's car. We dropped off June at Jamie and Gavin's nearby place en route to downtown Crown Point. The public square was featured in the film *Public Enemies*, starring Johnny Depp as the gangster who nearly took out Aunt Katie.

The four of us walked around the square Friday night before grabbing a table at Prime House. During our fun meal, we discussed family, careers, and legalized cannabis.

Jodie's a talented hairdresser. At one point, she described her beloved Uncle Mike as "a big ol' queen." She also said that, during an encounter with an old shipmate, the family learned Mike's nickname in the Navy was "Vitamins." I've yet to learn the story behind the moniker.

For what it's worth, I was also in the Navy. Trust me, I've heard all the jokes.

Of course, we'll never know for sure why the Weises made Mike persona non grata. The family reportedly referred to one member as the "bastard son," while a venerated Weis became monsignor after excommunicating his cousin Nancy Jane.

Joe tucked June into bed in Schererville while Jodie drove us back to Hammond. Edie got some quality front seat time with her cousin on the way to Paula's, where more Mike stories awaited.

My wife's grandfather wanted six hookers and a champagne fountain at his funeral, and a springboard in the coffin to make him sit up every so often. I also learned that his sister Sophie—the lone Lukaczyk with no kids—was the "idiot aunt" who dissuaded Mike from searching for Susan, telling him a daughter belongs with her mother.

His innate drive to find her was tempered by concern for her wellbeing. Paula said he didn't want to make life worse for his daughter. It's almost like he knew any sort of effort to reunite with Susan would be unpleasantly visited upon her in some form by Nancy Jane.

Nevertheless, Paula still wondered why Mike didn't go after them. We can only speculate, but maybe he was also worried about a dangerous reprisal against him. Perhaps he was fearful Nancy Jane might open a door, one countless Americans for centuries have desperately tried to keep shut by denying who they are, lest "civilized" members of early '50s society use the closet's contents to justify beating him to within an inch of his life.

Susan revealed that her mother once said of Mike, "He preferred having relationships with men instead of women." Nancy Jane capriciously excising Mike from his daughter's life sounds exactly like something an excommunicated Catholic—who stands next to priests in family pictures, and whose well-documented status in society was paramount—would do after learning that her husband was a "big ol' queen."

As much as we had learned about Edie's grandfather so far, the Golden Child and I had a pair of long-awaited gatherings that weekend with a horde of enthusiastic Ukrainians bringing all their Uncle Mike stories. We needed to rest up.

27

Yaha-Maha

Saturday morning was fairly chill at Paula's place, at least until we saw updates on Tropical Storm Florence, predicted to rapidly intensify into a major hurricane before slamming the Carolinas. Paula was a bit troubled by the news, and even more so by Carole's refusal to even consider evacuating.

"Headed your way!" Edie texted Susan near 1 p.m. At their hotel, the five of us assumed the same seating as we had on Thursday. Without Paula pointing out old neighborhood houses this time, I noticed Susan and her daughter holding hands next to me in the back seat on the way to Jodie's.

Knick didn't say a word. This didn't feel so much surreal as it did right.

We got to Jodie and Joe's over an hour before the scheduled start time of 3 p.m. so Susan could greet, upon their arrival, long-lost cousins who thought they'd be meeting only Edie and me. I was soon icing down beer in an inflatable pool raft on the deck, and placing a handful of unopened wine bottles nearby.

While I was outside helping the Guzmans knock out a few final details, our surprise guest of honor told the promoted guest of honor about her new, fancy wine bottle opener back in Metairie. Susan told Edie she'd have to show her how it works someday.

Skip overheard this exchange and interpreted it as an order of the highest priority to open a bottle of wine. Immediately.

I was coming back inside through the open sliding glass door when I saw Skip coming at me with a sense of purpose, a steely look of determination, and an even steelier-looking kitchen knife in his shaking hand, leading the march. A vocal Susan gave chase in a futile attempt to abort the misheard mission.

On their sliding glass door, the Guzmans had installed a screen that opens and closes along a seam lined by magnets as people walk through. I took no chances with my well-being, nor that of Jodie's screen, and stood aside from Skip's path against the outside wall, holding one half of the mesh curtain pulled open. As he went by me, still laser-focused on completing the unasked task, Skip told Susan to shush with her insistence that he put down the knife and leave the wine alone. While continuing her pursuit, I heard Susan reply under her breath, "Don't you shush me." She managed to stop him after opening only one bottle.

The first unsuspecting Lukaczyk to arrive was Aunt Theresa's daughter, Drea. Paula introduced the family historian to Edie and me, then to Susan and Skip, in the dining area where we were gathered. Her early arrival caught me flat-footed. I failed to record Drea's mascara-filled breakdown as she finally got to hug the cousin she'd known about her entire life.

I had my phone at the ready a couple minutes later when cousin Lois, from the Mother's Day photo, came in. Turns out Aunt Katie, who survived Dillinger as a kid, raised a cool customer. Still wearing her dark sunglasses, a smiling Lois gestured "hello" at me upon entering. I reciprocated. Over the next couple seconds, as Paula directed Lois's attention away from Skip and me, and toward our spouses to our left, the newly arrived guest's mouth steadily transformed from grinning to partially agape.

"Cousin Lois," Paula said, pointing across the table, "Edie and Susan."

In that instant, her jaw completed its drop. The gasp was audible from across the room as her head snapped back toward Paula for a split second, before finishing her double-take of Susan.

"Oh my God!" she trilled, then calmly stowed her purse on a chair.

"Hello, ladies!" Susan belted, drawing laughter from her cousins.

A youthful Lois removed her sunglasses. While she shed no tears —unlike mascara-streaked Drea across the room—a joyous Lois was genuinely shocked.

"This is like a..." Lois paused, searching for a word as she raised her hands toward slightly shrugged shoulders, "...moment." She completed her thought with a slight chuckle and a "hell if I know" gesture.

Giant smiles overcame everyone's faces as Susan made her way toward her older cousin.

"How are you, Susan?" Lois greeted her as the two embraced for the first time in two-thirds of a century.

"Nice to meet you," Susan said mid-hug.

As they unclinched, a wide-eyed Lois replied. "Nice to see you *again*," she emphasized with raised eyebrows and a hand flair. "I saw you when you were a little girl." Lois lowered her open palm toward the floor, maintaining eye contact as she pointed with her other hand at a beaming Susan.

Our latest guest then turned to Paula. "Was this a surprise or what?" Lois asked, her thumb pointing at Susan from near point-blank range.

"For who?" Paula replied off-camera.

"You," Lois answered, doubting her cousin's ability to keep such a thing from the rest of the horde. "She couldn't," was all Lois could get out before Paula's face revealed Susan's presence was no surprise to her.

With an almost indignant smile, Lois placed her hands on her hips as Edie busted out laughing and Paula broke into dance. This demonstration lasted for a few seconds, during which Lois's mouth grew agape once again. Agog at her younger cousin's ability to orchestrate such an awesome surprise sixty-five years in the making, she seemed even more amazed than when she first laid eyes on her long-lost cousin.

"She's tricky like that," Susan purred as Lois picked her jaw up off the ground for the second time in less than a minute.

While Lois arrived with potato salad in a bowl inherited from their Uncle Mike, cousin Misha showed up with photos. Lots of them.

Aunt Rosie's daughter represented the Lukaczyks' Library of Congress. Misha had tons of pictures and other artifacts attesting to the family's crazy-ass history. One was a trifold wedding invitation.

"Dr. William D. Weis requests the honour of your presence at the marriage of his daughter Nancy Jane to Mr. Michael Lukaczyk," it read in a fancy Old English font, "son of Mr. and Mrs. Andrew Lukaczyk on Saturday, the nineteenth day of June nineteen hundred and forty-eight at ten o'clock in the morning, St. Joseph's Church, Hammond, Indiana." The keepsake's flaps were fashioned to house future pics of the bride and groom.

The wedding reception in East Chicago, fifteen minutes away from Hammond, was scheduled for 7 p.m. I guess they wanted to allow plenty of time for passing trains along the way, given I'd never seen so many damn railroad crossings per square mile. Paula said one delayed Aunt Bernice's funeral procession long enough for multiple roadside cigarettes and a snack, at least for the Lukaczyks lucky enough to have found stray food in their cars.

Drea told us how Edie's great-grandmother Mary worked on the Trans-Siberian Railroad as a teenager to save enough money to come to America. Though her true maiden name was Sklarczyk, she met Andrew on the boat while traveling under the name Kolibowski. Her father, a general in the tsar's army, was killed when she was just a girl. As a result, Mary's status fell to that of future servant to the Romanov children. She managed to strike out on her own as a teen, working on the world's longest railway line, before the Bolsheviks in Russia overthrew Tsar Nicholas and executed his entire family, loyal servants included. Mary had changed her name for fear of reprisal.

She had her first child at the age of twenty-eight. Ten additional children later, the Lukaczyks' matriarch gave birth to her youngest when she was forty-seven.

My wife's great-grandma was a badass.

Mary's eleventh child was Theresa. She grew up to equip seventeen-year-old Drea with a fake ID for a trip to Las Vegas with a legally aged Paula. The family historian told us that—after some negotiations by members of the gangster-adjacent family in the city built by the mob—all three met Elvis.

A steady stream of cousins started flowing through the doorway, including Jamie and her husband, swole, bald Matt Damon (aka Gavin). Just like in Bothell, all the little kids were soon on the backyard trampoline, enjoying the cool, partly sunny afternoon.

Paula's cabbage rolls simmered on the stove. A few feet away, she fell in love with the hog's head cheese Susan and Skip had brought. The smoked boudin was a hit in the midst of kielbasa country, too.

Susan also brought a king cake—in September, which is nowhere near king cake season. I should know; it officially starts on my birthday, January 6. The Epiphany, or Three Kings Day, is the twelfth day of Christmas, heralding the start of Carnival. The season ends with what's known in certain quasi-banana republics as Mardi Gras, or Fat Tuesday, followed by Ash Wednesday, marking the start of Lent.

However, given the nature of the occasion, I—keeper of the rightful king cake season—granted special dispensation unto dozens of Lukaczyks gathered in the backyard for my Susan-approved primer on what the hell a king cake is. The tasty pastry—covered in purple, green, and gold sugar—went fast.

Far more important than any story I might've had to offer were all the ones about Mike. Throughout the afternoon and into the evening, mother and daughter learned all sorts of fantastic tales about the man they never knew. Their cousins described a true card who was all about making sure people, especially his nieces and nephews, had a good time.

Word was he'd supply all the fireworks for the horde's annual Fourth of July celebration. Mike didn't skimp on things that go boom. One year, when the cache accidentally went off all at once, Mike went out and bought more. He'd also bring bags of candy for the kids, in case some of them didn't catch any during the parade.

Mike's drink of choice was Chivas Regal. He tended the bar in his sister's backyard during many get-togethers, where he made drinks for the kids. If they didn't like his creations, they'd give them to their parents.

One of Mike's favorite words was "yaha-maha." While there's no exact definition, he seemed to employ it much like we South Louisiana types use the word "couyon" to refer (sometimes affectionately) to someone who isn't quite right. A foolish person, in other words.

Mike had to learn how to speak again following a stroke. Cousin Arlene, photographed as an eleven-year-old on those East Chicago steps, told us how she and her mother, the formerly hitchhiking Auntie Matza, tended to Mike three times a week during his recovery.

Around sunset, everyone gathered out back for photos. As in 1952, two groups were photographed: the nine cousins present from Susan's generation, and everyone gathered. The infamous Mother's Day picture and its decades of questions ached for an answer. Better late than never.

"A thousand words is not even enough for the foreword," I commented to Fort Worth.

The '52 photo featured thirty-three people; its long-awaited bookend captured twenty-eight. At least two of the nine first cousins were named John, including the next day's host, Johnny Mark.

When it came to Christmas decorations, we learned that nobody outdid Mike. After spending the 1945 holiday season in that San Diego hospital, following the war, he went full Kringle every year, starting with the family's Christmas celebration upon his return home in March 1946.

He also loved dogs. My wife's grandfather once picked up a pup belonging to a friend, drove around the block with the furry fellow, and dropped him right back off. Mike said he just wanted to say hello to the dog.

Of course, a night of lauding Uncle Mike would be incomplete without at least a couple of hustle stories. While Andrew, the patriarch, bootlegged for Capone, Mike and his siblings ran a somewhat more benign racket: illegal bingo.

Like her daughter, Susan had a father who spent time in jail for extra-legal endeavors that involved ensuring others had a good time. During a raid by authorities, the guy helping run the bootleg bingo walked out on Mike, leaving my wife's grandfather literally holding the bag.

Not an ounce of judgment was directed toward Susan and the unfathomably tough decisions she had to make in her life. Her enthusiastic cousins showered her with a love that screamed "we never forgot about you" and "we always knew we'd find you again." Nancy had done everything she could to block Mike from Susan's life. That night was a great start at filling the void. There was so much laughter, all night long.

At some point, one of Edie's kin told her, "You're so much prettier in person than in your pictures," unwittingly bolstering my wife's aversion to being photographed.

Cooling temps and a dying fire that evening drove the remaining mini-horde indoors to Jodie's kitchen and dining room area, where warm memories of Mike continued flowing.

In addition to the Fighting Irish, my wife's grandfather was a huge fan of the Chicago Cubs. His team jacket, like most things he owned, had his name on it. He evidently spent a little extra on the embroidery by giving himself a title.

Arlene's daughter, Tracie, recalled running into Mike, wearing his Cubs jacket outside Wrigley Field before a game. This sparked a flurry of talk about the steel mill worker and his exploits as a member of the Cubs' "Executive Staff."

The best story involved a bus full of fans pulling up to Wrigley for a game. Mike immediately jumped on board and began taking food orders—and cash—from passengers, obviously convinced by the jacket that someone from the team's organization was generously offering to make a lunch run before they'd be limited to stadium fare (which the Cubs make money on) for the next several hours. Mike returned with their food, the story goes, undoubtedly marked up by an enterprising "Executive Staff" member. I'm still not sure if the driver was duped or in on it.

The laughter from that account was ebbing just past nine o'clock when Jodie exited the room. She soon returned with something from Jack's closet. Joe had converted his stepson into a White Sox fan, Jodie insisted, before handing Mike's jacket to my bride.

"I know Jack would never wear it," she explained, adding how she felt a little sad thinking of Uncle Mike every time she put away her son's laundry.

The granddaughter Mike never knew existed soon donned his prized jacket. I managed to snap a pic or two of the newest Cubs fan before absolutely losing my shit. Right there in Jodie's kitchen, I was straight-up bawling. The company didn't matter. I was done.

"I lost it," Fort Worth learned with my latest photo. "The stories of Mike scream how much he's still so beloved by this family."

"Wow," Patrick replied after seeing his baby sister wearing the hell out of her grandfather's jacket. "That's amazing," he added. Yvette sent her love with a cat sticker.

Moments before our farewells, Edie and I invited Jodie and her family to celebrate Mardi Gras with us in the Spanish Town Parade, in return for their hospitality the last two days. In my spiel to my wife's cousin about what to expect, I dropped the term "spank bank."

Spank. Bank. Two words, innocent apart. Together, though, they make an Urban Dictionary entry.

Jodie reacted with a gasp louder than Aunt Lois's. Our hostess clutched her gaping mouth and doubled over with a mixture of laughter and disbelief. I quickly surmised we were among a small handful of people there familiar with the term.

It came while showing Jodie a video of a shitfaced Sunny and me "dancing" together in front of the phallic Louisiana State Capitol. Someone artfully shot the two of us doing "our thing" a couple hours before the Krewe of Spanish Town rolled through downtown Baton Rouge back in February. The video went viral among members of the city's gay community, as noted on the last episode of The Red Shtick Podcast, recorded the same day Edie first laid eyes on her father.

"I'm a forty-eight-year-old man," I reiterated my thoughts from the show to Jodie. "If I'm in somebody's spank bank, I consider that a source of pride. I don't give a damn who they are."

Jodie and Jamie wouldn't be able to make Sunday's gathering in Crown Point. We bid them goodbye around 10 p.m.

Susan and Edie held hands riding back to Hammond, as they had done en route to Schererville.

An excited Johnny Mark pulled up at Paula's just past 9 a.m. on Sunday morning. We loaded my gumbo ingredients, including a can of Tony Chacherie's from home, in his new Volkswagen SUV. The vehicle simultaneously occupied multiple eastbound interstate lanes for what seemed like mini eternities to me. My nerves settled down as we drove along the blight-riddled streets of Gary, Indiana, where we stopped by Michael Jackson's childhood home. For what it's worth, this was before *Leaving Neverland*.

Nearing Crown Point, my driver pointed out fields once worked by his family. John pulled into the driveway of their split-level home at the end of a cul de sac in a gated community around 10:30 a.m. Inside, I greeted Mira, who was preparing to attend a midday baby shower. She patiently acquainted me with her kitchen, before rewrapping a gift her young granddaughter thought was for her.

For the next couple hours, I chopped holy trinity (onions, celery, bell pepper), browned several pounds of meat, and created a dark roux. Throughout the attention-demanding process, John asked multiple times if he could show me something outside. He turned sixty-four that Sunday, and the birthday boy was dying to show his new cousin's husband from Louisiana all his toys, including one freshly detailed by his son Nick. John's "midlife crisis"—a black, fiftieth-anniversary edi-tion Mustang convertible—was parked in the driveway, just begging to be driven on a glorious summer day.

This is the part of the story where my culinary-averse mother would sing the praises of gumbo from a box.

"When are y'all coming home?" Patrick messaged Edie, back in Hammond, minutes after she finished a nine-minute call with Ducky.

"Also, did you tell Mom the details of your trip?" he wondered. "I've been avoiding calling her because I never know when I'm going to be interrogated about your situation."

"Just got off the phone with her," Edie informed him, "reminded her we're here."

"Okay, cool. Now I can call her," he laughed. "I'm so glad y'all are having this time."

"Ducky wanted to know if I had arranged lunch for her with Susan and Kellie."

"Of course," Patrick noted. "I'm jelly about that jacket," he added. "It's awesome."

Minutes later, Carole sent her first Facebook message to Edie. "What a fabulous week of Love!" she sent from the Palmetto State.

"So awesome!" Edie answered. "Your sister and her girls are the best," my wife raved. "Love my cousins!"

"And I'm grateful for my sister's detailed play by play with emotion that allowed me to see it, be there, and feel it!" Carole shared. "There is so much love for you all!"

Mira returned from the baby shower around the time I placed a lid on the simmering gumbo. A couple hours later, Paula and the rest of the gang from Hammond pulled up. Susan soon sampled and signed off on my creation, as did Edie.

Don't tell the rest of the horde, but those two were the only endorsements that mattered to me.

While we enjoyed some hot boudin in the kitchen, Johnny Mark was out by his pool grilling up its Eastern European cousin, a zesty Balkan sausage commonly spelled cevapi. The grillmaster pronounced it "CHEE-vahp."

After lots of buildup by John, and despite his bad back acting up, our host eventually fried up bologna like his dad used to make for him and his siblings. It lived up to the hype. It also involved ketchup.

That afternoon, we met two of Johnny Mark's nephews, Danny and Bob. The latter shared the name of their late father, Johnny Mark and

Gene's deceased older brother. I was fine with learning about a second Bob Lukas over an umpteenth John.

Bob and Danny's brother Mike Lukas was named in honor of Edie's grandfather. He lived in New Jersey, serving as CFO for Quest Diagnostics, the company responsible for Ancestry's DNA testing. As part of his job, Mike Lukas got a free DNA kit some time back. His results showed he had a close relative that he'd never heard of before.

The guy's name was Jim. He lived in Illinois. He also turned out to be the extramarital son of Johnny Mark's dad, the late John Lukas.

Back in July, Edie spoke on the phone for half an hour to her grandfather's namesake in New Jersey about the methodology used to figure out how Jim fit into the family. Since his father was deceased, cousin Mike Lukas asked his uncle Johnny Mark to submit his DNA to help triangulate their relationship with this Jim kin. The way the birthday boy in Crown Point told it, once they figured it out, Johnny Mark called his big brother in Victoria with the news.

"Hey," John said, "you have a half-brother."

Gene reportedly shot back, "What'd you do with the other half?"

This account came around the time John Lukas fielded separate phone calls from both Jim and Gene on Sunday afternoon. Cousin Nick would later confirm my suspicion that his father spoke with his two surviving brothers every day.

Back in January, around the time I taught my wife how to spit in a vial, the Lukaczyks welcomed Jim into the family. Sadly, an ailing Gene couldn't make the reunion, which is why the Texas Devil Dog was the first to meet the Golden Child.

Then in early May, John Lukas logged into his Ancestry account. Like his nephew Mike, he discovered a close relative he'd never heard of before, and decided to reach out to his gorgeous new cousin in Baton Rouge. Four months later, I was making killer gumbo in the dude's kitchen on his birthday, all while he wanted me to go ride in his bitchin' Mustang.

In some respects, we owe the late John Lukas a debt of gratitude. The father of Jim, Gene, Johnny Mark, and their late brother, Bob, left a DNA puzzle for the Lukaczyks to solve, which, in turn, led to Edie and Beth solving another.

During the weekend, we also learned about the late Bob Lukas's conception. In 1935, at the age of twenty-three, Andrew and Mary's eldest son knocked up a seventeen-year-old girl named Bernice. John Lukas then skedaddled.

The expectant teen didn't even know the father's name, but she knew what his sisters looked like. A very pregnant Aunt Bernice, the account goes, saw them walking down the street and hollered, "Your brother did this to me!" Since their only other brother, Michael, hadn't hit puberty, they knew Bernice was screaming about John. Their mother, Great-grandma Mary, was so livid, she made her son sleep in the attic until he married that girl.

Told you she was a badass.

The two got married in the church basement. The official cover story alleged they did so because John didn't want to give up his Byzantine rites by converting to a different form of Catholicism.

No reunion of Susan and her cousins would be complete without an incident involving Skip and a screen door. This particular one led to the sunlit backyard deck from a dim man-cave-like area, where a TV showed NFL opening weekend coverage. Skip ran clean through the closed screen door. Cousin Nick said he wasn't the first to do so, and probably wouldn't be the last.

Over in the Lukas living room, cousin Misha guided the gathered horde through her numerous photo albums stacked on the table. She noted how some aunts were sometimes missing from wedding photos because, at the time, they were mad at other family members. One of John's aunts—Sophie, if I recall correctly—skipped the wedding when he married Mira. I'm not sure whom she had beef with.

Misha also brought over more archives, including her Uncle Mike's ceramic candleholders, resembling a pair of angels. She gifted them to Edie.

Susan was sitting next to me at the table when one of her younger cousins, Aunt Katie's son Buddy, bid her goodbye. I heard him tell

Susan, "I'm so glad to finally meet the little girl at the bottom of the picture."

Naturally, Buddy's real name is John, because the family has more Johns than a brothel.

As the lovely afternoon turned into a cool, clear evening, Edie, and her generation of second cousins there, posed in front of the Lukas home for a group photograph. To the left, Nick's sizable younger brother Stevie stood next to Edie; the two each placed an arm around the other. Nick held his young daughter, Mallory, to the right of me and my camera. In between were Johnny Mark's nephews Bob and Danny, along with Lois's son Gregg, a fellow sports official who enjoys cooking.

"How did the gumbo turn out?!" Jodie texted Edie during our twilight photo shoot. "I'm sorry that I couldn't make it out today. I bet you're having a time with John & Mira's family!"

"It was great," Edie reported on the gumbo. "I made sure your mom took home enough for all of y'all!"

Paula had headed back to Hammond a bit before sunset, when Susan and Skip left in their vehicle for a final night at the hotel. We bid the couple goodbye knowing we wouldn't see them again until we were all back in Louisiana. Susan planned on visiting previously known kin in Michigan the next day before beginning the Oktoberfest trek. It was still too soon for Susan to tell her folks about the daughter no one knew she had.

Later Sunday evening, she texted Edie. "Just in case I haven't said it lately," Susan sealed with a kiss, "Thank you!"

"This has been a great week," her daughter answered. "I'm so happy we could experience it together. Love you!"

Moments later, Susan ranked my gumbo via text: a golden cup trophy with two exclamation marks. "Thanks for all of your hard work!"

"Awww, thank you!" I replied, a bit weepy-eyed. "So glad you think I set the bar high for those Hoosiers! This has been such an unbelievable trip!"

Sometime that Sunday, I was near Edie as she conversed with folks about her journey thus far—including the parts about her paternal and adopted families—and all the wonderful people who were now a part of our lives. "Just bringing more love into the world," is how she characterized it.

Never in my life had I felt so fortunate, so honored to have married Edris Ann O'Neal than I did right then. The hot, badass Marine OCS candidate who saw *Full Metal Jacket* as a chick flick was now bringing untold peace and love to recent strangers all around the country, and I could not have been prouder.

28

Dey Lyin'!

Once everyone had gone home on Sunday night, Edie and I settled into the man cave with Nick and his eleven-year-old son, Ryan, both wearing Bears jerseys. Together, we watched the second half of Chicago's season opener in Green Bay. The Bears ended up blowing a twenty-point third-quarter lead to the Packers, who were led by a practically one-legged Aaron Rodgers after he'd been carted off the field in the first half.

This lifelong Saints fan knew better than to talk shit about the Bears choking away the game to an ostensibly crippled legend before a national prime-time audience. I didn't feel like looking for a hotel room at 10 p.m. in Crown Point.

On the evening of John's birthday, he and Mira insisted we sleep in their big, comfy bed while they'd doze in a small room not occupied by their son or grandkids. Her paternal Serbian kin always gave up their beds for non-blood relatives, Mira explained.

Monday morning saw Nick dealing with a sick Ryan (it really was a gut-wrenching loss) and preparing his "Mallogator" for picture day at the kindergartner's school. Once Mallory had breakfast, Nick loaned me his White Sox jacket to contend with Chicago's touted wind off Lake Michigan that day, and to provide yang to the yin of Edie's inherited Cubs jacket.

With John back from the chiropractor for treatment that morning, we ate leftover cevapi for breakfast before our host drove us to Paula's in Hammond. By the time we arrived, though, she'd already left for the East Chicago station, where the 10 a.m. train had just come through. We soon met Paula there. She lobbied to wait for the 11:52 South Shore Line rather than trust John behind the wheel for a day trip to downtown Chicago.

We boarded the upper level of a double-decker passenger car with seats capable of facing either end. Edie and Paula chatted up front. John napped toward the back of the car, affording Mira some much-deserved quiet time. I occasionally enjoyed the perverse feeling of misplaced schadenfreude while passing lines of idling vehicles that were waiting for our steadily rolling train to pass. I lost count of how many times we were on the aggravating end of such interactions up there.

We disembarked at the line's last stop, Millennium Park Station. Drumming could be heard, louder and louder as we ascended the stairs leading to Michigan Avenue. It reminded me of the sound of plastic-bucket drummers in the French Quarter.

The five of us reached and exited the door. Like all of Chicago, we were awash in brilliant daylight. My eyes adjusted to see the rhythms coming from a full-on drum kit being played on the corner of a bustling downtown area during lunchtime. That's not something you normally see in New Orleans.

Any remaining delusions about this being like the Crescent City evaporated when the drummer stopped to give someone directions. That definitely never happens in NOLA, where music's far more important than directions in the city where one travels east to get to the Westbank.

A couple of traffic light cycles later, our pentet made it safely across Michigan Avenue. Our first stop in Millennium Park came at the Crown Fountain, aka the Faces Fountain. Imagine a couple of the obelisks from Kubrick's *2001: A Space Odyssey* standing on end, facing each other. On the surfaces are these giant, close-up videos of random people's faces. It looked like they were peeking at us through a pair of five-story-tall peepholes in the fabric of their obviously giant-populated quantum universe.

Water trickled down from their foreheads like profuse summer sweat the whole time, and sometimes squirted from the mouths of those creepy, giant faces. Kids and a few adults played in voluminous spit-takes scaled up to match that of someone large enough to eat them in one bite.

Nearby was the much-ballyhooed "Bean." The official name is Cloud Gate. It's a highly reflective, bean-shaped, metallic sculpture. It's like a funhouse that got reincarnated as a shiny legume, one large enough to feed a family of the fountain giants. It's great for trippy selfies.

By this point, the sun's unexpected warmth convinced me to carry Nick's black jacket. Edie wore Mike's light gray one a bit longer. It was the sort of Monday that would've led Ferris Bueller to ditch school for a day in the city.

While the older cousins futilely asked people in uniform about an alleged trolley to Navy Pier, which served as a World War II-era training site for sailors like Edie's grandfather, she discovered on her phone that the trolley only ran on weekends. Meanwhile, I scanned the area for parades featuring popular truant teens lip-syncing Wayne Newton's "Danke Schoen."

We soon squeezed into a taxicab. Paula's aching back earned her shotgun. John and Mira sat next to me in the back seat, where Edie sat on my lap. We clown-car'd our way through the City of Big Shoulders in a hybrid Camry to the lakefront some ten minutes away.

Before the driver even pulled away from us, John was guessing his nationality. The former chip salesman, who had called on shop operators of various ethnicities for ten years, prided himself on identifying accents.

We visited Navy Pier's Crystal Gardens, and its dancing leapfrog fountains, before taking a selfie with the nearly 200-foot-tall Centennial Wheel. It also goes by the name Ferris. (I knew we'd run into him.)

We stopped for lunch at Harry Caray's Tavern. Their patio overlooking the pier's promenade was made for days like this Monday. While

I walked in repping/schlepping the South Siders in a place named for the beloved longtime Cubs announcer, Edie and her grandpa's jacket were right at home.

A gaggle of bona fide, orange-clad Hare Krishnas soon walked by. I later tried making a Lettermanesque play on words about seeing Hare Krishnas at Harry Caray's, but our young waitress had never heard of the cult before. For enlightenment, I suggested she watch the movie *Airplane!*.

During lunch, I referenced something I had revealed that morning while waiting for the train. One cousin who had a bit too much to drink on Sunday in Crown Point couldn't shut up about how "weird" Uncle Mike was. He said it several times. "Weird." The best he could elaborate was with a couple of synonyms, like "strange," and "uh...strange." At one point, he actually pulled me aside to applaud the Weises for being mum about Susan all those years.

I told my lunch partners what's really weird: meeting people you never knew existed just weeks before, having them pick you up at an airport a thousand miles away, putting you up in their home, feeding you, lending you their brand-new car to drive around a strange city, and insisting you sleep in their bed on their birthday, while they and their spouse sleep in a converted storage room in the garage. Even stone-cold sober, that's just fucking bizarre.

Nevertheless, I informed our table of five, as weird as all those things may sound, that's how much it all felt right.

Moreover, the drunk cousin's "weird uncle" comments about Mike were meant as a pejorative in a conversation with a guy who proudly wears that same moniker. He violated the first rule of stand-up: Know your audience.

After lunch, Paula said she'd meet us out front when the rest of us got back from walking along the remainder of the pier, where we checked out shops and moored yachts. She soon messaged Mira, however, that her back wouldn't let her continue. Our former hostess took a cab back to her Kia in East Chicago. At home in Hammond, she hoped to alleviate pain severe enough to cut short a Bueller-worthy hooky Monday in the big city with the Golden Child and her entourage.

Our remaining quartet was approaching the series of wind-stiffened flags along Lake Michigan at the end of the 3,300-foot pier when Gene called. John actually spoke with him a few minutes before handing me the phone this time.

"Whatcha doing in Chicago?" the former Marine asked me.

"Asking around if they remember you and your exploits," I answered.

Our next destination was the John Hancock Center. During the cab ride there, we witnessed Chicago hotel workers in red union T-shirts picketing in front of the Ritz-Carlton. Our driver's accent was Caribbean. There were no guesses about his nationality upon exiting.

To reach the 360-degree observatory on the tower's ninety-fourth floor, we needed to go downstairs, a building concierge told us, and nothing more. After futilely searching for a way to go downstairs, we eventually realized that we had to go back outside and around the corner to the west entrance, where stairs led us down to the observatory ticket office. The drummer by the train station was proving more helpful than some folks in uniform.

The late-afternoon sun shone through much of the observatory, where, borrowing from John Glenn, the view was tremendous. We could clearly see industrial plants dotting the Indiana shoreline, where folks like John make supertall skyscrapers like this one possible. We also watched visitors pay for the privilege of holding on for dear life as they got tilted over the edge, giving them a clear view of the nearly thousand-foot drop to the street below. We passed on that attraction.

An hour after entering Chicago's fourth-tallest building, we were back out on Michigan Avenue just after 6 p.m. We hiked down the Magnificent Mile toward Millennium Park Station. Leftovers awaited us for dinner in Crown Point.

We made a few brief stops on our walk, like when Mira pointed out the historic Chicago Water Tower. Built two years before the Great Fire of 1871, its 180-foot-tall exterior looked like a fancy limestone chess piece belonging to one of the fountain giants.

At seven o'clock, standing less than a block from the train station entrance, we walked into Stan's Donuts ahead of the expected ninety-minute commute to the Lukas home. "I wonder what time the next train leaves," someone said as we nibbled on pastries.

Edie again conducted research on her phone, this time for something she had intended to look up earlier, but didn't. The time was 7:19 p.m., nine minutes after the last train had left. Since it was just past peak commuting hours, the next one didn't depart until 9:10 p.m.

Hopes of making lemonade, in the form of Chicago-style deep-dish pizza before the ride home, were soon quashed by the expected wait time at a busy Giordano's around the corner. Mira then led us to the train station's Chicago Kernel outlet, where we bought gourmet popcorn around 8 p.m., seconds before the young lady turned off the sign and locked up. To wash it down, my bride and I got a pair of Miller Lite tallboys in wino-sized paper bags at the station watering hole for a surprisingly reasonable $4.25 each.

Minutes later, the four of us were in the Windy City's third-busiest transit station, eating fancy popcorn and trying to charge our phones, all while Edie and I nursed big-ass beers in paper bags. And just like that, I was reminded of the French Quarter again, namely at 3 a.m., while you and friends try to get home without any accompanying music.

Just before our train pulled into the station, I accepted John Lukas's newly sent Facebook friend request. I figured it was the decent thing to do after the dude sitting next to me had let us sleep in his bed on his birthday.

We were just pulling out of the station when Edie replied to an earlier text from Paula. She apologized for having "snuck off" at the pier, and was soaking in the tub. She hoped to join us at Indiana Dunes State Park on the lakeshore before our flight out the next day.

"We had fun!" Edie sent back as we rolled along. "We missed the 7:10 train since we didn't think about checking the schedule," she reported, "so we're just now heading back!"

"You all must be exhausted!" Paula replied. "But in a good way!"

"Precisely," my wife confirmed.

Exhausted was right. I snapped a pic of a slouching John snoozing across the aisle to our left at 9:29 p.m. His sunglasses rested on the bill of his ball cap, which covered most of his face. The train momentarily stopped a couple of times to pick up more folks as we made our way toward the South Side. Nursing them to last most of the expected ride, our beers were still about half full.

Suddenly, nowhere near a station, the train slowed and came to a complete stop. An initial announcement a few minutes later said the train in front of us had mechanical issues.

Immediately upon the announcement's conclusion, a passenger sporting one of those red, striking-hotel-union-worker shirts melodically insisted with a Caribbean accent, "Dey lyin'!" He said it loud enough for the entire car to hear. "Dey ran da red signal. Dis same train—one month ago—ran da red signal."

An hour later, a follow-up announcement stated, "Transit lost power at the substation up ahead." As a result, other trains were stranded there. It was like a dead zone, apparently. Or at least to me it was.

"Dey lyin'!" red-shirt dude piped up again. "You watch. Come eleven o'clock, we stay right here."

About that time, the young conductor made an appearance in our car. He was a nice guy with rapport among regular commuters, and did his level best to pass along whatever info he was getting about the situation. Not everyone shared my assessment.

"I don't belieeeve you!" came booming from behind us.

The conductor just shook his head and exited to the car in front. A minute or two later, fake-news union guy followed him. Another minute or two later, a trio of transit cops passed through our car, heading in the same direction with a sense of purpose. Like crew members on *Star Trek*, we wondered aloud, would our red-shirted friend suffer a tragic fate?

By this point, John had moved to an empty aisle seat in front of me to stretch out a bit. Like many commuters, he passed the time watching videos on his phone. Unlike many others onboard, the yaha-maha had no headphones. Thanks to Edie's cousin, half the car got to learn about nineteenth-century happenings in South Central Asia.

"Dammit," I told Edie, "we should've gotten him earbuds for his birthday."

I looked over at Mira. Her face wore an expression equivalent to a shoulder shrug.

"Jaaahn!" she called to him from across the aisle. "JAAAHN!" Mira repeated, finally gaining his attention over the narrator's voice. "Turn that down!" she told him.

He, in turn, insisted he couldn't lower the volume because he could barely hear it as is.

"Everyone in this car can hear it except him?" I asked Mira, in a tone that she, and perhaps a few others, would hear.

"I can hear it," belted a lady seated several rows back.

Have I mentioned lately how patient Mira is?

We and the folks around us got a chuckle out of that exchange. We also speculated about what might've happened to red-shirt Alex Jones. What kind of mass transit conspiracy theories had he been spreading car to car on his one-man show "Train InfoWars"?

"Why you take my money so quickly right before it stops?" was one insightful question he posed to the conductor. "If dey don't have power, how come we have lights and da air?" was another from Rasta Tesla, who apparently failed to grasp that we had stopped short of the electrical dead zone.

"I hope a plane in front of us tomorrow doesn't stop in the air and we can't go around them," I said at one point.

As Monday's final hour approached, the transit folks made another announcement. They had received permission to back up to McCormick Place. There, we could either grab alternate transportation, or wait for the train to resume, whenever that might be. With my beer now finished, I successfully suppressed an urge to jump into the aisle and channel rapper Juvenile in celebration of CTA's decision to back that train up.

Back at McCormick Place, before the train's doors had opened, Edie and her phone again proved invaluable to Monday's travels as she snagged the last available Lyft in the area, within seconds of getting a signal. She and I hustled toward the designated pickup point as we disembarked with several other passengers willing to pay more to hopefully get home before Tuesday morning. Our driver called her at exactly 11 p.m. to see where we were. The two of us were quickly heading down some stairs to the street below, where his car was in view. John and Mira were somewhere behind us.

Edie and I claimed our ride as we waited for the rest of our party to catch up. Mira sat up front, next to our polite driver, a patient man named Sam. We informed him that we were going just around the corner to East Chicago.

"Indiana?" he asked, seeking clarification. The only landmark he knew was the area casino. "What makes you live out here?" he later wondered.

After chatting with the former chip salesman about his Middle Eastern accent, Sam dropped us off by the VW in the far back corner of the station's all-but-empty parking lot, where only a handful of spots had been available at midday. Five minutes remained before Tuesday.

We pulled into the Lukases' driveway at 12:20 a.m. On the ride from the station, I dozed off, something I almost never do, with or without John driving. I couldn't remember the last time I had fallen asleep in a moving vehicle without me behind the wheel.

I can only imagine how exhausted John and Mira were, but you never would've known it. For all of us, it was a fun adventure with newly reunited, long-lost cousins.

John fixed fried bologna sandwiches, which paired great at that hour with leftover potato salad and beer. Our heads hit our pillows an hour after we drove up.

The sun arose in Crown Point a few hours before we did on Tuesday. Edie spent time that morning on the phone dealing with air conditioning issues back home at Earle's. Our flight was slated to depart Midway at 8:15 that evening.

In a text to Paula, Edie mentioned our "extended adventure on the train." She also asked, "How you doing this morning?"

"Still icing my back," a perturbed Paula answered.

"So scaling the dunes doesn't sound like a plan for today, huh?"

"Not for me!" Edie's cousin replied. "Have fun!"

My wife also touched base with Susan. She and Skip were on the first stop of their Oktoberfest tour in a Michigan town known for its Bavarian architecture and German roots.

"Frankenmuth has been a bit of a disappointment for Skip. It's not Oktoberfesty enough for him," Susan reported from the road. "You've heard the term 'on steroids,'" she added, "this place is more like 'on Geritol.'"

As midday approached, Edie and I finally got to take a spin with her cousin in his convertible Mustang on another picture-perfect day in the breadbasket of America. John still hadn't figured out how to drop the top. It didn't matter, however, as long as I was the one behind the wheel, although my wife might argue that made no difference in her tension during the ride.

Cousin Stevie and his daughter, Delilah, were at his parents' home when I pulled back in. The toddler was receiving an elocution lesson from her Baba Mira. Moments later, as we loaded our previously packed bags into the VW, the junior member of the family of thieves—which had stolen our hearts—attempted to make off with her cousin Edie's purse.

My wife and I soon joined our gracious hosts and their grand-daughter for a group photo out back by the pool. We then bid goodbye to Nick, Stevie, and his blonde cutie, before heading out with John and Mira for the lakefront.

There, on a glorious summer afternoon, we dipped our toes into Lake Michigan. A brisk wind came in off the water, rushing past the towering dunes, as I imagined how inhospitable this place would be in January. We gathered a few pebbles as keepsakes, cleaned the sand from our feet, and headed west for Midway around 3:30 p.m.

From the back seat with Mira, Edie fired up her Waze app just as we were about to miss the suggested route's exit—maybe a hundred yards or two ahead, and five lanes of traffic to our right. John traversed all of them in a couple of seconds.

"Call me when you get settled at the airport," Paula texted Edie that afternoon. "Unless of course John gets you there late!" she laughed.

We deeply appreciated the abundant hospitality and free transportation provided. Nevertheless, Edie and I agreed that we felt safer with eighty-seven-year-old Aunt Neenie at the wheel.

Since he made his living as a truck driver, I can only hope that Gene (and their grandfather Andrew, for that matter) was a better driver, the Shelley Winters wreck obviously notwithstanding. Paula had insisted on riding the train for a reason. A ride through downtown Chicago piloted by her cousin would likely have proven no less adventurous. To paraphrase his big brother, John's a bad driver. Good guy, good guy.

He safely negotiated the rush-hour traffic along the route to Midway. We got there with plenty of time to spare.

Edie and I hugged him and Mira at the curb. Twice. We couldn't wait to see them, Paula, and their families again.

Unlike our last flight home, we quickly made our way through security, thanks to PreCheck. Red and I grabbed dinner in the terminal. Washing down Irish fare with Harp draft at Reilly's Daughter, the former Miss O'Neal and I discussed another potential reunion of sorts, five days before she'd likely see Ducky. Edie anticipated another request to arrange lunch with Susan. We spoke about how best to finesse the tricky issue. She knew Susan wasn't near ready to meet the woman who had raised the child that—outside of Skip—no one from her life knew about.

Meanwhile, Susan and Skip were at the Lorelei Lounge at the Bavarian Inn Lodge in Frankenmuth. "We're waiting for the live music to start," Susan informed us. "Three buses of 'old farts' (Skip's description) came in and filled the place. We thought the music would be German, but the song the singer started with is 'Mr. Bojangles,' followed by 'Norwegian Wood.' I'm falling on my chair laughing at Skip giving the guy 'the look.'" With a wide-eyed emoji, she closed, "I think we're leaving shortly."

Upon boarding, we sat in the back of the Southwest aircraft amid a gaggle of women thrilled to be going to New Orleans. Just before takeoff, one ate an airport salad, likely the most healthy thing she'd put in her mouth for the duration of her trip, we predicted. We also noted never seeing anything close to that level of excitement on a plane bound for Baton Rouge.

"Hopefully you're on your way home now," Mira texted Edie during our ascent. "We just got in. A few wrong turns, drive down hooker row, complete with mattress on the side of the road," John's passenger added about their return trip, "pit stop at tollway oasis along the way. Sorry you missed that adventure. Safe travels!"

Our plane landed safely around 10:30 p.m. The shuttle brought us back to the Kenner hotel we last saw one week before. At two minutes into Wednesday, I parked the Rogue under our carport.

Edie would be back at work in eight hours.

In eight days, we'd be in California, meeting more family.

29

Nature vs. Nurture?

"I finally sat down and watched the video of you meeting Susan," Mira messaged Edie midmorning Wednesday. My wife shared it around the time our hearts recovered from John's multilane exit. "I love how you were giggling from the get-go, and hearing Susan gasping before she's visible on the screen! That was great," she said. "Thank you for sharing that incredible moment with me!"

"Thank you for opening your home and heart to us," Edie answered.

"It was a pleasure having you and Jeremy in our home," Mira insisted. "Our door's always open to you."

A couple days later, Susan asked for our shirt sizes in an update from the road. "If you're ever in Kentucky," she texted Friday, "this is called a Kentucky Hot Brown." Given the term is found in Urban Dictionary, I was pleasantly surprised by her totally safe-for-work photo of a savory dish covered in bacon and cheese. The NSFW version of the "Kentucky hot brown," incidentally, happens to be a close cousin of the "Chicago sunroof," made famous by Jimmy McGill during a nursing home bingo game on *Better Call Saul.*

The following Tuesday, Kellie texted her baby sister. "Mom's keeping me updated on your travels and experiences," she sent two days before our flight to California. "Have fun!"

That's what we were aiming to have in the Bay Area, some four months since Erica first said, "I'd love to meet up sometime this year and hang out."

"We'll be together tomorrow!" Rachel kicked off our Wednesday, the 19th. It ended with the two of us in the same Kenner hotel, on the eve of Edie's first gathering with both of her younger siblings. Rachel's morning flight was set to land at San Francisco International around the same time as ours, while the Harts would fly into Oakland later in the evening.

Before boarding, Edie and I marked the most important grocery item off our list at Louis Armstrong New Orleans International Airport: Community Coffee. Mardi Gras Blend, to be specific. "Cherish will love you forever!" is how Justin phrased it.

For the second time in as many weeks and a day, my wife and I were soon on an otherwise uneventful predawn direct flight across the country to meet new family. It had been a while since I heard Knick's voice. He remained silent that Thursday morning.

We deplaned and headed for baggage claim to catch up with Rachel. I walked up behind her, channeling *Sesame Street's* Super Grover. "Are you lost, little girl?" I asked in a lilted rasp. Rachel whipped around and hugged the two of us hello for our third-ever meeting.

An hour and a shuttle ride later, I was driving the three of us around in a heavily populated part of the country I had never been to before. My passengers were grateful that neither of them were behind the wheel. They were also the only ones included in Tuesday's email from LeMerle about our destination.

The nearly 500-word message had a stream-of-consciousness feel, not unlike dozens of others Edie had received over the past few months. Besides her and Clark's phone numbers, LeMerle mentioned lots of things, including Chinese flight delays, tai chi, junkyard art, and a docent speaking midday Thursday at their church about the San Francisco Museum of Modern Art's Magritte exhibit.

"If you would like to come," John Hart's sister wrote, "it should be very interesting." LeMerle offered to "pick up snacks. We usually get a muffin from our favorite bakery/store. We have Better Morning, or zucchini (whichever is still left). They also have blueberry. They also have ordinary muffins," she added, before continuing on about muffins, including cranberry orange and cornbread. "Could I pick up muffins for you?" Edie and Rachel's aunt asked them. "I'd need to know ahead of time what you prefer," she explained, "they disappear very fast!"

While LeMerle admitted it was a "long description for a simple question," nowhere in her email did John's sister mention an address for her and Clark's "Epworth Church." The closest she came to doing so happened parenthetically. "(The church is near Marin & the Alameda, on Hopkins—about half an hour from our condo)," wrote LeMerle, whose place we'd never been to before.

Had I been included in the thread before the trip, I would have replied seeking clarification regarding the address, to ensure accurate Waze-assisted routing. Then I would have immediately said "screw it," and impatiently Googled it myself before my maiden drive through a major metropolitan region.

But I wasn't in the thread, so I didn't. As a result, I was about to drive across the Oakland Bay Bridge with no idea where the hell we were supposed to go once we reached the other end.

My navigator checked her email from the passenger seat while her baby sister in the back scanned the area on her phone for a growingly needed lunch. A nearly 300-word email from LeMerle and Clark's joint Gmail account announced "WELCOME TO THE BAY AREA!" Whoever sent it around the time we landed signed off "LM & C."

"Please call when you get over the bridge (on 80 or 580)," the email read. "When you see Ikea, you are about a half hour from Epworth Church." In lieu of an address, LM and/or C continued with what I'm sure they thought were helpful directions. "Marin is, I think, next exit after University after Gilman, maybe (may say Buchanan). Few blocks," the sender estimated, "you could turn right on San Pablo & next right into Sprouts/Starbucks, Petco Parking Lot—another restaurant & other stuff. Sprouts may have something you could eat," at least one of the muffin connoisseurs mentioned. "I will get five or six muffins on the way to church. There will be fruits," we learned, "if you don't eat muffins."

I like fruit and muffins, as well as the French surrealist responsible for *The Treachery of Images*. I'd have been there for all of it in a heartbeat if not for not knowing where the hell they were.

"To get to church, go back uphill on Marin," the email continued, "right on the Alameda. You will see a library on your right. Turn left on Hopkins (service station on left). Church is a block down on the left. I give directions since it took us four years to find the church," wrote the octogenarian with the better sense of direction. "Kept turning the wrong direction!"

As we drove across the double-decker bridge I first learned about during the 1989 Bay Area World Series—when a span collapsed from a major earthquake hours before Game 1 between the two teams connected by the structure—my navigator Googled "Epworth Church Oakland," per my instructions. Professional sports and rap music had convinced me that everything on the east side of the bay was Oakland, not unlike folks who think Louisiana is nothing but New Orleans.

Shortly after setting course for the first of three results, Edie realized she chose correctly after discovering the street name, Hopkins, buried in the email on her phone. Turns out, we were headed to Berkeley, a city never mentioned in any of the messages.

We arrived at Epworth Methodist Church (1953 Hopkins Street, in the 94707) toward the end of the Magritte presentation. The remarkably youthful LeMerle and Clark met us in the lobby. As first noted by Justin back in May, my wife, indeed, resembled their aunt, whom Rachel was also meeting for the first time. She and cousin Erica had once connected in person some time ago.

Following hugs and introductions, we set off to grab lunch after perusing the junkyard art in the church's funky Berkeley neighborhood. Clark drove Rachel in their car; LeMerle became my shotgun-riding navigator. Her directions contained several confidence-inspiring qualifiers, like "maybe" and "I think so." Edie's uncle and sister followed us, while my wife whispered phone-aided directions to me from the back seat.

During this excursion, we learned that after moving there a few years earlier, the Milsoms had gotten the lay of the land by driving around, getting lost, and spending hours finding things, including their way home. It's an activity the retired couple still does after church on Sundays, after eventually figuring out how to get there from home.

"Did you pass by the Ikea on the way in?" LeMerle asked us.

Instead of saying, "I didn't notice because I was too busy trying to not get us killed while my distracted navigator scanned cluttered, punctuation-deprived emails, and her sister searched for food because all three of us were starving," I simply told Edie's aunt, "I think so."

Did I mention this was an exercise in patience?

On the way to lunch in Point Richmond, LeMerle offered more qualified directions. I managed to train my ear on Edie's quiet navigation over my right shoulder, over our rumbling tummies. We never did get any of those muffins.

The delightful couple insisted on picking up the tab at a nice Mexican restaurant. Back in our vehicles in the same configuration, we drove by the Richmond Yacht Club, where we saw spectacular boats and waterside homes on a lovely late-summer day in Northern California.

Minutes later, we reached their place in Richmond's Marina Bay community, where Erica and Ben also live. During our visit, Clark and LeMerle spoke glowingly about how diverse the community was. A lovely Russian couple lived upstairs, our hosts informed us. It reminded me of when Justin had told us that one of the main draws to Renton, when he and Cherish were house hunting, was that it's Seattle's most diverse suburb.

Meanwhile, Baton Rouge is in the record books for the longest-running desegregation case in U.S. history. I'm not sure if the kids in the myriad White-flight communities learn that in their "better" schools.

We three travelers hung out with our hosts and chatted for a bit until it was time to head north, ahead of the peak afternoon rush hour. Despite our earlier adventures, we still insisted on asking for suggestions regarding grocery stores outside the city, on the way to Kenwood in Sonoma County. There were no supermarkets near the AirBNB there, Justin had informed us.

LeMerle began rattling off names of different places to buy groceries for the weekend, complete with turn-by-turn directions. She even offered alternate routes in case the traffic was bad. No addresses were given.

"LeMerle," Clark gently chimed in with a smile, "they have Siri." We all chuckled.

Minutes later, we headed out the door. Clark began explaining to us how to exit the expansive development.

"Clark," his wife said, "they have Siri." LeMerle had delivered a top-notch, backhand callback with expert timing and delivery. That's when I completely fell in love with this adorable couple, both of whom are incredibly capable and independent. Most people I know in their eighties don't use email or ski the Rockies.

Nevertheless, LeMerle is also John's sister. Moments after meeting her aunt in Berkeley, Edie turned to me as we walked to our vehicles. "It's not the head trauma," she noted.

"Did you see Costco," LeMerle emailed about the wholesaler's Novato location, as we drove to the Safeway in Sonoma. The warehouse was on "Vintage Way, I think."

Two weeks after turning six, Hadley was headed to SEA-TAC with her parents minus a baby tooth, plus a loose one. Justin sent a pic of our niece and her new smile from the Tesla.

"We have arrived at our destination!" Edie announced within the hour. Nearly another would pass before sunset.

"You like?" Justin asked.

"C'est magnifique!" Edie confirmed. "Cherish is the bomb dot com!"

After learning of our visit with the Milsoms, Justin wondered, "Good time? Or kinda weird?"

"Great!" Edie answered.

He messaged again at 9:36 p.m. "We just landed in Oakland." After fetching their bags and rental car, he followed up, "Google says 11:39 arrival."

The three of us in Kenwood passed the time by playing Cards Against Humanity. It was one of the many games available in the house, in addition to the handful Rachel brought from her vast collection. "Have games, will travel" seemed to be her new motto.

The Harts pulled in precisely at the time Big Data had predicted. Edie and I were still wired from the large iced coffees we got six hours earlier from the Safeway's Starbucks. Rachel, a true night owl, had gotten tea.

The Renton gang walked in with a half-awake Hadley. We bid her and Cherish a quick hello and good evening just before midnight. For our bodies, it was closing time back home. Justin joined his older sister and me for a quick sip of the Elijah Craig I spotted at the store. My frugal wife had signed up for the Safeway membership discount in the store on her phone before checking out, even though their closest location to Baton Rouge was over 800 miles and a time zone away in Colorado.

Before bed, the four of us hugged one another again, not quite as weepy-eyed as when we and Rachel had greeted the Harts some half-hour earlier. Unlike our first nights in Washington and Indiana, the two of us were still too wired to sleep after retiring to our room. Edie and I stayed up to talk about that day and evening together with her baby sister. This third encounter already accounted for the longest time our trio had been together in one location. Thursday also saw the sisters' first one-on-one time, while I kept myself busy exploring the rental house's assortment of cool amenities.

"To call me verbose would be an understatement" was the first sentence of the fourth paragraph Rachel composed for her newly discovered sister back in February. "I could have a nearly continuous conversation for a whole day if given a chance" was the second.

You're not going to believe this, but in the hours since I greeted Rachel in a blue, furry superhero's voice, Edie did not talk nearly as much as Baby Girl did. As my wife and I laid in the dark, she brought up her sister's admitted verbosity, along with their father's five-hour phone call, and the loquaciously enthusiastic horde of Lukaczyk cousins.

"What the hell happened to me?" Edie laughed, loud enough I worried she'd wake up someone down the hall. She first noted this contrast as early as February, when we were just learning about Fran.

"Biggest example of nature vs. nurture?" Edie proposed in the Fort Worth thread on February 24. "John's five-hour conversation (that we had to spur the close of) and Fran's public Facebook profile vs. moi?" She winked at her comparative churchmouse state.

In that same opening email to her sister, Rachel said, "Please feel free to ask me anything from my opinions to my history. I am an open person." It's a position shared by the rest of their immediate paternal family. Though I don't frequent Reddit, I referred to John, Justin, and Rachel as the AMA Trio, because you can ask them anything.

Meanwhile, Edie's still trying to get used to talking about herself.

We'd been up for nearly twenty-four hours straight. Rather than sleeping in a comfy bed in a dark, cool room—under the same roof as her biological siblings for the first time ever—she was laughing about being a relative mute. All things considered, I'd say my bride was processing everything like a champ. If nothing else, her giggling sure as hell beat the uncontrollable crying I awoke to after first meeting their father.

Before midmorning Friday, we discovered Justin was right. Cherish loved the Mardi Gras Blend, and us for bringing it. We hugged her and Hadley, the only other ones up, since we didn't get to properly do so the night before. The four of us used the time to catch up on the last four months apart. It had been too long since I last saw my BFF. Hadley's gap-toothed smile made her even more ridiculously cute.

She and her mommy tested out the hammock, suspended between a pair of olive trees in the backyard, while the rest of us ate breakfast and took showers. With our two trios back in our rental vehicles, Justin and

I drove into the morning sun toward Emeryville, about an hour away on the bay's east side. As we had done on the drive up the previous afternoon, the sisters and I marveled at the terraces of grape vines on steep slopes looming over the endless acreage of vineyards below.

The gentleman at our destination's front gate found our names on a list. He gave us our passes and let us into cousin Erica's workplace, directing us to a nearby parking lot. There, in lieu of a traditional bicycle rack on the rear, we saw a Jeep displaying a life-size cutout of Elastigirl (aka Helen Parr) from *The Incredibles* racing on a bike. We all agreed it obviously belonged to an employee.

In the sunny Pixar Studios parking lot, I captured the first-ever image of John Hart's kids together. Just like the photo with Patrick at Conans Pizza in Austin, a taller Justin's arms wrapped around his two sisters flanking him.

A towering version of Luxo, the Pixar lamp, and its accompanying ball, greeted us in the bricked courtyard leading to the main building, named after Steve Jobs. The luminary from the company's logo (and first film) was a bit shorter than the multistory structure beyond it. Hunched and poised to pounce, the lamp looked down upon the rest of our dwarfed crew. The five of them posed in front of the yellow ball, with its blue stripe and two red stars, as I snapped away. The sisters barely had a head on the sphere. Atop her six-foot-one father's shoulders, Hadley was tiny in comparison to the dynamically inanimate objects. The ascending late-morning sun in the clear blue sky shone on them brightly at nearly the same angle that an illuminated Luxo would have.

Before even walking in, it felt like we had won a golden ticket.

We were greeted near the front desk by more Pixar figures, including Buzz Lightyear and Woody. They were made of 25,000 and 17,000 Legos, respectively. The entire Parr family was there, too. *The Incredibles* were much less blocky than their *Toy Story* cousins.

Erica, a director of films showing how major Pixar projects come to fruition, greeted us with hugs and a giant smile. She whipped out her phone to snap a few shots of her smiling kin, huddled tightly together. A few feet to her left, I captured her capturing the moment as Buzz and Woody looked on. I had documented the documentarian documenting her family.

She led us upstairs to begin our tour. The upper-floor offices were populated by people who create worlds brought to life by state-of-the-art animation. Artifacts from their latest blockbuster endeavor, *Coco*, lined the halls. We explored the nuances of the elements that made up the film's universe, particularly *Coco's* Land of the Dead, in the midst of the people who created them. We were in their work environment, where they were inventing more universes. Photography was prohibited on that floor.

From there, Erica led us to another building. The seven of us had lunch in the dining area surrounding an open-air kitchen dubbed Brooklyn. Following made-to-order paninis, we joined a few dozen other viewers for a screening in the building's theater. The essentially dialogue-free, animated short about a man in the harsh wilderness—desperately trying to keep alive a plant with lots of sentimental value—proved too scary for Hadley. She quietly exited with her mommy while the rest of us watched the remainder of the film. We didn't stick around for the entire Q&A session.

Moments later, Erica introduced the six-year-old to a sizable likeness of James P. "Sulley" Sullivan and his one-eyed buddy Mike "Waz" Wazowski from *Monsters, Inc.* They stood side by side, waving at everyone in Brooklyn's dining area across the way. In no time, Erica had her recently rattled little cousin high-fiving these smiling monsters, including one who could eat her for lunch, if not for the lack of a working digestive tract.

With a giggly Hadley amongst us again, we walked over to Erica's office a couple of buildings away. Our host gifted her guests with some cool souvenirs, including a copy of the *Brave* soundtrack for Red. Edie and I also bought a few souvenirs for her cool boss and a Friday night crewmate at the gift store back in the Steve Jobs Building.

Along the way there, through the shade-tree alley, we gawked at the campus's recreation area. Regulation basketball and sand volleyball courts lay idle near a giant hammock and a four-lane lap pool, all amid tall palm trees and immaculate grounds under the warm afternoon sun.

My BFF and I had fun running around the grassy amphitheater. We then headed back inside to check out whatever the lifesize rainbow-maned unicorn, seated a few yards from Buzz and Woody, was reading. We peeked over her shoulder to inspect the sheet of paper she held. Hadley and I were immediately sworn to secrecy by Pixar officials.

Erica joined us as we bid farewell to the magical campus by mid-afternoon. We departed for nearby Richmond, where we met Erica's engaging mutt, Spock. His right ear often folded down, and the left usually pointed up. As a result, the USS *Enterprise* chief science officer's canine namesake typically channeled Mr. Spock's "fascinating" raised eyebrow.

Clark and LeMerle soon joined us for a brisk walk along the bayshore. We nine people and one Vulcan-like dog enjoyed the strong breeze off the chilly Pacific, tempered by the reclining sun. Toward the orb's glow, haze shrouded the San Francisco skyline.

Back at Erica's, we met her equally buoyant husband, Ben. The Richmond City Council member was no less charming and intelligent than his wife and in-laws.

I soon accompanied Erica, Edie, and Rachel for a trip to "the Costco where people get shot" to kill Friday's dinner for ten. Back at the Milsom-Chois, their expanded table encroached into the living room area to accommodate our decade of people. My view from the end of the table was even more enjoyable than the lasagna and pizza.

The bottle of Suntory Toki whisky I grabbed at Costco was at least half full by the time the Harts left for Kenwood with Rachel after dark. Our octogenarians had retired to their home a bit earlier to rest up for their church's morning tai chi class. That left Edie and me with the homeowners and Spock, with whom we enjoyed every second of the next couple hours. Yes, we were those guests who stayed until our hosts began yawning.

With the name Choi, Ben's Korean. Nevertheless, he's often presumed to be of Pacific Islander descent. (Guilty as charged.) It also doesn't help that he plays the ukulele and sings like Don Ho.

At one point, our conversation shifted to John Hart. Edie mentioned that we had been together in Renton in May.

"Oh," a surprised Ben said. "So you've met..." He paused for a second or two before completing his thought. "...John."

"Yes," Edie confirmed. "Twice."

We headed out the door sometime before 11 p.m. with plans to reunite at a pool party the next day. The Suntory was gone before we were.

Justin kicked off our Saturday with his first-ever frittata, which he naturally hit out of the park. We enjoyed breakfast on the deck in the ample shade of a sycamore tree.

All that showbiz stuff on Friday evidently rubbed off on Hadley, who luxuriated on a deck chair by the pool like a boss. Five adults gawking and photographing her like paparazzi prompted the sun-drenched diva, enjoying a sleeve of cheap deli crackers, to pose more emphatically and emote even more adorable attitude through her sunglasses in our direction.

An hour later, I captured the sibling trio clinking glasses at En Garde Winery, a short jaunt away. The name, our engaging attendant told us, came from the Hungarian owner's reputation for stealthily refilling glasses.

We returned to the house near midday, not long before the Marina Bay foursome arrived there. Justin grilled chicken and opened Dusted Valley wine. Spock watched us play in the pool under the cloudless NorCal sky all afternoon. At our behest, Ben serenaded us a cappella on the patio. His impromptu aria was on par with the lovely one we heard atop Rattlesnake Ridge back in May.

So perfect was this afternoon, I was all but oblivious to the day's bevy of football games, including Louisiana Tech at LSU. My compliments to whoever wrote the script for this computer simulation we call a universe.

Clark, Cherish, and I took turns photographically documenting the family reunion under the deck's string of lights after sundown. We bid adieu to our affable guests around 8:30 p.m., ahead of their hour-plus drive back to Richmond. Watching Erica's parents depart with nary a sign of fatigue after spending a picturesque afternoon and early evening with us in wine country, I decided that I want to be like that when I'm Clark and LeMerle's age.

Cherish began getting Hadley and herself ready for bed around 9 p.m. The rest of us gathered in the living area. I piled on one of the two comfy couches, opposite the three sibs together on the other. Edie sat in the middle, still wearing her floral-print swimwear wrap.

Rachel, who doesn't usually drink, had consumed some alcohol. Justin, hours after En Garde, clearly had been caught off guard by Mr. Elijah Craig. That's the moment Edie began to more fully appreciate her role as big sister. As I snapped those cherished memories from across the room, she was definitely the most put-together of the bunch.

Moments later, a freshly bathed, ebullient little delight crashed the drunken photo shoot. Hadley continued to steal the spotlight until her ever-patient mother wrangled her into bed before 10 p.m.

Any hangovers on Sunday were remedied just past daybreak in the hot tub. I joined the sibs for a soak while Hadley walked around the jacuzzi in her pajamas. The diva dined on more deli crackers.

Holding my phone just above the bubbling water, I managed to get a killer photo of my wife. Some might deem it spank bank material. Steam rose past her illuminated auburn crown, into the brilliant California sun behind her. In a word, it's hot.

Justin had persuaded his cracker- and scenery-eating daughter to exit the frame before I lost the shimmering backlight. Hadley would ditch the crackers and jump into the pool with her mommy a little later, after Cherish returned from mixing some work into her vacation at a nearby heart walk.

Around the corner at Palooza Brewery & Gastropub, we enjoyed a late brunch on their patio with Justin's former colleague, Sara, who traveled nearly an hour from Novato to join us. But for a passing glance, I ignored TVs tuned into Week 3 NFL games that Sunday. Without an ounce of regret, it marked the second time that nascent season that I didn't see a single down of a Saints game.

Back at the rental house, we swapped last-minute photos in the backyard before throwing our bags into the cars. Check-out time was 3 p.m. We ended this reunion not one minute sooner than required.

Justin and Hadley had an early evening flight out of Oakland. Cherish would stay in the city for work the next day. The rest of us had a couple of red-eyes home from San Francisco.

Following extended hugs, Rachel, Edie, and I got in our rented Jeep, while Justin and Cherish secured Hadley in the back of their car. We waved goodbye and drove off in another direction, heading for the Golden Gate Bridge.

During our travels that weekend, I recall Jungle's new song "Heavy, California" playing as I drove around NorCal with my wife and her baby sister in a Jeep we picked up Thursday from Hertz's garage in a parking spot numbered 420. Heavy, indeed.

On Sunday afternoon, the elder Milsoms emailed their nieces and nephew to suggest a stop at the Pacifica Taco Bell, across the Golden Gate, for easy parking and great views of the ocean. "Happy trails and pleasant flights and delightful dreams as you snooze en route to your homes with lots of good memories of times we enjoyed so much with you!" Clark and LeMerle signed off, "Til next time."

Not that we had time for the diversion anyway, but we missed their lovely email. No one in our vehicle was checking their accounts while I drove us down unfamiliar, curvy, hillside roads at speeds some of us found a bit unnerving. My passengers grew increasingly uneasy as the Jeep whipped back and forth a bit, descending toward the Robin Williams Tunnel. In my defense, I was just blending in with the rest of the traffic.

The Golden Gate Bridge was nothing short of breathtaking, especially when you imagine humans completing what was deemed an impossible feat in the 1930s. We three hoodie-clad Southerners walked out a couple hundred yards across the fog-free span, over the turbulent strait, before turning around to hit the road again. The stiff, cold breeze was surprisingly taxing, and made the cloudless photographs taken there a bit interesting, at least for those of us with hair. While driving across the iconic structure, at least one of my uptight passengers let me know that she didn't care for me taking in the marvelous view.

My childhood interest in designing bridges may have led me to initially major in civil engineering, but it was the zoology graduate in our household who was building them on this journey.

Unlike Thursday, I drove the hilly roads of San Francisco minutes later. Residential garage doors, hung squarely with gravity, lined the steep streets at weird angles. Parallel-parked cars framed the extremely graded thoroughfare. "Can you imagine trying to do that with a stick shift?" I wondered aloud.

Approaching cross streets was interesting, namely because we couldn't see them over the hood, which was pointed up at the sky. Not until our Jeep halted at the flattened intersections could we see the stop signs again. It may be one of the most expensive places in the country to live, but at least San Francisco residents don't have to spend extra money on roller coasters.

With better than five hours before our SFO boarding times, Rachel met her second Catholic High School of Pointe Coupee alumna at a Bernal Heights eatery. Edie's classmate Estelle had been insisting for years that we visit her in San Francisco.

We returned the rental and checked our bags. After TSA, Edie and I caught back up with Rachel in the secured area for a few minutes. For the third time in their lives, the two sisters bid goodbye to each other. While less teary-eyed, the hugs were no less intense than those of their first farewell in June.

The Austinite headed for the Alaska Airlines terminal while Edie and I proceeded to our gate. We closed down the nearby bar. A little later, we were the final two passengers to board.

Because this trip couldn't possibly be perfect enough, we found a completely empty row. Separated by the aisle, we each laid out on a triplet of seats and snoozed in the dimly lit cabin. A full moon, peeking through unshuttered right-side windows, followed us all the way back to the Big Easy.

"Love you guys!" Justin texted his sisters before his flight. "And even though our visit was short," he smiled, "I really appreciate how much we did and shared."

"I just got out my phone to say the same!" Rachel soon replied. "I feel like this vacation, time crunch aside, has been as good as I can ask for!"

"It has been a fabulous weekend," Edie declared with heart emojis. "Love my family."

30

Twinsies

"Our weekend together was one of the best family reunions I have ever had," Justin wrote back to Clark and LeMerle. "Thank you so much for spending time with us."

Edie caught up with the Milsoms' daughter a couple days after returning home. "Hey cousin!" she messaged Erica. "Can we PayPal you to help out with the groceries?"

"AWWWW." Erica insisted it wasn't necessary. "When I come to see you in Louisiana," she requested in return, "I expect some po-boy action!"

"We can definitely hook you up!" Edie promised.

"But man," Erica continued. "That was so great! I love meeting you and Jeremy," she said, "and I know Mom and Dad and Ben did, too. Lots of love," she sent. "Welcome to the family!"

Edie thanked her cousin with a heart.

During our incredible four-day weekend, Susan messaged Edie.

"Finally having some time to reflect," she wrote after getting home from their post-Indiana travels, "I think I owe you a couple of apologies. First," Susan lamented, "we never did get around to our tea party. I guess we could count the pierogi-making session as girl time, but it wasn't quite what I was thinking.

"Second," she wrote, "I think I may have accidentally overstepped our agreement about hugging by grabbing your hand and holding on through our ride back from Jodie's. I just did it without thinking, and I'm sorry if it made you feel uncomfortable. The only time I usually hold anybody's hand (except Skip's) is when I'm trying to lend support or comfort them. It was just an unconscious thing and I hope it didn't upset you. I love you!" S signed off.

"Omigosh," Edie replied after we put Erica and Ben to bed Friday, "please don't fret over this! I was so happy just to get to be with you at Paula's. We are in California now visiting with other recently discovered relatives," she revealed, "and as I was responding today to an inquiry from the biological half-brother who kickstarted this whole discovery process, the thing I mentioned as most significant to me about the whole time in Indiana was that moment when you grabbed my hand. I love you, too!" Edie closed with a single emoji, composed of two hearts.

AncestryDNA kicked off October with an update to its members' ethnicity estimates, spurring a comparison between Patrick's and his sister's new genetic profiles. With nearly two-thirds of his genes coming from Great Britain, Cottontop was even Whiter than before.

"Also," he added that Monday, "I have big news, but I've been sitting on it while I process it." Patrick proposed a phone call. "I want to hear about your trips and discuss my news."

Suggesting a couple days for a call, Edie reported, "I'm no longer Scandinavian."

"I guess I got that covered now," Patrick replied.

The next morning, Edie shared news with me. "Susan's DNA is in: It's official." The update drew my shocked reaction.

"Hey," Edie smiled at Susan on Facebook Messenger, "there you are on AncestryDNA!"

"Ah, yes," Susan replied to her now-Ancestry-confirmed daughter. "It appears we have a bit in common." Edie loved Susan's message, which came at the end of a larger back-and-forth between the two.

"Have you had time to decompress yet?" Susan asked, eight days after our return from California. "It took me a couple weeks to get over our trip after we got home, and you did more traveling after that." Susan also mentioned that she and Skip had weekly Oktoberfest plans, both in Manchac and at New Orleans's Deutsches Haus.

"Whew," Edie answered, "I can't believe it's already October! I'm not sure I remember what normal is at this point," my wife winked. While she wasn't sure if we could Oktoberfest with them, Edie added with hearts, "Would love to see you again sooner rather than later."

That same Tuesday evening, during the bottom of the eighth inning of the National League's one-game playoff between the Cubs and visiting Rockies, I photographed Michael Lukaczyk's granddaughter bouncing around our living room in shorts and the "Executive Staff" member's jacket. Edie nervously sipped Suntory as she rooted for the home team, down 1-0 late in a game wherein the loser was done that postseason.

Literally within seconds of me sharing that picture with all of our Indiana hosts, the Cubs' Terrance Gore scored the tying run off Javier Baez's double.

"She wears it well," Jodie replied with a heart as Gore crossed the plate.

"It brought good luck," Paula noted.

"Damn right it did!" I insisted.

Alas, Colorado ended up winning in the thirteenth inning. Neither of us in Baton Rouge could stay awake until the end to continue the rally.

During that Tuesday night exchange, Paula mentioned that every time she saw Chicago manager Joe Maddon, "I think of Uncle Mike."

The next day, Susan passed along their Oktoberfest plans. "Skip is already mumbling negative thoughts about Deutches Haus parking."

"Hm," Edie replied Wednesday evening, "maybe consider using Uber or Lyft to avoid the parking scenarios?"

"That would make sense. Have you met Skip?" Susan eye-rolled Thursday. "Actually, there is a kind of logic behind having our car there. We tend to load up on German food and other stuff." If they drove, she explained, "We can just put it into Rubbermaid containers and load everything in the cooler as we buy it."

"Ah," Edie realized, "that does make sense, but I love your initial response," she winked.

"Okay, so here's a thing to think about," Susan soon followed up. "Uncle Joe's (one of our neighborhood bars) has a 'Diva Day' twice a year. It's a day when they get a bus or limo to take ladies to the French Quarter." Their fall edition was two Sundays away, on October 14. "Skip has said I can't go because I can't walk on my own like I usually do. My knee is messed up, and I don't stay with the group," she said, "but if it's a day you might want to spend time together, we could. Then again, we could just wait until the spring trip and I might be better company. It's a great excuse for a girls-only day. I guess we shouldn't need an excuse, but we both love our guys," Susan added, "yet we still haven't had too much time for us to figure out 'us.'"

"Indiana was easy," she continued, "because I was Uncle Mike's daughter and you were Uncle Mike's granddaughter. Every other place you went, you were either a sister or cousin. When it's just you/Jeremy and me/Skip, we talk about everything else. When you're home with your family, I don't (and shouldn't) exist. Life is complicated. I'm sorry."

"You most definitely exist," Edie shot back. "And I want it that way. You're right that we didn't get to have 'us' time in Indiana. My second favorite part of that trip was getting a few minutes sort of alone with you while we peeled potatoes. I love the idea of Diva Day. Jeremy and Skip can each survive on their own for seven to ten hours," my wife assured her mother that same Thursday. "Put me down for it and let me know when and where to meet you!"

The following Tuesday marked just over two weeks since our return from wine country. "I feel like it has already been ages since we got together in Sonoma," Justin emailed Edie on the eve of his late mother's birthday. "I have been thinking about her a lot. I suppose I have been dwelling on regrets a little, too, or feeling sad, anyway, about how things could have/should have gone differently. It's fleeting," Justin allayed, "not like I am moping around, and I suppose I just miss her."

He also said that, after conferring with Rachel, he had a "good working plan" for their sister and the Renton Harts to visit us in Baton Rouge the weekend before Fat Tuesday in early March 2019. The plan included the four of them riding with us in Spanish Town and catching parades in New Orleans.

"It does seem like ages," Edie wrote her baby brother back that same Tuesday. "And of course your mom would be on your mind and heart at this time. I'm sorry I didn't get to meet her," she shared with a heart, "but I'm so glad your quest brought us together." Regarding her nascent relationship with her own mother, Edie revealed, "We plan to spend the day together this Sunday in New Orleans—first time it will be just the two of us." She also shared a link to a rental home in Beauregard Town, within walking distance of the Spanish Town route, since we didn't have room at our place to accommodate our Mardi Gras newbies.

"I wish you could have met my mom, too," Justin responded on Wednesday morning. "I know she would have been blown away by you and your story. Rachel got to meet her once or twice. I recall Rachel feeling a lot of kinship with her." He explained how Shirley reminded Rachel of her own mother, Elizabeth, furthering Justin's theory that their father was drawn to women who, "like himself, were deeply wounded."

Regarding Susan, Justin wrote, "I hope I can meet your mom someday," though he understood if that wasn't "feasible or comfortable. I just think it would be interesting to meet her. I have no expectations in any way." He also liked his sister's idea of renting a place for the Mardi Gras gang.

"My mom would love to meet you," Edie told Justin about Ducky, "and we might be able to swing that depending on the eventual timetable. And I appreciate your observation about John's pattern of attraction." She added, "I appreciate the consideration you put into your relationships, and especially how you are able to process and share your experiences, helping yourself, but also others like me. I've often tried to just lock away or distract myself from anything uncomfortable," Justin received with a heart, "so that's something I admire in you."

Minutes later on Friday evening, Edie messaged Susan. "I'm so excited we get to be together again Sunday! And since I've so little diva experience," she asked, "anything special I should know? I typically dress casual for the Quarter."

"Casual is cool," Susan assured on Saturday. "Some of the ladies spruce up and/or wear hats. I'm not much of a sprucer," she mentioned, "but I'll bring us a couple of hat options just in case."

She later texted her daughter a picture of Red as a child. Susan had found the heart-melting image of my future wife on Facebook. "I love this picture of you so much!" she wrote with a heart in lieu of "love." Six-year-old Edie's adorable nose provided gentle terrain for countless freckles, some hidden by a handful of curly locks hanging down to a pair of big brown eyes trained slightly off-camera. Her barely ajar mouth was enigmatic. It could easily be the immediate prelude to a smile or a furrowed brow. I get a similar face whenever I substandardly crack wise.

With Maringouin business already handled, Edie left our place for Metairie before eight on Sunday morning. She met up with Susan at Uncle Joe's in time for a nine o'clock bus. It wasn't actually scheduled to depart until ten, though, affording mother and daughter an extra hour of initial one-on-one time.

Once in the French Quarter, the two split off from the main group. The pair paid visits to Johnny White's Corner Pub, Harry's Corner, and Pat O'Brien's. They also spent time shopping together in the French Market. Susan seemed to innately know Edie's tastes, including her badass sensibilities.

She told her daughter that she believed, at least at one time, that she didn't deserve to have another child. Susan also said she knew that she couldn't let Nancy Jane know about her granddaughter. She wasn't about to let the woman who capriciously expunged Mike from his only child's life oppressively control everything.

Edie reassured Susan that she did the best she could given the situation and era. Susan is awesome, her daughter informed her, and had nothing to apologize for. Edie also explained how she could relate to the fear of a matriarchal figure (from my family) exerting undue, unwelcome influence on our hypothetical kids.

My bride spent most of the day looking at Susan's face and seeing herself, mesmerized by the novelty of something many of us have regularly experienced since our formative years. As Edie would later tell me, "I never looked at myself in the mirror until I saw myself outside the mirror."

Their waiter at Pat O's asked if they were twins. *Separated at birth?* Edie thought, but didn't utter. She and Susan just smiled.

Both were sporting tiny, bluish-gray alpine hats, trimmed in little blue and white ropes and feathers, from Oktoberfest in Georgia. They looked like fedoras that'd be ideal for a house cat named Tom Landry. All day in the Quarter, random people complimented the pair on their matching headwear.

The camera-averse duo ended up taking unprompted selfies back in Metairie. Susan's friend at the neighborhood bar was understandably shocked. She asked Edie how she knew Susan. Following a moment of silence, right as the friend was ready to begin offering her guess, my wife quipped, "Susan and I go way back." The friend then volunteered to take their picture together.

"Gonna send it to our relatives," they told the photographer, sitting across the table from the side-by-side pair who visually shared way more than just matching hats.

"Oh, so you're related," the woman concluded. She never seemed to figure out that her previously childless friend suddenly had a daughter.

Back in Baton Rouge by sundown, Edie told me all about the fantastic Sunday with her mother, including the drama involving Skip and his keys. Long story short, he ended up spending most of the day outside on their Metairie porch.

From our kitchen, Edie soon sent Susan a selfie. Still wearing her feline-sized hat, she had managed to affix a pink version to my bald

THE LITTLE GIRL AT THE BOTTOM OF THE PICTURE | 357

head for the occasion. "Home!" my partner texted with the pic. "Thank you for such a fabulous day with you, my twin, my heart who I am so happy to be reunited with. I love you so much."

The following morning kicked off a week of civic obligation.

"Good luck with jury duty," Susan texted Edie. "I've decided I can't do Diva Day by myself again, ever," she winked. "I absolutely need a chaperone from now on. You are the only one who meets the specific qualifications for the job, so be prepared!"

The criminal trial's prospective juror sent an update on Tuesday. "They kept me."

"You're just too irresistible!" Susan offered, along with some sage, motherly wisdom. "Maybe just tell them about your association with *The Red Shtick* and they might send you home?" She also noted recently seeing Tony Shaloub portray Monk serving jury duty. "Hope yours went better," Susan said. Aside from Patrick and Yvette, in-laws deftly dropping pop culture references is still a novelty for me.

After exchanging messages on Wednesday, and a text-free Thursday, Susan checked in with Edie on Friday afternoon, just as we were meeting up with the rest of our officiating crew. Following the high school game, a crewmate from the country—who knew my wife years before me, and fondly remembered Doc O'Neal—predictably put his big ol' arm around me and made me promise to "take care of his home girl."

As we drove home, our clock operator saw Susan's text wondering about jury duty. "Oops," Edie replied, "I was so happy to get out of there, I forgot to tell you they dismissed me Wednesday afternoon." With digitally clinking mugs, she asked, "Oktoberfest tomorrow?"

Saturday, the Cavells joined us in New Orleans. They, in turn, joined Celeste from The Bulldog as the only people in our lives to have met Susan. Unlike Celeste, Shannon and Mike knew the backstory.

In addition to daily beer-stein-holding contests, the Deutsches Haus Oktoberfest celebration featured dachshund races. Edie shared photos with Shannon. "How have I never been to this?" asked the dog-loving, festival-going beer lover married to a home brewer, who often parks at Deutsches Haus for Jazz Fest.

Susan sent directions to the table under a tent they'd grabbed moments after the gates opened. "Can't miss Skip." She was right. Skip was in his element—namely, bundhosen and an alpine hat. His wife wore jeans and an Oktoberfest T-shirt, similar to the ones we wore from Helen, Georgia, courtesy of Susan.

Additionally, mother and daughter soon donned matching copper-and-leathery-cork bracelets. Susan had bought them from Queork in the six-day interim since their visit to the French Quarter shop. She presented the jewelry upon our arrival. Edie's matching coffee-bean ring, worn to honor our deceased artist friend who designed it, helped Susan pick just the right twinsies accessory.

As they took sips of Riesling brought by Susan, the pair stuck out their right arms for a side-by-side photo. Susan had far fewer freckles than Rachel. Edie's definitely came from John.

Once the intermittent rain began clearing out, a tuba-playing frau led a Bavarian version of a conga line. Skip fell in and followed, serpentining and oom-pa-pa'ing behind three children and an older lady. Behind him were members of the 610 Stompers, a tongue-in-cheek all-male dance group sporting Interstate-sign-colored knee-high tube socks, snug powder blue coach's shorts, white tees, and red sweatbands. The self-described "ordinary men" with "extraordinary moves" also have an all-female support team billed as the 610 Splits.

Mike Cavell was excited to meet the guys, who marched by their house in July and have provided memorable halftime entertainment at Saints games. In fact, the group inspired Mike, and a few other Baton Rouge friends, to form a similar group called Men at Twerk. It's a far better name than the regional-chemical-industry-related moniker I came up with: The Cancer Alley Cats.

As the drizzly Saturday afternoon drew toward evening, Skip had Oktoberfested more than enough for one day. I snapped a few final pics of his wife and her daughter to my right. Both beamed brightly at me and my phone as Edie leaned her head against Susan's. They hugged goodbye within earshot following the last photo, which I soon shared with Fort Worth.

"Seconds after this," I retold overhearing Susan quietly tell her child, "'You have brought so much peace into my life.'" I continued, "More than she thought she'd ever have on this Earth. I'm about to bawl at fucking Oktoberfest."

"Awwww man," Patrick replied. "Enjoy the moment."

"So beautiful!" Yvette noted.

Minutes later, as Skip drove her home, Susan texted Edie. "Thank you for sharing time with us. Be careful going home," she offered with a heart. "It was great meeting Mike and Shannon. Hope we weren't too crazy for them."

"You are awesome," Edie replied around seven with twin red hearts. LSU and Mississippi State had just kicked off following our Baton Rouge foursome's walk around a soggy Uptown, eleven days before Halloween in New Orleans. "We went by the skeleton house at St. Charles & State," a pun-filled attraction, "and just got to Cooter Brown's to watch the game. I loved the chance to be with you today!"

Around that same time on Saturday evening, Susan texted me, as well. Initially requesting the photo I took of her and her daughter, she quickly followed up with a concern. "If for any reason you doubt my feelings for your wife," I read in the noisy tavern, "please don't. There's no way on Earth that I would ever do anything to hurt her."

I had no idea why she sent that. No exchange that day, to my recollection, would have warranted such a plea. Puzzled, I waited until I was sober on Sunday morning in a quiet house to reply.

"Susan," I emphatically responded, "there is no way I could ever doubt your feelings for Edie. While I consider myself fairly discerning regarding the authenticity of sentiment, Edie's abilities to judge the trustworthiness and realness of others is nothing short of astounding. Even if for some reason I had doubts (which I certainly don't), the fact that she doesn't have even the tiniest scintilla of hesitation with respect to y'all's relationship is all I would need for me to realize I was wrong.

"BTW, I overheard you tell Edie that she has brought more peace into your life than you ever thought you'd have on this Earth. It was all I could do to not start bawling in front of everyone else at Oktoberfest. Edie's reaction was: 'Mission accomplished.'" I told Susan, "I'm a jaded, cynical A-hole, and I start to tear up every time I think about it.

"Also," I added, "we had fun yesterday! Thanks for the passes!"

"My bad," Susan responded Sunday evening. "I must have read your 'I'm-not-going-to-bawl' look wrong," she said about my resting bitch face desperately trying to hold back tears. I'm guessing it's akin to Clair Danes's ugly-cry mug, only with more eyebrows and testosterone. "I was totally sincere," she said of her overheard goodbye, "but when you looked away, I thought what I said bothered you in a completely different way. Sorry for the misunderstanding. I happen to think you're pretty great," Susan noted, "and not an A-hole at all. If you'll recall, that name is reserved for my ex," she winked. "So glad y'all could come and be with us in Fest-mode in spite of the rain. Oh," she added, "in case Edie forgot to tell you, thanks for loaning her to me last Sunday!"

Her daughter had not forgotten. Also, after over a quarter-century of marriage to one woman, it's strange to suddenly have your wife's mother seeking your approval.

"Just finished gleaning through this thread," I shared in the Fort Worth chat thread on Tuesday, after I had begun curating source material for this massive project. "Archived March through today," I posted. "I'm a mess now."

"I bet," Patrick responded. He and Yvette were driving to Maringouin on Friday for the weekend's annual group celebration of four O'Neal birthdays (Ducky, Kellie, Cindy, and Edie). My wife soon confirmed that, like the Texas couple, the two of us also would stay at Ducky's most of the weekend to maximize our time together.

On Wednesday, Susan forwarded to her daughter an email from Kat at Queork, allaying concerns about their bracelets' magnetic clasps possibly damaging nearby tech equipment.

"Good to know as I've been wearing mine all week!" Edie replied with a wink and a heart. "I love it," she said, "but not as much as I love you. It's special to me that you took the time to find something for both of us from the cool spot we visited." She also mentioned Uptown Halloween decorations. "If you haven't seen the skeleton house yet, all the puns really tickled our funny bone," my wife quipped a*head* of a skull emoji. "Sorry, had to do it."

"Wasn't planning to mention it," a reluctant Susan responded, "but I slipped on some wet leaves in our rock garden when I was rushing around the van to get everything out Saturday. Just a couple of very purple, swollen knees," she reported, "and they've been changing colors daily. Must be an indication of Fall. (I did owe you a pun)," Susan winked. "Skip's been a great nurse."

One day after learning of her mother's unfortunate fall, Edie received news about her father's latest tumble.

"FYI," Justin mentioned late Thursday evening, "John is in the hospital. He fell, he is probably okay, just scraped and bruised," Justin relayed, "but due to his head injuries, they are doing full CT scans and X-rays of his upper body." John's most recent mishap occurred while bringing his iPhone to the Apple Store after leaving it out in the rain.

"Oh no!" Edie replied two nights after speaking with John.

Two nights later, Patrick was driving his mother, wife, little sister, and me from Maringouin to Stab's Steakhouse in Baton Rouge. Wade and Cindy pulled in behind us, as did Kellie and her husband, Mike.

A number of things were discussed at the table that Saturday evening. Cindy's nephew won a boat, complete with motor and trailer, by catching a 6.5-pound trout, we learned. Kellie, seated next to her mom, educated Ducky about the PG-13 lyrics that Tiger Stadium's student section consistently roared whenever LSU's band played Cameo's "Talkin' Out the Side of Your Neck." Knowing what was coming, I briefly considered videoing Ducky's aghast reaction to her oldest daughter whispering into her ear, "Suck that Tiger dick, bitch."

Ever vigilant to not steal thunder, bio fam was off the table. The closest any of us came to the topic was during my brief, quiet aside to our waiter when ordering Sangiovese with sea bass. Some of my recent wine education had stuck, was the gist. That earned me a nudge from my wife, along with that enigmatic look from six-year-old Edie. Our waiter's invitation to tour the restaurant's wine cellar only further agitated her. I wisely declined the offer.

Back in Maringouin by 11:30, Ducky went straight to bed after dozing on the ride home. Near midnight, the rest of us were in the same living room where all this started ten months earlier on Christmas evening. The brother Edie described as "responsible for getting me to dive into the gene pool" briefed his sister and me on his Ancestry discoveries.

Weeks earlier, we had learned that Patrick and his birth mother's sister, Gayle, had communicated. Besides Patrick's mother, his aunt was the only one who knew Dyan had a blond son when she was nineteen, during a break from her longtime sweetheart. The couple would later reunite, marry, and have three children, completely ignorant of a half-brother who doesn't mind his anonymity from their family one bit. Dyan was widowed in 2017. She and her sister were set on taking the secret to their graves.

Gayle had recently told Dyan about communicating with Patrick, he told us in Ducky's living room. Gayle informed him that his biological father was definitely dead. Furthermore, Patrick was strongly advised against investigating his paternal family. It's not a good idea, we learned by the time Patrick and Yvette left for Fort Worth on Sunday morning. As horrible as that situation seems, at least Dyan, unlike Susan, had a sister with whom she felt comfortable enough to share her undoubtedly devastating secret.

The following Sunday, Edie received news involving her aunt, Susan's lone surviving sibling. "I've been doing a lot of thinking about sharing you with the family," Red read. "I didn't want to do anything to stir up drama or create stress, but I've been so happy since I met you, and felt like I needed to share that. Anyway, I told Sharon about you today," Susan revealed, "and her response was very positive. I hope that move was okay with you, too. It kinda opens a door for y'all to meet if/when you're ready for that.

"I had to send her a picture to show her how beautiful you are," she added, "and she was actually shocked by our resemblance. Sorry, but I love it! Hope I didn't overstep." Once again, S closed with a pair of hearts.

"I'm so happy you got a positive response from Sharon!" Edie answered early Monday morning, upon our return from the Saenger Theatre with the Cavells. "That's got to be a huge relief for you, and I'm so happy it went so well. And you certainly aren't overstepping at all." My wife told Susan about our late-night ride back from New Orleans, "I could barely keep my eyes open while Jeremy was chauffeuring us, but hearing that you were able to open the door to this new chapter without any undue drama will surely lead to sweet dreams. Love you!"

A few hours later, Edie began an otherwise uneventful work-week, the first full one of November. By Saturday afternoon, she was having withdrawals. "Hi," Edie messaged Susan with their now-almost customary twin hearts, "I miss you!" It was their first communication since early Monday morning. "Hope you're starting to feel a little better at least."

Frustrated that she still wasn't "back to 100%" since her fall, Susan soon reported on a recent conversation with Sharon. "She made the point of saying she needs to come over this way after the first of the year so the three of us can get together. That's you, her, and me," Susan clarified, "not her, me, and Skip."

"Hey," Edie winked, "you've given me a jump-start on goals for the new year: meeting my aunt!"

"I can't wait that long for another Edie fix," Susan insisted. "I think it's our turn to drive up there."

"If y'all want to come up on a Sunday," my wife proposed, "we could hang out at The Bulldog again." She also brought up Pinetta's, the European restaurant Susan had previously mentioned, "but they aren't open on Sundays," Edie said ahead of a long-awaited proposal. "Pinetta's is quiet, because they're just a dimly lit, small restaurant that plays local radio," she explained about the eatery, "no TV or German music to entertain Skip, so maybe that might be a better option if we want to set up a meeting with Ducky someday."

"I used to love Pinetta's lasagna," Susan recalled. "Hmm, do we dare make the trio into a foursome (you, Ducky, Sharon and me)? That may be too much for a first meeting," she conceded. "Anyway, I could come up for a meeting with Ducky."

The U.S. Marine Corps turned 243 years old that same Saturday, November 10. My wife drank a traditional rum and (Diet) Coke to celebrate her beloved Corps's birthday, among other things.

She heard back from Metarie the following evening. "Think about you, Ducky, and me doing lunch for your birthday," a flexible Susan advised her child, born on the month's final day. "Figure out what works for y'all and let me know. I think it's time to celebrate your birthday (or close-by day) together?" Susan's birthday was just three days before Edie's, which fell on a Friday less than three weeks away.

"I will!" Edie responded. "I was thinking it would be awesome if we could celebrate our birthdays together!" My wife then posed a question. "How about lunch at Pinetta's on Saturday, December 1?"

"Sounds great!" Susan soon replied. "Do you think Ducky is ready for meeting me?"

"I already called her," Edie revealed with a heart. "She is almost as excited as I am!"

From our office, I gave Fort Worth real-time updates during the exchange. "She's on the phone with Ducky now," I posted. "December 1 at Pinetta's," I quickly confirmed. "The three of them."

"Wow," Patrick replied. "That's amazing."

Yeah. It sure was.

Edie messaged Beth: "I just booked the meeting of Ducky and Susan." Beth sent back: "!!!!"

"And her sister wants to come in after the new year to meet me," my wife added.

"How do you feel about that?" her friend wondered.

"Most anxious about the three weeks of anticipation," admitted Edie, who was "kinda nervous about how mom will handle it."

"How IS she handling it?" Beth asked of Ducky.

"She's always said this is what she wanted, but that abstract concept," Edie noted with an incomplete sentence, "and the reality that I've now got a relationship with someone new."

"Completely different," Beth accurately finished her friend's thought.

Edie worried, "It's going to be a heavy tightrope not hurting feelings on both sides."

"Yeah."

31

Red Letter Day

"They had some big-ass holes," Edie's previously incarcerated father told her during a sixty-nine-minute call in mid-November. John's Florida Gators had lost some key defensive football players, he elaborated on speakerphone that Tuesday night. As the two of us tried stifling our giggles, I shared the line with Fort Worth.

"And he just dropped a pair of F-bombs in rapid succession in discussing Kemp in Georgia," I reported. Not surprisingly, John was no fan of the Peach State's Republican governor-elect.

Two mornings later, I updated the Texas O'Neals on what Edie donned for warmth on a nippy Thursday. "Today would've been Grandpa Mike's ninety-third birthday," I shared. "Guess what Edie's wearing today."

"She repping the Cubbies?" Patrick correctly guessed.

Edie also observed the occasion by changing her Facebook profile photo to one of her wearing the "Executive Staff" jacket in Chicago.

"Hey cuz!" Paula texted near midday. "Been thinking about you," she said. "Hope all is well!"

"Hey there!" Edie replied with a heart matching Paula's. "So glad today is chilly enough that I get to wear Grandpa Mike's jacket on his birthday."

"I'm so happy you have something of his you can use!" Mike's niece beamed, explaining the jacket would require layers up there following their first snowfall of the season.

By late afternoon, Susan texted me. "I've been trying to figure out what to give Edie for her birthday, and I need your help," she told me sixteen days ahead of Pinetta's. "I've been looking at some of my jewelry that I want her to have, but my taste in jewelry has been kind of weird (like me) over the years." Susan wondered, "Do you think she'd mind 'used' jewelry?"

"At least 95% of her jewelry collection is used," I answered, "passed down predominantly from Ducky and Earle. I am more than confident she would cherish your contribution."

After second-guessing herself, Susan decided, "She's getting some jewelry anyway. Can't help it," she winked.

"She would absolutely cherish jewelry you've worn," I reassured my wife's mother. "Trust me."

"Any advice you can give me about a first meeting with Ducky?" an antsy Susan further inquired.

"Just be yourself," I maintained. "You'll be fine."

"Thanks," she rolled her eyes. "I'll try."

"If that fails," I teased, "she's a sucker for good scotch."

"Aha!"

Six days later, on Thanksgiving Eve, Edie called Susan. After nearly five months of numerous emails and texts, and multiple encounters, their initial phone call lasted fourteen minutes.

In contrast, during the first five months she communicated with her father, Edie had spent over eight hours—an entire workday—on the phone with John. In that same amount of time, she and Susan barely had a coffee break.

"Thanks so much for calling today," Susan messaged later that Wednesday afternoon. "I think of you every day, but don't want you to have to roll your eyes when you see a call or text from me pestering you." She sealed with a kiss, "You could never pester me."

"I've thought about calling for days," Edie admitted. "Thanks for indulging my need for a fix."

Around the time of that Wednesday exchange, Edie phoned Austin to wish John a happy Thanksgiving. That call lasted forty-seven minutes.

Kellie; her husband, Mike; and their youngest, Natalie, joined the two of us in Maringouin at Ducky's for Thanksgiving. My mom, as well as Mike's mother, were also there.

Edie sent midmorning wishes to a host of folks who hosted us—in Renton, Austin, Richmond, Crown Point, Hammond, Schererville, and Metairie—despite not knowing us last Thanksgiving. John's three kids were especially thankful to have found one another.

"I am so grateful to have you in my life," Rachel replied to her sister. "Like the Grinch," she grinned, her heart "grew three sizes. Except, you know, not starting from evil."

Edie then messaged Susan. "I am so happy we have been reunited," she winked, "and it feels so good!" With love for her mother and Skip, Edie offered twin hearts.

"Happy first Thanksgiving 'together,'" Susan answered around the time we finished eating at Ducky's, "or at least 'connected!'" Her twin hearts were paired with a chain-link emoji.

"Hope y'all had a great day," her daughter replied. "Thankful we get to see each other again soon!"

Later that afternoon, Fort Worth learned of my gratitude for a wife who channeled her father's wokeness in Ducky's living room. It came in response to a straw-man argument involving NFL players kneeling during the national anthem. "So not sorry I missed it," Patrick joked.

On Saturday, Susan sought to confirm that Ducky was fine with Pinetta's, one week before the gathering there. Edie brought up a related issue that she'd been grappling with for two days. It involved a request by Ducky.

"At Thanksgiving," Edie told Susan, "she asked about including my older sister, Kellie, but I said the first meeting is just for the three of us. Even if we're at a round table," Red noted, "I don't want it to feel like we're two opposing sides. Maybe next time we can add Kellie and Sharon."

"I was going to suggest including Kellie," Susan responded. "Not a problem as long as I have you there," she insisted. "Include Kellie if that's okay with you."

"Ok," Edie came back after calling Abita Springs, "sounds like Kellie is in."

"I'll stop harassing you for today," Susan said. "I'm just anxious and excited. Since you'll be coming separately," she asked her child, "do you think we could meet afterward to chill together?"

"Absolutely!"

"You're so wonderful!" Susan proclaimed. "Thanks for being my Edie!"

"Happily yours and forever and so glad we're together again!"

Moments later, as we talked it through, the two of us realized that Kellie both deserved and needed to be there. With thirteen years' seniority on her little sister—not to mention insanely strong maternal instincts—Kellie's first baby was Edie.

By that Saturday evening, Fort Worth learned, "So now the plan is for both Mom and Kellie to meet Susan at lunch next Saturday."

Three days later, on Susan's sixty-ninth birthday, Edie sent her the same photo of a crimson and gold daylily that she'd taken and shared on August 12. "I couldn't find a card I wanted to send more than this picture of our lily from the day we reunited," my love messaged Tuesday's birthday girl. "Looking forward to seeing you this weekend! Happy birthday week," Edie wished. "Love you!"

"Love my special card from my special Edie!" her mother replied. "Thanks for being such a wonderful new part of my life," Susan gushed, "and sharing your birthday week with me."

Minutes later, she was texting me. "Okay," I read in a doctor's exam room with my bronchitic mother, "now I need to know what I can win Kellie over with."

"She's a gin person," I reported after confirming with Edie. "She's a nurse who likes Dr. Bombay," I said, workshopping a *Bewitched*/geography bit on my wife's newly discovered birth mother. "I don't think they've changed the name to Mumbai Gin yet."

"Thanks for being my inside source," she said. "I really appreciate it!"

"No worries!" I insisted, "The gifts are totally unnecessary for them to love you."

"Yeah," Susan countered, "but nothing breaks the ice better than a bottle of something."

"This is true," I concurred, "especially in the O'Neal family."

As I write this, I realized that I failed to wish Susan a happy birthday that Tuesday. Oh well, at least I nailed the crap out of that "Mumbai Gin" bit.

Her special day wasn't an hour old when John sent their daughter a pair of emails. At 340 words, the subject of the first was relatively straightforward: "news." Two of Edie's aunts were included in the update about their brother's health. In the wake of last month's fall, John's cardiologist found a minor valve issue, thankfully in no need of immediate action.

He sent his second message solely to his eldest child. "Good Morning!" read the ninety-word email's subject line.

"Hoping that you and Jeremy, Susan, her husband, had a GOOD time!" he wrote in past tense four days before Pinetta's. "Hearts and minds open," an admittedly exhausted John shared. "Hugs, love, and may your heart continue to merge with the body of your mind, processing, internalizing, and embracing what arrives, and guiding you patiently along the journeys. I appreciate deeply your sharing with me. If Susan wishes," he offered, "she can contact me. I will do my best to hear, listen, and be patient with comprehension, supportive.

"Much love," John closed, "(Dad?)"

Hours later on her speakerphone, Edie's scientifically proven father made our Tuesday evening with a gift—for all of us, really—on Susan's birthday. "If you keep following the stars," the font of hippie wisdom observed, "you'll always be in the universe."

Our Friday began with a Facebook message from Patrick. "Happy happy birthday, sweet sister!"

"Thank you, dear brother," Edie replied. "Love you so much!"

"Big day tomorrow?" he asked.

"That's the plan," she confirmed, "unless the weather gets in the way."

"Fingers crossed," Patrick promised. "Sending you all the love," he closed, evoking Mardi Gras-colored hearts from Red, ahead of our hermana's "birthday hugs" sticker.

About an hour later, Susan emailed an animated Hallmark birthday card, set to the "William Tell Overture." In forty-eight years, it marked the first time she was able to pass along such wishes to her only child.

"Happy birthday!" Beth popped up midmorning.

"Thank you!" Edie replied at lunch. "I'm not stressing at all about Susan meeting Mom and Kellie tomorrow," she winked.

"BREATHE," her pal advised. "And keep me posted!"

After work, Edie used an orange marker to write the date on our kitchen's whiteboard. Below "NOV. 30" in quasi-gold, she added a green "90," then "days til STMG family weekend" in purple. She started the countdown to her paternal family's Mardi Gras visit hours before introducing her two mothers—and older sis—to one another.

On Friday evening, the Cavells joined the two of us at The Chimes near LSU for dinner, followed by Big Freedia opening for Tank and the Bangas next door at the Varsity Theatre. Along with the New Orleans musicians, the three of us tried to keep the birthday girl's mind on enjoying herself, and not on the what-ifs about tomorrow's lunch.

Do you think Ducky is ready for meeting me?

Sort of seems like a silly question, given my mother-in-law's insistence on such a gathering, upon first learning about Susan in July. Nevertheless, there was still a tiny, lingering concern that the reality of meeting her daughter's birth mother might be a far departure from whatever ideal Ducky may have envisioned.

Human beings are complicated. We have all sorts of genetically encoded hardwiring and evolutionary programming that compels us to do and feel all sorts of things that we don't necessarily expect or want to do and feel. It's the same reason why open relationships and

Libertarian utopias sound great in theory, as long as you don't account for basic human emotions.

Kellie drove in from Abita Springs some twenty minutes before Pinetta's opened on Saturday morning. Edie and I pulled in moments later, followed shortly by their mother. Ducky joined her two daughters and me in checking out the assortment of faded relics displayed on the eatery's storefront. Next door, sharing a small building dating back to JFK's lifetime, was a local bookstore that opened years before my wife and I enrolled at LSU.

At 11 a.m., we entered Pinetta's Old World atmosphere and grabbed a table under empty Chianti bottles. Numerous fiascos hung from the decorative wrought iron spanning the ceiling above.

Bright sunlight seeping into the dimly lit dining area through the front door made for a less-than-satisfying video of Susan and Skip's arrival moments later. She led the way in a floral blouse, and carried a pair of shopping bags.

Edie met them near the door, where she and Susan embraced. Kellie and Ducky quickly made their way there so mother and daughter could welcome Susan into their lives with gracious hugs. Skip and his giant grin got a pair of warm handshakes amid introductions made with the widest smiles. Edie then greeted Skip with a hug as the gang started to make their way toward me and the table.

Before leaving the ladies to enjoy lunch, I attempted to document the occasion by photographing them around the red-and-white-checkerboard-clad table, topped with a lit candle in the dim environment. Knick started to open his mouth, but didn't. The troublesome lighting was just distracting enough. The two daughters flanked the pair of mothers, who sat in the middle. After a couple of photos, Edie and Kellie swapped places so they could stand next to their respective birth mothers.

With a blue-and-white Lowenbrau Munich banner behind them—precisely five months after first contact—I captured my love with the incredible woman who secretly ceded her only child nearly five decades ago, along with the women who raised our equally incredible girl.

I said goodbye to Skip outside, and set off for a lunch just down Perkins Road. At Zeeland Street Market, I archived a tiny portion of this insane story's excessive source material, all while four ladies furthered the lovely narrative around the corner.

Ducky and Kellie appreciated the scotch and gin. Susan also brought a Doberge cake—half-lemon, half-chocolate, of course. Most of it would end up in our refrigerator.

Pinetta's owner-operator, my friend Diane, approached the table at one point. I had given her a heads-up about the special gathering. She gave the foursome a fiasco of Chianti. Failing miserably at holding back tears, she handed the gals a Sharpie to mark up the bottle in commemorating an occasion she was honored to host.

The nurse at the table lived up to her reputation when Kellie brought up Crohn's disease, and all its complications, before the meal. She did deliver on her promise to not embarrass her sister with anything political, though.

Also, for the first year of Edie's life, my then-teenaged sister-in-law feared the proverbial "they" would come any day to take away her baby girl. Kellie and her insanely strong maternal instincts were prepared to hide Red in the cattle catch pen in the O'Neals' back pasture.

Susan assured Kellie that she never considered making that year-long childhood fear of hers come true. Because that year was never capped with the promised paperwork needed to officially finalize Edie's adoption, Susan told the table, she never knew if her daughter survived birth.

Then, out of the blue, in late June, an envelope arrived from Baton Rouge. Susan's retelling of her truly Red letter day matched the one Skip provided weeks before, both at Gator's Den and the Schererville Lounge.

Susan thanked Ducky and Kellie for sharing Edie with her, and for doing such a bang-up job raising her child. There wasn't much quizzing; just four women having lunch. At one point, Ducky mentioned a friend who had sold her Alabama vacation home because she couldn't drive anymore.

"We're done," Edie texted me at 12:53 p.m. A couple minutes later, I greeted the squinting foursome exiting the restaurant on a sunny Saturday. A delighted Ducky and Kellie departed in their respective black Lincoln Navigators.

The two of us gave Susan a one-block ride to Ivar's, where Skip was parked at the end of the bar, a mere football field's length away from Pinetta's. If only the Schererville Lounge had been that close.

The three of us saddled up next to Skip and his beer. Over a couple rounds of drinks, his wife bequeathed to her daughter jewelry that had been passed down to Susan, along with some of her "hippie jewelry." These were all things Edie's mother had worn. The gorgeous assortment of necklaces, earrings, and bracelets hadn't just been stored away somewhere. In a sense, they represented a part of Susan's life.

A logo-covered cycling jersey on the wall reminded her of a relative who lived in Midland, Michigan. The Karpovas used that residence as a permanent address for things like passports, since Nancy Jane and their family moved around so much.

Susan's late brother, John, had earned his political science degree at Loyola University in New Orleans, we learned. He likely would still be alive had he not been smarter than the doctors, Susan lamented. She wished Edie could've met him.

She also said she was happy with how lunch turned out. Her daughter agreed. Edie said she didn't set any expectations beforehand. Susan, meanwhile, admitted she was fine once she got there, prompting my wife to wonder aloud how many times Susan thought about turning around en route. "That wasn't going to happen," Susan averred.

Just like the last time the four of us said goodbye, as she hugged Edie before leaving for Metairie with Skip, Susan said something within earshot of me. "I love having you in my life so much," I heard. Fortunately for all, my resting bitch face didn't waver too badly this time.

We had just begun driving home when Patrick called for his little sister's take on the lunch, after receiving a good initial report from Kellie. It was 2:38 p.m., the same minute Susan texted Edie.

"Thank you for a great time, great meal, and great memory," she sent her daughter, along with a postscript to thank Susan's "elf." She and Fort Worth soon received my pics from Pinetta's.

"Beautiful," Patrick replied.

From the Rogue's passenger seat, Edie updated her younger siblings. "Just had introductory lunch with mom, older sister, and Susan," she texted Renton and Austin, "and all went well!"

"That is amazing," Rachel responded. "Any new realizations or point of view?" she asked.

Edie mentioned thirteen-year-old Kellie's yearlong fear, and her plans to hide Red in the cattle pasture. "Susan related how she knew she was giving me up permanently," Edie added, "but didn't know until I wrote to her whether I had survived because she never got the follow-up paperwork after I was born."

"Just wow," Justin managed. "That is amazing," he remarked. "So glad you are having these experiences with them."

"Wow," Rachel responded. "Seriously."

A show at the Saenger the next day meant Edie took care of weekly business in Maringouin on Saturday afternoon. While there, she visited Ducky, just a couple hours after introducing her mother to her mom. My mother-in-law greeted her youngest by getting right in her face. Inches from Edie's nose, a bug-eyed Ducky expressed amazement at seeing so much of her baby in a nearly seventy-year-old woman.

My wife also fielded a couple questions that Susan answered at lunch. "Why did they move around so much?" Ducky asked, prompting Edie to remind her about Mr. Karpova's job. "I wonder how Susan felt when she got your letter," she also pondered aloud.

While we were concerned about them being too inquisitive, Ducky and Kellie were apparently too busy processing the emotions of the moment. My mother-in-law obviously didn't think to ask any questions at Pinetta's, because I know damn well that she wouldn't have been afraid to ask any of them.

On the way home, Red called Wade to tell him about the lunch with Susan. "Who?" he asked. Wade still didn't know Edie had found

Susan. He thought her birth mother was still an unknown entity. We still haven't figured out how the hell that happened.

Back home, Edie complied with Beth's demand to keep her posted. "Went well," she led her update.

"Hallelujah!" Beth replied. "I've been thinking about y'all all day. Was it weird?"

"It was weird how relaxed it ended up being," my wife reported, "or maybe everyone just didn't want to be the one to make it not relaxed." Edie added, "Mom thinks it's criminal that nobody ever followed up with Susan."

"So do I," her friend agreed.

"At her house tonight," Edie mentioned visiting Ducky, "Mom said she wondered how Susan felt when she got my letter; I avoided commenting 'That's what we were talking about today.' There were many emotions involved," she conceded, "and lord knows I've probably lost countless details along the way."

"That's what you and Susan were talking about today?" Beth sought clarification.

"At lunch," Edie explained, "Susan mentioned getting my letter, and how it was a good thing she was on her way to her regular doctor appointment so she could get some Xanax."

"So how DID Susan feel about your letter?" Beth asked. "I mean, nervous obvs."

"She never checks the mail, but that day she did, as she was walking out the door. She saw a handwritten, Baton Rouge address," Edie said. "She saw my pic and the name Leggio (OB-GYN), and knew, 'That's my daughter.'"

"My heart rate spiked just reading that," the mother of two girls shared.

"After lunch," Edie turned to our time at Ivar's, "she showed me some of the recent texts with her sister." Susan had sent Sharon a photo of Edie, prompting Sharon to remark on the resemblance between mother and daughter. Susan then told her sister, regarding Edie, "'And she doesn't hate me.'"

"!!!" Beth reacted.

"'Why would she?'" Edie cited her aunt's reply to Susan, Sharon's only surviving sibling. "'You're a good person who deserves good things.'"

"It honestly never occurred to me that you might hate her," Beth admitted. "Maybe because that's just not you."

Edie thanked her friend for the spot-on compliment and observed, "Just like Patrick and I never thought about having younger siblings!"

"I mean," Beth wondered, "why look through every suburban Chicago newspaper for a specific pair of cat-eye glasses to tell someone off?"

The two of us indulged in Doberge cake after supper, and polished off the Chianti from Pinetta's. Fort Worth received three photos of the partially emptied bottle, showing what the four women had written on the straw basket of Diane's gift.

"For the love of Edie!" my sister-in-law wrote under the Bell'Agio label. "Making memories," she added below. "Love you...Kellie." She double-underscored her name.

"Me too," Ducky declared to the right. "Love," she wrote on the next line, "Mom." Under that, my artistic mother-in-law drew a large heart.

"Ditto," Susan Sharpied her sentiments next to Ducky's, one word per line. "Love," she inscribed before closing with a small heart below, "your Susan."

On the basket's remaining quarter, my wife recorded her time on earth across three lines, "11-30-70 to 12-1-18," followed by "Hearts full" on the next. Below, Edie drew a modest heart before her name.

On Sunday afternoon, Kellie followed up with her baby girl. "Loved meeting Susan yesterday," she texted. "She's a lovely lady. I see so many similarities between you. The resemblance, brains, kind heart, quiet dignity," the nurse noted, "fun personality, but not trying to draw attention. She's great! Thanks for sharing her," Kel told Edie. "Hope we can get together again."

"Aw," her little sis replied, "I'm so glad you were there. Mom's thinking maybe we can get more of us together in Maringouin sometime."

"I knew she'd want to," Kellie said.

Two days later, Edie reached out to Susan about Gator's Den. "Is your friend bartending this Sunday?"

"Nope!" Susan replied that Tuesday. "We really don't need a 'baby-sitter' this time, anyway. Not quite strangers anymore," she winked.

A week and a day after Pinetta's, we were back in Manchac on a blustery late Sunday morning. Cold, choppy water lapped near the Rogue's parking spot. Seeing Susan and Skip made it that much warmer inside.

Like our first visit, Susan brought gifts for us: more vintage T-shirts from her collection for her girl, and a four-pack of Firefly moonshine for Susan's "elf." She also gave us a chocolate Elf on the Shelf Advent calendar. My wife taught this former Catholic how it worked, thus returning, nearly a year later, the favor of teaching her how to spit.

Kicking off at noon, the large TV behind the bar showed the Saints game. Any cheering Skip did was for the Buccaneers. The gathered Who Dats were totally chill. "Oh, don't mind him," seemed to be the attitude, "that's just Skip."

A growing, vocal crowd heralded our goodbyes early in the second half. We made it home in time to see the Saints clinch the NFC South title in Tampa.

"Oh, no," Susan alerted Edie in the fourth quarter, "we messed up big time." With hand over mouth, she exclaimed, "No pics-du-jour! I guess we'll just have to plan another get together."

In my defense for dereliction of my documentarian duties, I was focused on being in the moment, like Rachel was during our first trip to Austin. I defaulted to not disrupting Susan and her daughter's time together by doing something I knew they normally didn't care for.

"We will have to catch up on pics," Edie insisted. "Just pulled in at home. Getting to be with you is definitely the weekend highlight!"

"In case I haven't told you lately, I," Susan replied with a heart in the right spot, "you! Love," she wrote in closing, "Your Susan."

"I love you!" her child declared.

32

Ducky's Jam

"OHHH MYYY GAWD!" Justin messaged Edie while we were in Manchac. "John is regaling us with stories of him bartending in Baton Rouge back in the day when our cousin Nate's parents came to visit him," he mentioned their Minnesota kin, visiting Renton the day before a Vikings-Seahawks game. "I think it explains how you came to be. I will catch you up next call."

"Oh, that sounds epic!" Edie responded. "We just got back from visiting Susan," she reported, "confirming where I got my love of Twinkies and Mexican food."

That same Sunday, Rachel informed Edie that she'd received the AncestryDNA kit her sister sent in an envelope inscribed with a message: "Here's to making it official!!" To resemble a smiling face, Edie drew an upturned C below her twin exclamation marks, before closing, "Love you, sis."

Rachel's message arrived while we attended an annual Dirty Dirty Santa Christmas Party, hosted by our friends Tim and Leanne. A revelation by Susan hours earlier inspired me to snap and share pics of their decor.

Over the past several decades, Susan explained in Manchac, my hoarder-ish wife's mother had amassed a huge collection of Mr. Bingle dolls. The cuddly Maison Blanche department store chain mascot is

379

a New Orleans original dating back to 1947. In his annual iterations, MB's a nattily dressed, blue-eyed snowman with an ice cream cone hat, and a catchy ditty folks still fondly remember from childhood. "Jingle jangle jingle," I recall my mom singing when I was a kid, "here comes Mister Bingle!"

Like Susan, our estate-sale-loving friend Leanne collects Mr. Bingles. She had arranged her MB menagerie along her kitchen's bay window, where they sat atop an upholstered bench seat. I photographed the plushies, guarding the candy on the table from three small dogs. Another photo showed Tim and Leanne's Christmas tree, adorned with Mr. Bingle ornaments. Susan reacted with a shocked emoji.

I had a similar reaction two nights later when the patience of a Washington state angel had been tested. "Having a shit storm right now," Justin messaged ahead of Tuesday night's planned phone call, "need to reschedule." John, who was slated to regale us about "his bartending days in BR," had caused some havoc in Renton. "No one is hurt," Justin reported. "My car is slightly dinged up and I am all mad/flustered."

"No worries," Edie assured him about postponing the call.

"It's my fault," Justin asserted, explaining how he shouldn't provide John, who's eager to help, with even the easiest tasks. "He gets discombobulated and can't remember the simplest instructions," my brother-in-law said, "and then I end up dealing with the aftermath."

"Your patience is astoundingly vast," Edie assured, "as is your compassion, and it contributes to you being an amazing dad."

"Well, I don't know about the patience part," Justin countered. "I just about lost my shit. Not one of my shining moments."

"As someone who recently lost their shit with their parent," my wife referenced Thanksgiving's episode of John Hart-esque wokeness, "I'm a little relieved to know that I don't have impossible biological standards of innate patience to live up to."

"Word," Justin concurred with a chuckle.

"Or else I'm sorry for being the bad influence," Big Sis kidded.

Justin, Edie, and I spoke for close to an hour the following evening, but only after he had "idiot proofed" the Harts' garage. He still needed to buy a new washer. In addition to dinging up the Tesla, John had also overloaded their ailing machine on Tuesday.

While their father was "in the bathroom" on Wednesday night, and Hadley was headed to bed, Justin told us of John's Red Stick mixologist tales. One involved serving John's nephew "five liters of vodka" when Joe Ed's son came down to visit his black sheep uncle in early-'70s Louisiana.

Three nights later, Ducky, Kellie, and Edie enjoyed cocktails with dinner after checking into the Roosevelt Hotel in New Orleans. The trio spent Saturday night there after a mid-December concert at the nearby Saenger.

Mannheim Steamroller is Ducky's jam. She doesn't discuss music much, but when she does, it's most likely the neoclassical New Age group. If you walk into her house near Christmastime and music happens to be playing, it's most likely Mannheim Steamroller.

Edie had recently discovered they'd be at the Saenger. The show was her gift to her mom and sister. The all-girls weekend in New Orleans was lagniappe, courtesy of Duck.

Two time zones west, a bright little girl was also thinking about gifts.

"Hadley and I came up with an idea for presents for you," Justin messaged his sisters and me one week before Christmas. "Would you like to come and visit us sometime next year for a camping trip?" Sometime between May and October of 2019, Justin suggested, Mason and Odelle could join us for a three-day weekend of "beach camping, or just somewhere in our lush, beautiful forests." He added, "Just an idea, no pressure."

I was first to reply. Chris Farley repeatedly flipping up his shades in *SNL*'s legendary Schmitt's Gay beer ad seemed befitting. I was crushing on Justin at the time, although, in all honesty, things haven't changed much since.

That same Tuesday, Edie heard from someone a little closer to home.

"Hope you're getting some of my mind transfers, even when we don't get a chance to talk," Susan texted around midday. "I send them often and at random times. Here comes one now…," she typed before a trio of twin hearts.

Three hours later, she again thought about her daughter after seeing *Willy Wonka and the Chocolate Factory* on TV at a neighborhood bar. "Did I ever mention that I love that movie?" she asked with a heart serving as a verb.

"I hope it's the Gene Wilder version?" Edie wondered.

"Of course!" exclaimed the woman who'd found an amen corner in the daughter who found her.

"I mean, to me," Edie maintained, "that's really the only one."

"Kinda like you!" Susan quipped.

Thursday afternoon, five days before Christmas, Edie invited Susan to Maringouin. "I want you to know that you and Skip are welcome," she texted, "but I don't want you to feel obligated. There will likely be twenty to thirty people," Edie forewarned about "crowds and kids and noise." She suggested, "Smaller intros first would probably be less chaotic."

After learning about our busy holiday schedule, Susan joked, "I guess I messed up and you should have been triplets just to keep up! You're absolutely right," she addressed her daughter's invitation. "We need to stick to our baby steps. The Indiana plunge worked out so well because nobody knew anybody else," Susan observed. "Now we're down South," she reminded Edie, "and things here work better taken slowly."

"Agreed," her child replied, "except this would've been WAY wilder if there were four of us to reunite! In this case," Red winked, "I'm going to be selfishly glad I don't have to share you with wombmates."

"I guess I'll just have to remember that you deserve three times the love for keeping up with everything and everybody!" Susan also mentioned that we could get together a few days after Christmas under the auspices of a pre-birthday weekend get-together for yours truly. "Have a great weekend, super Christmas, happiest New Year," she told Edie, "and remember that we've only just begun."

"Your elf needs an elf," I texted Susan on Friday afternoon, after Edie confirmed the four of us would get together on the last weekend of the year. "What kinda booze should we get Skip?"

"Find an empty bottle of anything and fill it with colored water to match the original contents. He's crazy enough already!" Susan cracked. "To be a polite elf, I'll say peppermint schnapps," she shared. "That's what he has as a nightcap when he's sitting on the porch yelling at the people who don't stop at the stop sign."

Two nights later, Edie was texting my elf. "Happy Christmas Eve Eve!" she told Susan. "We're about to catch *Elf* at the Saenger with Mike and Shannon."

Apologies to Will Ferrell, but we'd never seen the film, which the Cavells attested was far better than the stage production. The best part of Sunday's show was the first twenty minutes, when half the audience (including me) not-so-slyly streamed the Saints game to watch them clinch home-field advantage throughout the playoffs by beating the Rams. From the stage, Santa acknowledged our collective fandom.

"We saw *Elf* last night without any prior knowledge of the story," Edie texted Justin the next day. "Buddy's mom was named Susan. If his dad had been named John," my wife said, "I might've lost it." When Justin offered her a DVD copy of the film, Edie laughed aloud. "Lemme get over the creepy factor first," she insisted. "But I am as excited as Buddy to have a 'little' brother," she added with a heart, "and sis, and niece, and Cherish."

She soon heard back from Susan that Monday afternoon. "Sounds like those tickets have brought you a lot of fun outings."

"I was a little edgy upon realizing it was the story of an orphan whose mom was named Susan," Edie texted back. "It made me that much happier that you and I are reunited!"

"Plus you know you'd never, ever have been an orphan." Susan emphasized, "That was NOT an option!"

"Merry Christmas, everyone," Edie texted her younger sibs late Monday evening from Ducky's, where we spent Christmas Eve. "I'm so happy we have found each other," Big Sis said, "and have happy times together to look forward to. Love y'all."

"We love you guys," Justin replied. "June 'glamping' is booked," he reported on their Christmas gift to us, which had been upscaled to minimize roughing it. Before that, though, was Mardi Gras. "I am looking forward to our next visit in March," he added, "making more memories."

I later thanked my brother-in-law for the upcoming two-day stay in Port Angeles with Mason and his wife, Odelle, on Washington's Olympic Peninsula, near mountains and hot springs. "Just got a good look at the AirBNB you booked," I gushed like a schoolgirl. "OMFG!"

"Really looking forward to spending some time relaxing and doing some fun stuff with you guys in all that splendor," Justin said. He was excited about finally having a chance to be together with all of his known siblings.

"Word!" Rachel replied.

"WOW!" Edie exclaimed. "Can't wait!"

I was sipping coffee on Christmas morning when Ducky busted up in her kitchen like a boss. "Let's get to work," she belted in a full-on Mrs. Claus dress, complete with an apron and elf hat. I complied by photographing a festive Ducky Claus, holding a glass of eggnog around 9:30 a.m.

"Ducky is dressed for the season!" Rachel commented.

Following a round of holiday greetings among John Hart's kids, Edie thanked her little sister for a gift Rachel had sent to both of her siblings: a 5x7 glass photo of the trio taken with Hadley on our last night in Kenwood. The image of the smiling quartet, huddled tightly together for my camera, accompanied an easel. It turned out to be exactly what my wife's work desk needed. "I love it and love y'all even more!"

"My life is so much fuller with you in it," Rachel shared. "I'm so lucky how well we work together when it could easily have not been the case." She later followed up, "I love my present, Edie and Jeremy! Won't say more in case Justin hasn't opened his."

Red had packaged Louisiana tea with Rachel and Justin's blue, full-sized coffee mugs, adorned with a collage of photos from the California trip. "September 2018" and "LOVE" accented images of the idyllic reunion. Edie got a mug for herself, too.

My group photo from Pixar, in front of the Steve Jobs Building, adorned Cherish's mug. John's featured the pic of Justin and Edie at Patterson Cellars in Woodinville. Both of their mugs were paired with Community Coffee, which John had fallen in love with as an LSU student.

He would later call while Edie was in the shower, so I answered. He thanked us for the "very thoughtful gifts," which also included a bottle of jalapeno garlic olive oil for Hallie. John told me he tried to empathize with what his two oldest kids were thinking in the winery pic on his mug. Later in the call, he said, "You're the best of good people." Of all the reactions to gifts from Edie, his was arguably the most enthusiastic. Except for maybe his granddaughter's.

"OHHH MYYY GAHHHHD!" Hadley emoted in Justin's video. My BFF showed off the 8x10 desktop plaque reading "YES YOU CAN" on its left half. To the right was a photo I took of Hadley attempting to move an immovable ball—taller than her—in the Pixar courtyard, as Luxo oversaw her cheerful efforts. "Thannnnk you!" Justin texted, mimicking his ebullient, pink-pajama-clad delight.

Additionally that December, Edie, Rachel, Odelle, and Cherish's sister, Milani, were apparently all on the same wavelength. "Funny note," Justin informed Edie, after conveying the Harts' sincere thanks for all the gifts, "all four of Hadley's aunties kind of got her the same gift—mermaid tails. She almost has one for every day of the week! She loves them so much," he texted, "it's really perfect and I think kind of weird while being awesome at the same time."

"Maybe we're all vicariously living out our mermaid fantasy lives through Hadley," Auntie Edie hypothesized. "I started to get her something more educational," my wife admitted, "but wanted her to have something fun and soft and pink and purple."

"I just want to say I am thankful for you and your presence in our lives," Justin volunteered, "because you have a very different story than I do, and I think you present a very different aspect to the very complicated story that is John's family tree." He told Edie, "Rachel is still very hurt and angry at John for not being there when she wanted him to be, and she doesn't accept his reasons (which he poorly explained in a letter ten years ago). I am hopeful knowing you and your story might help her in a way I can't," Justin said of their sister, "or in a way that is difficult for me because of my being 'in the middle' perpetually."

"I'm hopeful for the same thing," Edie revealed. "It's amazing to me to think of our three moms and the different choices they made, none of which were easy. I imagine it's not even easy when you have two awesome, committed people like you and Cherish with a whole support team," my wife noted. "Y'all are so incredible and I am so happy to have the opportunity to be part of your family."

"Aw shucks," a humble Justin grinned. "Thanks, Edie. It feels amazing to have a big sister. You and Jeremy are wonderful, and I am so thankful you found us. Each of our mothers had dramatically different circumstances," he agreed, "and our father was, to some extent, kind of (or completely) oblivious to the ramifications of his choices. He never really wanted or figured out how to be a parent. To his credit, he always knew that he wasn't capable of being a good parent.

"With your mom," Justin theorized, "I gather he never even knew or thought about anything beyond some moment of togetherness with her. With my mom, he really was trying to be a partner in bringing someone into the world," said Shirley's son, "but at the end of the day, he still did it because he thought that's what she wanted. With Rachel's mom," he said, "I bore witness to him simply wanting to help someone, wanting to give me a more comfortable place than the halfway house, and not really being good about boundaries with Elizabeth. He's a good man," Justin reiterated, "but a flawed and deeply hurt man who doesn't really understand the way other people work. I love John," his son said, "but he is certainly a handful." The perfect emissary added with love, "I am honored to know you and have you as a sister."

Edie's warning to Susan was accurate. Including my mom, Laura, there were around a couple dozen people on hand Tuesday for the O'Neal present exchange in the poolside cabana where my in-laws had hosted our wedding reception. The Christmas morning excitement was a bit overwhelming for my mom. She'd previously met most everyone there, and is about as shy as I am. I could only imagine what it would have been like for Susan.

Kellie's kids continued their longstanding tradition of after-dinner naps, both on furniture and the floor, near the fireplace in Ducky's living room. We spent the rest of the day there, in the same room where—exactly one year before—Edie decided to embark on this insanely beautiful journey. Her nephew and nieces, who had learned of their aunt's mother the night before, were crashed all around us when Susan texted.

"Merry first Christmas 'together'!" she sent her child.

"Merry Christmas!" Edie replied. "I hope y'all have had a fun, peaceful day," she added. "We're pooped!"

In three days, we'd return to Diane's place for a Friday lunch. "Just want to see y'all once more before 2019 if possible" is how Susan put it. "The guys didn't get to do Pinetta's with us," she noted.

One of the gifts her child got for Susan was an 8x8 photographic tile. On the Diva Day bus, Edie snapped a selfie of the smiling twinsies in their matching miniature alpine hats. Red got a photo tile for us, as well. To this day, I catch myself staring at it in amazement.

My wife also treated herself to a 3x5 of Hadley's upside-down, orchid-adorned tiara on my stubbly dome in Renton. When the magnetic photo arrived a week earlier, I slapped it on our office's filing cabinet before sending Edie a pic to confirm its arrival. With little hearts, she replied, "I.AM.IN.LOVE."

The twenty-sixth marked our twenty-sixth anniversary. In 1992, the day fell on a Saturday between semesters.

A quarter-century and a year later, my AncestryDNA results came in on a Wednesday. Edie had gotten me a kit with Rachel's.

"DNA Story for Jeremy" the heading read, next to a mostly yellow pie chart. The key under "Ethnicity Regions" led with a yellow dot next to "France" on the left, and "84%" to the right. Below was "Migrations," which listed "Acadians," a group of exiles from Nova Scotia who settled in Louisiana before it was a state. With a screenshot—and a particular shithead of a seventh-grade P.E. teacher in mind—I informed some of my in-laws I'd be "printing this on cards to hand out to assholes who insist I'm not Cajun because my last name isn't LeBlanc. I mean, I'm literally French enough to make a Pac-Man pie chart."

"My friend, you are FRANCH!" Patrick replied. "Happy anniversary, guys," he added.

"Crazy!" Rachel commented on my uber-Franco genes. "I've heard it's really rare for someone whose family is in the U.S. for several generations to have such a high percentage of anything."

"My peeps didn't leave Indiana," Edie noted. "His didn't leave down da bayou."

"Well," her little sis observed, "y'all are bringing people together!"

Two days before our return to Pinetta's, my wife's Wednesday started with an anniversary eCard from Susan. Edie answered that afternoon with a photo taken on Tuesday before Kellie's slumbering kids occupied most of Ducky's living room. Wade and Kellie wore elf hats and smiles in front of the hearth with their sister and festively dressed matriarch.

"Ducky is so cool!" Susan replied. "YOU are gorgeous (but you know that already)."

The two of us enjoyed our anniversary dinner at home, watching a bowl game officiated by our buddy Bradford from the New Orleans hotel lobby. My wife was right; we were pooped.

Friday morning arrived with an admonition from our lunch date. "So there's no discussion," Susan texted, "this is your anniversary present from us. Polite people do not argue about presents. As a wise woman named Ducky once told me, 'You shouldn't have, but thank you.'"

"I will strive to be as gracious," Edie promised. "Thank you!"

We and the Metairie couple arrived at Pinetta's near 11 a.m., and snagged the same table from four weeks earlier. Counter to what Edie previously said, German music was playing. Sadly, even after our server turned it up, Skip could hear nary an "oom" nor a "pa-pa."

I attempted to make up for the unheard Deutsche musik with peppermint schnapps, the last one on our neighborhood liquor store's shelves that morning. In return, the woman who brought my wife into the world presented me with a bag of confectionaries. I never imagined being so thankful to get a fruitcake for Christmas.

Packaged with an easel, Edie gave Susan her behatted twinsies photo tile. Susan reciprocated with a gift for her girl.

"Tradition says the person who gives it wants you to smile," she explained while pulling from a bag a pair of super-soft, jingly Mr. Bingle dolls, identified by the year embroidered on the soles of their right feet. Mouthless Mr. Bingle 2017 was the seventieth-anniversary edition. He was supposed to be the final addition to Susan's collection; but then came along the daughter she thought she'd never see in this life, so she bought dapper Mr. Bingle 2018 for Edie. She also bequeathed her 2017 Mr. Bingle so MB 2018 wouldn't get lonely. My wife graciously accepted both.

"Thanks for the time and great company," Susan texted as Skip chauffeured them home. "And especially the picture!"

"Thank you for lunch, and goodies," Edie replied, "but time with you most of all! Love you so much!"

"Ditto!" her mother responded. Later that afternoon, Susan texted both of us a pic of her and Skip at Uncle Joe's. "Oops," she commented, "we forgot pictures today!"

In this binary-based digital world, you can either document a moment or be in it. Again, I blame my photographic lapses on striving to focus on the latter in all encounters with Susan.

"Your turn...," Susan continued.

"Awake and already sampled the fruit cake!" Edie replied with a selfie we shot in our kitchen, some time after European comfort food and midday red wine had conspired against my eyelids.

"He looks very well rested," Susan noted.

"I talked to Rachel this morning," Edie alerted Justin on the second-to-last day of the year. "She said she's looking forward to Mardi Gras. I also gave her a trigger warning about seeing 'John Hart is your father' when she gets her AncestryDNA results." Based on the arrival of mine, she expected Rachel to get hers within a week.

"We got our tickets for Mardi Gras!" Justin emailed us the following afternoon, with under eight hours remaining in 2018. "Flying into Houston, driving to BR from there," he smiled. Rachel and her new Volt would meet them at Bush International on Thursday evening before Fat Tuesday.

"WOOHOO!!!" I gushed. "This is gonna be so awesome!"

The two of us joined the Cavells on Monday night at Shannon's family's compound in Ascension Parish for their annual outdoor gathering. While a local news crew covered the giant bonfire that took several industrious cousins over a week to build, we bid a fond farewell to what Edie recently described as "this amazing year."

"Happy New Year!" she sent Susan and Paula with a pic of the walkable, soon-to-be-ignited replica of the area's chronically damaged Sunshine Bridge. "We are at our friends' family bonfire. Had a cardinal visit at home earlier today," Edie referred to the bird long seen as a departed loved one watching over kin. "So happy this year brought us together," she said, "and looking forward to what our future has in store for us! Love y'all!"

Paula replied with a heart.

"Gorgeous bonfire!" Susan remarked. "So glad your grandfather found his way South for a visit," she said, alluding to Edie's red visitor. "I'll be on the lookout here. Paula, we'll send him back up there when it gets warmer." Susan said, "2018 was amazing as a year of surprises and uniting with missing parts of my family/heart. Can't wait to continue the adventure in the new year!!"

33

All Three Worlds

Susan started 2019 with a text. "First time this year," she told Edie, "I love you!" She also said she'd place their twinsies picture tile "in 'my' room so it's what I see first every morning. It's gonna be a great year!"

"Yes indeed!" our girl agreed that same Tuesday. "I love you!"

Two days later, Edie alerted Mira about a gift set to arrive on the eve of Ukrainian Christmas that Sunday, January 6. "Good stuff coming your way for the celebration this weekend," she sent with a FedEx link to track the king cake, just like the one en route to Paula's. The two cultural traditions meshed together perfectly on my birthday. Jodie's enjoyment of king cake for her birthday that same weekend at her mom's was lagniappe. "Y'all get special dispensation to enjoy it a day early," Edie decreed.

January 3 also saw John's first two emails of the new year. The times at which he sent them—12:38 a.m. and 12:53 a.m., respectively— proved a bit freaky that Thursday morning. Updating my spreadsheet, I noticed that he had sent 2018's last two emails to Edie, days before her birthday, at the exact same times, fifteen minutes apart.

"So four different messages," Edie asked in the thread with Justin, "but two pairs at the exact same times?!"

"Yep," I confirmed.

"Obviously, he has fingers of fury when it comes to typing," Justin replied. "We had to get him a keyboard made entirely of steel."

"Even more impressive," Edie noted: "Today's pair of emails were sent from his iPhone. It takes something like initial contact from a newly discovered relative to get me to even consider trying to type an email on my phone!"

Laughing, Justin speculated, "I wonder if he finally figured out how to use speech to text."

"I'm guessing no," she said. "Check your email."

"You guessed correctly," he soon confirmed. "Although, given the timing of the emails," John's son added, "he may just be half asleep."

Edie had her first conversation of 2019 with their father the following Tuesday. I listened on speakerphone as John talked about his Christmas gift some two weeks after receiving the mug depicting his two eldest children, smiling at him every morning. The winery pic prompted John, ever searching for meaning, to bring up our anniversary photograph from Hugo's Cellar.

"John's interpretation," my bride messaged me during the call, to ensure I heard it: "You have a happy life, and it gets happier—that's the wine in that picture."

"The rose represented us being beautiful people," I noted.

Edie touched bases with Susan the ensuing Friday, before Mardi Gras madness took over our lives. "Didn't want the weekend to come and go without checking in," she texted. "Jeremy's started trying to round up the krewe to start working on parade prep, so it's feeling like it's going to be kinda nuts around here for a while." Edie added a trio of Carnival-colored hearts.

"Nuts is okay," Susan insisted. "I live with it full time."

"Any word from Sharon about her heading this way?" Edie asked. It had been two weeks since our lunch at Pinetta's, when Susan mentioned potentially meeting her sister sometime in early 2019.

"Not yet," Susan texted back. "Whenever is good is good," she maintained. "We don't have to try to make any bad time work."

"No need to press," her child concurred, reciprocating Susan's caring sentiments. "Just want you to know I'm thinking of you, and love you!"

Halfway through the month, I sent our rookie revelers a primer on Spanish Town Mardi Gras. We wanted to make absolutely sure the new fam knew what they were in for. Edie followed up days later with an email thread to plan the rest of their four-day South Louisiana visit. The tentative itinerary included a possible Lundi Gras (Fat Monday) brunch at Ducky's, just before the gang would head back to Houston for the Harts' evening flight home.

"I hope we can meet Ducky!" Rachel gleamed. "I'm excited to get swept up in your town and traditions!"

"What Rachel said!" a beaming Justin dittoed.

That same Sunday afternoon, we learned that Rachel's Ancestry-DNA results came in with no (new) surprises. Ninety-four percent British Isles, the ethnicity estimate said, with three percent Norwegian for lagniappe Whiteness.

Moments later, as the Harts headed to a friend's cabin in the snowy mountains, Justin photographed an adorable sea creature in his Tesla's back seat. Wearing her newest auntie's Christmas gift, "H the mermaid said she has to stay well hydrated." With a wink, Justin told Edie, "See what you have started!?"

Following an eleven-minute phone call with Ducky about a potential Lundi Gras gathering—for which Edie suggested a simple brunch with easy vegetarian options—Red began inviting her older siblings to Maringouin for a chance to meet her younger ones at the now-confirmed gathering.

"Just in case y'all might be free for Mardi Gras weekend," she messaged Fort Worth, "wanted to let y'all know that Justin, Cherish, Hadley, and Rachel are coming in for the festivities."

"I just spoke with Mom and she told me," Patrick reported. "I'm so happy that they're coming. And Edie," he said, "she was so thrilled that you called her. She was very touched. She said she'd cook them all their meals!" Patrick was doubtful he and Yvette could make it. "But we'd love to meet them if we can. And," a chuckling Patrick added from his call with Ducky, "she said, 'Pat, they only eat vegetables.'"

As the ensuing workweek wrapped up, and the calendar flipped to February, Edie received word on possibly meeting her aunt. "I did reach out to Sharon," Susan texted that Friday, "and suggested a meeting in Lafayette. She really wants to meet you!"

"I'm looking forward to meeting her, too!" Edie replied. "Lafayette is no problem for me," she said of the hourlong drive from Baton Rouge, "since I go halfway there every weekend already to pay Earle's sitters."

"Have I told you lately that I love you?" Susan wrote. "Can't let you know too much. Lost too much time."

"I love you, too!" her daughter reciprocated. "Now and always. And we can have fun together now without all the rough spots!"

Susan shared good news the next morning. "Got a thumbs up from Sharon for 2/10," Susan sent Saturday.

"Yay!" Edie exclaimed. "Looking forward to it!"

February 10 was the following weekend. In the interim, Mardi Gras prep was in full gear, as evidenced by the ongoing exchange with Justin and Rachel. His attempt to nail down details for our June trip to the West Coast was beginning to cause a bit too much anxiety for the project manager's sisters.

"One crisis at a time," hinted Rachel, who was "so excited for Mardi Gras."

"Crisis = trip planning?" Justin's query earned a pair of fair, freckled thumbs-up. "I hope it isn't too hectic/troublesome to figure out travel plans," he tried to reassure his sisters. "It's supposed to be fun or exciting!"

While Edie was "looking forward to hanging out" with her new family, she half-joked, "I'm on the fence about inviting a couple dozen nieces/nephews who want to meet y'all."

"Ooooh, I got it!" Justin picked up what the sisters were putting down. "The invasion of your other family," he realized was the issue. "That's panic-inducing."

Edie admitted, "I was skirting that until someone brought it up today."

That someone was me, because I know my wife and her skirting prowess. We damn nearly eloped because of it. For my bride, it seemed easier than addressing our "small" wedding's exploding guest list. Decades later, she could completely empathize with her little sister, the one raised in a tiny family.

"I'd love to meet them," Rachel insisted. "But yeah," she giggled, "maybe a half-dozen at a time."

"Jeremy's mom jumped on the bandwagon today, too," Edie noted.

"Did the bandwagon appreciate being jumped on?" Justin asked.

"Only when dressed in pink or flamingos," Baby Girl replied, bringing it full circle back to Spanish Town.

Edie continued the thread's circular theme on Groundhog Day. "I am having entirely too much fun for a Saturday morning."

"Oh?" a curious Rachel wondered.

"We ordered 300 pink urinal cakes for custom handouts from the krewe," her big sis explained, further ensuring they knew what awaited them. "And because no one expects the Spanish Inquisition or fruit-scented urinal cakes, I tweaked the label design to include a warning."

My fully corrupted wife had created stickers for the individually wrapped pucks. They included our krewe name, a pissing flamingo, and the warning "DO NOT EAT!!"—complete with a pictogram indicating inedibility. It all fit the theme of our float and the parade, set to roll precisely one month later.

"Y'all will meet our friends Mike and Shannon," Edie mentioned the Cavells, "who ride on our float and lead our trivia team. Mike is making two kegs this year since we tapped the one last year well before we rolled," Edie said of our krewe brew, which our brewmaster promised to be potent. "'Measuring in around 8% ABV.'" She quoted Mike channeling Dave Chappelle portraying Samuel L. Jackson hawking beer, "'Mmm, mmm. It'll get ya drunk!'"

The next day was Super Bowl Sunday. The Saints undoubtedly would've been in Atlanta if not for a recent, egregious no-call that led the NFL to radically change its replay rules the following season.

"Jeremy and Edie can be proud of me," Rachel announced in our group chat thread. "I've watched multiple plays of the Super Bowl."

"Don't say that too loud," I earnestly replied. "Most of the state is boycotting. Saints got fuuuuuuuuuuucked. Personally," I added, "I'm glad the game is crap."

"Yes, even at my distance from following football," my sharp sister-in-law laughed, "I've heard there were shit calls, and the person in charge just kinda said, 'We're human—too bad so sad.'"

While tinkering with his AncestryDNA account, Justin discovered he had about ten percent more DNA in common with Edie than with Rachel. "I just found that interesting," he passed along to his big sis.

"I noticed that, too," Edie replied. "I share a wee bit more DNA with John than I share with Susan," she noted, "but I'm not sharing that with them."

"Why wouldn't you tell them that?" Justin wondered. "Just curious."

"I don't want to stoke competition," my wife explained. "I love them both, and feel so honored to have some of both of them within me. They are both amazing people. I don't know what their relationship was, and don't have the capacity to accept that it was just to put me here." Edie revealed, "John offered again this week to talk to Susan if she wanted. I don't bring John up with her because I don't know the circumstances," she explained, "beyond her apologizing to me because she knew she couldn't make a family with 'the father.'" My love added, "But I am so grateful to have the best of all three worlds."

"I see," he smiled. "Also," Justin asked, "since I look a bit like John did as a young man, do you think if I meet her it might be upsetting or disturbing?" He wondered, "Maybe I will remind her who he was."

"We haven't talked about it," Edie reported, "but I had our three siblings plus Hadley pic as my profile pic for a while. Granted," she conceded, "seeing us all together in person would probably be more significant.

"I am just so in awe of what she was able to do," Susan's daughter lauded. "And I was thinking the other night—if she and I are as much alike as I feel we are—how much she doesn't want to hear that," my compliment-averse wife winked, citing Susan's response to the "young and beautiful" line from Edie's initial letter.

"It's amazing this hasn't even been a full year yet," Red beamed. "I am so grateful for you. And to you," she added. "My brother Patrick probably won't be able to come in for Mardi Gras, but I can't wait till y'all meet. No girl could dream of having such wonderful brothers."

"Ah shucks, and wow!" a confused Justin responded. "She wouldn't want to hear how much you feel you two are alike?"

"No, sorry," Edie clarified about Susan, "I meant I have trouble accepting compliments, and that appears to be one of the things she and I have in common." Edie said, "We like our commonalities."

"Amazing how DNA can translate into not just physical traits," her brother grinned, "but behaviors and self-awareness, as well. Hope you have a wonderful day, sis."

"You too!" she closed their Sunday exchange. "Love you."

That same weekend, the two of us joined the Cavells at the inaugural Mid City Gras Ball. The new krewe's theme was "Peace, Love, & Nuts." I threw on a Mardi-Gras-colored, tie-dyed shirt, sandals, and a red-white-and-blue sweatband with an attached curly mullet. Some folks were apparently trashed enough to think I had miraculously grown eight inches of hair in a few weeks, exclusively on the back of my head.

Edie wore one of countless outfits bequeathed by Ducky. The purple-flower-bodiced, sheer brown dress was the closest thing to "hippie chic" in my wife's closet.

"Loved the pic on Facebook!" Susan texted Monday morning. "You looked so retro-glamorous!"

"Thanks," Edie chuckled, "I like that a lot better than the 'sixty-five-year-old art teacher' description someone else gave me." My notoriously youthful-looking wife added, "We had fun."

Back in November, Susan asked if Edie was familiar with Pat's of Henderson, an eatery just east of Lafayette. Her daughter confirmed the seafood restaurant was one of our go-to places to eat after officiating postseason games in the Acadiana region.

Two and a half months later, the pair finalized plans for the upcoming weekend. Susan and her sister would spend Saturday night at an area hotel after spending the day with Sharon's friend from college. "Sunday, 11-ish, Pat's in Henderson OK?" Susan texted that Tuesday.

"Sounds great to me! Can't wait to see you," Edie sent with twin hearts. "I'm excited to meet Sharon, too, of course, but I'm gonna need our hug ASAP."

Five days later, Susan alerted her girl about the construction she drove through the day before. "Sharon is so excited about meeting you," she added that Sunday morning, "and I have sooo been needing an Edie fix."

"Thanks for the heads up," Edie answered. "Hope y'all had a good day yesterday. Can't wait to see you!"

During the ninety-minute lunch with her daughter and little sister, Susan revealed how, as a teenager, she was a chaperone for a bunch of younger kids in Europe. She once packed thirteen of them into a little beat-up Volkswagen, with one rule: no more than three up front besides her. At fifteen years old, Susan became a de facto taxi driver; Nancy never drove anywhere again.

The VW had one working headlight and one functioning windshield wiper. If it was dark, someone would usually hold a flashlight out the passenger-side window to help light young Susan's way down the road.

While the company was lovely, my wife was distracted by repeated calls from Maringouin, where she was set to visit Earle on the way home from lunch. Just as Edie was meeting her aunt, the woman long seen as her other mother was in need of medical attention. She excused herself to take at least one call, and constantly glanced at the phone in her lap for updates.

Before leaving Henderson, Edie took a handful of selfies of the trio in the restaurant's parking lot, just before Sharon departed for Houston, and moments before Susan gifted her daughter with more stuff from the back of her van. She and Edie managed to prevent the regular bevy of cats loitering around the waterside seafood place from jumping into the vehicle.

"Thank you for coming!" Susan texted a little later. Edie had finally met her aunt. More importantly, Susan's only surviving sibling had graciously and enthusiastically embraced her older sister's long-held secret. "Sorry our visit was so short," Susan followed up, "but we have the meet-and-greet behind us now. Whew! I just had to share how wonderful you are with someone in my family besides Skip."

"I was so happy to get to see you today and to meet Sharon. Love you," Edie sent Susan with pics of the trio. Later, after briefing me about their lunch, my wife added, "Jeremy apologizes for the last couple visits, and promises to try to remember to get a pic next time the four of us are together."

One of Susan's gifts that Sunday turned me into a giddy little boy from down the bayou. "Mais dat's a really good king cake, yeah," I texted her in Cajun parlance.

"High praise from a king cake connoisseur," she replied, "and my favorite king cake storyteller."

While I gushed to Susan about the sweet treat, Edie elaborated to her younger sibs on the confection's deliciousness. "So Susan gave me a traditional king cake this weekend from one of our local grocery chains," she raved to our soon-to-be Mardi Gras newbies, "and it is the most fabulous way to become diabetic I never imagined. It has been added to our weekend lineup."

Less than a week later, with carnival-colored hearts, my wife would update our kitchen's whiteboard countdown to their arrival: "10 days!"

34

The Pink Maw

Saturday, February 16, brought the Spanish Town Mardi Gras Ball, followed Sunday morning by the Mystic Krewe of Mutts Parade. Amid the plentiful pups parading through downtown Baton Rouge was a young man with a pair of leashed Doberman pinschers. An image of one with a German flag adorned his T-shirt, which declared, "I know a little German." The full-grown dogs wore lederhosen, complete with cutouts for their docked tails.

"Skip loves it," Susan responded to my pic of the canines.

One week later, our friends Case and Rachel hosted several revelers, including the Cavells, at their home, a short walk from the Mid City Gras parade route. We arrived that final Sunday of the month with Edie's second iteration of a boudin king cake. Like the first one she made for the MCG Ball, the savory creation appeared inspired by Georgia O'Keeffe. My wife's gynecologically shaped, meat-filled treat was devoured in the vegetarian home an hour before the parade kicked off.

"Where are you going to be for MCG?" Beth texted Edie just past noon. "I need to hug your neck." Along with her girls, and their rescue dog Penny, our ninja soon met up with us along the route for the parade's sophomore effort on a lovely sunny afternoon.

Even more strikingly gorgeous than the weather was my wife. While I donned the same tie-dye shirt from the MCG ball, she wore a floral-print hippie dress, bequeathed by Susan in Henderson. The full-length garment wrapped around Edie as though it were tailored for her. I've never seen my wife handle so many compliments from so many so well.

"She'd have made a great hippie!" Susan said of an image that instantly became one of my favorites.

"Everyone absolutely loved Edie's hippie dress," I later wrote back, "and Edie wearing the hell out of that dress. I just sat back and smiled, knowing they will eventually flip out when they read the rest of the story behind how she came to wear it."

No less eye-catching than my wife were Men at Twerk, although they weren't nearly as elegant as Edie, particularly gangly-ass Case. With moves that resembled every clutz in the "Has this ever happened to you?" part of an infomercial, he twerked down North Boulevard like a six-foot-one marionette of Abraham Lincoln.

The diverse crowd roundly hooped and hollered as Case, Mike, and the rest of the eight-man ensemble gyrated by Steele Boulevard in Dickies and hard hats. A female cop posted across the street walked backward for a spell with her phone trained on the dance group. A few members had energy after the parade for an encore in Case and Rachel's front yard.

During a phone call with Justin the next afternoon—three days before the gang's Thursday arrival—Edie sent him a picture of our late friend Jim Work, co-founder of both the Spanish Town Ball and the float krewe we inherited from him. Like John Hart, Jim was a hippie Vietnam vet with lots of insane stories, as was his partner in crime, Lonnie. The two also spent time in 1970s Baton Rouge dealing and partaking in illegal substances, as evidenced by the venerable moniker they coined: "Royal Mystic Krewe of Generic Yo-yos."

"He does kind of look like the guy I met with John back in 1990," Justin remarked. "Of course, my memory of him is a little hazy. I will ask John about him." Spoiler alert: Jim didn't deal with John back in the day.

On Thursday afternoon, I stocked the Beauregard Town AirBNB with groceries, and shared pics of the loaded pantry and fridge with the folks en route. "Holy moly!" an excited Cherish responded after landing in Houston. "The food and booze fairies visited!"

"Get ready for lots of fairies this weekend," my sly bride said, earning a giggle from Cherish.

That evening, with the Cavells in New Orleans to catch the Muses parade—and hopefully one of the all-female krewe's signature decorated shoes—the two of us joined our teammate Kym in repping our trivia team, Betty White Lives, at The Bulldog. Edie scored fantastic Muses swag at work earlier that week, courtesy of her cool boss, a Muses member parading Thursday night through a sea of people screaming, out of habit, "Throw me something, mister!"

Multiple rounds of bar trivia distracted us from increased antsiness about seeing the gang again, as well as from concern about them driving through hours of nighttime rain on sketchy roads amid sketchier drivers. As runners-up at Port Royal, Edie and I got to pick a bottle of wine from the bar. Seeking Justin's input proved difficult since he was behind the wheel of Rachel's Volt.

They quietly parked the hybrid just down the street from the rental house maybe twenty minutes after we arrived. The front door's locking mechanism unexpectedly came alive. Two steps inside, Hadley made a beeline for Auntie Edie on the couch. Seconds later, I got to hug my BFF after she spotted me sitting behind the front door. We similarly greeted the rest of the quartet near midnight.

Despite the hour and the drive, there was much giddiness to overcome. Hadley had caught her second wind following a three-hour nap, which came after a bout of car sickness in Houston. Two fully sugared king cakes on the kitchen table did nothing to abate our late-night buzz.

Justin broke out the Woodinville bourbon he'd brought, and opened our trivia prize. Cherish tried out the wine. Her face indicated we chose poorly. On the bright side, though, we had gotten all the less-than-enjoyable alcohol consumption of an epic Mardi Gras week-end out of the way, right up front.

Hadley was still up when Edie and I finally went home, just after 2 a.m. Friday morning. None of us got to bed before three.

"Hadley is raring to go," Cherish texted just after 9 a.m., "everyone else is slow."

"Hadley might be our pacesetter this weekend," Edie replied as we grabbed muffins to go with king cake for breakfast.

The Friday before Mardi Gras is always one of the most awful traffic days in Baton Rouge. Half of Texas uses our already overcrowded, poorly designed roads to go see titties in New Orleans. It's why we strongly urged the foursome to come in the night before. I've been stuck on the west side of the river on that day before. Twice. Both times, it took several frustrating hours and a ride across the out-of-the-way Plaquemine ferry to get back home, which is why we didn't dare venture across the Mississippi to visit family Friday. We had a forty-foot float to finish decorating, on which our krewe would load no less than a couple tons of throws that afternoon. Our day centered around LSU and downtown as the interstates transformed into parking lots.

Friday was also the first chance for the siblings to be together alone. Justin sat behind his sisters in the Rogue while I drove Cherish and Hadley in Rachel's Volt. At LSU, we met up with the Cavells. They joined us as tour guides that morning.

First, we visited Mike VII, the same lounging live tiger mascot I'd sent Justin and Rachel photos of the day before Edie first met Susan in Manchac. The regal Siberian-Bengal hybrid snoozed on an expansive bed of tree-shaded pine straw near the fence, partially obscured by vegetation. A waterfall crashed down a rock wall on the far end of Mike the Tiger's $3 million habitat. After partially waking up the 350-pound feline, Hadley saddled up on his bronze representation, a few yards from the plate glass holding back tons of water in Mike VII's personal pool. Countless riders like our niece had polished the statue's ears and back.

Our entourage passed by the LSU Campus Mounds on our way to the Greek Theater. Hadley joined her weird uncle on the ninety-three-year-old amphitheater's stage—in front of a handful of strangers and mostly empty concrete pews—as he did half-assed pliés in a boonie hat.

Our campus tour's final stop came at a place instrumental to this insanely fortunate dude's marriage. Edie and I met largely due to her position as chair of what was then called the Pop Entertainment Committee, part of the LSU Union Program Council. We later had our first meal as an engaged couple at the Union, moments after I proposed in my un-air-conditioned dorm room, because I'm a goddamn romantic.

The LSU Union is also where Free Speech Alley is found. As I walked through the area with his children, my thoughts turned to John, along with Carl Tickles, and the blood they mingled in front of the most infamous neo-Nazi, right there, before any of us were born.

Soon, it was time for a late lunch at the venerable Louie's Cafe, just outside the campus's north gates. The old-school diner's signature hash browns prompted Rachel to bring up Tony Chachere's, and how TSA at SFO told her in September that if the unopened eight-ounce can Edie gifted her were any larger, they'd be forced to confiscate the popular spice mix as a potential bomb.

Moments later, our guests were learning about an actual bomb that seriously damaged the Louisiana State Capitol's Senate Chamber on a Sunday afternoon in 1970. The locals among us pointed out the blast-impelled shrapnel still lodged in the Senate's fifty-foot ceiling, from an explosion connected to right-to-work legislation being debated at the time.

It took two trips for the building's original, upper-level elevators to ferry the eight of us to the observation deck on the twenty-seventh floor. There, surprisingly calm winds and a 360-degree, bird's-eye view of Greater Baton Rouge awaited. A mile-wide Mississippi steadily rolled along below a gridlocked I-10.

Security closed the deck thirty minutes before we had to vacate the building, so we made our way downstairs to the House of Representatives, where we bumped into a longtime Gridiron Show castmate who worked at the Capitol. Rather than going home on the Friday before Mardi Gras, he assumed the role of tour leader. Guards shouted a steady countdown to closing time as our friend Mike Hasten lived up to his name by speeding through how Governor Huey Long—the corrupt firebrand populist who built the still-tallest state capitol in the nation—was shot by...somebody. It could've been Dr. Carl Weiss (no relation to my wife), as the official account maintains, or it could've been Huey's bodyguards, who indiscriminately shot dozens of bullets into the young physician, the marble walls standing next to us, and possibly the Kingfish himself.

Following a brief stop at the rental house, our octet headed for our annual Spanish Town Eve decorating/loading party hosted by longtime Yo-yos, the Boudreauxs. My wife rode in the Cavells' back seat with Hadley, strapped in her relocated car seat. They passed the WBRZ-TV studios on Highland Road. "That's where Poppa John used to work," Auntie Edie pointed out.

"I don't care for ABC News very much," the six-year-old bluntly replied. This came after expressing issues she had with the prevalence of "y'all" in local parlance, including mine.

During Friday night's festivities, as excited krewemates arrived to load their many bags of throws, Cherish texted us. "Hadley quote: 'This is the lifetime, man.'"

Rachel and the Harts were riding with me back to Beauregard Town when Edie messaged the group from the Cavells' vehicle. "I think she's out," Auntie Edie texted at 9:25 p.m.

"I am not surprised," Hadley's dad smiled. His big sis shared a pic of our "pacesetter" zonked out in Mike and Shannon's back seat.

Before dawn on Saturday, I met our driver, Barry, and followed the taillight-free float to the downtown staging area. Heavy fog diffused the ever-present interior lighting of Tiger Stadium into a purple haze as we drove by on River Road.

Up before dawn like me, Edie was in Beauregard Town by 7:30 a.m. to lead her brother and sister on the twenty-minute walk to the converted cotton trailer painted to look like a forty-foot claw bathtub.

With working plumbing on the front, the Yo-yos were once again staged near the start, right in front of Huey's giant, mist-shrouded erection.

Cherish would later show up with Hadley. My BFF wasn't feeling all that great, possibly because last night's food was spicier and richer than she's used to. Their arrival at the float was further delayed because the 450-foot-tall landmark that Cherish was told to head for was still concealed by midmorning fog. Instead of riding in the back seat of Barry's truck for two hours, mother and daughter decided to be spectators with Beth and her young girls, all dolled up in pink. Edie had already invested in tickets for restroom access in the Louisiana State Museum, just a quick trot from our spot.

Beth brought a "funny pink feather headband for Hadley," but only after asking Edie for permission the night before, for some reason. The accessory complemented Hadley's teal outfit, emblazoned with dozens of pink flamingos. Sporting a rainbow-accented flamingo mask painted on her face, my bestie looked like an adorable mascot for the Paradise Park beer in the Cavells' cooler.

Her mommy opted for a pink-and-white iris, blooming from Cherish's left eye. It went beautifully with her pink fedora.

The float's uniform of the day was bathwear; the pinker, the better. Most krewemates followed our suggestion and wore pink bathrobes or kimonos. Like us, a handful dangled pink bath poufs around their necks, to my mild surprise. I thought for sure we had bought every last one in Baton Rouge to hang above the depicted tub, loaded with rubber duckies portraying Trump cronies.

Pink rollers highlighted Mike Cavell's beard. Rachel also threw on a shower cap and one of the many rubber-ducky necklaces she bought to throw. That was in addition to the numerous grosses of beads Edie and I provided our two Mardi Gras virgins from our ample stash.

Besides family, there was another new Yo-yo onboard, who'd requested (and was enthusiastically granted) permission to deviate from the prescribed dress code. Three years after rolling with another krewe as Spanish Town King, Chris Frink—who never goes to Spanish Town not dressed as a woman—graced us with his massive presence. Before Queen Elizabeth II's reign in 2016, other outrageous get-ups included Paula Deen and Octomom. For 2019, Frink let his freak flag fly as a six-foot-five, 300-plus-pound blond straight from a high-class Russian house of ill repute, sporting a constant stream of simulated urine.

Three hours before the parade's noon start, Hadley's daddy and aunties completed a task I had saved especially for them: dressing a pair of naked, Russian-flag-tattooed blow-up dolls in pink fishnets and nothing else. In front of our phallic (albeit still-shrouded) State Capitol, Justin hoisted an inflatable commie whore's bare ass as his two sisters hiked slutty lingerie toward a sorry excuse for a plastic vagina. "Family bonding," I yelled with camera in hand from the truck's flatbed as they drew attention from the growing crowd. Dozens of nearby staged floats blasted out a cacophonous soundtrack of Carnival and club music.

Outfitted and topped off with air, the girls were mounted face-up (and tied down) on the front of the float. They flanked an image of the president dressed as an LSU Golden Girl in the shower. A video camera and a grinning Vladimir Putin, through separate peepholes, peered at Trump's orange, white-leotarded ass.

From three gold cans, Mike Cavell ceremoniously emptied fifteen gallons of water—made bright yellow with food coloring—into a concealed plastic bin where a pump rested. A hidden hose was set to carry the water up a few feet to a showerhead, also spray-painted gold.

Before activating the actual plumbing, Mike attempted to install simulated plumbing by inserting glisteny gold wreath spray into the dolls' slits. I heckled my friend like he was Garret Graves as the father of two struggled for minutes, trying to find a Russian whore's snatch.

Like the showerhead, phones were aimed at the president, in front of a deep-red state's always-hard seat of government. "Three, two, one," we yelled, cueing Mike to power the pump. Enthusiastic cheers and bright, golden liquid poured forth.

Flowing on the back of the float was Mike's "Peeneaux Greedio" homebrew. Next to the two kegs stood stacks of red cups wrapped in stripes of blue and white duct tape, roughly depicting a 360-degree Russian flag.

We were balls-deep in 2018 parade prep when AncestryDNA suckerpunched Edie at work. A year later, siblings who didn't know we existed the last time we rolled were parading with us on this awesome Saturday. And they half-stepped nothing. Months after Justin first mentioned visiting for Mardi Gras, Edie's new family fit right in with the rest of our eclectic krewe of committed, fun-loving subversives of all ages, from the barely legal to long-retired Boomers.

Before alerting riders to make their final visit to the float's port-a-potty, around a half-hour before parade time, Hadley briefly boarded the float. Our pink-and-teal Yo-yo's two aunties held her up on either side as Justin leaned in over Rachel's shoulder for a photo. Along with Beth's girls, and thousands of other kids along the route, Hadley was moments away from going wild, catching all sorts of trinkets, and seeing all sorts of...things. Auntie Edie and I had already donned our pink toilet-lid sunglasses and large, matching shower caps. Uncle Jeremy was extra weird that day.

Police sirens wailed, amping the throng to full throat at noon. The boisterous six-figure crowd lining the route—more than a dozen deep in spots—commenced its two-hour crescendo as we zipped into parade formation amid the first handful of seventy-five floats. The procession slowly rolled through the opening gauntlet of narrow Spanish Town Road, scraping its canopy of late-winter trees.

Our first-time riders experienced a massive dose of exhilaration that Edie and I had absorbed annually on the float for nearly a decade. We had since assumed the roles of safety-mandated float walkers. The experience is no less thrilling, plus it allows for more intimate dancing and carousing with thousands of strangers. Whether walking or rolling, costuming provides anonymity amid the pink masses, making Carnival a perfect way for introverts and privacy-lovers like Edie to feed off a massive crowd's palpable energy.

Too trashed to count, we witnessed innumerable mouths in the crowd go from smiling to gaping as we drew closer. Many of their owners nudged neighbors, pointing with raised eyebrows as they processed the presidential golden shower vignette on the front of our approaching float. Gratifying, raw reactions like these were precisely why this only child spent years doing stand-up comedy instead of writing a big-ass book.

Edie and I playfully snapped pink towels at the matching throng, keeping them back while Justin, Rachel, and the other forty Yo-yos joyously fed a couple tons of beads into the pink maw. Sporting a thick beard grown since the last LSU football practice in late December, I took selfies with revelers who caught my eye, like the guy wearing a red, Soviet-era "CCCP" hockey jersey, à la the 1980 Miracle on Ice. Down the route, I saw Santa Claus with an authentic white beard far more impressive than mine.

We neared the judge's stand on North Street at Sixth when Dave, our float's sound engineer, cranked up Public Enemy's "Fight the Power." That cued our krewe to collectively climax by firing off most of the fifty golden streamer cannons my still-fully corrupted bride had found online. I was pleased with how many of our wasted riders were cognizant enough to blanket the block with a golden shower.

We pulled back onto Spanish Town Road around 2:15 p.m., in front of the now fully exposed Capitol building. Krewe members deboarded, raving as though they had just ridden the greatest Carnival ride ever, like they do nearly every year. Overall, Spanish Town 2019 was a consensus top-three, even among veteran Yo-yos.

With the float's abundant trash bagged, Barry hauled away the rental an hour later, marking the end of our float-related responsibilities. Brief drama over a lost phone and keys—and an even briefer visit from an unwelcome guest later that afternoon—made the otherwise fairytale day a bit more believable.

Following several miles of walking, and even more hours of day drinking, our gang of eight enjoyed a respite in Beauregard Town. It was time to make Edie's now-signature boudin king cake, which turned out a little less erogenous-looking. When asked, the small-portions guy who lived in Japan for four years said he ate about six pieces. As his sister's sous chef, Justin made the savory dish extra-spicy by piling on the cracklin dust (bagged kettle scrapings), and washed it down with Strawgators. The half-and-half blend of Abita Strawberry and Andygator proved popular with our gang's beer drinkers.

My mom, Laura, also paid a visit that afternoon. She made sure the out-of-towners knew that she wanted to meet them so badly that she actually got on our city's post-parade interstate on Spanish Town Saturday. As she departed, we told her how she could get home on surface streets with only three right turns.

Sometime after sunset, the locals left so our guests could rest ahead of Bacchus Sunday in New Orleans. Edie and I joined the Cavells at Pastime for boudin pizza, then a nightcap at a downtown bar where their son worked.

"Happy pre-Mardi Gras weekend!" Susan texted Edie earlier that afternoon. She needlessly apologized for not finding a "headband that would have been a perfect accessory for our flower child" in time for the Mid City Gras parade. "Sorry I messed up on your dress accessory."

"Are you kidding me?" Edie replied on Saturday evening. "Your dress is awesome and got more compliments than I ever remember. Today has been a great day," she proclaimed, "and I hope y'all enjoy a peaceful weekend. I love you and can't wait till next time."

"Temp will drop tonight after rain," I texted the gang in Beauregard Town before 9 a.m. Sunday. "Should be cleared out by the time Bacchus rolls by."

"Woohoo!" Rachel answered my weather update.

On their third consecutive day with our gang, the Cavells reprised their roles as chauffeurs by ferrying our two younger guests to New Orleans, where Shannon's kin would host us on the neutral ground (aka median) of St. Charles Avenue at Euterpe. During the hour-plus drive, we in the Rogue learned to never trust Waze during Mardi Gras in the city that care forgot. The navigation app sure as hell didn't give a good goddamn about barricaded roads, much less allegedly two-way streets barely wide enough for a single vehicle to get through. Amid negotiating the plague of crater-esque potholes, a fresh crash involving a bus and an NOPD cruiser forced me to drive on the wrong side of a boulevard, toward oncoming traffic, for some distance. "Welcome to fucking New Orleans," I blurted to the Renton residents in our back seat.

We safely parked in a church lot and hauled chairs, coolers, and a tent to a spot secured every year by Shannon's cousin Daniel LeBlanc and his equally fun wife, Beth. Near the idle streetcar tracks, a few feet from the curb, they had erected four ladders. Secured atop one of them was a bench wide enough for three small children, complete with railing and lap bar, not unlike a Ferris wheel seat. There, Hadley safely sat better than six feet above the tarp-covered muck and growing crowd. Her dad stood behind her on the rungs.

The LeBlancs had also brought a couple of homemade "First Mardi Gras" signs for our newbies, enjoying their first Bacchus Sunday, just like Edie and I had done the previous year. That number of rookies also included lanky-ass Case's future mother-in-law, who agreed with my assessment of his twerking. All told, there were about fifteen of us in our festive urban encampment.

Rolling a few hours before Bacchus, the Krewe of Thoth threw their signature colored hats and matching toilet paper. The latter streamed in the breeze from branches and power lines, brightly accenting the route.

The sisters and I headed toward Avenue Pub, across the parade route, for drinks, restroom passes, and a chance to see Edie's culinarily gifted coworker pass by on the crab-themed float, the twenty-fourth in the expedited parade. Authorities had stripped out all marching bands and the 610 Stompers in hopes of completing the procession before a line of strong thundershowers moved in ahead of an approaching cold front.

The last float passed before 2:30 p.m. The hourlong rain arrived by three. Five minutes later, a grinning Cherish texted that she and Hadley were "hanging" in their raincoats under an eave around the corner at a Walgreens that was quickly selling out of warm clothing. The rest of us huddled under a tent, attempting to avoid the increasingly chilly, wind-blown rain. At one point, with lightning popping about, five of us held down our metal-framed shelter to keep the gusts from taking it, as they evidently had done to the umbrella of some completely drenched woman walking down the sidewalk, still holding up its scraggly metal skeleton with moxie. Another young lady's boyfriend carried her through calf-deep water awaiting pedestrians at the curb. Some people busted their drunk asses running for cover. Others, with wind-whipped plastic bags on their heads, looked like they were being strangled by ghosts.

Forty minutes or so into the downpour, rain ebbed enough for Hadley and Cherish to join us in dodging growing lakes of cold, muddy water under the tent. Following the lead of NOPD cops who threw a football with revelers earlier during Thoth, my BFF and I played catch as the rain subsided.

With cold air rushing in, Edie and I headed for the Rogue, where we threw on warmer clothes, including dry socks and shoes for my frigid, sandal-shod feet. Over my long-sleeve tie-dyed Carnival shirt, I donned Justin's recent gift: an "I make pour decisions" T-shirt. Edie transformed into a "Pour'n star."

We soon realized the two of us had missed a walking parade known for creative getups and free alcohol. "Box of Wine just came through," Justin texted at 4:30, while we were still changing. A photo showed his squatting wife's head fully tilted back as a Kelly green fairy (green hair, green lycra bodysuit) held a Black Box spout millimeters from Cherish's open mouth, taking in the red.

Another peculiar wine-pouring marcher in the minutes-long parade had offered Cherish white wine. "It's too golden," she protested. Everyone there agreed the guy pushing it looked genuinely offended.

We returned in time to catch a few vino-toting stragglers heading back up the route. I managed to get some red wine in my mouth, on my beard, and on my new wine-themed shirt.

A local vendor selling the hell out of some popcorn came rolling by. Mike bought a bag solely because of the guy's rhyming pitch. So good was the hustle, a woman was seen videoing it.

Mike offered some of his impulse buy to Hadley. "My mommy said I could have cotton candy," she replied as the vendor pushed his cart uptown.

I had been near Cherish for some time, and I didn't hear that exchange. "Oh crap," I thought, "we're a horrible influence!" When I tried to apologize for obviously corrupting their previously perfect daughter into a blatant fibber, the Harts admitted that they disagreed on the cotton candy matter. Cherish indeed had said yes. Justin then explained that he was worried Hadley would get sick from the voluminized sugar.

"So?" his wife shot back. "She's riding in Mike's vehicle. We don't have to worry about it."

That sent me walking away, doubled over, as I laughed my entire ass off. After catching some of my breath, I circled back to tell my sister-in-law, "I like you."

Mother and daughter dueled with plastic swords under overcast skies, which were occasionally abuzz with U.S. Coast Guard choppers cruising by, maybe a couple hundred feet above the route. Their frequency and the crowd's energy increased as parade time approached an hour after sunset. Fifty years after its first parade, Bacchus made it to us near 7 p.m. with much fanfare and illumination.

The weather had thinned out the crowds just enough. No douchebags or overly aggressive assholes were in our area, just folks enjoying Mardi Gras. A cadre of young people were seemingly ill-dressed for the cold, but they were from Chicago, they said, so it was all good.

Mounds of beads formed a walkway through the water, leading to the curb where I joined Edie, my two sisters-in-law, and everyone else on the front row. There, we dodged trombone slides and tuba bells rhythmically and emphatically swaying within inches of us. I'm confident I wasn't alone in feeling a bass drummer's glancing backswing or a dancer's twirling baton.

Rachel's excitement level spiked when the float of the superkrewe's king came by. Jensen Ackal was the latest in a long line of celebrity monarchs to reign over the wine god's parade. Baby Girl's a huge fan of *Supernatural*. Neither she, nor her sister, nor Cherish were shy about walking right up to the massive floats, where they were handed all manner of light-up Bacchus swag.

Several rows of people behind us sat Hadley, her legging-clad gams dangling in the cold, damp wind. Daddy was right there with his outdoorsy girl, an absolute trooper, both loving life so much that they screamed and waved their hands for nearly two solid hours.

Before nine, though, Justin and Edie huddled tightly with my BFF under the tent, covering our niece with dry towels. Hadley was shivering, Justin said, though she uttered not a single complaint. Rather, our little champ soon reported that she was getting warmer, so we headed back to the vehicles with all our gear. Street sweepers trailing the final float flung beads at unsuspecting ankles.

As a new big sister, Edie later recounted being compelled by an aunt's imperative to protect Hadley from the cold. She also told me that she could relate to Wade, by simultaneously wanting to protect her brood of younger siblings, while also being a bad influence in making sure they all had a good time.

A nightcap awaited in Beauregard Town, where the temp had dropped thirty degrees in twelve hours. Edie and I stalled saying our final goodnights of the trip by resorting to discussing the perversions of our deceased cats.

Justin rode shotgun with me to Maringouin in the Rogue on Monday morning. The ladies were in Rachel's hybrid, in need of refueling. Since we forgot to get cracklin dust for him to take home, I grabbed Justin a consolation bag of gas-station cracklin in Grosse Tete.

Before the stop, he and I chatted about future family travel plans to Hawaii. For the rest of the way to Ducky's, we discussed writing, his poems, and decoding John. Justin mentioned his first kiss came as an eight-year-old, from his dad's girlfriend at the time. John was supplying her with "good" coke while she was on the lam from her abusive pimp. It was a very maternal gesture on her part, Justin explained, in that she was trying to help him learn how to deal with women. My brother-in-law honored the woman by writing a poem in her voice, he told me. I encouraged him to resume writing at least one of the books about his life that he had started.

We arrived at Ducky's near 10 a.m., a couple hours before the Harts' flight time necessitated their departure for Houston. Limited vacation time at Justin's still-new job meant they couldn't join us for Wade and Cindy's annual Fat Tuesday celebration in New Roads. The town boasts a pair of parades, with one route starting right in front of the O'Neal home.

My giddy mother-in-law greeted us at the door to meet her baby girl's lagniappe family. Awaiting inside was Wade and Cindy's youngest, Ali, and her three little ones. While Renee couldn't make it, Cindy brought her eldest daughter's two little children. Hadley soon joined our grandnieces and grandnephews and their copious toys, all laid out in Ducky's living room. Our newest niece was the oldest of the bunch, but not by much.

I made my bride a bloody Mary from fixings available on the self-serve bar. With mimosa in hand, I then led Justin and Rachel on a tour of the house their sister grew up in, including Ducky's garden near the cabana, out by the covered pool. While showing them Ducky's pimped-out enclosed patio off the master bedroom, we spotted her skittish black cat, Zulu, trapped between us and the housekeeper vacuuming inside. The feline named for the historic Mardi Gras krewe darted under my mother-in-law's sizable bed.

Moments later, we gathered in the large dining room. Ducky requested that this recovering Catholic ask the blessing. Thankfully, Ali and her mom were still busy tending to the kids at the children's table, near one end of the formal dining room table, capable of seating a score of adults. I used that precious time to search for words befitting the joyous occasion that wouldn't betray my (less-than-)religious sensibilities, nor those of anyone else present.

"We are so thankful for everyone who is here to share in our...," I opened before pausing, staring straight ahead at the table centerpiece. In a room with a half-dozen kids eating sugary food, there was dead silence for a good ten seconds as I did everything in my power to prevent the tears quickly welling up in my eyes from gushing forth. After swallowing hard, I resumed, "...share in our new discoveries."

Relieved that I managed to get that out without another Cubs-jacket-gifting scene, I concluded with the standard O'Neal family blessing. "And as they say in Rome," I prefaced, before prompting them to join me in uttering the familiar words, "Lord, thank you for these gifts, which we are about to receive from thy bounty, through Christ, our Lord. Amen."

I'm not sure if it was Ali, Cindy, or Ducky, but one of them told me I was about to make them all cry.

Justin told Ducky that he appreciated her shrimp and grits, because the latter half was the only Southern dish his mom ever made for him. He also talked about his stepfather raising him and Mason after Shirley took off, when Patrick Hadley was still in his twenties.

Despite the distance, and a recently overcome fear of flying, Ducky said she wanted to visit Justin's wine cellar, all 1,200 bottles or so, even if only half of them were his. She absolutely fell in love with Red's new family, especially Rachel. Ducky saw so much of her baby girl in my wife's baby sister. At one point, while holding Rachel's face in her hands, an amazed Duck exclaimed, "Look at you!"

The feeling was mutual. Rachel felt so welcomed by everyone there, a feeling made even more impactful by the size of the gathering. Growing up in a relatively tiny family, she had never before had such familial love coming at her from so many beautiful, smiling faces at any given time in her life.

Five more of those faces later showed up from Lafayette in the form of Jamie, Jenni, their almost-six-year-old twin boys, and nearly two-year-old daughter. In the twenty minutes that Dr. and Mrs. James Wade O'Neal IV got to know Edie's new fam, Jenni discovered they shared a love for the band Fleet Foxes.

By midday, Edie and I were outside, tearfully seeing the foursome off to Houston. The hugs seemed longer and more emotional as we soaked in the moment. We embraced the embrace, so to speak. It marked the first time we were forced to watch any of them—much less all four—depart without the distraction of a long drive or flight ahead of us. In short, we had plenty of opportunity to think about how much we'd miss them.

Rachel soon texted her sister a series of hearts and crying emojis. Edie responded by relaying something her mom had just said to her: "'I love your little sister! She is so sweet!'"

"I love Ducky, too," Rachel replied. "I don't know," she noted, "I just felt a connection to her right away."

Hours later, Edie asked her, "Did y'all make it to the airport?"

"Yep! Just dropped them off," Rachel answered with digital tears. "It's easier when they're rushing to get inside and I'm watching approaching traffic. Too distracted to cry," she laughed. "I MISS YOU ALREADY!"

"Love you, sis! We'll be together again soon," Edie promised, following a screenshot of our booked June flights to SEA-TAC. "I'm glad you're with friends tonight, and hopefully getting to rest up before the last leg home tomorrow," she told the Austinite, who was spending the evening in Houston. "Have fun!"

Minutes later, Justin texted the group. "Thanks so much for a wonderful, fantastic trip!" he exclaimed. "Loved meeting your family, Edie and Jeremy, and your friends, and seeing your home and town. We are grabbing a bite in the airport before our flight," he reported. "Rachel is off to visit her friend. See you in June and talk to you soon!" he closed, ahead of Cherish's preflight hugs.

"Love y'all," Edie shared with a heart quartet, "and we're so glad y'all were here to make our happiest time of the year so much more joyous!" Wishing the Harts a restful flight, my wife again alluded to our June trip. "We'll be starting the countdown to Port Angeles soon!"

"It was wonderful!" Rachel followed up late Monday evening. "My heart is so full! We've got each other and it matters more than anything to me. Cheesy saying from my mom and me as a kid," she prefaced the following sentiment: "'I love you as high as the sky and as wide as the world forever and ever and ever.' It explains how I feel more than anything else I could say."

35

Port Angeles

Fat Tuesday fell on my dad's seventy-fifth birthday. He and I talked about the Saints, on March 5, during a twenty-minute phone call from Wade and Cindy's pier.

The Cavells joined Edie and me for Mardi Gras in New Roads (where Ducky cajoled beads from float drivers who had none to throw) in part because Baton Rouge has no parades after Saturday. Spanish Town is the peak, heralding the exodus of partygoers to New Orleans and other festive destinations.

"Y'all look tired," Jenni told us at Ducky's the day before. The two of us needed something chill, like a pair of family-friendly parades in a city with nothing wider than a three-lane road running through it.

That evening, Edie messaged her brother in Washington. "I wore your shirt again today to have you with us for New Roads Mardi Gras," my Pour'n Star informed Justin.

"I should make pink Pour'n Star shirts for next year!" Justin replied with two photos of Cherish. With their parade haul covering her torso, our sister-in-law went from smiling to dying under the weight of "all the beads at once."

"It was really great to meet some of your family this week," Justin told us. "I sincerely wish we would have had a little more time to visit with them. Next time," he vowed, and asked about Ducky visiting up there. "I would love to take her for a wine tasting or two."

"Omg," Edie winked, "if you had said that, I would not hear anything else from her until I had booked the trip and confirmed details with her three times, minimum."

"Well, I try to be discreet," he humbly said. He also extended the same invitation for my mother.

"Jeremy's mom may have a minor crush on you," my wife alerted him about the tree that dropped a nearby apple.

"He is so handsome!" my mom said after meeting Justin. "Most people look better from far away. But him," she explained, "the closer you get, the better he looks!"

Edie and Justin discussed Ducky potentially hosting a future visit by the Harts, including John. Around that same time, Patrick spoke with my mother-in-law.

"Mom seemed genuinely touched and excited about meeting Justin, Rachel, and the crew," he reported on Ash Wednesday. "She raves about Jeremy's blessing."

Of all the ways that I could've dreamt of impressing my mother-in-law, prayer would not have been near the top of my list.

"I really want you to meet my brother (you will in June) and stepfather," Justin messaged the two of us on Thursday. "You would probably love them."

"I will love them more than I already do without meeting them," Edie avowed.

"WOOHOO!" Rachel emailed her siblings and their spouses on Friday. "I'm officially booked!" she screamed about her June flight reservations.

"WOOHOO indeed!" I replied. "Can't wait to see y'all again!"

"Really looking forward to more time together," Justin wrote. "One week back at work and I am ready for another vacation already!"

Three months later, Edie and I were flying out of BTR, where TSA dusted bags of cracklin crumbs for bomb material. Like our first trip to Washington, we connected through DFW on a Tuesday, hours before

Cherish followed us home from a Dallas work trip. Hadley was asleep with Auntie Jen in Renton when Justin picked up his two sisters and me at SEA-TAC in the Tesla.

He previously mentioned the possibility of us walking Hadley to and from school our first full day there. "If the school will let her go with her weird uncle Jeremy," the love of my life noted.

On Wednesday morning, my brother-in-law and I ended up escorting Hadley for the four-block trek, in the middle of Pride month. After passing several rainbow flags along the way, an approaching Asian couple smiled and nodded at us, two handsome men walking a cute little girl to school together.

"We should hold hands," I said.

"I was just thinking the same thing," the perfect emissary replied.

As in California, I chauffeured my wife and her little sister around the late-morning streets of a major city that I'd never driven in before. We checked out Jimi Hendrix's Renton grave before heading out for an adventure to see Kurt Cobain's somewhat secluded former home in Seattle.

My navigator then set course for a post office on Broadway Avenue to run an errand for Justin: shipping yet another cell phone to John. On average, he'd gone through two phones a year, although he seemed to be breaking them much more frequently as of late.

Minutes later, I snapped a selfie of our trio on the sidewalk with the street sign behind us. "It's official," my social media post read, "My Posse's on Broadway," I wrote, referencing an early song by my favorite Seattle rapper, Sir Mix-a-Lot.

Once again, my apologies to Macklemore.

At my BFF's urging that afternoon, this grandson of a homebuilder constructed a styrofoam pergola on the patio out of packing material for Jen's new fridge. Scotch tape and my wife proved far more helpful than I ever did for my Paw Paw. As such, my cursing was held to a minimum.

On Wednesday evening, after Hadley and Cherish went to bed, Edie and I joined her brother and sister in rewatching the first episode of

Star Trek: Discovery. "I love talking about *Star Trek*," Rachel reminded us a few weeks earlier, "and the more the merrier!"

As we prepared Thursday for the two-and-a-half-hour drive out to the scenic Olympic Peninsula, to the west of Puget Sound, Justin packed full-stem wine glasses in special packaging. He didn't want to "diminish the experience" with lesser drinkware.

With the sibs bonding in the Tesla, and Hadley in the Volt's back seat, I rode shotgun in the hybrid, where I noticed the handy Bacchus knob on the back of Cherish's iPhone. She used it to navigate us to Port Angeles, taking us across the Tacoma Narrows Bridge 2.0. Like the Oakland Bay Bridge, its original iteration (aka "Galloping Gertie") had a spectacular collapse. As an engineering grad, I find it a bit strange crossing bridges best known for their association with structural failure.

Our Volt trio enjoyed locally made ice cream in Discovery Bay while the sibs stopped to juice up the Tesla at a charging station a couple miles away. We soon met up at the AirBNB, where a chill Mason drove in from Olympia with a vibrant Odelle. We finally got to meet them and their two adult labs, Pliny and Piper.

A zipline stretched out a few hundred feet from our cabin, to a tree standing about fifty feet shy of the sandy bluff, which dropped several stories to the Strait of Juan de Fuca; wind-whipped waves crashed against the rocky beach below. Cherish was the first to go for a spin on the small wooden seat attached to a rope dangling from a pulley whizzing along the line. My sister-in-law is adventurous like that; after all, she did willingly take on John Hart as her father-in-law.

Following one or two tandem runs with her mother, Hadley was zipping down solo toward the large tree, but not before my first trip. "Screw you guys," I said to the nearby camera, "I'm ziplining to Canada." I then lifted my feet off the concrete deck while flashing my middle finger. "Kiss it, Trump!" I declared as gravity sped me away. Throughout the rest of our stay, Hadley yelled various iterations of her weird uncle's departing words, even when she wasn't ziplining. At one point, Cherish had to explain to her daughter why she should steer clear of saying "Kiss me, Trump."

My ass grazed the tall grass early on the way down. Justin's had even less clearance, prompting him to advise his slightly larger brother against trying out the ride. Fortunately, the bungee cord serving as a brake managed to stop our momentum each trip, despite later discovering that it was substantially frayed.

With the novelty of the contraption worn off, Justin asked me to take a photograph on the balcony facing the bluff, to memorialize the first time he and all three of his known siblings were together. The gorgeous late spring day along the water on the Olympic Peninsula seemed like an ideal setting for the occasion. Moments later, we noticed the first of numerous deer—up to four or five at a time—that we'd see over the next two days, traipsing through the couple dozen spindly trees smattering the football-field-sized expanse between us and the drop-off.

Friday commenced with my bundled bride and me drinking coffee on the bluff. Nearby was the giant, bricked fire pit, which had warmed us as Thursday's temperatures dropped with the sun. Calm morning winds greeted the two of us, standing near the same grassy ledge where Cherish and I had our faces sandblasted by the updraft the day before. Edie and I could barely make out buildings in downtown Victoria, British Columbia, past a seemingly tiny oil tanker headed out to sea toward our left. A thick, gray, marine-layer ceiling extended across the water to our newest sister-in-law's home country, some twenty miles away.

Odelle is a science-minded air quality specialist back home in Thurston County, where she regularly attempts to talk down chemtrail-triggered conspiracy theorists. She told us how some residents would regularly post online pics of Bob Ross-esque, fluffy white clouds, accompanied by the hashtag #CrimeAgainstHumanity.

After burning off the marine layer, the sun shone brightly on us as we enjoyed brunch. The Hadleys are no less competent in the kitchen than the Harts.

The eight of us, plus the two dogs, burned off some calories hiking the Madison Creek Falls trail. Justin later took his wife and daughter back to the cabin as the rest of us rode up to Hurricane Ridge in

Olympic National Park. Unlimited visibility afforded us a breathtaking, eye-level view of every peak in the Olympic Mountain Range.

Like Cherish, Mason's a soft-spoken, cool customer. From the front passenger seat, I witnessed the graphic designer calmly drive their SUV (with a back seat full of nervous passengers, and at least one gassy dog) up and down the sharply winding, occasionally guard-rail-equipped hillside road leading to the mile-high ridge. He was way more chill than I was driving through Cobain's old neighborhood and its curvy, narrow streets, graded as steeply as those I drove in San Francisco. I'm sure it also helped that no one—like, say, a pair of sisters—screamed at him while he was driving.

By early evening on Friday, Justin, Edie, and I joined Mason, sitting on the rocker swing overlooking the water near the bluff's edge. The four of us shared the brothers' hefty binoculars as three cruise ships, likely headed for Alaska, grew larger, then smaller again, as they zigzagged the channel, steaming for the sun setting in the gathering purple haze.

Edie and I washed off smoke from that night's fire in an outdoor shower on our room's private patio. The chilly, nighttime air expedited our entrance into the hot tub with Justin and Rachel; I could feel my core temperature rise after settling in. Through binoculars, we peered at a bright Jupiter and its four visible moons. A nearly full, waxing moon was not far away in the sky, still partially illuminated by mid-June twilight at 11 p.m.

We bid our newest family goodbye late Saturday morning. Mason, Odelle, Piper, and Pliny headed back to Olympia, while the rest of us made our way back across the sound. Cherish and I used the travel time to introduce Hadley to Public Enemy, Kamasi Washington, and Del Tha Funkee Homosapien. My sister-in-law, raised as a Jehovah's Witness, knew all about "Mista Dobalina."

While Justin recharged the Tesla, and his sisters caught Pokemon, the three of us in the Volt made a side trip to where *An Officer and a Gentleman* was filmed. In Fort Warden, we saw folks dressed as killer whales dancing to Rebirth Brass Band's "Do Whatcha Wanna" at Orca Fest 2019.

The six of us headed toward Mount Rainier, then Renton, before making our way to Dusted Valley in Woodinville. During our pre-dinner wine tasting, Rachel got to meet Aunt Neenie; cousin Jennifer; her hubby, Dave; and their twins, Lincoln and Ellie. They and Hadley didn't recall meeting at the Memorial Day gathering in Bothell, but were strangers for maybe a minute. The trio of cuties had a blast eating their dinner of noodles and cheese at the Hollywood Tavern, where I managed to grab a selfie capturing the entirety of our near-dozen diners.

Sunday was no less gorgeous. Under the warm, midday sun, Justin and I assembled his new Traeger grill. It came with an app for his iPhone.

A little later, we all gathered in the Harts' TV room to watch the moving video from Cherish and Justin's 2000 wedding. The then-gap-toothed groom walked down the aisle with three women who served as Justin's mothers, each in her own way. Inez and Paula joined Shirley in escorting their handsome son.

John met Inez, his future common-law spouse, in San Francisco after Shirley split in 1974. "They broke up for good somewhere be-tween 1980-1982," Justin estimated, "before John last went to prison." Inez was "the only other person who had any sort of consistency" in Justin's life with his dad.

Paula was his stepdad's second wife. She wed Patrick Hadley when Justin was fifteen, and they divorced when he was sixteen. Mason wasn't yet a teenager. "That really broke my heart," Justin later revealed to me. "We loved her so much, and she really was beneficial to our recovery from a lot of emotional scarring and heartache."

In the video, Patrick Hadley sang and played guitar near the large, outdoor fountain serving as the altar's backdrop. He performed Kate Wolf's "Give Yourself to Love." My brother-in-law's musically gifted stepdad makes an instrument called the array mbira. It's a hand-crafted, five-octave thumb piano owned and used by the likes of Imogen Heap, Sting, and Björk.

For the occasion, the groom had written a poem about love, read in tandem by his friend Adam, and Justin's nine-year-old goddaughter Allison. The duo deftly delivered the exchange of verses.

A much younger John was there, as well. At the reception, they actually gave him a microphone. The video's editor included a snippet of him delivering some hippie wisdom.

Justin soon prepared for us a recent creation of his: salmon cracklin. We've since agreed to offer it as a side item with all the boudin we plan on selling up there.

On Monday morning, Rachel, Edie, and I caught the bus into downtown Seattle, where we enjoyed Thai food, MoPop's Prince exhibit, and a tour of KEXP's studios. A massive mural from their recent Six Degrees of Prince Day covered an entire wall of their sizable gathering space. Our guide, a volunteer at the first radio station to ever play Nirvana's *Nevermind*, held up their original vinyl copy of the groundbreaking album, protected by a plastic lining. This former radio DJ dug the stickers showing contemporaneous comments, shared amongst station DJs, adorning the sleeve's famous artwork. None of them covered the swimming baby's penis.

Back in Renton that afternoon, Justin washed dust from Port Angeles's gravel roads off the Tesla. He told Edie and me that John's phone—the one we shipped Wednesday—was already useless. He didn't break it; John just left the package on his table inside his home in Austin, which apparently lured a robber who ransacked the place, because of course it did.

As my wife's kid brother wiped down his whip on the driveway, on a glorious Monday 2,500 miles from Baton Rouge, it hit me: It didn't feel like we were away from home, I told Justin and Edie.

Later, at dinner on the patio, Cherish completely gut-punched Rachel and me when she told Hadley how, as a teen, she'd fly out to stay with Auntie Rachel, as well as with Auntie Edie and Weird Uncle

Jeremy. "That little thing is going to freaking grow up!" I reeled, echo-ing Rachel's thoughts.

As we kissed my BFF good night a few hours before our red-eye home, I noticed Auntie Edie's "YES YOU CAN" plaque and its Pixar pic, prominently displayed by Hadley's bedroom door. Her fancy Sty-rofoam pergola was still standing tall when we left, a testament to fine craftsmanship.

"Much less traumatic venture through TSA & Terminal D this time," my travel partner messaged her sibs from the gate.

One of the lasting images from this trip—aside from the couple smiling at an obviously gay couple walking their adorable daughter to school—was my presumed lover's face when I brought up paying for our share of the AirBNB. I had totally forgotten that the stay was all a Christmas gift from the Harts, dating back to a week before the holiday when Hadley thought of the gift. And what a gift it was.

While in Port Angeles, I observed Odelle lead a discussion with Rachel about the wall between her and John. Later that weekend, I learned how it went up in response to John's only communication with his youngest. At twenty-two, Rachel was living with Justin and Cherish at their current Renton home, while wrapping up her school-ing at Antioch University in Seattle. The campus in Yellow Springs, Ohio, had closed; she moved in, just over a year after first meeting her brother as an adult in Boston. Adventurous Cherish took her in after one visit.

John had lived with the Harts at their previous house, where all the bedrooms were upstairs and small. They bought their present, larger Renton home with plans for John to live downstairs, in Jen's digs, just before he met Hallie on a trip back to Austin. Their resulting marriage and cohabitation left the Harts with extra room for Rachel.

It was around this time, when Justin was trading familial house-mates, that John wrote a letter for Rachel. Before delivering it to her, Justin asked their father if he was sure that the words contained therein represented what he wanted to say to his estranged daughter. John said yes. Justin tried to prepare Rachel by mentioning that John sought her forgiveness. She figured he'd ask her to forgive him for not being a part of her life.

"He said, 'Please forgive me, I never wanted you to be born,'" Rachel recalled. John also placed blame on her mom, Elizabeth.

Up until that point, Rachel had friends citing John's age and health, telling her she'd be sorry if she didn't try to communicate with him. "Maybe I'm just being a twenty-two-year-old idiot," she thought before receiving his letter. Then, without alerting Justin, Rachel read it "for herself." She insisted, "I have no problem telling stories about my life," but this was different. John's letter made her so furious, she shied from discussing him just a year before at a pizza place. "Fuck that guy," she said in the Harts' TV room.

Rachel couldn't even sleep in the same bed her father had dozed on downstairs. Rather, she slept in the same upstairs bedroom where we stayed. She even temporarily moved out of the house a couple times when John stayed downstairs during visits for VA treatment. She jokingly worried she'd have to sleep in her car. After Rachel moved in with a friend in Austin, a few different folks lived downstairs in Renton before Jen moved in.

The only reason she'd consider having anything to do with her father, Rachel said, would be for Hadley's sake. She imagined how it might go at her niece's future graduation ceremony. "You sit way over there on the other side of the auditorium," she jokingly pretended to instruct John.

Back in Beauregard Town, after the parade, Rachel had joined Hadley and Mike Cavell on the porch. "You don't like Poppa John, do you?" her niece flatly asked. Drunk Mike's face got even redder with an "Ooooh, there's gonna be a fight" look.

Rachel told us in Renton that she knew she couldn't handle John— and everything that goes with having him in one's life—on top of everything she's already dealing with.

"There's a reason they tell you on the plane to put your oxygen mask on first," I endorsed her logic, "before you try to help someone else with theirs." You're no good to anyone else if you don't have air to breathe, I explained.

A year after clamming up at Conans Pizza, Rachel was much more comfortable talking about John. "More comfortable," incidentally, does not mean grief-free.

One week after her little sister opened up about their father, Edie reciprocated. She painstakingly drafted an unusually frank email to her new sibs after coming across an advice article by Heather Havrilesky that resonated with her. My wife had me review the revealing message several times before finally deciding to click send. As the only one of John's three kids who grew up in what's considered by many to be a "normal" family—the only one without decades of John-related baggage, the sole offspring he never disappointed as a father—my wife was processing more than her fair share of survivor's guilt.

"When we were together last week," Edie wrote Rachel and Justin, "I referenced how I often have to remind myself that it's unproductive to look through the lens of guilt at the different circumstances each of us grew up in. None of us had any choice or control over those situations. But I was a kid raised by a Catholic dad who grew up during the Depression," she noted, "and I always felt like I was supposed to feel guilty or ashamed of having anything that someone else didn't.

"Now, trying to grow beyond that," their big sister explained, "to focus more on making things equitable rather than perpetuating our disparities, I am trying to detach myself enough to be able to appreciate various perspectives, and focus on bringing that mindfulness into our relationships with each other." Edie mentioned that she and I were witnesses at the adoption proceedings for our oldest niece's son, and how that event a few years ago "was the first time I really deeply felt what it might have been like for my own adoptive parents. And yeah," she conceded, "I realize a lot of this still starts with things related to my own situation, but it's got to start somewhere; it's a continual shifting of looking inward to be able to change the way I look at the world, and seeing other people's perspectives to shift the way I see myself."

Circling back to the article and her bouts with guilt, my wife said, "It doesn't seem like the proper big sisterly thing to burden y'all with sharing that I have been/am in that mindset often. I've never even shared that with my older siblings, and only recently with Jeremy (as he said, the family I grew up in doesn't talk about anything difficult). But don't worry," Edie allayed, "as close to the edge as I've ventured, I'm not going all the way over the cliff. This article was a positive reminder to me to not hang on to the painful perspectives of what's past, but to enjoy the journey of life that I'm glad we're on together.

"Back at an extreme low point in college," she revealed, "before Jeremy and I met, while I was working up in Wisconsin, Patrick sent me a letter that included a line about how I seemed to have this inordinate ability to feel and magnify pain, and how it might make the world a kinder place if more people shared that trait, but it must make things awful for me. I think I held on to a lot of pain as part of my identity," her new siblings read, "and despite the intense hurt, it was also my comfort zone. It took a long time for me to reach a point where I was willing to let that go, getting so close to the point of going over the edge that I realized that I didn't really want to give everything up but just change the situation I was in, and changing my perspective was a big part of that.

"I lived so isolated inside my own head as a kid," Red recalled, "that I'm still trying to let go of obsessing over what I think other people are thinking about me or expecting of me. But with help from you, Jeremy, and some good friends, I'm trying to focus on learning from the experiences I've had, enjoying the experiences life is offering us today, and contributing to making better experiences for our tomorrows." With love, she closed, "I wanted to share this article in case it may be as helpful to you or someone you know as it is for me in that journey."

My remarkable bride continues to do a bang-up job of figuring out this still-nascent big-sister gig, featuring an age span larger than that between herself and Wade. We remain hopeful for future sibling gatherings where Edie can grow more comfortable in her exciting new role.

430 | JEREMY WHITE

She wished her baby bro a happy forty-sixth birthday a couple days after getting back home from Washington. A day later, she called their father to wish John a happy seventy-sixth. He was so thrilled to hear her voice. "I love having you in my life," I heard him say over the speakerphone. "My job now is to be your friend."

He again brought up abuse by BRPD. This time, it was when the cops were surprised to find him still alive after throwing him in a paddy wagon with a bunch of Black men, who had been told by the police that John was "messing with their old ladies."

There was also a "my art got me out of jail" story. The narrative had a few holes. We didn't press John for more details.

He seemed to finally realize that he indeed fathered my wife with a woman he was simply incapable of recalling. He wanted to, so badly, but couldn't. John said he's open to getting together to talk about it with Susan, but only if she wanted to. Not remembering her hearkened back to his Jekyll and Hyde days, when cops accused him of horrific acts he couldn't recall (due to massive head trauma), but feared he may have done.

"I'm awkward," he emphasized at one point in the call. "I know I'm awkward." An MRI showed multiple sections of brain damage, he added. The women in Vietnam called him their "beaucoup dinky dau deaf guy."

He had been hoping that Edie's mom was Fran because she was so open, said a man not on Facebook. Imagine the arc of that woman's life—from passionate lover of the super-woke pot saint Johnny Gingerweed to regular poster of the right's latest batshit propaganda.

John held not an ounce of resentment against anyone for not knowing about his oldest daughter. After all, he didn't want Fran around him, lest association endanger her life, too. I'm sure he'd feel the same way about Susan, if only he could recall her.

He also addressed the Rachel issue during the call. As with Susan, he said he's willing to meet with her if and when she's ready. Without getting into too much detail, let's just say it's complicated. Because of course it is—it involves John and a woman.

Justin later explained how he believed their father's messy bound-aries (e.g., repeatedly returning to a woman he later claimed coerced him into impregnating her) stemmed from all the abuse he suffered growing up. We heard from John multiple times how, as a small child, his older sister stopped him from shooting their abusive father. Justin called John a "battered person" who "didn't think he had any choice or power to act. He doesn't know his worth," John's son said. "He doesn't know how to stand up for himself (only others)." He also mentioned how John's drive to help people further blurred any semblance of boundaries in their father's life, like keeping "Susie the Floozy," the woman who gave Justin his first kiss, plied with "good" coke.

"I appreciate you finding me with an open heart and an open mind," John told Edie over the phone. "I really appreciate that."

36

Ducky's Jelly

Just over a month after John's birthday, on the final Thursday in July, we flew into Chicago's O'Hare to fulfill a promise. The twenty-fifth Pierogi Fest, Indiana's third-largest festival, was that weekend.

After landing that morning, we explored Wrigley Field's exterior before mon cher finally got her long-overdue deep dish fix. Leftovers from our meaty legend at Geno's East odorized the rental car while we checked out nearby Oz Park. Moments later came a visit to Emerald City Coffee on a lovely, unexpectedly L. Frank Baum-themed, mid-summer afternoon. And no, it never crossed my mind that Seattle is the Emerald City.

During dinner at Paula's Thursday evening, Edie revealed that she wanted to hug Susan upon reading her first email. Later, though, she was mindful to meet her somewhere safe, with distractions available in case things got awkward with Susan. Of course, none were needed.

Paula told us how Nancy Jane had called Mike about allowing John Karpova to adopt his only child. He categorically vetoed the proposal, yet she proceeded. We also learned that our hostess once took a class in standup comedy, which helped Paula's eulogy at her Uncle Mike's wake.

Following a night at our Hammond hotel, we drove back to Paula's, where she gave us coffee mugs her Uncle Mike bought at the 1994 NCAA Final Four in Charlotte, North Carolina. She then drove us to

Whiting, where 119th Street was lined with ninety vendors ahead of that night's wacky parade.

Not thirty seconds after passing under a banner welcoming us to the town's twenty-five-year-old claim to fame, a Duke's Mayonnaise booth triggered my "Oh HELL no!" reflex. To entice folks into grabbing tiny jars of the white stuff, they displayed a sign showing their logo, website, and an image of a dish labeled "BATON ROUGE-STYLE POTATO SALAD." As I later explained to Mira, some marketing douche at Duke's evidently reached way up their ass, and pulled out "BATON ROUGE-STYLE POTATO SALAD." It sounds exotic while offering zero appeal to visit and find out that there's no such goddamn thing as "BATON ROUGE-STYLE POTATO SALAD."

Three hours later, that same reflex was going nuts at a booth advertising "Big G's Famous Crawfish Boil." Some genius decided it would be a fantastic idea to cook mudbugs in a huge wok, where they soaked all damn day, getting god-knows-how mushy in undoubtedly underseasoned water. Even North Louisiana, Dallas Cowboy-rooting rednecks would consider whipping someone's ass over the abomination we witnessed that Friday.

Closer inspection revealed further horrors. Aside from perfectly acceptable sausage, they had thrown in three things I have never even heard a rumor of anyone defiling a crawfish boil with: carrots, broccoli, and—everyone's favorite Cajun staple—cauliflower.

Suddenly, amid my unbridled shit-talking about the affront to my people, I saw festivalgoers walking by, eating roasted corn on the freaking cob. A booth down the block had pallets of sacks of fresh corn getting shucked by unhappy kids. They were obviously upset that, in a state filled with the stuff, those folks at Big G's didn't have the goddamn decency to throw an ear or two in there. I guess I should be thankful they didn't call them "crayfish" or "crawdads," else I'd still be in jail for murdering someone.

While we enjoyed the pierogis, our favorite ethnic food was the Dragobobs (tasty meat on a stick). When an opening band played polka music, Paula handed me her phone and told me to video just her dancing feet. I started to ask if it was for extra cash on an Eastern European foot-fetish site. The Ron Smolen Orchestra, for their part, made up for the crawfish boil's lack of corn. "We've had some requests," the gray-haired trio's accordion player said, "but we're going to keep playing anyway."

Multiple TV reporters from Chicago came in to do live shots that morning, including one doubting her career choices as the buscias (women dressed as grandmas from the old country) fixed her up with rollers and a headscarf on air. Besides Reggie, the purple mascot for Whiting's newly opened Mascot Hall of Fame, there were food-themed mascots, like a six-foot-tall cabbage roll. And of course, there was Mister Pierogi, who arrived during a live shot to a murmur of people whispering, "Ooh, there's Mister Pierogi," and, "Hey, that's Mister Pierogi!"

We later bumped into cousin Gregg, the fellow sports official, wearing an Obi Wan Pierogi T-shirt. Lois's son joined us for that evening's parade, which celebrated Eastern European culture without taking itself too seriously. When a trio of guys with boxes of vino on bikes passed by under the banner "Tour de Franzia," Edie and I looked at each other, knowing what the other was thinking: namely, someone in Whiting had been inspired by our favorite New Orleans walking parade. Jamie and Gavin were also nearby for the sunset procession with Paula's three youngest grandkids. Joss, Decky, and June had somehow gotten even cuter over the past year.

We saw them again Sunday for another Lukaczyk family reunion, where we got to meet a few more cousins who couldn't make either of the previous year's gatherings. Jodie graciously hosted again, despite having to fly out to California that evening for a last-minute, career-related golden ticket of sorts. That was on top of worrying about Jack, Jodie's teenage son with a broken foot and wrist from a recent moped crash.

As in 2018, we all took a group photo on the Guzmans' deck. Misha, being a Lukaczyk through and through, earned ten bucks by ensuring the occasion was memorialized with Johnny Mark sprouting rabbit ears.

Minutes after the picture was snapped, one more cousin whom we hadn't yet met arrived. It was Jim, Johnny Mark's recently reunited half-brother, the one who had popped up when his nephew Mike Lukas, of Quest Labs in New Jersey, got his DNA results.

Like his older brother Gene, Jim was a Marine. Like Edie's father, Jim served in Vietnam. His wife's stepmom hailed from Baton Rouge. Even more intriguing, Jim's a retired Cook County detective. The former Chicago cop blended right in with the gangster-adjacent Lukaczyks, a term that cousin Nick confirmed as apt for his folks. Nick also had me demonstrate for the horde how much my Chicago accent had improved since his dad handed me his phone in Paula's kitchen.

Edie and I were excited to meet Jim. After all, he's the reason his little brother was on Ancestry, where Johnny Mark found and contacted his gorgeous, long-lost cousin in Baton Rouge. Simply put, without Jim, we might still be looking for Susan.

The two newly discovered cousins were missing from the latest official Lukaczyk family photo. Ever since the 2018 trip, Susan had been looking forward to returning with us for Pierogi Fest. Health issues, though, kept her in Metairie with Skip. Everything turned out fine, but Susan didn't make it to Indiana, much less set up a Reuben pierogi food truck for the festival, like she and Paula had discussed.

Nevertheless, throughout 2019, Susan and her daughter managed to get together a few times, including once on the phone, in late March. "I have got to have looked like the craziest woman on Earth," Susan texted shortly after they hung up that afternoon, "driving down the street after talking to you, smiling like the Cheshire Cat. So good hearing your voice!"

"Heehee," a giddy Edie giggled, "I did a little happy dance in my office."

Weather forced the cancellation of Spring Diva Day in early April, so mother, daughter, and their husbands met up later that month at Gator's Den for their annual Spring Fling, a Special Olympics fundraiser. Along the way to Manchac that Sunday morning, we listened to KUTX in Austin as they celebrated Willie Nelson's birthday with a collaboration between the Redheaded Stranger and Ol' Blue Eyes. "Heading out to meet up with Susan and Skip," Edie reported to Fort Worth from the Rogue's passenger seat, "heard the ultimate Jim O'Neal song: Willie & Frank teamed up for 'My Way.'"

Our early arrival allowed us to park within 100 yards of the place, just a little farther than Skip and Susan's Dodge van. Dozens of vendors offered all manner of South Louisiana cuisine for a dollar a serving. In addition to all the food for sale, we brought something for Susan: strawberry jelly Ducky had made that weekend.

Once the crowd got too thick and rowdy, it was time to leave with bellies and Rubbermaids full of tasty fare. Parked cars lined the highway for hundreds of yards past our SUV. The Dodge van was now one of the closest vehicles along LA 51.

"I'm not walking," Skip emphatically told Susan as we headed past the dunking booth near the entrance. Seconds later, he had secured a ride for our quartet with a deputy driving the Tangipahoa Parish Sheriff's Office Special Response Team van. Susan's bad knee meant she rode on the doorstep with her legs dangling outside.

We remembered to take a picture this time. After the brief ride, I handed the helpful deputy my phone to photograph us standing next to the bedroom-sized metal box on wheels.

"Our very own SWAT team," Susan quipped when I later shared it. "Thank you both for a fun visit. Time just seemed to fly by. If we had the hourglass from Harry Potter," she said, "the sand would have stopped flowing, because the conversation was so great. Hope you enjoyed the food," Susan added. "Our refrigerator is totally full!"

"We were so happy to be with you again and hope (no pressure) we don't have to wait so long for the next time!" Edie winked. "The food was good, but my Susan time is the best!"

The four of us would also get together that spring at the New Orleans Greek Fest. "Skip will have on a navy Greek sailor's hat," Susan alerted us, "in case I'm off collecting treats."

Edie replied with an update on Earle, who had just gone through a bad Thursday. "Hopefully we will be able to enjoy our time as planned with you and Skip," my wife wrote Susan, "but we're kind of taking each moment as it comes at this point—something of a callback to when you and I were trying to plan our first meeting last year," she wrote, citing Susan's kin's stay in ICU. "We know that all will be well," Red assuaged, "and we just celebrate life and love and practice patience along the way."

"Please do what you need to do for her," Susan insisted that Friday. "We'll be blessed with more times to play ahead, and I wouldn't want you to have any regrets. I just feel so lucky having you in my life," she shared, "in person or in spirit."

The next day, Susan met Edie's cool boss, as well as her husband, a proud Greek and longtime fellow football official. Shortly after our arrival that warm Saturday, Skip went off to wrangle some food, while my wife headed to the baklava stand to tell her boss hello. As Edie strode away in the distance, Susan, seated across the table from me, shook her head. She verbalized that she still could not believe her only child was in her life. I reached out and grabbed her hand. She squeezed mine tightly.

"We forgot pictures again!" Susan texted Edie minutes after she and Skip left with stacked boxes of Greek confectionaries. "You're the only person I take them with, so it's hard to remember. Thanks for coming," she added. "I enjoy every second I get with both of you."

"J says we need to book a photographer for next time we're together to make sure we don't lapse again," my wife shared.

"I love you so much." Edie's mother revealed, "I was kinda depressed this morning thinking about how many years we missed, but spending that little bit of time together was like you providing a big bandage to hold my heart together. Thank you!"

"We have plenty of days together ahead of us," her child assured, "and I cherish each one. Loved being with you today."

Susan also asked if she was "family" enough to get Ducky's jelly recipe. "I tried to take a little taste," she said, "and it didn't work. Do you know how awesome it is over ice cream?"

"You are definitely FAMILY enough," a chuckling Edie ensured. "Ducky will be thrilled."

Days after receiving the coveted jelly in Manchac, Susan followed up with the history behind a gift she had given Edie that Sunday: a bracelet she'd received for her thirtieth birthday. "Since I missed yours," she explained, "I thought you should have it."

That same week, Edie discovered some freaky timing when our titular character helped me with this book project. "Susan scanned and emailed the initial letter I sent her for Jeremy's source material," my wife alerted Beth, "the letter that I wrote on the birthday of the parents who raised her. I was unaware John Karpova and Nancy shared a birthday," she added, "much less the timing."

Upon learning that her friend reached out to her birth mother on the birthday of Susan's two parents, who never knew she ever had a child, Beth reacted, "That's crazy." Indeed it is. Yet, for this saga, it's par for the course.

That same spring, Paula texted her two Louisiana cousins, "Uncle Mike is at Opening Day!" The Cubs were shutting out the Pirates at Wrigley. "He has the best seats in the house!"

"Hopefully he's saving one for me!" Mike's daughter chimed in. "We've got a lot of catching up to do..."

On another occasion, Susan mentioned a cardinal Skip had spotted. "We have so many special angels," she told her daughter. "I didn't notice all of them until you and I connected. Thanks for waking me up."

The pair further connected upon discovering they shared a unique hobby growing up. "I brought milk cartons home from school as a kid," Edie revealed to Susan and Paula. "I don't know why."

"Side confession between us," Susan exclusively messaged her daughter. "I also saved milk cartons to make candles."

"Oh wow," Edie answered the former Girl Scout troop leader, "I love it. I never did anything but stockpile mine."

Following a discussion about Red's playhouse, which became Doc's home medical office, Susan remarked, "Nothing makes me feel quite as good as hearing happy things from your childhood."

Edie later got to enjoy a bit of Susan's childhood in the form of a black-and-white photo she had recently received. Taken in December 1960, eight years after she was similarly photographed in East Chicago, an eleven-year-old, wide-eyed Susan looked at something off-camera. "I must always be interested in whatever is to my left," she surmised.

April showers brought May flowers, including lots of striking day-lilies in our front yard. "Two debuts today," Edie sent Susan with a pair of pics on the third day of the month. Four afternoons later, Edie was "trying to get home to see today's bumper crop." She shared a trio of flower pics from that Tuesday morning.

"I love all of my forever flowers," Susan said in a heart-filled text. "Thank you for being my flower lady!"

The following weekend, on Mother's Day Eve, my wife sent Susan more daylily photos. "Had thirty-two of the fancy ones today."

"They're so beautiful," her mother replied. "Give Ducky and Kellie hugs from me when you see them."

"Will do," Edie vowed.

Susan closed by blowing a kiss to her daughter. Two weeks earlier, Edie had invited Susan to join us in celebrating Mother's Day in New Roads.

"I'm so honored by your invitation to celebrate this special day with you," Susan replied after a week of deliberation, "whether it be on the day or on another day. I've been battling with my conscience about it since you brought it up, and, as much as I don't want to ever say 'no' to you, I have to this time.

"This holiday is a celebration of the women who were always there for you," she explained. "I'm so happy to have learned that you were blessed with at least three of them—Ducky, Kellie, and Earle. As much as I wish I had been part of your life between the day you were born and the day we finally met, I wasn't, so I just don't feel like I'm qualified to be part of this particular holiday.

"I think we could come up with a special day of our own that would better represent the special bond we have. It could be the day you reached out to me with your wonderful letter, the day I responded, or possibly the best day of my life—when we first got to hug each other.

"I love you, Edie. I always have, and I always will. We belong to each other in a very special way. Is it okay with you to keep 'Our Day' separate and distanced?" she asked. "Your Susan," she closed with a flurry of hearts.

"Of course it is absolutely more than OK for us to celebrate our relationship in the manner of our choice," Edie insisted, "and not just on any one day. I hope you don't mind that I've been celebrating every day, even though we're not together, and that's why I take even more joy now in appreciating each day's new blooms, and sharing them with you."

"I have loved all of the pictures you've shared! They're much better than live flowers," her mother asserted, "because they can be saved and looked at over time. They don't wilt away into distant memories; they're always fresh and smiling in their glory." Susan concluded, "So glad you understand about tomorrow. Every bit of time we spend together is special. Love always, YS."

Edie and I were out by Wade's pool with Ducky when Susan texted me on Sunday afternoon. "If you get a chance today, please pull your wonderful wife aside and give her a Susan hug. I've been smiling all day," she blew a kiss my way, "and wanted to share the feeling. Thanks!"

"Awww, will do!" I confirmed. "Ducky was just asking about you a little while ago."

"I was going to send Ducky a Thank You card today," Susan admitted to me, "but wasn't sure. I sent a hug with Edie anyway."

"Ducky was happy to receive your hug," Susan learned from Edie, moments before she shared that Sunday's daylily pics, "as I was to receive yours."

Shortly after blowing that kiss at me, Susan sent me scurrying from the poolside crowd in an attempt to not lose my shit in front of my in-laws. "Sharon sent this message to me this morning: 'I hope your heart is finally at peace with this holiday,'" Susan shared with me. "Guess what—it is!"

A few miles away that same Sunday, another motherly figure in Edie's life was receiving hospice care at home. Ninety-six-year-old Earle had grown rarely lucid.

"I know how special she is to you," Susan previously told her daughter. "It's so hard when things happen that you can't easily take care of or fix. Praying for the best."

Before the month of May was out, my wife sent Susan an update. "Happy Wednesday," Edie included with a spectacular shot of a daylily bursting in bright pink and yellow. "This one is from me and Earle, who is finally at peace as of 3 a.m. Monday."

After seven years of being cared for by my heart—the girl she always treated as her own—Earle Wagley finally went to be with Poppa in the wee hours of Memorial Day morning.

"A couple months ago, she asked me how she got me," Edie continued. "Now she knows."

37

Cottonwood

Near June's end, two days before the anniversary of receiving her daughter's letter, Susan alerted Edie that she wouldn't make it back to Indiana for Pierogi Fest.

"Oh no!" Edie texted back. "Sorry to hear that. We'll have to figure out another fun get-together just for us!" she winked. "But in the meantime, I was actually thinking about calling you to get my Susan fix..." She opted not to call, likely because the woman who worked in telecommunications for decades wasn't all that comfortable talking on the phone.

"Time has just been going by so fast," Susan shared with mixed emotions two days later. "I'm in the middle of an optimist/pessimist, half-empty/half-full state of mind. Can you believe we've *only* been connected for almost a year? Can you believe we've *already* been connected for almost a year? Everything is crazy," said the woman living with it. "I feel so lucky, but I feel sad, too. I love you so much, and I'm so happy we've become part of each other's lives. I'm so sorry it took so long to happen. Crazy, huh?"

"Absolutely crazy," Edie affirmed that Saturday, "and unbelievable that it's already/only been a year. Our first contact anniversary! And I can't believe I haven't seen you in over a month. I miss you!"

"I feel so blessed to have you in my life," Susan wrote one year from her Red Letter Day. "Thank you so much for finding me and reaching out. It had to be crazy for you. Heck, it was crazy for me," she said, "but the best kind of happy crazy ever!"

"I am glad we both get to enjoy this happy crazy ride together," Edie shared. "I love you so much. Thank you for checking your mail that day and responding and giving us this opportunity to be together."

On Monday, July 1, Edie revived a one-year-old email thread. "Happy anniversary to us!" she sent Susan in the "Surprise" thread with a pair of hearts. "Best is yet to come."

"The already been/only been thoughts are still in full debate in my mind. Whichever," Susan insisted, "it's all been wonderful! Thank you for bravely reaching out and enriching my life." With a single big red heart, she closed, "Always! S."

Five weeks later, we met up with Susan and Skip at Gator's Den on Sunday, August 11, one day before another major anniversary: first hug. We and the Cavells would see them again at Oktoberfest 2019, hours after the Hard Rock Hotel collapsed in New Orleans, entombing two construction workers and nearly taking out the Saenger Theatre. The Cavells also joined us the following February for a spirited lake-front brunch with Susan and Skip to kick off our Mardi Gras weekend in New Orleans. It would be our last pre-COVID-19 meeting with my wife's birth mother.

By March 2020, the pandemic forced us to cancel a gathering planned for the following month in Austin. Ducky had hoped to meet John Hart, and spend more time getting to know his other kids. As consolation, my mother-in-law met her baby's daddy over the phone in early June. For a couple minutes, I videoed Ducky discussing gardening with Johnny Gingerweed, just before he meandered into a rambling story about his first roommate in Baton Rouge, a Woodrow Wilson Fellowship finalist with the best résumé they'd ever seen.

On October 10, 2020, one month before his Marine Corps's birth-day, cousin Gene quietly passed away. "Lasting eight days without dialysis," Mira shared on Facebook, "having his pacemaker turned off, talking and eating until the end, he totally amazed us all, including hospice nurses. Gene was truly a larger-than-life character. His last days and the week that followed (funeral service story for another day) were truly as unique as Gene. To the craziest brother-in-law a girl could ever have, rest in peace."

Just up the road in Austin, on New Year's Day 2021, Rachel's mom suffered a stroke. Elizabeth was in hospice care within a week. Nearly a year would pass after her death before Rachel could hug her brother and sister.

We saw her in person before COVID when Rachel and her partner, Matthew, joined the Yo-yos for Spanish Town Mardi Gras 2020. The two of them also enjoyed Bacchus, as well as Mardi Gras in New Roads with Ducky, Cindy, and Wade. My oldest brother-in-law got to meet Red's baby sister mere weeks before lockdown. Rachel later joined us for online trivia with the Cavells, many of our friends from The Bull-dog, and our bobtailed ginger tabby, Waffles, whom we adopted late that same year.

We had begun connecting with new family just before we couldn't even responsibly visit old family. That's when this story began to read like one written in another age, when air travel was far less perilous, and we could safely hug strangers. As much as we missed visiting loved ones we'd just discovered, though, we're thankful Edie didn't further put off submitting her DNA by, say, a couple years. Besides never getting to know Gene or Elizabeth, COVID-19 would've meant discovering new relatives with no responsible way of meeting them for the foreseeable future.

Throughout our yearlong-plus isolation, Edie and I grew to more deeply appreciate the little things, like listening to KEXP and KUTX. They offered connections to those who introduced the radio stations to us, people we couldn't wait to see in person.

Every day, on the old player piano from Ducky, we've seen the fleur-de-lis that Edie painted with my mother-in-law in December 2019, as well as a Mr. Bingle painting she did with Susan that same month. My wife's creations, made with her mothers, flanked a photo album from our silver anniversary Vegas trip, which seems like a lifetime ago.

Little did we know how much we needed that getaway for us to more fully bond, to prepare for what awaited. Neither of us had a clue how much our lives were about to change, in so many ways, both as a couple and personally.

By the middle of 2019, a few months into writing about this insane journey, I realized the world could stand fewer assholes being assholes for the sake of being assholes. COVID-19 and the rest of 2020 confirmed that realization, and many others gleaned along the way. This book project taught me that in order to be real with the world, you must first be real with yourself. At the risk of being accused of plagiarizing John Hart: It's a hell of a lot more rewarding illuminating the abundant beauty residing in others, which in turn may help more folks discover unrealized beauty within themselves.

Nevertheless, as a tenured cynic, I can't imagine any true, lifelong Cubs fanatic coming back as a living, feathery mascot of rival St. Louis. Then again, maybe the eccentric who wanted a send-off with hookers and a springboard in his casket would get a kick out of the irony, and perhaps the colorful plumage.

Barely one-third into my first draft, I discovered how much I still had to learn from my wife, and our shared experience, when Susan first learned of the book via Facebook. I posted a Google doc screen-shot showing the word count. In the background was the passage about Grandpa Mike dying without knowing about his granddaughter, and Johnny Mark's assertion, "He'd have cut off his right arm just to hold you in his left."

"Is Jeremy writing a book about your discoveries?" Susan asked Edie. "I saw something on FB that came as a bit of a shock to me. Have I missed something?"

Susan managed to keep her creation's existence secret for nearly fifty years. Meanwhile, I couldn't wait to crow about the one I had just started working on. It was a pathetic attempt at a cheap, selfish fix for a recovering only-child-turned-mediocre-stand-up-comic traversing the gratification desert known more commonly as writing a book.

"I need to have a refresher course with him on discretion," my bride replied.

"I'm too sensitive," Susan insisted. "I just love you so much, but our relationship is so complicated. We understand without questions, but nobody else could. I've never been good at letting people in. You wouldn't know," she maintained, "because you're not just a 'people.'"

"I can definitely relate to not letting people in," Edie assured. "I think (aside from all the monumental stuff) that's a big part of what's blown his mind," my wife referred to all my new in-laws, noting "how different this has been in that regard."

Edie continued, "We are complicated, and I don't want you to feel any pressure or stress from us. I love you entirely and forever." Susan's daughter told her, "All of us have choices to make in life, and there isn't a right choice. No matter which paths we choose, a thoughtful person may consider 'what if?' We do our best. We consider our choices and our consequences and let them inform our subsequent actions. Hopefully, things work out and we love life and the people in it, or at least we keep working toward that." She added, "And that doesn't even scratch the surface of the choices you have to make as a result of other people's choices that you had no control over." Edie avowed, "You made a thoughtful, beautiful, selfless choice. I am so glad we finally found our way back to each other. I love you."

Around the time of that exchange, I sent my apologies to Metairie. "Susan, I am so sorry for blindsiding you with that regrettable post yesterday," I texted a woman with stress-related health issues. "I knew better but did it anyway. But yes," I confirmed, "I am writing about our journey. Numerous folks have insisted I should do so, pretty much since the first few discoveries. I feel it's a mesmerizingly beautiful story the world today needs to hear. However, I am also sensitive to privacy needs. I had planned to approach you about that issue once the first draft was written. I don't want to create unwelcome drama in anyone's life, especially someone I utterly respect, and whom my wife absolutely adores. My deepest apologies."

"I'm all for the book," Susan promised. "From the snippet I saw, it's going to be wonderful. Seeing it on my FB page was just disconcerting." She explained, "The two of you have learned so much over the past year, and I think that documenting that journey is wonderful. I started trying to find my father right after my dad's passing. Unfortunately, the tools we have today weren't available.

"I know I'm just a cameo player in your saga," my titular character wrote, "but I'm available for questions if you have any." With a wink, Susan assured, "It's my problem. I've always been a private person. Maybe it's because I've juggled so many different sides of my life for so long."

As surreal and emotional as the journey was the first time, the experience was even more mind-altering when I took a trip down the same path, but with a glimpse into Edie's point of view along the way. The colossal amount of source material afforded me a peephole, deepening my adoration of her with every keystroke. Much like the subject matter of our favorite Kate Bush song, this was an unprecedented opportunity to immersively see things from my love's perspective.

Back on that Friday morning in Renton, before Justin drove the two of us to Woodinville, Edie saw something I couldn't. I heard distressed birds, but I couldn't figure out why. Not until I abandoned my perspective for hers did I finally understand what was causing all the trouble.

Less than forty-eight hours later, I awoke to another disturbance Sunday morning. My wife's sobs alerted me that, like the birds on Friday, something was distressing her. While I knew it was John-related, I couldn't figure out exactly what was the matter, at least not until I later made a concerted effort to understand what she was experiencing. Echoing Edie's post-Port Angeles email to Rachel and Justin, sometimes all you need for an epiphany is a change in perspective.

On a related matter, why does it always have to be a midlife "crisis"? Why can't it ever be a midlife epiphany?

My second trip down the path essentially put me in my wife's head during a surreal experience we intimately shared. The contrasts between my thoughts and attitudes at any given time along the journey were instinctively drawn against those held by her. Day after day, I was confronted with the need to empathize with my wife. And from that, I feel like I've been transfused with some of her abundant patience and discretion in coming to realize something about the woman I share a life with: The more important someone is to her, the longer it takes for her to say or do something that has even the slightest chance of upsetting them.

I mentioned how, despite the miles between her and Susan, the Red apple fell not far from the tree. This is particularly true with regard to how exceedingly cautious they both can be when it comes to making waves for loved ones.

"She just sounds like we have the same heart. Or at least the heart I hope I have," Edie told Justin, moments before a Louisiana congressman got heckled by some asshat with a bullhorn. "We both keep repeating how concerned we are about the possibility of hurting someone to the point of not wanting to take that risk."

En route to Gator's Den for Spring Fling, I likened mother and daughter to gorillas each handling a kitten, scared any wrong move might crush it. Meanwhile, the kitten is thinking, "Just fucking pet me already."

They came by it honestly. Susan and Edie shared more with Michael Lukaczyk than just his disdain for being photographed. Not unlike when he quit staking out the cemetery—because he didn't want to disrupt his only child's estranged life—Mike's progeny also demonstrate far more concern for their loved ones' feelings than for their own. In all three, you find a thought process that selflessly refuses to push an issue if there's a chance it might—MIGHT—make things unpleasant for someone they care about.

Such exceeding consideration—stemming from abundant empathy, discretion, and patience—is what allowed Edie to successfully dodge all the traps that could have turned our story into a darker version of the insane yet heartwarming tale that it is. Like Indiana Jones, my bride chose wisely.

This is the part where, like an advertiser, I'm obligated to issue a disclaimer: Results depicted herein are not typical. Like I mentioned in the opening chapter, and as demonstrated by Patrick's journey, most mothers don't give up their children for adoption because everything in their life is going fabulously. In talking with people about this insane journey, I've heard stories about other families' DNA-related discoveries. Most are less than inspiring. I told Fort Worth when starting this project, "DNA is this generation's Pentagon Papers." The old folks kept lots of secrets they never expected the kids to uncover.

Just like we couldn't have drawn up a more ideal emissary than Justin, it's hard to imagine someone navigating this journey better than Edie did. While there's no reference manual for handling such discoveries, her approach was nothing short of "textbook." In baseball parlance, she stepped up to the plate and hit it out of the damn park.

Along the way, Edie and I shared uncertainty regarding what lay ahead of us. Likewise, we aren't sure what awaits us going forward, particularly after this revealing portrait, centered around two intensely private women, goes public. As a testament to how out of the box this story is, they've both come to see that it needs to become part of the human narrative.

Meanwhile, with lessons learned, my wife stands to help untold folks on similar journeys, like our officiating buddy Bradford. His father was White, my proud Black friend eventually learned. Brad's maternal side descended from the Georgetown slave trade, a national scar researched and covered extensively by Maxine Crump, who happens to be from— wait for it—Maringouin, Louisiana.

"Were your ears burning last night?" Beth asked after Edie booked the first Pinetta's lunch. Turned out, one of Beth's friends was adopted. "She and her husband did 23andMe to make sure they weren't related," Beth explained. "So I told bits of your story." The researcher noted, "This has become a big thing this year." Citing several loved ones, friends, and colleagues connecting with new family via DNA, our ninja remarked, "Issa theme!"

"I am by no means a sherpa," Edie conceded, "but willing to listen to anyone who might need a sounding board."

Perhaps my mom best encapsulated my wife's growth through this journey when she said that Edie seemed to come more fully into her own as a person. It's an apt assessment of how successfully captaining such a wild adventure could affect someone like her daughter-in-law.

When I ventured back up the path—over a year and thousands of miles earlier—I had barely begun retracing our steps when I came upon a fork in the road. One path included Ducky's help in finding Edie's bio mom. The other would be just her, with me by her side, and our deep state ninja at the ready.

My Molly Marine decisively took charge, and ownership, of the journey. She knew she only had one shot at doing this right.

Had Edie accepted Ducky's help in finding Susan via medical records, it would've felt dispassionate, cold, and intrusive. In a word, it would've been clinical.

Just think, what if Edie had not eschewed her privilege of a resourceful, dogged Ducky, willing to plow a shortcut through the doctor's office, as opposed to how things almost organically played out? Imagine the pair finding Susan—only Susan—without a clue about the life she led, nor the life she was estranged from, and then introducing themselves to her.

No John. No Justin. No Rachel. No Cherish. No Hadley. No Clark and LeMerle. No Erica and Ben.

No crazy Ukrainian horde. No Gene. No Paula. No John Lukas, nor any of the umpteen other Johns. None of them in our lives.

No Grandpa Mike.

No Indiana reunion.

No Cubs jacket.

Conversely, look at how many people have been positively and beautifully impacted by my wife setting aside any reluctance she may have had, and spitting in a vial. Once I showed her how.

"Finding both of you is a joy greater than I had expected to come from this journey," Edie wrote John and Justin eight days after the epic five-hour phone call, "and it keeps me smiling every day."

I'm so thankful my wife adamantly refused to take a shortcut, opting instead to lead an uncertain journey, one proving that—in a rush-rush world—you never know who you'll run across on the scenic route. Some of them may share your nose, eyes, and even your heart.

With all the wonderful similarities we discovered, some notable contrasts also presented themselves along the way. Around the time of the Seattle trip, I realized one of the wilder aspects of this whole journey was the dichotomy between Edie's old and new families, with regard to normalcy. Between adopted and bio fam, they've got both ends of the conventionality spectrum covered, not unlike the two Indiana families who came together to produce Susan.

Case in point: Edie's biological father once sold weed to Bob Marley; Edie's oldest brother does not know who Bob Marley is, or at least did not know in 2005 after we all spent an entire day in Montego Bay, Jamaica. On the first leg of a cruise celebrating Ducky and Jimmy's golden anniversary, I mentioned the Jamaican demigod playing on the ship's PA system. Just like when Edie mentioned Susan after the luncheon at Pinetta's, Wade asked, "Who?"

You know who doesn't know who Bob Marley is? Conventional folks, that's who.

There are many words to accurately describe my long-known in-laws: family-minded, industrious, generous (please don't leave me out of the will), honest, and functional are just a few. Among the least apt descriptors is "eccentric." If you need help moving into a four-bedroom home in a day, or clearing out that same flood-damaged house in half a day, I highly recommend them. If you want to have a conversation involving pop culture references, keep looking. Conventionality not-withstanding, I love Edie's adopted family. They all played a part in making my wife the incredible woman she is today.

They raise awesome kids who end up raising awesome kids. Last time I checked, none of them have ever handed over their child to a coke kingpin as a promissory note on moving some bricks tout de suite. In addition to being conventional, the O'Neals are a very loving, stable family, which I hear tends to produce quality people and great parents.

Of course, the stable-home rule doesn't account for Justin. If he's an exception to the rule, he's an exceptional exception.

Additionally, the Harts' cordial relationship with Cherish's first husband, and Nancy Jane's estrangement from Mike, offered another striking contrast. Cherish's ex served in her wedding to Justin, and lived with the Harts for a number of years. Hadley knows him as Uncle Aaron. Justin gave him a ring, just like he did to all the important men in his life, during a prenuptial event in lieu of a bachelor party.

Cherish's ex is also gay. Admittedly informed by drastically different generational attitudes, Cherish and Nancy Jane present diametrical reactions to similar discoveries regarding one's spouse. Moreover, the openness of Edie's paternal family about everything—like our new sister-in-law being cool with people knowing her first marriage ended in such a manner—is a far departure from most of our kin back home, who tend to play the tough stuff close to the vest.

Unlike nearly all of the Ukrainian horde who stayed in Northwest Indiana, Susan's nomadic childhood almost seemed like an attempt to prevent anyone from tracking them down. "I'd almost forgotten about how active Mom always was in Newcomers groups," Susan emailed Edie two weeks after first contact. "She sure had a lot of experience at being new in town!" Thankfully, Nancy Jane didn't share her daughter's aversion to being photographed, especially for publication. Her many bespeckled newspaper appearances played a huge part in finding Susan, a self-described "very private person" who tried to hide in her *Gumbo* pic.

Incidentally, AncestryDNA eventually presented Michael and Nancy Jane's marriage as a hint to Edie, nearly a full year after first contact with Susan.

A few months later, after reading the first half of this account, Susan offered her own hint, in hopes of helping to solve another mystery. At

Oktoberfest 2019, she told us something related to Edie's conception. It involved an egg, because of course it did.

"Susan suggested I ask John if he recalls a holiday at an apartment where the refrigerator contained nothing but one egg," Edie emailed Justin and their father, "which he combined with bouillon in an attempt to make egg drop soup for two people?"

In telling us the story, Susan's face said John wasn't too successful.

"She is a puzzle person," Edie later explained to him over the phone about Susan. "She likes to solve puzzles," their daughter told John. "I think she also likes for other people to solve puzzles, and I get that from her, apparently." Indeed, my oft coy wife does.

John replied to Edie's egg hint with a pair of emails. Adjusted for a space bar that should've been in hospice care, he sent over 3,500 words to say he still didn't remember Susan. That fact didn't stop him, however, from detailing the hypothetical scene, replete with verse steeped in hippie wisdom.

"Susan, somehow, had a relationship where I felt halfway like a human being," John told us by phone. "And I can remember nothing, but it seems remotely familiar. It might just come to me in a dream."

His two emails and ensuing phone call, of course, included lots of familiar stories about his time in Baton Rouge, among other topics. One thing I've come to realize is that John's effusiveness permeates every aspect of his life. He gardens intensely, "in bursts." He goes at that keyboard with his entire being, the same way he advocated for women and called out injustice and inequality throughout his life.

His effusiveness is also what got him into trouble with the powers that be. The fact that he had a hand in the drug trade—as noble as John's intentions might have been—gave aggrieved members of the establishment legal means to silence him, to finally pluck that commie thorn from their side.

It's why no sensible weed guy actively does things that draw the attention—much less the ire—of cops. It's bad for business. Same goes for powder pushers and cocaine Christmas cards.

But John didn't see himself as a dealer in the drug business. From his perspective, he was a human rights activist who sold drugs to make sure people didn't get ripped off. Unfortunately, that's not how state and local authorities saw it.

It's been a while since I heard Knick's voice in my head. Maybe that's because, in 2020, surreal became the norm, as evidenced by a stir-crazy eight-year-old in Renton learning to play piano from her weird uncle two time zones away.

Nevertheless, while our new reality settles in with each passing day, surrealness is still present, if only in the background. I'm not sure if it'll ever completely go away. I often test to see if it has whenever I pass by the photo tile of the twinsies from their first Diva Day. I also still catch myself looking at both Susan and John in my wife's face. It's like a newfound glow.

"Some of the better parts of my nature come from you," Edie told John, "and come from Susan, and I appreciate getting to know that." During their conversation about his mysterious holiday egg drop soup, after John explained how fear of hurting people close to him meant he could never be intimate with anyone "in a realistic way," Edie assured him, "We're all in a good place now, and there's no need for any regrets."

John insisted he had none, although during a later call with his two eldest kids, he said he was sorry he wasn't around for the development of the one he didn't know about. However, he knew had he been there for Edie, she wouldn't have met me, and there'd be no Justin. John said both of those outcomes would be terrible.

"Your efforts have really helped me to feel a hell of a lot better about my hell I've been through," he told Edie in the fall of 2019, "and I feel I'm in a much better place each time because of what you've done, and what you've shared, and what you are."

With tears welling up in my eyes, John continued on speakerphone, "Thank you for being a husband who validates Edie, and everything you are, Jeremy. It's beautiful. And LSU's got a hell of a lot more depth," he said of the Tigers' recent win over Florida, his signature sharp change of course evoking laughter from the two of us.

In another call, John again offered to sit down with Susan, but only if she wanted to. Over a year earlier, back when everyone thought Fran was the one, he similarly offered to join in a group hug to help make her pain go away, because that's who John is. He fervently believes in the power of nurturing touch.

In the interest of generating more Hart hugs, Edie and I intended to visit more of her father's family before COVID-19. The declining health of John's sisters in Tennessee and Florida, though, meant Edie's cousins had more pressing matters to worry about. The pandemic only cast further doubt on meeting them.

Likewise, the virus dashed any scintilla of hope for a reunion between Edie's birth parents. Then again, maybe a more appropriate, poetic reunion of sorts already took place, one not revealed for over two months.

A few weeks before the sibs arrived for Spanish Town Mardi Gras, Edie learned I was attempting to corroborate some of their father's wild LSU stories, including the Free Speech Alley incident with Carl Tickles. At that point, we had only read Tyler Bridges's book about David Duke, which didn't name John. Just shy of a year after the epic five-hour phone call, and John's account of the encounter, she decided to see if the other book would finally load online.

"Holy shit!" she messaged me. "The Zatarain book names John!!!!" With a screenshot of the passage mentioning her father by name, Edie added, "ho.lee.shit."

"OMFG," I replied. "You share with Beth yet?"

"Just told her," she said moments later. "Now I think I want to buy the Zatarain book."

After work that Friday, she drove down Perkins Road to purchase both books from the one place in Baton Rouge that had them on hand. The bookstore had been around since before Edie and I enrolled at LSU. It shared a small building dating back to JFK's lifetime, next door to a venerable European restaurant run by our friend Diane.

It didn't take long for me to realize that two months earlier, when Ducky and Kellie were meeting Susan, John was in the building, on the shelves, just beyond a wall. Similarly, despite any partitioning, Susan, John, and the rest of the gang we discovered along the way all have cherished places in our hearts.

Oh, by the way, the name of the bookstore representing John's place in our lives? Cottonwood Books. As in the blooming trees we experienced in Renton with Justin, and again in Austin with Rachel. Because of course it is.

Maybe, just maybe, the book originally failed to load so that Edie would later have reason to discover that John was present—surrounded by innumerable words—when the wonderful woman he and Susan produced finally brought together the loving ladies who raised her, and the long-sought-after mother who gave her life, all with no judgment, nor jealousy, nor resentment.

Just love.

ABOUT THE AUTHOR

Jeremy White is a tenured cynic who penned a hopeful book. He founded South Louisiana's premier satirical publication in 2004, eight years before relaunching the award-winning *Red Shtick Magazine* as its all-digital progeny, The Red Shtick. The comic-turned-writer created and produced Baton Rouge's first and only weekly stand-up open mic for years, during which Jeremy hosted and produced *The Red Stick Comedy Block*, a locally broadcast, weekly half-hour TV show featuring area comics performing before live audiences around town. The passionate Cajun can often be heard on various popular radio shows as either a guest or a guest host. A longtime football official and Mardi Gras krewe captain, Jeremy earned a bachelor's degree in mechanical engineering at LSU, where he met his wife, Edie. They've been happily married since 1992 and live in Baton Rouge with their cat, Waffles.

www.ingramcontent.com/pod-product-compliance
Lightning Source LLC
Chambersburg PA
CBHW031544260326
41914CB00002B/263

* 9 7 9 8 9 8 7 5 3 9 3 0 9 *